Aristotle

Aristotle's Ethics and Politics

Comprising His Practical Philosophy

Aristotle

Aristotle's Ethics and Politics
Comprising His Practical Philosophy

ISBN/EAN: 9783337033439

Printed in Europe, USA, Canada, Australia, Japan

Cover: Foto ©Thomas Meinert / pixelio.de

More available books at **www.hansebooks.com**

ARISTOTLE's

ETHICS AND POLITICS.

VOL. II.

ARISTOTLE's
ETHICS AND POLITICS,

COMPRISING HIS

PRACTICAL PHILOSOPHY,

TRANSLATED FROM THE GREEK.

ILLUSTRATED BY INTRODUCTIONS AND NOTES;

THE CRITICAL HISTORY OF HIS LIFE;

AND A NEW ANALYSIS OF HIS SPECULATIVE WORKS;

By JOHN GILLIES, LL.D.

F. R. S. and S. A. LONDON; F. R. S. EDINBURGH; and
Hiſtoriographer to his Majeſty for SCOTLAND.

Magna animi contentio adhibenda eſt in explicando Ariſtotele.
CICERO FRAGMENT. PHILOSOPH.

IN TWO VOLUMES.

VOL. II.

LONDON:

Printed for A. STRAHAN; and T. CADELL Jun. and W. DAVIES, in the Strand.

1797.

CONTENTS.

ARISTOTLE's POLITICS.

BOOK I.

INTRODUCTION. - - - - - - *Page* 1
Nature and end of a commonwealth.—Analyſis thereof.—Monarchy the firſt form of government.—Domeſtic œconomy.—Slavery.—Accumulation of ſtock.—Riches, real and artificial.—Commerce.—Money.—Manufactures.—Monopolies.—Women.—Children.—Slaves.—Connection between domeſtic and political œconomy. - - - - - - - - 17

BOOK II.

INTRODUCTION. - - - - - - - 53
Plato's republic.—Community of wives, children, and goods.—Nature and neceſſity of ſeparate property.—Plato's books of laws examined.—Schemes for equalizing property.—Their futility.—Hippodamus.—His ideal republic.—Arguments in favour of political innovation.—Stronger arguments againſt it.—The Spartan government.—The Cretan.—The Carthaginian.—The Athenian.—Zaleucus.—Charondas.—Philolaus.—Diocles.—Phaleas.—Pittacus.—Androgamas. - - - - - - - - - 73

BOOK III.

INTRODUCTION. - - - - - - - 159
Citizen—How conſtituted.—Virtues of the man and of the citizen.—Their difference.—Different forms of government.—Their diſtinctive characters.—Pretenſions of democracy—Of oligarchy.—Monarchy.—Its five kinds—Arraigned—Defended. - - - - - - - - 165

BOOK IV.

INTRODUCTION. - - - - - - - 203
Different views of national happineſs.—Fair eſtimate thereof.—The beſt commonwealth.—Extent and nature of its territory.—Commerce—Naval power—Climate—Conſtituent members—Health—Marriage—Children. 215

CONTENTS.

BOOK V.

INTRODUCTION. - - - - - - *Page* 251
Education.—Its different branches.—How far to be cultivated.—Grammar—Drawing—Gymnastic—Music.—Exercises adapted to different ages.—Doubts concerning music.—Its different kinds.—Purgation of the passions. 253

BOOK VI.

INTRODUCTION. - - - - - - - 273
Governments—Their classification.—Democracy—Its four kinds.—Constitutions—One thing by law—Another in fact.—Materials respectively fitted for different governments.—Mixed governments.—Tests of good government.—How governments may be meliorated.—Sleights by which the nobles deceive the people—And the people, the nobles.—Analysis of the sovereignty—Constitution of its different branches—Agreeably to the different spirit of different governments. - - - - - - - - 279

BOOK VII.

INTRODUCTION. - - - - - - - 317
Causes of seditions.—Insolence and rapacity of men in power.—Secret combination of obscure factions, &c.—Particular causes in each form of government respectively.—How governments are to be preserved—By strengthening the middle ranks, &c.—Of laws relative to Democracy—Oligarchy—Monarchy—Tyranny. - - - - - - - - - - 333

BOOK VIII.

INTRODUCTION. - - - - - - - 385
Of republics of husbandmen—Of manufacturers and merchants.—Imperfections of democracy.—Oligarchy.—Military and naval force.—Branches of executive magistracy.—Magistrates for protecting commerce and contracts—Of police—Of revenue.—Courts of record.—Controllers of public accounts.—Different orders of priests.—Superintendants of education and morals. - - 401

ERRATA IN VOL. II.

Page 25. line 6 of the note, *for* τεχνοποιητ *read* τεχνοποιητικη
    122. — 11 of the note, *for* ...
    165. — 4. *for* enumerating *read* enumerating
    220. — 21. *for* often *read* open.
    222. — 8 of the note, *for* συςασεως *read* συςασεως
    247. — 15. *for* rites *read* tights
    269. — 4 of the note, *for* κατασκιυη *read* κατασκιυη
    329. — 3 of the note, *for* ηττης *read* ηττης
    401. in note, *for* βυλιντικη *read* βυλιυτικη

THE
WORKS
OF
ARISTOTLE.

ARISTOTLE's POLITICS.

BOOK I.

INTRODUCTION.

THIS Book embraces three subjects, the noblest and most interesting that civil science can boast: the origin of society and government; the distinction of ranks in a commonwealth; and a comparison of the best plans of political economy. On each of these topics I shall offer a few remarks, not with the presumption of interposing my own judgment, but with the hope of justifying or illustrating the decisions of my Author.

In explaining the origin of political society, Aristotle writes neither the satire nor the panegyric of human nature; which, by writers of less wisdom than fancy, have been alternately substituted for plain history. In this, as in all other inquiries, his first question is, what are the phænomena? His second, what is the analogy of nature? Building on these foundations, he concludes that both society and government are as congenial to the nature of man, as it is natural for a plant to fix its roots in the earth, to extend its branches, and to scatter its seeds. Neither the cunning cowardly principles asserted by Hobbes and Mandeville, nor the benevolent moral affections espoused by Shaftesbury and Hutcheson, ought, according to our author's notions, to be involved in the solution of the present question: since the first political societies are as independent of human intelligence, and therefore of moral determination [a], as the instinctive actions of plants and insects, tending to the preservation of their respective kinds, are independent of any intelligence of their own [b], even when they move and operate conformably to the laws of the most consummate wisdom.

Government, then, is coëval with society, and society with men. Both are the works of nature; and therefore, in explaining their origin, there cannot be the smallest ground for the fanciful supposition of engagements and contracts, independently of which the great modern antagonist of Aristotle declares, in the following words, that no government can be lawful or binding: "The original compact, which begins and actually constitutes any political society, is nothing but the consent of any number of freemen capable of a majority, to unite and to incorporate into such a society. And this is that, and that only, which could give beginning to any lawful government in the world [c]." From this maxim, which is perpetually inculcated in Locke's two treatises on government, is fairly deducible the unalienable right of mankind to be *self-governed*; that is, to be their own legislators, and their own directors; or, if they find it inconvenient to assume the administration of

---

[a] See vol. i. p. 109. & seq.; and p. 285. & seq.   [b] Ibid.
[c] Locke's Works, vol. ii. p. 185. Edit. of 1714.

affairs in their own perfons, to appoint reprefentatives who may exercife a delegated fovereignty, effentially and unalienably inherent in the people at large. Thence refults the new unalienable right of all mankind to be fairly reprefented, a right with which each individual was invefted from the commencement of the world, but of which, until very recently, no one knew the name, or had the leaft notion of the thing[d]. From this right to fair reprefentation, there follows, by neceffary confequence, the right of univerfal fuffrage, univerfal eligibility, and the univerfal and juft preponderancy of majorities in all cafes whatever.

Such is the boafted and fpecious theory begun in the works of our Locke and our Molyneux[e], continued in thofe of our Price[f] and our Prieftley[g], and carried to the utmoft extravagance in thofe of (I wifh not to fay our) Rouffeau[h], Paine[i], and the innumerable pamphleteers whofe writings occafioned or accompanied the American and French revolutions.

[d] According to the fyftem of Locke and his followers, reprefentatives are appointed by the people to exercife in their ftead, political functions which the people have a right to exercife in their own perfons. They are elected by the people, they derive their whole power from the people; and to the people, their conftituents, they always are refponfible. Of this doctrine, Mr. Locke is the firft or principal author. But reprefentatives, in the ufual and legal acceptation of the word in the Englifh conftitution, meant, and ftill means, perfons in virtue of their election exercifing political functions, which the people had not a right to exercife in their own perfons, and fo little refponfible to their electors, that they are not even bound to follow their inftructions. That the ancients were not unacquainted with reprefentation in the ufual and only practical fenfe of the word will be fhewn hereafter.

[e] See his Cafe of Ireland, reprinted by Almon, p. 113, and again p. 169. "I have no other notion of flavery, but being bound by a law to which I do not confent."

[f] Obfervations on Civil Liberty, &c.

[g] Effay on the firft Principles of Government.

[h] Du Contrat Social, ou Principes du Droit Politique.   [i] Rights of Man, &c.

ARISTOTLE's POLITICS.

BOOK I.

Such works, co-operating with the peculiar circumstances of the times, have produced, and are still producing, the most extraordinary effects; by arming the passions of the multitude with principle, fortifying them by argument, and thereby stirring into action those discordant elements which naturally lurk in the bosom of every community. It is not consistent with my design, in defending the tenets of my author, to answer his political adversaries with declamation and obloquy, (a rash and dangerous attempt! since the voice of the multitude will always be the loudest and the strongest,) but merely to examine whether the fundamental maxim of their great master Locke be itself founded in truth. To prove that government is merely a matter of consent, he assumes for a reality a wild fiction of the fancy; what he calls a state of nature, which he defines to be " men living together according to reason, without a common superior on earth with authority to judge between them [k]." But he himself seems aware that this supposed natural state of man is a state in which man never yet was found; and in which, if by violence thrust, he could not for a single day remain. Locke, I say, saw the difficulty, which, instead of meeting, he only endeavours to elude. " Where are there," he asks, " or ever were there, any men in such a state of nature [l]?" He answers, " that since all princes and rulers of independent governments, all through the world, are in a state of nature, 'tis plain the world never was, nor never will be, without numbers of men in that state [m]." But this, I affirm, is not to answer the proposed question; for princes and rulers of independent states do not live together, nor associate and " herd," as he himself expresses it, in the same society. If they did so,

[k] Locke's Works, vol. ii. p. 164.   [l] Ibid. p. 162.   [m] Ibid.

they

they could not subsist without government: for government and society are things absolutely inseparable; they commence together; they grow up together; they are both of them equally natural; and so indissolubly united, that the destruction of the one is necessarily accompanied by the destruction of the other. This is the true sense of Aristotle as understood and expressed by an illustrious defender of just government and genuine liberty. "As we use and exercise our bodily members, before we understand the ends and purposes of this exercise, so it is by Nature herself, that we are united and associated into political society ⁿ."

Locke, who so severely, and, as I have endeavoured to prove, so unjustly arraigns what is called Aristotle's Metaphysics, appears to have equally mistaken his Politics. Had he understood ᵒ that invaluable work, this idol of modern philosophers, and especially of modern politicians, would not, probably, (since he was a man of great worth as well as of great wisdom,) have produced a theory of government totally impossible in practice; a theory admirably fitted, indeed, for producing revolutions and

---

ⁿ Quemadmodum igitur membris utimur, priusquam dedicimus cujus ea utilitatis caussâ habeamus, sic inter nos natura ad civilem communitatem conjuncti & consociati sumus. De Fin. Bon. & Mal. l. iii. c. xx. Conf. de Officiis, l. i. c. xvi. & seq. Cicero does not say "communitatem" simply, but "civilem communitatem," which agrees with Aristotle's definition of man, ζῶον πολιτικον, not merely a herding, but a political animal. See the same doctrine in Polybius, l. vi. c. iv. vol. ii. p. 460. Edit. Sweigh.

ᵒ Among Locke's private letters, there is one to Mr. King, who had asked him for a plan of reading on morality and politics. "To proceed orderly in this," Mr. Locke observes, "the foundation should be laid in inquiring into the ground and nature of civil society, and how it is formed into different models of government, and what are the several species of it. Aristotle is allowed a master in this science, and few enter into this consideration of government without reading his Politics." How honourable a testimony!

sedition,

sedition, but according to which, as is evinced by all history, no political fabric ever yet was reared; or if it were to be reared, could ever possibly be preserved [p]. The neglect or misapprehension of some of the most important parts of the Stagirite's writings is indeed most deeply to be lamented. Of the many thousand authors who have copied or commented his logic, the far greater number omit his interesting chapters on language; deeming the consideration of words below the dignity of philosophers. His profound observations concerning the nature and constitution of a family have been equally overlooked by his pretended followers in politics. Yet as his analysis of language has been proved in the present work to be the sole foundation of logic, so his analysis of family, and his explanation of the causes through which its elements naturally and regularly combine, can alone enable us clearly to discern the analagous principles (principles continually insisted on by himself) which have raised and upheld the great edifice of civil society; "which is not a mass but a system, and which, like every system, implies a distinction of parts; with many moral as well as physical differences, relative and reciprocal; the powers and perfections of one part supplying the incapacities and defects of another. To form a commonwealth from elements of equal value, or of equal dignity, is an attempt not less absurd than that of composing a piece of music from one and the same note [q].

A difficult question follows, how far social inequality, whether civil or domestic, may be allowed to extend? It is with a trembling hand that I touch the delicate subject of slavery; an undertaking to which nothing could encourage me, but the utmost confidence in the humanity as well as in the judgment of

[p] Aristot. Polit. passim.   [q] Ibid.

my

my author. First of all, Aristotle expressly condemns the cruel practice prevalent in his own days of enslaving prisoners of war[1]: secondly, he declares, in the most explicit terms, all slaves fairly entitled to freedom, whenever it clearly appears that they are fitly qualified for enjoying it. But the benefits conferred on men, he observes, must in all cases be limited by their capacities for receiving them; and these capacities are themselves limited by the exigencies and necessities of our present imperfect condition. The helplessness of infancy and childhood, the infirmities of old age, and the urgencies attending mankind in every stage of their existence on earth, render it indispensably necessary that a great proportion of the species should be habitually employed in mere mechanical labour, in the strenuous exertions of productive industry, and the petty tasks of domestic drudgery. Nature, therefore, in whose plan and intention the system of society precedes and takes place of the parts of which it is composed, has variously organised and moulded the human character as well as the human frame, without setting other bounds to this variety, than are imposed by the good of the whole system, of which individuals are not independent units, but constituent elements. According to this plan or intention, the Stagirite maintains, that there is room for the widest of all discriminations, and the lowest of all occu-

[1] Locke says on this subject, "There is another sort of servants, which by a peculiar name we call slaves, who, being captives taken in a just war, are by the rights of nature subjected to the absolute dominion and arbitrary power of their masters. These men, having, as I say, forfeited their lives, and with it their liberties, and lost their estates, and being in a state of slavery, not capable of any property, cannot in that state be considered as any part of civil society." Locke's Works, vol. ii. p. 181.—We should imagine that the *liberal* Locke and the *slavish* Aristotle had interchanged their ages and countries as well as their maxims and principles.

pations,

BOOK I.

pations, domestic servitude, " a species of labour not employed in production, but totally consumed in use;" because solely but not unprofitably spent in promoting the ease and accommodation of life. In the relation of master and servant, the good of the master may indeed be the primary object; but the benefit of the servant or slave is also a necessary result; since he only is naturally and justly a slave, whose powers are competent to mere bodily labour; who is capable of listening to reason, but incapable of exercising that sovereign faculty; and whose weakness and short-sightedness are so great, that it is safer for him to be guided or governed through life by the prudence of another. But, let it always be remembered—" that one class of men ought to have the qualifications requisite for masters, before another can either fitly or usefully be employed as slaves." Government, then, not only civil but domestic, is a most serious duty, a most sacred trust; a trust, the very nature of which is totally incompatible with the supposed unalienable rights of all men to be self-governed[s]. Those rights, and

---

[s] Politics would not be a science, unless it contained truths, absolute, universal, and unalterable. One of these is that in the text; because essentially springing from the nature of society and of man. Another universal political truth is, that the good of the governed is the main end and aim of every good government. From these two premises, it necessarily follows, that this main end never can be effectuated on Mr. Locke's principles. But the good of the community (without supposing all sovereign power derived from the people at large, and of which each individual is entitled to share) may, under many given circumstances, be highly promoted by giving to the people at large a controul in the government. This controul in all large communities can only be conveniently exercised either by particular magistrates, or by representative assemblies. Things, therefore, that have not any necessary connection with the origin of government (so far from being its *only just principle*) may be found admirable expedients for carrying it on. It will be shewn hereafter that assemblies elected by the people to provide for their interests, and thence called their representatives,

and those only, are unalienable, which it is impossible for one BOOK
person to exercise for another: and to maintain those to be I.
natural and unalienable rights, which the persons supposed to be
invested with them, can never possibly exercise, consistently
either with their own safety, or with the good of the community,
is to confound all notions of things, and to invert the whole
order of nature; of which it is the primary and unalterable
law, that forecast should direct improvidence, reason controul
passion, wisdom command folly. I now proceed to examine
Aristotle's reflections on political economy, which are not less
adverse than his misunderstood and misstated vindication of
slavery itself, both to the theories long prevalent, and to others
which have begun recently to prevail among the civilised
nations of modern Europe.

The northern conquerors, who invaded and desolated the
Roman empire, long disdained to produce by slow industry,
what they gloried in ravishing by sudden violence. War was
their delight and their trade. They subsisted by rapine; and
therefore cared not how far they were excelled by others in
peaceful and productive arts; while gold, and all that it can
purchase, might be conquered by iron. But the spoils of
rapacity having supplied them with the instruments of luxury,
they began to relish the pleasures of repose; and instead of
courting new dangers abroad, to imitate at home those objects
and conveniencies which, though they had not the genius to

tives, are not so new in the world as is commonly imagined. In some republics we
shall see a double row of delegates, representatives of representatives; in others, we
shall find representation and taxation regarded as correlatives; and even in some democracies, we shall meet with persons elected by the people, and representing them in
the most useful sense of the word, " that of acting for the people at large, as the people
at large, if the majority of them was wise and good, would act for themselves."

invent,

invent, they gradually acquired the taſte to approve, the vanity to diſplay, and the deſire to accumulate. Manufactures then were eſtabliſhed: navigation was exerciſed for the purpoſe not only of war but of traffic: an extenſive commerce was introduced; and colonies were planted. The avowed purpoſe of all thoſe operations, was to augment in each country the quantity of gold and ſilver; ſince, with thoſe precious metals, all other coveted objects might uſually be procured. The buſineſs of each individual merchant is to get money; and commercial nations, it was thought, could not reaſonably have any other end in view. This falſe principle was regarded as the baſis of all found political arithmetic; and the moſt concluſive reaſoning of Ariſtotle, in the book now before us, would not perhaps have ſufficed to prove, that national wealth conſiſted not in gold and ſilver, had not the ruined ſtate of Spain confirmed experimentally the ſame important truth.

For many years back, political writers have acknowledged, with our author, that the real wealth of nations conſiſts in the productive powers of their land and labour. They acknowledge alſo, with him, that the precious metals, in contradiſtinction to other uſeful commodities, have only the peculiar advantage of ſerving as the fitteſt inſtruments of exchange, and the moſt accurate meaſures of value; but that the quantity or number in which they ought to be deſired or accumulated is, like the quantity and number of all other meaſures or inſtruments, naturally limited and fixed by the ends and operations which they are employed to anſwer or effect [1]. Yet, while they

[1] It is worthy of remark that Locke is one of the moſt ſtrenuous aſſerters of the now exploded doctrine concerning money, which he conſiders "as the moſt ſolid and ſubſtantial

they reason thus justly respecting gold and silver, the same writers have not sufficient enlargement of mind to generalise the theorem, and to perceive with our author, that property itself is as much an instrument as money, though serving for a far more complicated purpose; and therefore, if it be collected in greater quantities than that purpose requires, the surplus will be at best useless, most commonly pernicious; will inflame desire, foment luxury, provoke rapacity, and produce that long train of disorders, which made our philosopher declare, "that the inhabitants of the Fortunate Isles, unless their virtue kept pace with their external prosperity, must inevitably become the most miserable of all mankind." In the fashionable systems of modern politicians, national wealth is considered as synonimous with national prosperity. To the increase of productive industry, and the augmentation of public revenue, health, education, and morals, are sacrificed without apology and without remorse; since that trade is universally held to be the best, which produces most money with the least labour. But according to Aristotle, it is not the quantity or the value of the work produced, that ought to form the main object of the statesman's care, but the effect which the producing of that work naturally operates on the mind and body of the workmen. In the praises of agriculture and a country life, our author's sentiments, and even expressions, have been faithfully and generally copied by the most judicious writers of antiquity; many of whom mark, with as much reprobation as Aristotle himself,

---

stantial kind of wealth, regarding the multiplication of the precious metals as the great object of political economy." See the passage quoted and refuted in Smith's Wealth of Nations, v. ii. p. 140. 8vo. edit. It is time that, with regard to subjects still more important, men should return from the school of Locke to that of Aristotle.

BOOK I.

himself, that species of traffic cultivated, not for accommodation but for gain; since such a traffic, universally diffused among a people, has a tendency to pervert their feelings, and to confound their principles, to make them value as ends, things only useful as means; and to debase and corrupt every part of their character; because wherever wealth is the primary object of pursuit, luxury will naturally afford the principal source of enjoyment. In agriculture and pasturage, the energy of nature co-operates with the industry of man. They are, of all occupations, the most beneficial and most necessary, as well as the most agreeable and most salutary; conducing, with peculiar efficacy, to the firmest and happiest temperament of the mind and body: and the property acquired by them is intrinsically more valuable, because essentially more useful, than any other property whatever. Our author likewise maintains, that those natural and primeval pursuits are of all the least likely to engender sloth, intemperance, avarice, and their concomitant vices; and that nations of husbandmen, in particular, afford materials susceptible of the best political form, and the least disposed to disturb, by sedition, any moderately good government under which it is their lot to live. In consideration of so many advantages attending it, he concludes that rural labour ought to be the most favoured branch of national industry; an opinion which nothing but the intrepidity of ignorance, fortified by false system, could venture to contradict. Yet, how far other methods of accumulating stock, beside those proposed by our author, ought to be admitted and encouraged, or discouraged and rejected, must depend on circumstances and events, the force of which the philosopher's experience could not supply him with the means exactly to appreciate. From the

the artifices and shifts which he explains, (and he is the only writer that explains them,) as practised by the republics and princes of his own and preceding times, for the purpose of raising money, it was impossible for him to conjecture that, in a future age of the world, monarchical government should attain such stability as rendered the public revenues a safe mortgage to creditors; that the immense debts contracted through the facility of borrowing, would have a direct tendency, by interesting a great number of powerful individuals in the permanence of constituted authorities, to augment that facility itself, and thereby still farther to accumulate the national debt; for discharging the interest of which, heavy taxes must necessarily, but not altogether unprofitably be levied, since they would, in some measure, repay, in public security, the burdens which they impose on personal labour, or rather the sums which they withdraw from private property. But taxes to a great amount cannot possibly be raised, except in countries flourishing in such resources as agriculture and pasturage alone were never yet able to afford; resources, which can only be acquired by war and rapine on the one hand, or obtained, on the other, by the powers of national industry, assisted and multiplied by the most complicated machinery, and an endless subdivision of allotted tasks; each individual performing his part quickly and dexterously, because each has but one, and that a small part, to perform; while the diligence of all is perpetually stimulated by the bait of gain, supplied from the exhaustless fund of an enlightened commercial spirit, as extensive as the world, and as enterprising as those renowned adventurers who discovered and explored its remotest regions. It is in vain to inquire whether the plan of political economy proposed by Aristotle be in

itself

ARISTOTLE's POLITICS.

BOOK I. itself preferable to that which some modern nations pursue. Nations, circumstanced as they are, may derive armies chiefly from agriculture, but must principally depend for supplies on manufactures and commerce. The option of their own or a better system is now no longer in their power: the question of expediency has ceased: they must obey necessity [*].

This seems to me the only firm ground of defence for what is called the commercial system of economy; a system which has often been defended by very inconclusive arguments. "Public wealth and prosperity," Mr. Hume observes, "is the end of all our wishes;" and this wealth or prosperity, both he and his follower, Dr. Smith, maintain, is only to be promoted by encouraging, with equal impartiality, all kinds of lawful industry; for though food be the great want of mankind, yet one man may

---

[*] It is not difficult to explain why the doctrines of speculative politicians respecting the wealth and economy of nations, should also differ so materially from the theory proposed by our author. Among the Gothic nations who subdued the Roman empire, every thing most valuable and most interesting is connected with the improvement of arts, and consequent extension of commerce; which were the only engines that could counteract without violence their peculiar and unnatural arrangements with regard to landed property. Previous to the refinement and luxury introduced by commerce and the arts, the great landholders, who had engrossed whole provinces, dissipated the superfluous produce of their grounds in maintaining idle servants and worthless dependants, ever ready to gratify the wildest and wickedest of their passions; to abet their insolence, to uphold their haughtiness, to encourage and second their violence and rapacity; and the governments of Europe, ignorantly termed aristocracies, formed the worst species of oligarchy; an oligarchy consisting, not in the collective authority of the whole body of landholders, but in the prerogatives and powers of each individual lord over his respective vassals and retainers. In such a condition of society the expensive allurements of luxury, produced by what Aristotle condemns as over-refinement in arts and manufactures, had the most direct tendency to remedy evils greater than themselves; to undermine the exorbitant power of the few, and to bestow consideration on the many. This particular case has been, by a very usual fallacy in reasoning, converted into a general political theorem.

may produce as much food as will maintain many [x]. But this assertion is not true in the acceptation in which it must be taken, in order to recommend the commercial system above the agricultural. In agriculture, as we above observed, nature operates in concert with man; and though one family co-operating with nature, may, in a given piece of ground, produce as much food as will serve six, yet six families labouring the same ground, will not reap a proportional increase; and twenty families labouring the same ground, may find it barely sufficient to supply their own nourishment. The more that the land is laboured, it will be the more productive; and the more fitly and fairly it is divided [y], it will (other circumstances remaining the same) be the more laboured; and the same country or island will thus maintain the greater proportion of inhabitants employed in that kind of work, which, according to Aristotle, is the most favourable to health, morals, good government, the unfolding of intellectual as well as corporeal powers, and the attainment of that measure of happiness which the general mass of mankind can ever hope to reach.

[x] Hume's Essays, vol. i. Refinement of Arts; and Smith's Wealth of Nations, passim.

[y] Does our author, therefore, propose an Agrarian law? No; he knew better. The second book of his Politics is, of all works ever written, the best adapted to prove to levellers themselves, that the measures from which they expect so much good, would, if carried into execution, infalibly terminate in their own ruin and that of the community.

BOOK I.

ARGUMENT.

Nature and end of a Commonwealth.—Analysis thereof.—Monarchy the first form of government.—Domestic œconomy.—Slavery.—Accumulation of stock.—Riches, real and artificial.—Commerce.—Money.—Manufactures.—Monopolies.—Women.—Children.—Slaves.—Connection between domestic and political œconomy.

EVERY political society forms, it is plain, a sort of community or partnership, instituted for the benefit of the partners. Utility [a] is the end and aim of every such institution; and the greatest and most extensive utility is the aim of that great association,

---

[a] The first sentence of the Politics may be translated literally thus: "Since we see that every commonwealth is a partnership, and that every partnership is established for the sake of some good, (good, real or apparent, being the cause of all human action,) it is plain that all partnerships have good for their end and aim; and especially, that the sovereign good must be the aim of that sovereign partnership, which comprehends all the rest, and which is known by the name of a commonwealth, or of political society." The word utility in the text is therefore taken in its most extensive signification; utility in the strict sense, constituting but one branch, and that the lowest of το αγαθον. See the Ethics, l. i. & x. passim. Plato uses the word utility nearly in the modern sense. καλλιστα γαρ δη τουτο και λεγεται και λελεξεται, οτι το μεν ωφελιμον καλον, το δε βλαβερον αισχρον, Plato de Repub. l. v. p. 655. Edit. Ficin. "This is most excellently said, and will ever continue to be said, that whatever is useful is honourable, and whatever is hurtful is shameful." In the Gorgias, p. 324. το καλον is analysed into pleasure and utility; a system revived by Mr. Hume in his Inquiry into the Principles of Morals. In both these significations "utility" is different from το χρησιμον, denoting what is good or desirable, not in itself, but as useful or subservient to some desirable purpose.

VOL. II.   D

ciation, comprehending all the rest, and known by the name of a commonwealth [a].

A commonwealth is not to be confounded with a family, as if a large family were nothing different from a small commonwealth; nor ought we, as too many do, to confound the functions of kings and magistrates with those of superintendants [b] or masters. Magistrates rule by an established rotation; kings reign for life [c]; and considered in reference to the number of those

---

[a] As I shall frequently have occasion to use the words republic and commonwealth, the signification of which has been of late years strangely altered, I cannot better explain Aristotle's meaning of those terms than in the words of Cicero. "Respublica res est populi, cum bene et juste geritur," &c. " A commonwealth is the wealth of the people, when it is well and rightly administered, whether by a single prince, by a small body of nobles, or by the people at large. But injustice converts the nobles into a faction; the prince, into a tyrant; the people, into tyrants. In all these cases alike, the republic is not only corrupted, but annihilated; since that cannot be called the wealth of the people which is administered by a faction or a tyrant; nor can that multitude be called the people, which is not associated on principles of justice and public utility." Fragm. de Republic. l. iii. Alluding to the sense above given to the word "commonwealth," James I. said to his Parliament in 1603, " I will ever prefer the weal of the public and of the whole *commonwealth* to any particular and private ends of mine."

[b] The οικονομος was a person appointed by rich men to manage their domestic concerns, and particularly to superintend and direct the labour of their slaves. When the δεσποτης, or master, was a poor man, he performed the office of οικονομος himself; for this reason Aristotle says, διοτι, αν μεν ολιγων δεσποτη· αν δε πλειονων, οικονομον. " As if there were no other distinction between a master and a superintendant, but that the former had the government of a few, and the latter of more."

[c] The original says, οταν μεν αυτος εφεξης βασιλικον· οταν δε κατα λογους της επιστημης της τοιαυτης, κατα μερος αρχων και αρχομενος, πολιτικον. The Latin translators all mistake the passage, " Esse quidem regem, si ipse praesit," &c. But Aristotle says, " when the same person perpetually presides, the government is regal; it is, on the other hand, republican when power changes from one hand to another, and the citizens rule by vicarious succession, according to the established principles of social arrangement." What these principles

ARISTOTLE's POLITICS.

those subject to their authority, the jurisdiction of superintendants is commonly more extensive than that of masters or fathers, and always more limited than that of magistrates and kings. These, however, are but accidental distinctions; others, more invariable and more scientific, will result from analysing (according to our usual mode of investigation) that complex object, a commonwealth, into its constituent elements; those simple and ultimate principles, that admit not of farther resolution.

In this analysis, we shall proceed most satisfactorily [d] by viewing society in its growth. Those parts or elements, then, will naturally force themselves into union, which cannot continue separately to exist. The necessity of perpetuating the species, forms the combining principle between males and females; a principle independent of choice or design, and alike incident to animals and to plants, which are all naturally [e] impelled to propagate their respective kinds. The same imperious necessity which compels association, naturally [f] produces government. Communities could not subsist without foresight to discern,

BOOK I.

Analysis of political society.

---

ciples are, we shall afterwards see. It is sufficient at present to observe that they are totally incompatible with the new-fangled doctrines concerning universal suffrage and the right of majorities. The learned reader will perceive that I have here changed the order of the words, the better to express the sense. The significant brevity of the Greek particles knit firmly together distant clauses and sentences. But their force could only be expressed in other languages by tiresome circumlocutions.

[d] Aristotle says, " in this, as in other inquiries, we should speculate most successfully, could we contemplate society in its formation or genesis." This is that comprehensive and sublime analysis which Aristotle has applied with such unremitting patience to the most important subjects of philosophy; and which is well illustrated in mathematics by the learned Barrow in his Geometrical Lectures; the principles of which probably laid the foundation of Newton's great discoveries.

[e] See Analysis, p. 109.   [f] Ibid.

BOOK I.

discern, as well as exertion to effectuate the measures requisite for their safety. Men capable of discerning those measures, are made for authority; and men merely capable of effectuating them by bodily labour, are made for obedience; but if safety be their common concern, the good of the governors must correspond with the good of the governed, and the interest of the servant must coincide with the interest of the master.

Why women and slaves are confounded by barbarians.

It is found by experience, that those instruments are the most perfect, which are each of them contrived for its specific use. Slaves and women, though confounded in one mass by barbarians, are therefore naturally different; for nature works not after the niggardly fashion of Delphic cutlers [g], who shape the same knife for various and often dissimilar offices; and if women are by barbarians reduced to the level of slaves, it is because barbarians themselves have never yet risen to the rank of men, that is, of men fit to govern; wherefore the poets say, " 'Tis right the Greeks should govern the barbarians."

Origin and progress of society.

Of the associations abovementioned, that of a family is the first in its origin. "A house, a wife, and a labouring ox," these, together with the husband or master, form the elements of the first community; for a poor man must be contented with a labouring ox instead of a slave. This primary association founded on daily exigency, Charondas [h] distinguishes by a word denoting those fed from the same board, and Epimenides [i] describes

---

[g] Delphi, as the seat of the oracle, being continually frequented by strangers, exhibited a perpetual fair or market, where each customer might be supplied with wares agreeable to his taste, and suitable to his purse. History of Greece, vol. i. c. v.

[h] Commonly reputed the legislator of Thurii, anciently Sybaris. Diodor. Sicul. l. xii. p. 485. Edit. Wesseling. He is mentioned afterwards by Aristotle. The sublime preface to his laws is contained in Stobæus. Serm. 42. p. 289.

[i] Probably in that work of his mentioned by Laertius, and entitled Περι της Κρητης πολιτειας.

describes it by a word denoting thofe warmed at the fame hearth.

Next in order follows the affociation of a canton or village, founded indeed on utility, but not on daily exigency, and moft naturally formed by colonization from the firft houfe or family. Such a community therefore is juftly expreffed by a word denoting thofe nourifhed from the fame milk. It is the affociation of kinfmen under the authority of their common progenitor, whofe jurifdiction flowly extends with the gradual multiplication of his family[k]. Cities therefore were firft fubject to kings; and to fome kind of monarchy, many nations have invariably adhered; for all of them have grown to their prefent magnitude from feeble colonies or fcattered tribes, originally fubfifting under patriarchal government, in which (according to the poet),

"Each ruled his race, his neighbour not his care[l]."

That

Why monarchy was the firft form of government.

πολιτας. On the government of Crete. Apuleius fays he was Pythagoras's mafter, and Plato relates that he came to Athens ten years before the battle of Marathon, or five hundred years before Chrift. (Plato de Legibus, l. i.) According to Plutarch (in Solon.), Cicero (de Divin. i. 18.), Paufanias (Attic.), Epimenides had made a journey from Crete to Athens near a century before that period, and had prepared the way, by his expiations and predictions, for Solon's legiflation. He is believed to have lived above 150 years (Corfin. Faft. Attic.). The catalogue of the works afcribed to him, particularly of his theological and myftical poems, is given by Fabricius, t. i. p. 37. & feq.

[k] The judicious Polybius agrees with Ariftotle in maintaining that government is the work of nature, and that monarchy is the firft kind of government. πρωτη μεν ακατασκευως και φυσικως συνισταται μοναρχια. "Firft of all comes monarchy, which is eftablifhed by the bare work of nature, independently of any preparation or defign." Polyb. l. vi. c. iv. vol. ii. p. 460. Edit. Sweigh. It is worthy of remark, that in the age of Polybius, Ariftotle's opinions were only known by tradition; his works, as we have had occafion to relate, ftill remained unpublifhed. Polybius therefore was not acquainted with Ariftotle's Politics, the perufal of which would have enabled him to avoid feveral errors into which he has fallen in his fixth book.

[l] Odyffey, ix. 115.

BOOK I.

Chap. 2.

A commonwealth congenial to the social nature of man;

That this is not a fiction, but an hiftorical fact, is attefted by that univerfal confent which has tranferred monarchy from earth to heaven. All nations believe the gods to be governed by a king; for men who have made the gods after their own image [m], are ever hafty in afcribing to thefe celeftial beings, human manners and human inftitutions.

The union of various villages forms, at length, a city or commonwealth, that finifhed fabric of fociety reaching, as near as may be, the bound of perfectnefs; felf-fufficient and complete, conftituted for fafety, and productive of happinefs. A commonwealth is not lefs congenial to human nature than the affociation of a family or village. It is the goal to which all preceding affociations tend; their natural refult, and their higheft maturity; and the perfection of civil fociety, being the matured ftate of man, is like the perfection of every other progreffive object, that ftage of his exiftence which peculiarly afcertains, characterizes, and effentiates his nature [n]. Whoever, therefore, is unfit to live in a commonwealth, is above or below humanity.

"Curfed is the man and void of law and right,
"Unworthy property, unworthy light [o]."

Such

[m] Εν ανδρασιν, εν θεων γενος
Εκ μιας δε πνεομεν ματρος αμφοτεροι.

"The fame is the race of men and gods; both of us received animation from the fame mother." Pind. Nem. Ode i. v. 1. The fame doctrine had prevailed, at leaft, from the time of Hefiod's Theogonia.

[n] The word is fometimes ufed in the fame fenfe by the Roman writers. Thus Tacitus alluding to the dark and livid colour of the Britifh pearls, which rendered them a lefs tempting prize to the avarice of the Romans (Vid. Sueton. in Jul. Cæfar, c. xlvii.), fays, "Ego facilius crediderim, naturam margaritis deeffe quam nobis avariciam." Tacit. in Agricol. c. 12.

[o] Iliad ix. v. 64.

Such a wretch can only delight in carnage, a folitary and ravenous vulture; but man delights in fociety far more than do bees or herds[p]; fince nature, which never works in vain, diftinguifhes him by the power of fpeech, not merely to fignify his pains and pleafures, a purpofe limiting the vocal communications of other animals, but to defcribe his advantages and inconveniences, to explain his rights and wrongs.

A participation in rights and advantages forms the bond of political fociety; an inftitution prior, in the intention of nature, to the families and individuals from whom it is conftituted[q].

and the caufe of his virtues and perfections.

What

[p] While tranflating this chapter I happened to look into an agreeable compilement, intitled, The Philofophy of Natural Hiftory, and read the following paffage: "Some writers, as Ariftotle and a few moderns, implicit followers of his opinions, deny that man is naturally a gregarious or affociating animal. To render this notion confiftent with the actual and univerfal ftate of human nature, thefe authors have recourfe to puerile conceits and queftionable facts, which it would be fruitlefs to relate." Smellie's Philofophy of Natural Hiftory, c. xvi. p. 415. Who thofe followers of Ariftotle are, I know not; but if any fuch there be, how unworthily has that philofopher been treated by his difciples as well as by his detractors!

[q] Ariftotle's words are, ὅτι μὲν ἦν ἡ πόλις φύσει πρότερον ἢ ἕκαστος, δῆλον· εἰ γὰρ μὴ αὐταρκης ἕκαστος χωρισθεὶς, ὁμοίως τοῖς ἄλλοις μέρεσιν ἕξει πρὸς τὸ ὅλον. "That a commonwealth is prior by nature to each individual citizen, is plain; for if each individual, when feparated, is incapable of fupplying his own wants, it is evident that he muft bear the fame relation to the community, as other parts bear to the whole or fyftem to which they appertain." Nature, our author obferves, has always fome end in view, and always employs the beft means for attaining it. "This end or purpofe is the firft thing in the intention of Nature, though fhe is often obliged to effect it by a long fucceffion of intermediate operations, each of which, except the laft of all, is both means and end, means with regard to that which follows, and end with regard to that which precedes it. Thus Nature, or rather the God of nature, willed the exiftence of fuch a creature as man, whofe characteriftic diftinction fhould confift in his perfectibility, or his capacity of being difciplined from a mere animal or favage, into a moral and intellectual being. But man is only to be difciplined by civil fociety; and civil fociety requires, for its materials, the fmaller affociations

ARISTOTLE's POLITICS.

BOOK I.

What members are to the body, citizens are to the commonwealth. The hand or foot, when separated from the body, retains indeed its name, but totally changes its nature, becaufe it is completely divefted of its ufes and of its powers. In the fame manner a citizen is a conftituent part of a whole or fyftem [r], which invefts him with powers and qualifies him for functions for which, in his individual capacity, he is totally unfit; and independently of which fyftem, he might fubfift indeed as a folitary

affociations of tribes and families. Thefe laft again refolve themfelves into individuals, diftinguifhed by the relative appellations of hufband and wife, father and fon, mafter and fervant, and conftituting the elements of families." Ariftotle here fpeaks as if civil fociety itfelf, confidered as a whole or fyftem, complete in all its parts or members, perfect, happy, and felf-fufficient, formed the end for which man was created. But in the twelfth book of his Metaphyfics, in the feven laft chapters of the third book of his Treatife De Anima, and even in his Ethics to Nichomachus, l. x. c. viii. he intimates that man has a ftill higher deftination than that of acting his part well in political fociety. Plato, in his Thæatetus, had faid, "That the main object of human purfuit ought to be ὁμοιωσις τῳ θιω κατα το δυνατον. ὁμοιωσις δι, δικαιον και ὁσιον μετα φρονησεως γινεσθαι. "a refembling God as much as poffible; and to refemble God is to imitate his juftice, his holinefs, and wifdom." Ariftotle holds the fame doctrine in the paffages above alluded to; maintaining, however, that the moral virtues may be ultimately refolved into the intellectual; or, in other words, that wifdom and goodnefs, though they do not keep pace in every ftep of their progrefs, yet finally coincide.

[r] The maxim that citizens are parts of the community had long been confidered as a practical principle, and had become a fruitful fource of laws in the republics of Greece. The wretch guilty of fuicide was punifhed with infamy, as robbing the ftate of a member [1]. The ftate refented injuries done to individuals, as inflicted on itfelf. Infults offered to women, children, or even to flaves, might be refented, profecuted, and punifhed by every citizen [2]: admirable inftitutions, Plutarch obferves, for preventing wrongs; the whole community warmly fympathifing with the indignant feelings of the fufferers [3]. Turpitude, or bafenefs, alone diffolved the connection between a citizen and his country. He who committed actions unworthy of a man, was divefted of his political rights, and fevered from the community, as a gangrened member which might infect and deftroy the fyftem [4].

[1] Ariftot. Ethic. paffim. [2] Demofthen. in Mid. p. 610. [3] Plutarch in Solon, p. 88. [4] Idem ibid.

solitary savage, but could never attain that improved and happy state to which his progressive nature invariably tends. He, therefore, who first collected societies, was the greatest benefactor to mankind. Perfected by the offices and duties of social life, man is the best, but rude and undisciplined, he is the very worst of animals. For nothing is more detestable than armed improbity; and man is armed with craft and courage, which, untamed by justice, he will most wickedly pervert, and become at once the most impious and the fiercest of monsters; the most abominable in gluttony, the most shameless in venery. But justice is the fundamental virtue of political society, since the order of society cannot be maintained without law, and laws are instituted to declare what is just.

BOOK I.

Cities or commonwealths are composed of families; and the management of a family is properly termed œconomy. A family, to be complete, must consist of freemen and slaves [s]; and as every complex object naturally resolves itself into simple elements, we must consider the elements of a family:—the master and servant, the husband and wife, the father and children; what all of these are in themselves, and what are the relations which they naturally and properly bear to each other [t]. We shall then consider the acquisition of property and the accumulation of stock, which

Chap. 3.

The nature and branches of domestic œconomy.

---

[s] This sounds harsh; but hear him to the end.

[t] The relations of authority and subjection subsisting between the master and servant were expressed in the Greek by the substantives δισποτια and δυλια. But the analogous relations subsisting between the husband and wife, the father and children, had not in Greek, Aristotle observes, any appropriate names. He therefore denotes them by the adjectives ή γαμικη (conjugalis societas) and ή τικνοποιητικη; which latter, in chapter twelfth of this Book, he calls πατρικη, to which joining αρχη, we shall have the patria potestas of the Romans.

ARISTOTLE's POLITICS.

BOOK I.

The nature of domestic slavery.

which by some is treated as a branch, and by others as the most important branch, of œconomy. Let us begin then by examining the relation of master and servant; and by investigating the nature of servitude itself, endeavour to form more salutary and more correct notions on this subject than those which generally prevail. By some writers, that part of œconomy employed in the management of slaves has been dignified with the name of science; by others, slavery is considered as an institution altogether unnatural, resulting from the cruel maxims of war. Liberty, they assert, is the great law of nature[1], which acknowledges not any difference between the slave and the master; slavery therefore is unjust, being founded on violence.

It is the business, then, of œconomy to procure the comfortable subsistence of a family; and all arts and employments require proper instruments for effecting their respective ends. Of these instruments, some are inanimate, and others are endowed with life. The sailor, as well as the helm, are instruments of navigation; since they are moved and impelled by the will of the pilate, for effecting the purpose of his art. Under this aspect, any piece of property may be considered in relation to the art of œconomy. It is an instrument to be moved and employed for the purpose of comfortable subsistence. Property at large, therefore, is merely an accumulation of many such instruments; and even a slave is, in this view, a moveable instrument, endowed with life, which, impelled by the will of another, communicates motion to other instruments less excellent

---

[1] The Scholiast on Aristotle's Rhetoric has preserved a saying to this purpose of Alcidamas, the scholar of Gorgias of Leontium (See History of Ancient Greece, vol. ii. p. 337.): Ελευθερος αφηκε παντας θεος· ουδενα δουλον η φυσις πεποιηκε. "All come free from the hands of God; Nature has made no man a slave."

lent than himself. The statues of Dedalus, and the tripods of Vulcan, moved, we are told, spontaneously.

"Wondrous to tell, instinct with spirit roll'd
"From place to place, around the blest abodes,
"Self-moved, obedient to the beck of Gods ⁿ."

Did this usually happen, did the shuttle thus weave, and the strings of the harp thus play, the artist would not need the assistance of workmen, nor the master require the labour of slaves.

Among the various instruments subservient to the comfort of human life, there is this material distinction; that the work performed by one class, consists in production; and the work performed by another, is totally consumed in use. A shuttle produces a web; a couch, or a suit of clothes, produce nothing; they respectively afford, however, the convenience of wearing the one, and of reposing on the other. As use and production are things specifically different, the objects or instruments that are relative to the one must, with respect to their ends and purposes, be essentially different from those relative to the other. A domestic slave is relative to use; his labour is totally consumed in promoting the ease of his master. He is merely the possession and property, or, as it were, the separable part of that master; and every part, whether separable or inseparable, is to be used and employed, not according to its own interest or caprice, but in subserviency to the general good, and suitably to reason. It is to be regarded merely in relation to that whole or system to which it appertains. A slave is simply the property of his master; but the master stands in many other relations beside

ⁿ Iliad viii.

BOOK I.

The analogy of nature evinces flavery to be juft and ufeful.

befide that of proprietor of his flave. Such is the nature and the function of fervitude. We proceed to examine whether this inftitution be wife and juft.

To determine this queftion, it will be fufficient to contemplate the ordinary courfe of nature, and to deduce from our obfervations clear inferences of reafon. Government and fubjection, then, are things ufeful and neceffary; they prevail every where, in animated as well as in brute matter; from their firft origin, fome natures are formed to command, and others to obey; the kinds of government and fubjection varying with the differences of their objects, but all equally ufeful for their refpective ends; and thofe kinds the beft and moft excellent, from which the beft and moft excellent confequences refult. In every compofition whofe parts are harmonifed into any regular whole, the neceffity of government and fubjection evidently appears, whether this whole or fyftem be continuous or difcrete, animated or lifelefs; for even in mufic, there is a certain principle of rule and fubordination: but fuch fpeculations are perhaps foreign to the prefent fubject. In compofitions endowed with life, it is the province of mind to command, and the province of matter to obey. Man confifts of foul and body, and in all men rightly conftituted, the foul commands the body; although fome men are fo grofsly depraved, that in them the body feems to command the foul. But here the order of nature is perverted.

In the human conftitution, therefore, mind governs matter abfolutely and defpotically; but reafon governs appetite with a far more limited fway; ftill, however, it governs like a juft and lawful prince, and the little community of man is thus held together and fuftained; whereas, were the fubordinate parts to ufurp usurp authority, or even to assert equality, all would speedily be undone, and the system would fall in ruins.

The same observations apply to the various tribes of animals, which rise above each other in excellence, in proportion to their tameness and docility; and which are all of them benefited by their subjection to man, because this is conducive to their safety. In the different sexes also, we see the male formed for government, and the female for submission; and a principle prevailing thus universally in every region of nature, cannot but apply to an institution so natural as is that of political society.

Those men, therefore, whose powers are chiefly confined to the body, and whose principal excellence consists in affording bodily service; those, I say, are naturally slaves, because it is their interest to be so. They can obey reason, though they are unable to exercise it; and though different from tame animals, who are disciplined by means merely of their sensations and appetites, they perform nearly the same tasks, and become the property of other men, because their own safety requires it.

In conformity with these observations, Nature, we see, has variously moulded the human frame: some are strongly built, and firmly compacted; others erect and graceful, unfit for toil and drudgery, but capable of sustaining honourably the offices of war and peace. This, however, holds not universally; for a servile mind is often lodged in a graceful person; and we have often found bodies formed for servitude, animated by the souls of freemen. Yet the distinction itself is not frivolous; for were part of the human race to be arrayed in that splendor of beauty which beams from the statues of the gods, universal consent would acknowledge the rest of mankind naturally formed to be their slaves.

What are the requisites which fit men for servitude.

ARISTOTLE's POLITICS.

BOOK I.
Chap. 4.

The mistakes on this subject caused by

The difference of minds, though less obvious, is far more characteristic and more important; whence we may conclude that slavery is founded both on utility and justice [x]. This decision, however, has been arraigned with considerable plausibility: for slavery may be taken in two senses, in one of which he is a slave who submits to the law of war, commanding the vanquished to become the property of the victors [y].

This

---

[x] Aristotle founds slavery on different principles from those assigned by Justinian, which have been universally followed by one party, and universally controverted by another, since the time of that Emperor, or rather since the Roman jurisprudence became a fashionable study. Servi aut fiunt aut nascuntur; fiunt jure gentium aut jure civili; nascuntur ex ancillis nostris. Inst. i. 3. 4. According to Justinian, therefore, there are three origins of the right of slavery: The law of nations; the civil law; and birth, that is, descent from servile parents. By the law of nations, a conqueror was thought entitled to kill his enemy, and having spared his life, might afterwards deal with him as he pleased, and therefore reduce him into slavery. This, indeed, was the practice of ancient nations; but the practice, how universal soever among them, was abusively termed a law, since irreconcileable with justice. In war the victor has not any right to kill his enemy but in cases of absolute necessity, for self-defence; and there is a clear proof that this necessity did not exist, when, instead of killing him, he made him prisoner. Even the right of killing would not infer the right of enslaving; since to many slavery may be worse than death. Justinian says, secondly, that slavery may begin "jure civili," when one man sells himself to another. But every sale implies a price, a quid pro quo; whereas in the case of strict slavery, the seller gives every thing; life, liberty, property; and the buyer gives nothing. Of what validity then, says Judge Blackstone, can a sale be which destroys the principles on which all sales are founded? Lastly, as to slaves by birth, it is plain that this foundation of slavery rests on the two former, and must fall with them. If neither captivity nor sale can enslave the parent, much less can they enslave the offspring. See Blackstone's Commentaries, vol. i. p. 424. Aristotle, as we shall see, might, consistently with his principles, have subscribed to the liberal conclusions of this excellent author.

[y] Aristotle says, ὁ γαρ νομος ὁμολογια τις εστι εν ᾧ τα κατα πολεμον κρατουμενα των κρατουντων ειναι. "That law is a certain agreement, according to which all belonging to the vanquished becomes the property of the victors." This was universally the law of nations in Aristotle's time; a law which his humanity abhorred, and his courage arraigned.

Instead

ARISTOTLE's POLITICS.

This is acknowledged to be law; but the law itself is accused of iniquity[a], and impeached, like the orators of Athens who have perfuaded the affembly to pafs unjuft decrees. On this fubject, wife men hold different opinions, proceeding from the different views which they take of the queftion. Some confider fuperiority as the proof of virtue, becaufe it is its natural effect; and affert that it is juft, the victors fhould be mafters of the vanquifhed, as being their fuperiors, and therefore their betters; while others deny the force of this argument, maintaining that nothing can be truly juft, which is inconfiftent with humanity[a]. Superiority in war, they fay, cannot furely be a proof of juftice, fince wars are often unjuftly undertaken, and fuccefsfully, though wickedly, carried on and concluded. It is harfh, befides, to affert that he ought to be a flave who is unfit for fervitude; and that perfons of illuftrious birth or illuftrious merit are rendered flaves by falling into the hands of an enemy. To avoid this confequence, the advocates for fubjecting the vanquifhed to the victors, propofe limiting this law to the cafe of Barbarians vanquifhed by Greeks; for the nobility of Barbarians is confined to their refpective countries, but the nobility of Greece is as extenfive as the world. But in this mode of reafoning, they abandon their own doctrine, and acknowledge the principle which we have above eftablifhed, that flavery adheres to the character itfelf, is independent of accident, and that

BOOK I.

confounding the kinds of flavery.

fome

Inftead of being accufed of abetting the harfh law of flavery, he ought rather to be refpected for deftroying the falfe foundations on which this law was eftablifhed.

[a] The orator, who had perfuaded the Athenian affembly to pafs an unjuft or a bad law, was impeached by the γραφη παρανομων. Hiftory of Ancient Greece, vol. iii. c. 32.

[a] The text is corrupt. The word is ιυκια; and on the margin ευχμια. I conjecture the true reading is επιικεια, equity; that is, humanity moderating ftrict juftice, the juftice founded on law.

BOOK I.

Differences of the two kinds of slavery.

some are every where slaves, and others, like the Helen of Theodectes [b], are every where free;

"Sprung from the immortal gods, on either side,
"Who dares reproach me with the name of slave?"

Such, indeed, seems to be the intention of Nature, who, as she produces man from man, and beast from beast, wishes likewise to generate illustrious descendants from illustrious ancestors; but here Nature often fails in accomplishing her own purposes [c].

There are, thus, two kinds of slavery, the one founded on nature, the other established by law, or rather produced by violence. The first kind can only take place when the master is as fit to command as the slave to obey. It is then profitable both to the slave and the master; whose interests, rightly understood, become as inseparable as the interests of soul and body. This communion of interests naturally engenders mutual good-will [d]; but in the slavery contrary to nature, occasioned by war, and

[b] A native of Phaselis in Lycia, the scholar of Plato and Isocrates, author of fifty tragedies, and of the Art of Rhetoric in verse. See Fabricius, l. ii. c. 19. & l. iii. c. 10. Cicero, Athenæus, and Suidas say, that he was a scholar of Aristotle's. The remains of his works consist in a few short fragments.

[c] See Analysis, vol. i. p. 110.

[d] The author advises masters to secure the fidelity of slaves by the pledges of wives and children, and to indulge them with the enjoyment of festivals and diversions, of which their condition stands more in need than that of freemen. De Cura Rei Familiaris, l. i. c. v. p. 494. In most countries of Greece, slaves, indeed, were merely the lowest class of inhabitants, a sort of servants for life, and not always for life, since they were entitled on many particular grounds to demand their freedom, and even to recover it by purchase, if frugal in the management of their peculium, or separate property. Comp. Plato de Legibus, l. vi. Aristoph. in Ran. v. 706. Terent. Phorm. act i. sc. 1. Xenoph. de Repub. Athen. The Athenian slaves, when harshly treated by their masters, found an asylum from cruelty in the temple of Theseus, and were allowed to pass into the service of

another

and created by force, slaves and masters must always be hostile to each other.

The principles above established shew, that a diversity in the nature and relations of things necessarily occasions various kinds of subordination. According to the differences of those subjected to its authority, government, therefore, is found to vary, to be more or less absolute, and, as it were, to fluctuate between monarchy and liberty; monarchy, where one man rules always, and sometimes absolutely; liberty, where different men hold the offices of magistracy by vicarious succession: but the management of a household must always be of the first kind, and entrusted to one only, if we wish it to be well regulated.

A master possesses a property in his slaves, and a right to employ their industry; yet it is not from his particular skill in directing this industry that he derives his authority. This authority is founded on the general superiority of his character; since it is their respective qualities and characters that class mankind under the different denominations of freemen or slaves. Did the government of a household consist, as some writers have imagined, in any particular skill or craft, this skill or craft must evidently be relative to the labour required, and the

Different kinds of subordination founded in nature.

Peculiarity of the relation between master and slave.

another master less tyrannical. Demosth. in Mid. Plutarch de Superstit. Demosthenes having cited a law which forbade the striking of a slave, proceeds thus: "You hear, Athenians, the humanity of the law, which prevents the offering insult even to a slave. What, in the name of the Gods! do you think would be the sentiments of those nations, from whom slaves are purchased into Greece, should they be told that there were certain Greeks, men so gentle and humane, that notwithstanding the accumulated injuries received from Barbarians, and a natural and hereditary enmity to their race, yet did not allow their countrymen to be ill-treated even in servitude, but had enacted a law expressly prohibiting insults to slaves, and had punished the violators of this law by death? Demosth. Adverf. Mideam. p. 392.

BOOK I.

the services exacted. At Syracuse there lived a man who exercised for hire the trade of teaching the various branches of domestic servitude; which are recommended by different degrees of necessity or utility, but which are all of them too mean and sordid to be understood by masters of families; whose proper function contains in it nothing very deep or mysterious, since its sole requisite is, that the master know how to command, what the slave knows how to perform. Masters unwilling to stoop to such petty cares employ a superintendant, who manages their houshold, while they themselves cultivate the liberal arts; plunge into politics, or pursue philosophy.

Chap. 5.

Of the accumulation of stock in general.

Slaves form the most valuable, indeed, but not the only kind of stock. Of the accumulation of stock in general, we proceed now to treat. First of all, is the art of accumulation the same thing with œconomics, or merely something subservient to this science; and if merely subservient, is it in the manner that the trade of shuttle-making is subservient to that of weaving, or as the art of founding brass is subservient to the art of sculpture? for shuttles are the *instruments* of weaving, but brass supplies the *materials* of sculpture. To accumulate stock, is to provide whatever is thought necessary for the purpose of comfortable subsistence; but œconomy consists in employing or managing the necessaries thus provided, in the manner best adapted to the attainment of the end in view. As the arts of accumulation and of œconomy cannot therefore be the same, let us consider whether the former be a branch of the latter; and there being many kinds of stock or riches, let us begin with examining the stock supplied by agriculture, or, in general, the art of providing food, the great and principal want of all mankind.

It

It is chiefly this want, and the various means employed for supplying it, that produces the wide variety of manners and modes of life, in men and animals. By the constitution of nature, different animals delight in different kinds of food; some delight in herbs, others in flesh, while a third class seek nourishment from both; and in subservience to the facility of acquiring such food as is agreeable to their respective natures, some animals are solitary, and others are gregarious. The life of man is wonderfully diversified by the same circumstance, and of all *his* modes of life, the pastoral is the most simple, the most easy, and the most indolent. Possessing a sort of living farm spontaneously productive, the shepherd roams at large with his herds, which supply him with all the necessaries of subsistence, independently of any labour on his part, but the pleasing care of conducting them to fresh pastures. Another part of the human species resembles, in its mode of life, the various animals of prey, and subsists by hunting and fishing, by war and robbery; but far the greatest proportion of mankind derives subsistence from the earth, and its cultivated fruits. Such, then, are the different forms of human life, all resulting from the different contrivances for procuring or producing food. Commerce, indeed, produces nothing; but it exchanges and distributes, as conveniency requires, the objects and commodities already produced and accumulated. A commercial state of society, therefore, presupposes a superabundance of productive industry. It is founded on the primary modes of acquiring the necessaries of life, which we have above enumerated; and which, seldom existing apart, are variously combined and blended, hunting and war often supplying the deficiencies of pasturage and agriculture.

BOOK I.

The different modes of procuring the necessaries of life.

BOOK I.

Distinction between real and artificial riches. The right of property founded in nature.

One kind of property, a property in the provisions necessary for life, is visibly established by Nature herself, who supplies all animals, at their birth, with necessary food, and afterwards furnishes them with the means of procuring it. When the young are separated from the parent in the form of eggs or worms, these organized germs contain in themselves the materials of their first nourishment; in viviparous animals, these materials are supplied by the teeming breasts of the mother. In their advancement to maturity, none of the living tribes are abandoned by the kind care of Nature. Herbs and plants are copiously furnished for the use of animals; and animals themselves for the various exigencies of man; almost all of them supplying him with food, while the tame serves him as instruments of industry, and the wild furnish him with useful articles of clothing, and innumerable other conveniencies.

A property in things necessary for subsistence being established by Nature, the means of acquiring this property must be natural and just. Hunting, therefore, is entitled to these epithets; and war, which is a species of hunting, and which may be justly employed against wild animals, and savage men, who spurn servitude, though incapable of freedom. The arts of acquiring this property are essential to every community, whether civil or domestic. They supply that genuine wealth, the accumulation of which serves as the instrument productive of comfortable subsistence, not that factitious riches stigmatized by Solon—

" No bounds to riches ever were assigned."

To real and natural riches bounds have always been assigned; since, like all other instruments, they are limited, both in magnitude and number, by the ends for which they serve, and the

effects

ARISTOTLE's POLITICS.

effects which they are intended to produce. But that factitious wealth which is often confounded with them, is indeed boundless, and will appear necessarily to be so, when we have investigated its nature.

Firſt of all, then, it is to be obſerved that every piece of property may be employed for two diſtinct purpoſes, the purpoſe of uſe, and the purpoſe of exchange. A pair of ſhoes may be worn, or they may be ſold. This ſecond purpoſe, though it is not the original and proper end for which ſhoes were made, is founded on a principle both natural and neceſſary, the diſpoſition to truck and barter, by which men part with their ſuperfluities, in order to ſupply their deficiencies. In the community of a family, there is not any room even for barter, becauſe this community is ſo cloſe and ſo intimate, that all kinds of property are conſidered as common ſtock. But when men ſeparate, at a diſtance, in ſcattered families, the varieties of local ſituation, and innumerable other circumſtances, muſt introduce that kind of exchange or barter, which we ſtill ſee practiſed among primitive and ſimple nations, who truck wine for corn, and any one commodity of which they have too much, for another of which they are in want. This firſt and natural mode of exchange gave occaſion to a ſecond far more refined and more artificial. The goods neceſſary to man, as the inſtruments of comfortable ſubſiſtence, were found not to be (many of them at leaſt) either of eaſy conveyance, or of conſtant uſe. The beſt, perhaps the only, markets, however, often lay at a diſtance. It became neceſſary, therefore, to think of certain commodities, eaſily manageable and ſafely tranſportable, and of which the uſes are ſo general and ſo numerous, that they enſured the certainty of always obtaining for them the articles wanted in exchange.

BOOK I.

Chap. 6.
The nature of commerce, its different kinds.

The uſe of money, on what principles founded.

BOOK
I.

change. The metals, particularly iron and silver and several others, exactly correspond to this description. They were employed, therefore, by general agreement as the ordinary standard of value[e], and the common measure of exchange; being

[e] The subject of money is treated above, vol. i. p. 269. & seq. In that passage compared with the Magna Moralia, l. i. c. xxxiv. p. 165, we find the fundamental principles of the modern œconomists. In both chapters the author is treating of commutative justice ; which, as he clearly shews, always depends on the equality of ratios, and therefore implies four terms ; namely, two persons and two things, or two works ; in the exchange of which, " he who has laboured much, receives much ; and he who has laboured little, receives but little :" τον μεν πολλα πεπονηκοτα παλλα λομβανειν, τον δε ολιγα πεπονηκοτα, ολιγα λαμβανειν. But different quantities of labour are, like other causes, best known and ascertained by their effects ; that is, by the works which they produce ; works so complex and so dissimilar that their relative values to each other can only be appreciated by the means of a common measure. The circumstances mentioned in the text as belonging exclusively to the precious metals, point them out as the fittest of all objects for supplying this function, and measuring the exchangeable value of all other commodities, which being all commensurable with money, are thus rendered commensurate with each other. But even the metals are not correct measures, (γινεται ΠΩΣ μετρον,) since they themselves vary in value in proportion to their plenty or scarcity, the more or less labour requisite for procuring them, compared with that requisite for procuring other objects of desire, and a variety of other circumstances, all expressed by the word χρεια ; the desire of possessing, and the difficulty of acquiring them. It is this varying relation which regulates the price or exchangeable value of things ; and beside this, no other standard can ever possibly be discovered. Had Montesquieu (Esprit des Loix, b. xxii. c. i. & seq.) and Hume (Essay on the Balance of Trade) paid due attention to our author's principles concerning money, they would not have fallen into the error of maintaining that the introduction of paper currency diminished the exchangeable value of gold and silver exactly in proportion to the quantity of paper circulated. Dr. Smith, who has ably refuted this doctrine (Wealth of Nations, v. i. b. ii. c. ii.), falls into the contrary error, when he asserts (p. 298.) that paper currency has not any effect in lowering the value of gold and silver : which value, he thinks, depends entirely " upon the proportion between the quantity of labour necessary to bring a certain quantity of gold and silver to market, and that necessary to bring thither a certain quantity of any other sort of commodities." It may be answered, that the introduction of paper currency supplying, or at least diminishing

being themselves estimated, at first, by their bulk and weight; and afterwards stamped, in order to save the trouble of measuring and weighing them.

The diminishing one of the uses of gold and silver, namely, that of circulating commodities, renders those metals less requisite for that specific purpose, less objects of desire, and therefore cheaper. In other words, it must diminish the exchangeable value of all the precious metals which have been accumulated by the labour of hundreds of ages. This, I say, it must do, other circumstances remaining the same, precisely for the same reason that the introduction of glass vessels and of pastes has diminished the exchangeable value of gems and diamonds. But as the precious metals have many and various uses, none of which, besides that of serving as a measure, can be supplied by paper currency, their exchangeable value will not be diminished in proportion to the quantity of paper circulated. One use of an object may be totally destroyed; and, notwithstanding this, the other uses for which it serves, may still entitle it to great value in exchange. Paper currency, indeed, lowers the precious metals on the whole, but lowers them on the whole by diminishing one only of their uses. Were this adventitious use of them, as Aristotle observes, entirely set aside by that kind of tacit convention which established it, they would still bear a great price on account of their many natural excellencies. The agreeable and useful properties of the metals, their brilliancy, durability, divisibility, &c. which recommend them peculiarly as a *measure*, render them also a *pledge*; and their exchangeable value is, according to Aristotle, more invariable than that of any other commodity (see above, vol. i. p. 271.). Dr. Smith, b. i. c. v. p. 51. on the contrary, maintains " that the exchangeable value of corn varies less, from century to century, than that of gold and silver." *Ibid.* The discovery, indeed, of the New World lowered exceedingly the exchangeable value of the precious metals in much less than a century; but this particular case ought not to be converted into a general theorem. In pursuance of his notion of the greater stability in the exchangeable value of corn, than in that of gold and silver, Dr. Smith observes, " that every other commodity will at any particular time purchase a greater or smaller quantity of labour, in proportion to the quantity of subsistence which it can purchase at that time. A rent, therefore, reserved in corn, is liable only to the variations in the quantity of labour which a certain quantity of corn can purchase. But a rent reserved in any other commodity is liable, not only to the variations in the quantity of labour which any particular quantity of corn can purchase, but to the variations in the quantity of corn which can be purchased by any particular quantity of that commodity." *Ibid.* p 53. The variations in the quantity of corn that can be purchased by gold

ARISTOTLE's POLITICS.

BOOK I.

Their abuse introduces artificial traffic; not for accommodation, but for gain.

The metals thus stamped are called money; and the invention of money necessarily precedes that artificial traffic, of which the main object is not comfort, but gain. To get money is the business of the merchant; with him wealth and money are synonymous; and to heap up money is in his mind to acquire all worldly advantages. By several œconomical writers, this opinion of the merchant is treated with contempt, and considered as mere dotage. They deride the notion of that being the most substantial or only wealth which, to him who should accumulate it in the greatest quantity, would only realize the fable of Midas, and thereby expose him to the danger of perishing through hunger. Money, properly so called, they observe, is founded merely on convention; its currency and value depending on the mutable wills of men, which may with inconstancy abolish what they have capriciously established. Such reasoners, therefore, recommend the acquisition of a wealth more absolute and independent; and think the productive arts by which such wealth is accumulated[f], far more deserving of attention than

gold or silver, are occasioned by the plenty or scarcity of corn, or by the plenty or scarcity of the precious metals; but far more frequently by the former circumstances than by the latter. The plenty of corn, or the little labour with which corn may be brought to market, diminishes its exchangeable value with regard to all other commodities, as well as with regard to gold and silver. When the rent is reserved in the precious metals, its exchangeable value, therefore, at different times, that is, the quantity of other commodities, or of the labour producing them, which this rent can at those different times purchase or command, will not be at all affected by the variation in the money prices of corn; because this variation, resulting from the plenty or scarcity of corn, enhances or reduces the exchangeable value of all other commodities precisely in the same proportion as it enhances or reduces the exchangeable value of gold and silver. The money price of corn was higher in the last century than in the present; yet the money price of labour was lower in that century than in the present.

[f] On the subject of political œconomy, and particularly on this subject of money, Aristotle's

than exchange or traffic, especially than that kind of traffic of which money is the end and object as well as the element and principle; a traffic ultimately centering in the augmentation of factitious riches, applicable to no other use than that of indefinitely multiplying themselves.

BOOK I.
Of traffic.

Of such factitious riches, the desire, as Solon said, must necessarily be boundless; the blindness of avarice mistaking for an object agreeable in itself, and as such indefinitely desireable, that which is barely an instrument, and of which the desire ought to be strictly limited by the purposes which it is fitted to serve. There is a limit, therefore, to accumulation for provision, but none to accumulation for gain.

Its abuse.

Yet the providence of a good master of a family, as well as the avarice of a merchant, is often strenuously employed in the pursuit of getting money; and when their activity has acquired it,

The confusion thereby occasioned.

Aristotle's opinions are totally different from those of Child, Mun, and particularly of Locke, who is by many regarded as his greatest metaphysical rival. Locke, as quoted by Doctor Adam Smith, Wealth of Nations, vol. ii. p. 140. remarks a distinction between money and other moveable goods. "All other moveable goods," he says, "are of so consumable a nature, that the wealth which consists in them cannot be much depended on, and a nation which abounds in them one year, may, without any exportation, but merely by their own waste and extravagance, be in great want of them the next. Money, on the contrary, is a steady friend, which, though it may travel about from hand to hand, yet if it can be kept from going out of the country, is not very liable to be wasted or consumed." Gold and silver are, therefore, according to him, the most solid and substantial part of the moveable wealth of a nation, and to multiply those metals ought, he thinks, upon that account to be the great object of its political œconomy. The poverty and misery of Spain and Portugal notwithstanding all their gold and silver, and the riches and happiness of England, a commercial country, without mines, as well as the riches and happiness of Switzerland, an agricultural and pastoral country, which disdains working its mines, more strongly fortify Aristotle's conclusions, than a thousand finespun arguments of the French œconomists.

it, their similar exigencies frequently compel them to use and employ it exactly in the same manner. But the merchant, if faithful to his principles, always employs his money reluctantly for any other purpose than that of augmenting itself. Yet, political writers, deceived by an agreement in accidental pursuit and occasional application, confound the endless drudgery of commerce with the salutary duties of œconomy, and regard the accumulation of wealth as the main business of both. At the name of money, they recall all those deceitful enjoyments of pride and voluptuousness which it is fitted to procure, and in which, wishing for ever immoderately to indulge, they cannot fail inordinately to desire that which promises to gratify their inordinate passions. If money is not to be obtained by traffic, the purpose for which it was first instituted, men thus minded will have recourse for obtaining it, to other arts and other contrivances; prostituting even skill and courage in this mean and mercenary service. Victory over the enemies of his country forms the proper ambition of a general; the health of his patients ought to be the main pursuit of a physician; yet how many military and how many medical men have no other end in view but that of gratifying their senseless, because unbounded, rapacity?

We thus see that there are two modes of accumulating stock; the one natural, productive, and strictly pertaining to œconomy, because essential to the purpose of comfortable subsistence; the other neither natural nor productive, and nowise pertaining to œconomy; and as justly blameable as the other is highly laudable. When we speak, however, of any kind of human industry as productive, we mean not that in the strict sense of the word it really produces any thing, but only that it

selects

selects and arranges the gifts of Nature, suitably to the exigencies and demands of human life. The manufacturer makes not the wool, but the cloth; and for the food of animals, Nature, at their first formation, provides a superabundance of those elements from which they are constituted, and with the same bounty copiously furnishes the materials of their future subsistence.

A question here arises, why the art of procuring subsistence and accommodation, any more than the art of procuring health, should be regarded as a branch of œconomy? We say, that both of them appertain to œconomy, political as well as domestic. The statesman and the physician, however, do not exercise the same talents, the one in providing for the health of his fellow-citizens, the other in providing for the health of his patients. The business of the former consists in general superintendance; that of the latter in minute and particular detail; and in the same manner the function of the statesman, respecting the provision for comfortable subsistence and accommodation, is totally different from the subservient offices of the labourer and manufacturer.

We have reprobated that species of artificial traffic which adds nothing to the common stock, but only enriches one man or one nation at the expence of another; and which, being subservient to no useful purpose, terminates in no definite end. But of all modes of accumulation, the worst, and most unnatural, is usury. This is the utmost corruption of artificial degeneracy, standing in the same relation to commerce, that commerce does to œconomy. By commerce, money is perverted from the purpose of exchange to that of gain; still, however, this gain is obtained by the mutual transfer of different

The function of the statesman respecting health.

Usury.

BOOK I.

The theory of œconomy applied to practice. The chief branches of husbandry.

Other modes of accumulation.

objects; but usury by transferring merely the same object from one hand to another, generates money from money; and the interest thus generated is therefore called "offspring," as being precisely of the same nature, and of the same specific substance with that from which it proceeds.

Having thus explained the theory of œconomy, we now proceed to the practice; observing that, as the theory is a liberal study, the practice is a necessary occupation. Whoever, therefore, would surely and honourably augment his substance, must acquire an experimental knowledge, first, of the various kinds of cattle, particularly horses, oxen, and sheep; he must examine their many and excellent qualities and uses, all subservient to the purposes of human life; he must consider and compare their respective advantages in their relations to each other, as well as to the local circumstances in which he happens to be placed. Having provided himself with cattle, which are the living instruments of agriculture, he will next direct his attention to this most useful art; distributing the labour of his household as circumstances require, among the various branches of tillage and plantation; without neglecting those advantages which offer themselves spontaneously from bees, birds, and fishes.

Such are the first and most natural contrivances for augmenting our substance. Exchange or traffic follows next. Of this the most conspicuous kind is that carried on by means of ships or waggons, by adventurous navigators, or stationary storekeepers; whose employments differ greatly in this, that some yield most profit, and others afford most security. To commerce, strictly so called, we have already referred that mode of accumulation named usury; and under the same head may be

classed

classed the letting to hire that labour or that skill of which we have the command; from which, blended with that mode of accumulation first mentioned, result many mixed modes, as the various kinds of mining and quarrying; in all which human labour is exchanged for things fruitless and lifeless, yet many of them highly useful. To enter into a more minute detail of the various modes of productive industry might indeed be useful, but certainly would be tiresome. It may be observed in general, that all such occupations partake the more of art, the less they are dependent on fortune. Those of them are vile and sordid, which hurt the health or deform the body; those are truly servile, which may be exercised by the corporeal powers alone; and those are the meanest and most contemptible, which require not any vigorous exertion of either mind or body. Chares of Paros and Apollodorus of Lemnos have exhausted the subject of agriculture, having treated both of planting and tillage. Other arts have been explained by other authors, to whose writings those curious after such knowledge may have recourse.

Persons eager for wealth may collect likewise and imitate, with much advantage to themselves, the dextrous contrivances by which other men have obtained great and sudden opulence[g]. Such, for instance, is the honest artifice ascribed to the

Monopolies.

---

[g] In a copious, but corrupt and mutilated fragment of Aristotle's, intitled ανακρισων τε 2, "the Second Book of Œconomics," we find intermixed with the just principles of political œconomy, the greatest part of those financial tricks which have been revived, and so often repeated in modern times: the debasement of the coin; not paper, indeed, but iron currency and credit; venality of justice; mortgaging the revenues; and innumerable contrivances, by which the republics and petty princes of Lower Asia impoverished and ruined their subjects. Aristotle does not explain these dangerous artifices with a view to recommend them (for he begins by declaring the only fair and certain means

BOOK I.

Exemplified by Thales of Miletus.

the invention of Thales the Milesian. The poverty of this great philosoper was thought to upbraid his studies, as serving no gainful, and therefore no useful purpose. But Thales, by his skill in meteorology, contrived to wipe off the reproach; for as this science enabled him to foresee that next season there would be an extraordinary crop of olives, he hired in the winter all the oil presses in Chios and Miletus, employing his little fortune in giving earnest to their respective proprietors. When the gathering season approached, and the olives were seen loading the branches, all men wished to provide oil presses at the same time, and suddenly. But Thales, being master of the whole number, let them separately at a high price, and thereby accumulating vast wealth, proved that philosophers might be rich if they pleased, but that riches were not the object of their pursuit.

The contrivance of Thales consisted in procuring for himself a monopoly; which, in general, is a gainful project, and as such has sometimes been employed by sovereign states, when distressed for want of money.

By a Syracusan banker.

In the time of Dionysius, a banker in Sicily bought up all the corn, and without greatly raising the price of that article, sold it to foreign merchants at the profit of fifty talents. Dionysius, when apprised of this transaction, allowed the monopolist to retain his profit, but banished him from Syracuse, as employing

means of augmenting domestic and national wealth, " produce much and consume little"); neither does he describe such unwarrantable political sleights (as has been suspected of Machiavel) with a design to satirize and disgrace those concerned in them. He treats the matter merely as an abstract question of political science. You wish to get wealth—Thus, and thus, may it be obtained: but take care; you will acquire it at too dear a rate (as I have proved in innumerable parts of my works) if you purchase it by any kind of dishonesty.

employing a mode of accumulation inconsistent with the public interest. Yet the knowledge of this, and such like contrivances, may often prove useful both to families and to states, particularly to the latter; wherefore some statesmen consider the art of improving the public revenues as the only object worthy of their study.

The three branches of œconomics, or domestic œconomy, may be illustrated by the three forms of government. A master commands his slaves like an absolute monarch; a father rules his children like a king; a husband governs his wife like a republican magistrate. The principle on which the master's authority is founded, has been explained above: that of the husband results from the natural pre-eminence of males; and that of the father, from the natural superiority of manly age to unripe youth. In republics, indeed, which aim at equality, the citizens govern by vicarious succession: yet those who happen to be in office wear a peculiar dress; the language used to them is respectful; they are distinguished by appropriate honours; honours paid, indeed, not to themselves, but (as happened to the laver of Amasis [h]) to the situation which they hold, and to the functions which they perform. The authority of a husband,

Chap. 8.

Analogy between the three branches of œconomics and the three forms of government.

[h] Amasis was a man of low extraction, but distinguished merit, who having gained the favour of Apries king of Egypt, found means to succeed to his master's throne. The meanness of his birth exposing him to the contempt of his subjects, he converted a golden bason in which he used to wash his feet, into the statue of a divinity, which he erected in one of the most conspicuous places of his capital. The superstitious Egyptians flocked to worship the image. Amasis told them that the object of their veneration had once been nothing better than a vile utensil. It is the same case with myself; I was once a plebeian, but am now your king; take care, therefore, to yield to me the respect due to the situation which I now hold. Comp. Herodot. l. ii. c. 172. Diodor. Sicul. l. i. c. 68. Athen. Deipnosoph. l. xv. p. 680.

BOOK I.

husband, therefore, over his wife, is precisely that of a magistrate over his fellow-citizens, but of a magistrate always remaining in office. The authority of fathers, founded on seniority and cemented by affection, resembles that of kings; and Homer justly characterizes the regal dignity of Jupiter, in addressing him as the father of gods and men. For kings ought to differ from their subjects, not in kind, but in perfection; and this is precisely the difference between the father and his children.

Relative importance of these branches.

It is manifest, from the observations already made, that the objects of political œconomy rise above each other in dignity; that men are more important than mere property; that the statesman ought to bestow more attention in exciting the virtues of the former, than in augmenting the mass of the latter; but that the discipline and improvement of freemen chiefly merits his most serious regard. And here a doubt occurs, whether a slave can be said to partake of any other virtue than merely the power of performing bodily service. If he is endowed with temperance, courage, and justice, wherein does he differ from a freeman? If he is entirely incapable of such excellencies, how can he be called a man? The same difficulty presents itself respecting women and children, whether the several virtues can be fairly ascribed to them or not? Can a woman be dignified with the epithets of temperate, courageous, or just? Can such virtues, or their contrary vices, belong to a boy? In one word, can that which is formed for subjection, exercise virtue in the same sense with that which is formed for government; or if we admit the affirmative, why is the one entitled to command, and the other bound to obey?

Difficulties respecting the virtues and duties of slaves, children, and women.

General solution of these difficulties.

This difficulty cannot be solved by saying, that both of them partake of virtue, but partake of it in different measures; for command

ARISTOTLE's POLITICS.

command and obedience are things *specifically* different, not merely different in degree or in quantity. And yet it sounds harsh, to allow virtue to one class of mankind, and to deny it to another. If he, who is unadorned by wisdom and justice, cannot possibly be a good master, is it possible for him, who is debased by profligacy and cowardice, to be a good servant? It is manifest, therefore, that certain virtues must be ascribed to both, but virtues as essentially different, as are the natures and perfections of those by whom they are respectively cultivated. Steadily to pursue a virtuous course of life, implies the habitual preference of this kind of life to every other. But every act of preference implies desire and comparison; and every act of virtuous preference implies propriety in the desire, and accuracy in the comparison[h]. Both circumstances must concur to produce virtuous determinations; and this concurrence cannot uniformly or steadily take place but in minds duly exercised, and highly perfected. In slaves, the faculties of deliberation and resolution may be considered as little better than null; in women they are weak and dependent; in children they are unripe and defective.

Of each class of mankind the virtues must be relative to their powers, and ought to be competent to their offices. The man fit to command may be compared with the architect, who adjusts the plan and directs its execution. *His* skill must extend to every part of the work; *that* of his workmen is limited by their respective tasks. In the work of government, reason is the architect; it is the part of reason to command, and the duty of weakness and of passion to obey. Thus the various distinctions of mankind necessarily discriminate

BOOK I.

Respecting women.

[h] See vol. i. p. 289.

BOOK I.

minate their virtues. Self-command in a woman is not the same thing with self-command in a man. The juſtice and courage of the two ſexes do not, as Socrates[1] thought, coincide; and were we to enumerate, after the example of Gorgias, each particular excellence, inſtead of contenting ourſelves with vague definitions of virtue in general, we ſhould clearly perceive that what the poet ſays concerning ſilence, is univerſally applicable to all qualities whatever.

"In woman, ſilence is an ornament,
But the ſame ſilence adds no grace to man."

There is not any quality ornamental in the one ſex, which, if exhibited preciſely in the ſame degree, would be graceful in the other.

Children. Children, we have obſerved, are unripe and imperfect; their virtues, therefore, are to be conſidered not merely as relative to their actual ſtate, but principally in reference to that maturity and perfection to which nature has deſtined them. They are diligently and modeſtly to hearken to their teachers, and obſequiouſly to obey their directors; the premature affectation of manhood, would diſqualify them from ever acquiring manly virtues.

Slaves. From the deſcription that we have given of ſlaves, it is plain that the catalogue of their perſonal excellencies is not extenſive. Extreme timidity, or exceſſive profligacy, is totally incompatible with their duties. To theſe duties they muſt carefully be trained by the maſter himſelf, and not by the overſeer who aſſigns to them their reſpective taſks, and who teaches them ſkilfully to perform their ſervile employments. It is falſe that ſlaves are to be governed merely by fear. They are capable of liſtening to reaſon, though naturally unable to exerciſe its energies.

Our

[1] Apud. Platon, in Republ.

Our slaves, therefore, are to be admonished, instructed, and disciplined not less than our children. A doubt here occurs, whether the virtues of artisans ought to coincide with those of slaves? The same vices of idleness and intemperance often prove alike ruinous to both these classes of men. Yet there subsists between them this material difference. He who is properly a slave, is such habitually and permanently through the imbecility of his nature. His servitude is perpetual and complete. The mean mechanic, on the contrary, submits to the tiresome drudgery of distorting, painful, and unwholesome labour; but he encounters these hardships for the sake of performing a particular task, which is accomplished in a limited time. His virtues, therefore, ought to coincide with those of slaves, in as far only as he partakes of a servile condition.

Difference between mechanics and slaves.

In every treatise of Politics, it is necessary carefully to examine the relative duties of husbands and wives, fathers and children [k]. These, we have said, are the elements of families, and families are the elements of states; and, as in every system the parts ought to conspire by their respective excellencies to promote the perfection and harmony of the whole, so the principles and habits of women and children must be fashioned by

The connection between domestic and political œconomy.

---

[k] There remains but imperfect fragments of Aristotle's First Book of Œconomics; in which he treats of women, children, and slaves. See Aristotle, edit. Du Vall. p. 492. & seq. The defect may be partly supplied by the remains of the Pythagoreans preserved in Stobæus, and by the fifth book of Xenophon's Memorabilia, intitled, De Administratione Domestica. Aristotle, doubtless, treated the subject more scientifically than his predecessors; since he made the rules of domestic œconomy depend on the nature and object of the national policy. Such were his just and extensive views, that, as Strabo observes (l. xiii. p. 608.), his works, even when imperfect, taught profound and practical knowledge, in opposition to shadowy embellishments and scholastic trifling.

BOOK I.

by the intereſt of that government, to the ſafety and happineſs of which they are alike eſſential; women forming the one half of the preſent, and children affording the ſole hope of the future generation. In conformity to the plan of the community, individuals, we ſay, are to be educated; and in ſubſerviency to this great and general object, all their particular virtues muſt be moulded [l]. The nature of political ſociety and the forms of civil government muſt, therefore, be clearly underſtood, before we can explain and aſcertain the fluctuating and dependent rules of domeſtic diſcipline [m]. We now enter on this vaſt ſubject, beginning with the important queſtion, which form of government is the beſt.

[l] Ariſtotle gives the reaſon, την δι τη μερης προς την τη ολη δι ὁριπιν αριτην. "The virtue of the part muſt always bear a reference to the virtue of the whole." The continual referring of particular truths to general maxims has an air of pedantry in modern languages. It certainly is uſeleſs, where the particular truth is as evident as the general one. But the diſlike or diſguſt which it excites ariſes from this, that the ſchoolmen adopted many maxims that were falſe or obſcure, and the pedantry of theſe ſcholaſtics has been long held in juſt contempt.

[m] The relation between government and education, and the ſubſerviency of the latter to the former, were ſtrongly expreſſed by Pythagoras. Being aſked by a certain Xenophilus, How he might beſt educate his ſon, he replied, Send him to live in a well regulated ſtate. Diogen. Laert. viii. 16.

ARISTOTLE's POLITICS.

BOOK II.

INTRODUCTION.

IN this Second Book, we see the intellectual exertions of the deepest thinker of antiquity strenuously exerted in solving the most important political question that can possibly be agitated. With affectionate respect for his master Plato, but with still greater veneration for truth, our author examines and refutes his ingenious, but fanciful opinions concerning the best form of government; and in detecting the errors of that admired philosopher, as well as in exposing the dangerous systems of polity recommended by Phaleas of Chalcedon and Hippodamus of Miletus, he arraigns by anticipation the extravagancies that have been proposed, approved, and many of them in our own days carried into execution. From the speculations of mere theory, he passes to those plans of legislation which have actually been established in the world; collected from the description of upwards of two hundred commonwealths; and presenting, when his work was entire, the most valuable series of political experiments that ever was exhibited. But concerning the republics of Asia and Magna Græcia, as well as those of Africa and Gaul, we must now be contented to gather our information from mutilated or doubtful fragments.

Yet

ARISTOTLE's POLITICS.

BOOK II.

Yet let us rather congratulate ourselves on the riches which remain, than peevishly regret losses which cannot possibly be repaired [a]. In the Book before us, we have the result and general conclusion of all our author's comparisons and reflections; which is, that the institutions of Crete, Sparta, and Carthage, though far from being perfect in theory, were the best and wisest that ever were carried into practice. In these governments, therefore, we may contemplate the term and limit of the civil wisdom of antiquity. With them, each nation may compare its domestic polity; and each individual may be contented, if the constitution under which he lives, can stand in honourable competition with those boasted models [b]. To satisfy his mind completely, the reader must himself make the comparison: and the English reader will finish this useful task, cherishing his country, and blessing the memory of his ancestors.

Aristotle is the only writer that describes with fulness and accuracy the commonwealth of Carthage. He does more; he predicts her melancholy fate, and points out the lurking seeds of her decay and ruin, even during the most vigorous period of her health and prosperity. But besides the malignant poison which destroyed that republic, there was a deep and radical error in the constitution of all those denominated the *free states* of antiquity; an error which our author in some passages hints

---

[a] Fabricius, vol. ii. p. 196. & seq. gives a copious list of the commonwealths described by Aristotle. Cicero says, that this indefatigable author " explained the institutions, manners, and discipline of almost all the republics of Greeks and Barbarians." Omnium fere civitatum non Græciæ solum, sed etiam Barbariæ mores instituta ac disciplinas expofuerat. De Fin. l. v. c. 4.

[b] The objection arising from the supposed ignorance of the ancients with respect to representative government, will be answered in the sequel. It will be shewn that the Greeks were acquainted with representation in the usual and practical sense of that word.

hints at, but which he no where completely explains. This evil confifted in the faulty conftruction of what is now called the executive power; which, inftead of being fovereign, permanent, and indivifible, was exercifed by affemblies and fenates, or by them delegated to an almoft indefinite number of mutually independent minifters and generals. The deplorable effects of this arrangement, with regard to liberty as well as juftice, I endeavoured twenty years ago fully to illuftrate from ancient hiftory; and as the obfervations then made could not be influenced by the events which have fince happened in Europe, and the actually fubfifting ftate of public affairs, I think it better to tranfcribe a few paffages from the work alluded to, than to repeat the fame opinions in other words. " In confidering the nature and tendency of any government, there are two principal queftions to be refolved; how far it protects the lives and liberties and properties of individuals, and what duties it requires them to perform in return for this protection? Both queftions are eafily anfwered with regard to the ftates of Greece; they required every thing, and they performed almoft nothing. Such a political arrangement gave extraordinary energy to their military enterprifes [c]; and this, if it may be confidered as a good effect, was the principal advantage with which their plan

of

[c] "Such nations," Ariftotle obferves, "fhine in war; in peace they ruft with their fwords." This truth ftrongly impreffed the author's mind, while it was yet a queftion of political expediency, what means fhould be ufed for avoiding a defperate conflict with a people, whofe ambition under defpotifm, firft fubjected their neighbours to the neceffity of keeping on foot mercenary ftanding armies; and whofe more dangerous ambition under democracy, was likely to fubject them to the ftill harder neceffity of becoming armed nations. The lively and profound fenfe which he thought it his duty to exprefs of the military energy of democracy, was ftrangely miftaken and grofsly mifreprefented, by *fome perfons* or *perfon*, who, at the time alluded to, affected to treat all thofe as enemies to peace at home, who were anxioufly zealous for peace abroad.

of policy was attended. The state enjoyed an absolute command over the personal services and the wealth of its subjects; and could on every occasion call forth their most strenuous exertions. The authority exercised over the rich and the poor was equally unlimited. But the condition of the former seemed peculiarly unhappy, because their estates, as well as their personal services, might always be required of them; and, without danger of inevitable destruction to their owners, could not possibly be withheld. They not only supplied the whole expence of the navy, but furnished such extraordinary contributions as any sudden emergency demanded. In all the following pleadings, there is scarcely one example of a rich man venturing to appear at the bar of the public, without being able to prove that he had expended the best part of his fortune in the service of the community. But this was a matter of necessity, not of choice. For the Greeks were tyrants in one capacity, and slaves in another; and that impervious line which ought to be drawn between the exercise of power in the sovereign, and the enjoyment of liberty in the people, was a secret undiscovered in Greece, and is still concealed from every country but our own [d]."

" But the Athenian institutions, distressing as they were to individuals, who loudly complained of their injustice, yet enabled the republic to exert itself with vigour against its foreign and domestic enemies. The exorbitant and uncontrolled jurisdiction, assumed by the Grecian states over their colonies and allies, tended still farther to promote the same end. The enormous exactions of the Athenians from their tributary isles, as well as the heavy taxes which they imposed on their Asiatic

---

[d] Introduction to the Orations of Lysias, &c. p. 17.

Asiatic colonies, have been already described. Sparta exercised, in this respect, an authority equally tremendous. In the beginning of the Peloponnesian war, that republic demanded from her colonies in Italy and Sicily, five hundred ships, and large contributions in money; and during the course of the same war, she made many similar applications, which were seldom ineffectual. But it is not from particular acts of extreme rigour and severity, that we must appreciate the intolerable servitude of the countries which had the misfortune to become subject to those ambitious republics. While human nature continues the same, the right to exercise power will always be attended with a strong propensity to abuse it. Unless this dangerous prerogative, on the one hand, be balanced by the invaluable privilege of defending liberty on the other; unless the line of separation between these two be boldly marked and accurately defined; unless the interests of that part of the constitution which tends to corruption, be invariably resisted by those of the generous portion which sustains its political life; it is of little consequence, whether a country be governed by one tyrant or a thousand. In both cases alike, the condition of man is precarious, and force prevails over law [e]. It shall be proved that the institutions of those ancient republics, as well as

[e] To see clearly the cause of the peculiar evils inherent in all kinds of popular assemblies vested with government, we must have recourse to the trite proverb, "Set a beggar on horseback," &c. Men not used to power are the most likely to abuse it; and when this power centers in one assembly, however constituted, it is found by universal experience, that the majority will for ever tyrannize over the minority; and will execute its unjust and wild resolutions more zealously and more ardently, exactly in proportion to the opposition which it has encountered. In its ungovernable career, the obstacles which could not check and resist, will wonderfully encrease and accelerate its headlong impetuosity.

as the manners refulting from them, both of which have been injudicioufly extolled by many learned men, approach nearer to Oriental defpotifm and the manners refulting from it, than can well be imagined. The principal difference between the citizens of the one and the flaves of the other is, that a greater number of the former might expect at fome future time to inflict the fame calamities which they had previoufly fuffered. But between the foreign dependancies of republican and defpotic ftates, there is no diftinction whatever. The moft rapacious Turkifh governor, armed with all the tremendous power of his mafter, never acted with more cruelty and injuftice, than did the magiftrates of the Athenian republic under the fanction of popular decrees[f]."

Thefe obfervations are confirmed by the juft theory of political arrangements, and illuftrated by the moft extenfive furvey of thofe denominated free ftates, both ancient and modern. In every well-regulated community, the people ought to have a control in the government, but ought not to adminifter it; for power vefted in the people at large, or in an affembly delegated by them, muft, in nations ordinarily circumftanced[g], neceffarily degenerate into the tyranny of a faction. Difcontent, fedition, confpiracy, and revolution, form the miferable train of confequences; pourtrayed in characters of blood in the melancholy annals of republican hiftory[h].

The

[f] Introduction to Lyfias, p. 18.

[g] What the *extraordinary* circumftances are which alter the nature of republicanifm, will appear in the progrefs of this work.

[h] I atteft not only the republics of Greece, but the Italian republics of the middle age, whofe tumultuary tranfactions and fanguinary revolutions crowd the defultory pages of Machiavel, Guicchiardin, Nerli, Varqui, Malavolti, Ghirardacci, Fioravanti,

The evil is not accidental, it springs from a perennial source. With the constituent elements of every commonwealth, naturally grow up two parties, distinguished by different names in different countries, but whose essential characteristics are uniform and unalterable. The nobles and the people, the rich and the poor, will always respectively entertain many particular views, and always allow themselves to be governed by many seemingly incompatible interests. When these jarring orders are united in one sovereign assembly, whichever party prevails, the majority will tyrannize over the minority, and tyrannize the more outrageously, because the same persons who have made unjust decrees, are invested with the awful power of carrying them cruelly into execution. Even in the wildest democracies such a monstrous arrangement never was durable[i]. But its continuance, however short, was long enough to be feared and detested; since to whichever side the balance inclined, either the weight of authority degenerated into despotism[k], or the flame of liberty blazed into conflagration[l].

As

vanti, Portenarli, &c. As a modern Italian writer observes, " These republics were all of them exposed to almost daily revolutions, and seldom did the system of administration continue a whole year the same." Denina's Revolutions, &c. c. v. sect. 10.

[i] It seldom happened, in the republics either of ancient Greece or of modern Italy, that the whole exercise of government was vested in one council, in one assembly, or in the committees of either; but as the legislative body, whether senate or people, itself governed by the capricious will of a tyrannical majority, directed and controlled the exercise of all executive and judiciary functions, the matter was not much mended; since all power proceeded from one centre, and flowed from one source, a power unbalanced and unresponsible, and therefore, as Aristotle observes, not made for man.

[k] The most prominent examples are the tyranny of the four hundred, and afterwards of the thirty, at Athens. History of Ancient Greece, vol. iii. c. xxi. & xxiv. Likewise the tyranny of the Decemvirs at Rome. T. Liv. l. iii. c. 32. & seq.

[l] All republican histories abound with examples of this kind. Those of Athens and Florence contain little else for near a century preceding what is called the extinction of their liberties.

BOOK II.

As by univerſal conſent, therefore, all legiſlators or reformers of free ſtates divided the ſovereignty between the two orders, convened in diſtinct chambers; the one forming a ſenate to deliberate and propoſe; the other, an aſſembly of the people to approve and confirm. This, doubtleſs, is one great point gained: the two ſovereign chambers ſerve to check each other; the one divides and the other chooſes [m]; and while each reſts ſatisfied with its preſcribed ſhare of power, their meaſures will be harmonious, and their government will be happy. But the paſſions of men, as our author frequently obſerves, are indefinite and inſatiable; and ſcarcely a ſingle example occurs in hiſtory, of either a ſovereign ſenate or a ſovereign aſſembly, which did not frequently abuſe its power, and continually endeavour to aggrandize it. How is this evil to be remedied? What authority is to be interpoſed between contending factions? What hand is fit to hold the balance, and to render the energy of law ſuperior to the violence of party rage? Ariſtotle will tell us " that the middle ranks muſt be encreaſed and magnified; that veneration for the conſtitutional laws muſt be inſpired; in fine, that a king muſt be eſtabliſhed, whoſe office is a pledge and ſecurity, that the few ſhall not be plundered and oppreſſed, nor the many inſulted and enſlaved." In proportion to the degree in which theſe advices have been complied with, free ſtates have flouriſhed. Even the republican Machiavel will vouch, that the commonwealths of the middle age never enjoyed

[m] In this, according to Harrington, conſiſts the whole myſtery of government; "a myſtery brought unto light by two ſilly girls. For example, two of them have a cake yet undivided, which was given between them; Divide, ſays one unto the other, and I will chooſe; or let me divide, and you ſhall chooſe." Oceana, p. 13. edit. 1656.

joyed any tolerable meafure of profperity or tranquillity, when the factions of the nobles and the people were not reftrained by the authority of fome virtuous, prudent, and powerful citizen [n]. Into this form, of two deliberative affemblies with an executive magiftrate at their head, all the moft renowned republics, both of ancient and modern times, have fhewn a continual tendency to throw themfelves; and that independently of contrivance and theory, or rather in oppofition to them; fo true it is, that "government," to ufe the words of Ariftotle, "is the work of nature; and all good government, the refult of time and experience."

But innumerable obftacles, both without and within, prevented free ftates from attaining the juft perfection of political arrangement. The republics of antiquity were too jealous of liberty to entruft the executive magiftracy with fuch a fhare in the legiflature as is effential to its own defence. The archon, the conful, the fuffetes, the king, or by whatever other name

---

[n] L. iv. fub. init. Machiavel has branded with indelible impreffions of indignation and contempt, the inftitutions and governments of modern Italy. Their hiftory is not, however, he obferves, without its ufe. "E fe nel defcribere le cofe feguite in quefto guafto mondo, non fi narrera, ò fortezza di foldato, ò virtu di capitan, ò amore verfo la patria di cittadino, fi vedra con quali inganni, con quali aftutie et arti, i principi, i foldati, i capi delle republiche per mantenerfi quella riputatione che non havevano meritata, fi governavano. Il que fara forfe non meno utile che fi fiano l'anticne cofe a conofcere; perche fe quelli i liberali animi a fequitarle accendono, quefte a ruggirle & fpegnerle accenderanno." L. v. Delle Hiftorie, fub init "In defcribing the tranfactions of this degenerate country, I fhall not have to fpeak of the bravery of foldiers, the fkill of generals, the patriotifm of citizens; but there will be frequent occafion to recount the flights and artifices by which tofe who were at the head of civil and military affairs, kept poffeffion of that confiveration to which they were by no means entitled. The exploits of antiquity fire noble minds with the defire of imitating them; the tranfactions of a recent date, will fire the noble minded among pofterity with a defire to avoid and fpurn fuch ignominious examples."

BOOK II.

name the firſt magiſtrate was diſtinguiſhed, judged cauſes in perſon, and commanded armies in perſon; his power did not conſiſt in appointing thoſe by whom cauſes were judged or armies commanded. In conſequence of theſe unfavourable arrangements, the wiſe and equitable adminiſtration of the laws depended on the inſtability of perſonal character, not on the ſoundneſs of the conſtitution; and diſcontent with the adminiſtration, naturally produced a revolution in the government. Among the modern nations which conquered and divided the weſtern provinces of the Roman empire, the nature of the kingly office came to be better underſtood; but as their kings were entruſted with the uncontrolled command of armies continually augmented through the fear or jealouſy of ambitious, and often hoſtile neighbours, it was eaſy for ſucceſſions of ſuch kings to overawe both nobles and people by the right of the ſword, and to unite in their own perſons the ſupreme legiſlative with the executive power. In Great Britain alone, whoſe inſular ſituation rendered the public ſafety dependent on that kind of national force which is moſt formidable to enemies abroad, but which can never be conveniently employed as an inſtrument for deſtroying liberty at home, the progreſs towards the higheſt perfection of political arrangement was left free and unincumbered; unchecked by the timid jealouſies of the people, unobſtructed by the overwhelming power of the prince[o]. Two legiſlative aſſemblies, the one popular, the other ariſto-

[o] In populous countries, the encroachments of power cannot be regularly reſiſted by the people collectively. The people, therefore, muſt act by their delegates. But theſe delegates will uniformly and heartily unite with the general maſs of the community, in maintaining equal laws and public liberty, when they are thoroughly convinced that the power which they reſtrain can never become their own. Hence the ſingular advantage of an indiviſible and ſovereign executive, whoſe functions can be legally

ariſtocratical; the former entruſted with the control of the national purſe and the inqueſt of public grievances; the latter judges in matters of impeachment by the Commons; but both orders or aſſemblies totally deprived of all conſtitutional means of hurting each other, ſince the exerciſe of government centers in one ſovereign magiſtrate, defended by a negative on the paſſing of laws, and inveſted with the whole prerogative of naming thoſe by whom they are carried into execution.—This diſtribution of power, the reſult of experience operating on fortunate circumſtances, is the nobleſt contrivance that ever was deviſed for killing thoſe ſeeds of ſedition which lurk in the boſom of every commonwealth; for enſuring the continuance of equal and uſeful laws; and for rendering the juſt authority of thoſe laws prevalent over the blind fury of contending factions. Other modes of polity have ſucceeded in countries peculiarly circumſtanced; but this applies univerſally; and free ſtates have flouriſhed in peace and proſperity, exactly in proportion* to their approximation to this perfect model.

BOOK II.

It legally exerciſed only by reſponſible miniſters; and hence the wonderful ſtability of the Britiſh conſtitution; a ſtability (humanly ſpeaking) unalterable, becauſe founded on the indelible and beſt underſtood intereſts of men, the cleareſt dictates of reaſon, and the warmeſt paſſions of the heart.

* *Other circumſtances being the ſame*; words which ought always to be underſtood in ſuch general propoſitions. The nature of the country, exacting induſtry and frugality, conſpired with the authority of the Stadtholder in giving proſperity to the Netherlands. The United States of America owe their happineſs, under their preſent executive, not merely to the great perſonal weight of their preſident, but to their extenſive poſſeſſions, offering the ſtrongeſt incitements to agriculture, to the enjoyments and virtues of domeſtic life, and to the improvement of their private fortunes; all which circumſtances have a tendency to render men eaſily governable. Theſe republics, as well as the Swiſs Cantons and their allies, preſent, doubtleſs (I ſhould ſpeak of Holland in the paſt tenſe), a picture of more tranquillity and ſtability than did moſt ſtates of ancient Greece, or the Italian republics of the middle age; and that not merely in conſequence of their political arrangements, but of many other cauſes, both moral and phyſical.

BOOK II.

It has been the fashion, however, of late years to maintain that the misfortunes of the Greek commonwealths did not originate in the source above explained, but in the general ignorance of all the free states of antiquity with regard to representative government, the highest improvement of republicanism. As this doctrine is very sedulously inculcated on both sides of the Atlantic, by those who having overturned their own hereditary constitutions, are desirous of encouraging other nations to imitate their example, it may not be improper to examine how far such assertions are warranted by history; especially as the examination will serve to illustrate several of our author's remarks in the following Books of his Politics. That the Greeks were totally unacquainted with representative government, can not be maintained by any who have the least tincture of learning. I need not mention the Amphictyonic council¹, and the Achæan league ʳ, both of which representative bodies I have described in another place. But I may observe, as a fact less generally attended to, that in the commonwealth of Mantinæa, persons chosen from the people at large ˢ were invested with the power of naming the magistrates. In this Arcadian republic, there was not only representation simply, but a double row of representatives; delegates of delegates; and it is not reasonable to conjecture that an arrangement so obvious should have remained undiscovered among a cluster of free states, where all sorts of propositions

¹ Compare the History of Ancient Greece, vol. i. c. iii. p. 107. & seq. and vol. iii. c. xxxii. p. 467.

ʳ Ibid. vol. ii. c. xi. p. 14.

ˢ Aristot. Polit. l. vi. c. iv. The author mentions other republics on the same plan, particularly that of Teleclcs the Milesian; and in his Fourth Book, where he treats of the sovereignty in a state, maintains that elective, as well as deliberative assemblies, should consist of only a part of the citizens, acting for the whole by an established rotation.

fitions were made, and all kinds of experiments were tried; where nothing was rejected which had not been previously refuted; and where inftitutions, feemingly the moft unpromifing, were condemned or approved in proportion only to the mifchief or benefit vifibly manifeft in their effects. This is fo true, that the fuppofed modern maxims, refpecting reprefentation and taxation, were held and practifed by the Lycians; a people not obfcure nor inconfiderable, but eminently illuftrious both in war and peace, from the earlieft to the lateft period of their hiftory. The Lycians inhabited the fouthern coaft of the Afiatic peninfula, and were furrounded by the territories of Carian, Pamphylian, and Cilician pirates; wretches who deformed thofe feas by their rapacity and cruelty, and whofe cities were marts of booty and flavery, particularly of captives, born free, reduced into inextricable bondage [t]. The Lycians alone difdained this abominable traffic; and though they often commanded the fea even to the coaft of Italy, yet they never were convicted or even accufed of facrificing honour to gain [u]. Their equity and innocence protected them againft the juft vengeance which often fell on their neighbours from the Syrian and the Roman power. From the age of Homer to that of Brutus [x] and Caffius, they continued to flourifh under their hereditary inftitutions in domeftic tranquillity and national independence. Within a circular peninfula, nearly an hundred miles in diameter, and with upwards of one hundred and feventy miles

---

[t] Strabo, l. xiv. p. 664 & 665. from which this account of the Lycians is almoft wholly copied.

[u] Idem ibid.

[x] See in Plutarch's life of Brutus, and in Appian (De Bell. Civil. l. iv. p. 633, & feq.), the memorable refiftance of Xanthus and Patara to Brutus.

miles of sea-coast, Xanthus, Patara, Pinara, with three equal, and seventeen inferior cities, formed from time immemorial a federal and representative government. The national convention or congress consisted of deputies from the several members of the union; the greatest cities having three votes; the middling, two; and the smallest only one vote in the election of magistrates and all public concerns. In the same proportion they paid taxes and incurred other public burdens; their taxation and representation being regarded by them as correlatives[y]. They had one common archon or stadtholder[z], whose office became in later times elective, but which may be conjectured, from the analogy of their history with that of their European brethren, to have been anciently hereditary[a].

In

---

[y] ἀναλογον δε και τας εισφορας εισφερουσι, και τας αλλας λειτουργιας. Strabo, l. xiv. p. 665.

[z] λυκιαρχης. Ibid.

[a] The Lycians were a happy people. Did they owe their happiness to their representative government? History will shew us that they owed it to their virtuous manners, which could alone render that government either beneficial or permanent. In confirmation of this, the following statement of facts may be given. Among the Gothic conquerors of the Roman empire, elective princes having gradually raised themselves to the rank of hereditary kings, their jealousy of the nobility naturally led them to protect, encourage, and insensibly to exalt to power, the industrious and peaceful inhabitants of towns and cities; of whose participation in the legislature, the first clear evidence that occurs in the history of France is the reign of Philip le Bel in 1301. In 1484, Charles VIII. summoned deputies from the country, from which time the States General, consisting of three independent chambers, each of which had a negative on the proceedings of the other two, were appointed in the manner seemingly the best adapted to unite the whole wisdom and patriotism, as well as to collect the real sense of the nation. The inhabitants of each parish sent deputies to the jurisdictions; and these deputies again sent the persons deemed best qualified to represent them in the States General. There were thus two orders of deputies; or deputies of deputies, an institution which Mr. Hume (Idea of a perfect Commonwealth) proposes as the highest improvement in representative government; and which, Dr. Price (see Appendix to his Sermon on the French Revolution) greatly extols the *French republic* for

being

In examining the other Greek republics, we shall find that power exercised by delegation formed a leading feature in every one of them. Athens itself, which became the moſt democratical of them all, was in its beſt times a government of repreſentation as well as of rotation; and in reading its laws, we ſhall be often tempted to believe that we are peruſing the code of a certain modern repreſentative democracy. In the former commonwealth, which from the time of Theſeus breathed a peculiar ſpirit of freedom, the comitia or ordinary aſſemblies of the people were not ſummoned as at Rome by a conſul, nor by any analogous magiſtrate, as in many neighbouring Greek ſtates. At Athens the political machine moved, as it were, ſpontaneouſly, with the revolution of the ſeaſons. The aſtronomer Meton, who reformed the calendar ten years before the Peloponneſian war, regulated the commencement of the Athenian year by the firſt new moon after the ſummer ſolſtice [b]. The year was divided into twelve months, conſiſting of twenty-nine, and of thirty days, alternately; and each month was divided into three decades [c]. On the days immediately preceding the firſt decade of

being *the firſt ſtate* to carry into execution. Notwithſtanding all this, the States General of France contributed nothing to the benefit of that country. The aſſembly of 1484 was diſgraced by multiplied quarrels among the chambers. The five aſſemblies which followed, exhibited alternate ſcenes of civil diſcord and ſanguinary ſuperſtition. The States were ſummoned for the laſt time in 1614; and this aſſembly, like moſt of the preceding ones, broke up as abruptly as it had deliberated uſeleſsly. Eſſais Hiſtoriques ſur les Commices de Rome, les Etats Generaux de France, & le Parlement d'Angleterre, v. ii. p. 189, & ſeq.

[b] Conf. Petit. de Leg. Attic. p. 186. Diodor. Sicul. l. xii. p. 96. Liban. Argum. in Demoſt. Orat. in Androt.

[c] Julius Pollux, &c. apud Potter. Antiq. v. i. p. 26.

of the first month, called Hecatombaion, in allusion to the numerous sacrifices by which it was distinguished, the Athenians from the wards in the city, and the districts in the country, amounting collectively to one hundred and seventy-four in number[d], assembled in the public market-place of the capital, in order to elect the senate, the archons, and other annual magistrates. For the purpose of conducting these elections, as well as other public matters, with the greater regularity and expedition, the people voted by divisions, called tribes; which were four in the time of Solon, but raised to ten by Clisthenes[e], who restored the republic after the expulsion of Hippias. From persons properly qualified[f] in point of age, character, and fortune, each of the ten tribes chose by lot fifty senators, who formed collectively the senate of the five hundred for the succeeding year. To the senate thus constituted, another body was aggregated[g], to supply the place of those senators who might be removed by death, or dismissed for malversation in office. The whole senators, actual and supplemental, were divided into ten classes, representing the ten tribes; each of which enjoyed presidency in rotation[h]. The order of this pre-eminence was also determined by lot. The fifty presiding senators were entitled the Prytanes; the hall in which they assembled and dined, the Prytaneum; and the period of thirty-five days, during which they held their dignity, was called a Prytany[i]. This period was divided into five weeks; and the fifty Prytanes into five companies, each consisting of ten persons, and each presiding in the senate during

---

[d] Strabo, l. ix. p. 396. [e] History of Ancient Greece, v. ii. c. xiii.
[f] Lysias adverf. Philon. [g] Harpocrat. in Επιλαχοντις.
[h] Suidas in Πρυταν. Liban. Argument. in Androt.
[i] Pollux. l. viii. c. 15. Demosth. de Corona.

during its respective week ᵏ. From these presidents of presidents, a single person was chosen by lot to preside in the senate for a single day, during which he was entrusted with the command of the citadel, the key of the treasury, and the custody of the public seal of the commonwealth ˡ. The nine other tribes attained the honour of the Prytany, each in the order which had been established by lot; and their presiding companies, as well as the president himself, were appointed precisely in the manner above described ᵐ. With this representative body, Solon lodged the most important branches of sovereignty. The senate convened daily ⁿ: it prepared all matters of deliberation for the popular assembly °; no measure could be lawfully enforced by the people which had not been previously approved by the senate ᵖ; and the senate, independently of the people, made laws which had force for a year, that is, during the period of its own existence ᵠ. The presidents of the senate also presided in the popular assembly; summoned its extraordinary meetings by their authority; put the question to a vote; collected the suffrages; and having declared the will of the majority, dissolved the assembly ʳ. The senate, therefore, enjoyed the principal share in the *legislative and executive* powers of government; but the judicature was merely a temporary commission, exercised by juries chosen by lot from the people at large ˢ. These juries were directed in their proceedings by the nine

---

ᵏ Liban. Argument. in Demosth. Androt.   ˡ Suidas in Επις.
ᵐ Suidas & Harpocrat. in Πρυτρει & Επιςαται.
ⁿ Petit. Leg. Attic. 183.   ° Harpocrat. in Προεδρ. Demosth. in Leptin.
ᵖ Idem ibid. & Plutarch in Solon.   ᵠ Plut. ibid. & Demosth. in Aristocrat.
ʳ Æschin. de Falsa Legation. & Aristophan. Concionatric.
ˢ Plutarch in Solon. Demosth. in Aristogeit.

BOOK II.

nine archons[1], who were annually appointed at the same time with the senate, and from persons of the same description with those qualified to sit in that council[n]. In the stated assemblies held at the end of every year, and commonly during the last four days of it, the people also appointed the military commanders, the surveyors of roads and buildings, the commissaries and controllers of accounts, and a variety of other officers; each department of office commonly containing ten citizens, that the ten tribes might be respectively represented, each by one of its own members[a].

Solon could not foresee the events which destroyed this political arrangement. He foresaw, however, that it was extremely liable to destruction. He was fully apprized of the danger of tyranny, by which the republic was first assailed[y], and of the danger of democracy, by which it was finally ruined[z]. The regulations which he established were admirably calculated to prevent both those evils. I shall not here dwell on the judicious plan of public education which he prescribed and enforced[a], or on the admired authority of the Areopagus, which he extended or confirmed[b]; institutions respectively adapted to maintain the equality of freedom on the one hand, and to uphold a fair and moderate aristocracy on the other. This aristocracy was still farther strengthened by the laws regulating the mode of proceeding in the popular assembly,

---

[1] Ulpian in Demosth. adversus Midiam. Demosth. in Neær. Pollux. l. viii, c. ix:

[n] Pollux. l. viii. c. vi. Æschin. in Ctesiph. Pelit. de Leg. Attic. p. 237.

[a] Compar. Æschin. in Ctesiph. p. 429. and p. 432. Harpocrat. in λογισται. Pollux l. viii. c. ix.

[y] History of Ancient Greece, vol. i. c. viii.   [z] Ibid. vol. ii. c. xiii.

[a] Ibid.   [b] Ibid. & Isocrat. Areopagit.

bly, which subjected to a rigorous perquisition the lives and characters and qualifications of the orators entitled to address the people [c], and which gave a legal precedency in every debate to those speakers who had past their fiftieth year [d]. But these wise regulations, all breathing the same spirit, were unable to resist the storms by which a republic enriched by commerce and elated by conquest must ever necessarily be assailed. They could not prevent the multitude assembled in a large and luxurious city from yielding to the perfidious voice of demagogues, while they encouraged the people at large to become managers of their own affairs [e]; to act on every occasion as their own ministers; and thereby to destroy that line of distinction between the sovereign and the subject, on the unalterable continuance of which the stability of good government will ever most firmly rest, under every fluctuation of external circumstances, of prosperity or adversity, simplicity or refinement.

[c] Æschin. in Timarch. Suidas & Harpocrateon in ἐντοφυς γεαφη.
[d] Æschin. ibid.   [e] Demosth. passim.

ARISTOTLE's POLITICS.

BOOK II.

ARGUMENT.

Plato's republic.—Community of wives, children, and goods.— Nature and necessity of separate property.—Plato's books of laws examined.—Schemes for equalizing property.—Their futility. —Hippodamus.—His ideal republic.—Arguments in favour of political innovation.—Stronger arguments against it.—The Spartan government.—The Cretan.—The Carthaginian.—The Athenian.—Zaleucus.—Charondas.—Philolaus.—Dioiles.— Phaleas.—Pittacus.—Androgamas.

IN order to discover and ascertain that form of society under which those would prefer to live, who were at liberty to choose a mode of civil existence completely agreeable to their wish, we must not only consider the most admired political institutions that have actually prevailed in the world, but likewise examine those imaginary plans of perfect governments, which fancy has devised, and which philosophy has highly approved. Such an examination will enable us to determine the hitherto undefined limits of justice and utility, in matters of society and government; and will thus rescue the present work from the reproach of being undertaken for the unworthy purposes of ostentation or censure [a].

Every

BOOK II.

Chap. I.

The subject, and the end or purpose of this inquiry.

[a] σοφιζεσθαι ευλομενον. I resolve the first word into the two motives by which the sophists were usually actuated.

BOOK II.

To what objects the partnership of a commonwealth ought to extend.

Every commonwealth being, as we have said, a partnership, it follows, that in every commonwealth men muſt be partners in ſome things or in all [b]. Some things they muſt poſſeſs in common, ſince the community could not otherwiſe ſubſiſt. The advantageous ſituation of the capital and of the territory is neceſſarily a part of the common ſtock; and all men who inhabit the ſame city and country muſt breathe the ſame air, and enjoy the ſame climate. A queſtion therefore ariſes, how far this community ought to extend? Whether the partnerſhip of a commonwealth has its defined limits? Or whether, as Socrates maintains in the republic of Plato, all things ought to be common, wives, children, and poſſeſſions?

This extraordinary innovation, which is ſo different from every thing that has hitherto prevailed in the world, is attended with innumerable difficulties. Were it reduced into practice, we deny that this novelty would anſwer the purpoſe which its author means it ſhould ſerve; we deny likewiſe, that this purpoſe, which Socrates ſays ſhould be the end and aim of every commonwealth, is in itſelf deſirable.

Plato's opinion refuted.

According to this philoſopher, the main object of legiſlation is to promote the union of the citizens, " to unite them as much

[b] Ariſtotle's diviſion is threefold. He ſays, it is neceſſary that the citizens ſhould enjoy all things in common; or nothing in common; or ſome things in common, and other things not. But he immediately adds, that the ſecond branch of the diviſion is impoſſible, ſince, if nothing were common, a republic would not be what he has defined it, a community or partnerſhip. In compliance with the general rules which he lays down concerning diviſion, he introduces a part or member, which the nature and definition of the particular ſubject of inveſtigation obliges him immediately to reject. The inventor of method could ſcarcely be held guilty of pedantry in exemplifying his own rules: his ſcholaſtic imitators indeed are frequently liable to this reproach; but even the pedantry of method is ſeldom a very grievous fault when real inſtruction is the aim.

much as possible; and to reduce them, as nearly as may be, from many to one." Yet it is plain, that this project of uniting, when carried beyond certain limits, would totally deſtroy the community, reducing a commonwealth to a family, and a family to an individual ᶜ. But a commonwealth muſt, from its nature, confiſt not only of many individuals, but of individuals differently endowed, and differently employed ᵈ. It is not an alliance in war, operating by the mere ſtrength of numbers; it is not a nation living in ſcattered families, remote, detached; and, in civil concerns, totally unimportant to each other. But it is a ſociety of men united by their mutual exigencies, and their reſpective acquirements; ſo that the very circumſtance itſelf which, in one ſenſe, unites a city, that is, harmoniſes it into one body or ſyſtem, neceſſarily infers a multiplicity of wants, a diverſity of talents, and a diſtinction of property. The reciprocation of good offices, reſulting from all theſe varieties, upholds ſtates;

By the nature of political ſociety.

ᶜ Vid. Platon. de Republic. l. v. paſſim. Ariſtotle's reaſonings never ſeem to us leſs worthy of himſelf than when he combats the exceptionable doctrines of his maſter; not that he does not ſufficiently refute them, but becauſe he refutes at too great length, extravagancies that neither merit nor require ſuch patience of examination, and ſuch perſeverance of oppoſition. Yet to the contemporaries and immediate ſucceſſors of Ariſtotle, the paſſages which to us appear tireſome and frigid, probably ranked among the moſt intereſting parts of his work. Such was the great fame of Plato, juſtly earned by the ſublimity and truth of many of his doctrines; and even by his paradoxes themſelves, ſo naturally introduced, ſo ingeniouſly ſupported, with ſuch power of arrangement, and ſuch charms of ſtyle, that under his plaſtic art, the moſt ſhapeleſs crudities received form, beauty, and brilliancy. That fanciful writer became a philoſopher by choice, but always remained what he had been originally, a poet by nature; and like men of a ſimilar ſtamp in modern times, often perplexed thoſe ſciences which he ſought to adorn.

ᵈ This doctrine is beautifully illuſtrated by the greateſt of all ſyſtems in the Treatiſe de Mundo. Ariſtot. p. 608, & ſeq.

BOOK II.

states[e]; and the more numerous are the varieties that within certain limits prevail, the more completely will that purpose of comfortable subsistence be obtained, for which civil society was instituted[f].

In

---

[e] Aristotle here refers to his Treatises on Ethics, in which he has explained with great accuracy the doctrine of justice, both moral and political. See vol. i. from p. 257 to p. 284. Comp. Ethic. Eudem. b. iv. from beginning to end. Magna Moral. b. i. c. 34. In pursuing his first comparison of government to a partnership in trade, he observes, that it is easy to regulate the shares of the profit by those of the capital. But when the greater skill or the greater labour of one partner is to be set in opposition to the greater capital of another, the distribution of profits then becomes more difficult; the matter, however, may, for the most part, be pretty accurately adjusted. But in the great partnership of civil society, how many intricate proportions are to be unravelled, before the jarring elements of birth, wealth, talents, industry, can be harmonized into any lasting system of equitable policy? This, however, must be done, not indeed with scientific accuracy, but according to those liberal principles of moral geometry, which are the only rules that the practice of civil life either requires or admits. When this great work is effected, and the interests of the many are thus reconciled with the fair pretensions of the few, distributive or political justice will then have performed its office; and room will be left for the impartial exercise of justice, commutative or corrective; which is to be regulated not by geometrical analogy, but by the simpler kind, called arithmetical (ὁ κατα την αναλογιαν ἐκεινην αλλα κατα την αριθμητικην.); in which the terms of any numerical series increase or decrease by a fixed and given difference. This, therefore, according to Aristotle, is the only kind of justice and the only kind of virtue which admits of precise and definite rules; for as in any series of terms in arithmetical proportion, the common difference always remains the same, whatever be the terms, so in commutative or corrective justice, whatever be the quality or the merits of the persons concerned, the contracts and the injuries defined by law are considered as things fixed and invariable, and having fixed and invariable equivalents. See vol. i. p. 265, & seq.

[f] ὅτι μὲν γὰρ εἶναί πως μίαν, καὶ τὴν οἰκίαν καὶ τὴν πόλιν, ἀλλὰ ὁ παντως. ἐτι γαρ ὡς ἐκ ἰσας πρεπουσα πολις, ἐτι δ' ως ἐσαι μιν, ἐγγυς δ' ουσα τῳ μη πολις ειναι, ἐσαι χειρων πολις. Literally, "both a family and a commonwealth ought to be in *some* respects one; but not in all. For a commonwealth, when it attains perfect unity, ceases to be a commonwealth, and as it approximates this ultimate limit, it will continually become a worse commonwealth than it was." The thought is finely illustrated by Cicero, " Ut in fidibus ac tibiis, atque cantu ipso ac vocibus, concentus est quidam tenendus ex distinctis sonis, quem immutatam

In proportion as labour is divided, arts are perfected; and the various branches of industry are all of them best cultivated, when the same individual is strictly confined to the same branch of art. In matters of civil government, the same principle is applicable; but justice prohibits, that, in such matters, this principle should always be actually applied. In some communities the citizens are so nearly equal in merit [a], that it would be highly unjust that one portion of the state should be continually debarred from offices of magistracy; it would be equally unjust that another portion should exclusively appropriate them. Whether government be a good or a bad thing, it is fair that men of equal abilities and virtues should equally share in it; that they should receive the advantage of it as their right, or bear the burden of it as their duty. But as they cannot all of them exercise magistracy at once, it is necessary

BOOK II.

Reason why the great principle of the division of labour cannot be applied to government.

immutatam ac discrepantem aures eruditæ ferre non possunt; isque concentus ex dissimillimarum vocum moderatione concors tamen efficitur et congruens: sic ex summis et infimis et mediis interjectis ordinibus, ut sonis, moderata ratione civitas consensu dissimillimorum concinit; & quæ harmonia a musicis dicitur in cantu, ea est in civitate concordia." "Concord in states is like harmony in music. The one results from the differences and relations of distinct and most dissimilar sounds; the other, from the distinction of ranks among the citizens; the high, the low, and the middle order, which is interposed between them." We shall learn from Aristotle, that it is this middle order which binds and cements the political edifice. Men of this class understand better than any other, how to deal with the multitude. They have many interests in common with both of the extremes; their superiors, and their inferiors. Whence Aristotle maintains, that those states are the best and happiest, and most secure, where the middle ranks most abound.

[a] This is here the force of the word φύσις. "They have so equally attained the perfections of their nature." See vol. i. p. 22. This equality among the citizens implies the sameness of education and pursuits, as our author afterwards explains; and, therefore, infers that the arts of productive industry should be exercised, and the exigencies of bodily accommodation should be supplied, by those who are not citizens.

BOOK II.

Chap. 2.

Arguments againſt the community of wives and children.

neceſſary that they ſhould govern by vicarious ſucceſſion, each ruling and ſubmitting in his turn, and thus aſſuming and laying down ſuch important prerogatives, as render them, in their civil capacities, at different times, altogether different men.

Should we allow the propriety of the end at which Socrates thinks that every legiſlation ought to aim, yet we could not admire the propriety of the means by which he thinks this end is likely to be attained. For this purpoſe, he propoſes the abolition of the diſtinction " mine and thine," and maintains that the citizens of his ſuppoſed commonwealth would be perfectly unanimous, if all of them could apply the word " mine" in ſpeaking of the ſame objects. In this remark there is an evident fallacy. The word " all" may be taken diſtributively, or collectively; if taken diſtributively, it is plain, that on the ſuppoſition of the community of goods, the word " mine" could not be applied by any body; no *one* of the citizens could juſtly ſay this is my wife, my ſon, or my property; and though all collectively might, indeed, ſay ſo, yet their doing this would not be found conducive to concord.

Farther, that which is a common concern is very generally neglected. The energies of man are excited by that which depends on himſelf alone, and of which he only is to reap the whole profit or glory. In concerns common to him with others, it is with reluctance that he employs ſuch a degree of attention and activity, as even his own intereſt requires. He neglects that of which he thinks other men will take care; and as other men prove equally negligent with himſelf, the common intereſt is univerſally abandoned. Thoſe families, beſides, are commonly the worſt ſerved, in which the domeſtics are the moſt numerous. In a commonwealth where each father had a thouſand thoufand fons, and each fon a thoufand fathers, it is plain that neither fathers nor fons would be very zealous in performing their relative duties; and the condition of a nephew [h] would be more eligible under an ordinary government, than that of a fon in Plato's republic.

In the interior parts of Africa, geographers tell us that women are common, but that each man appropriates the children which moft refemble himfelf. Among quadrupeds, fome females have been obferved to bring forth young wonderfully refembling their fathers. The famous mare of Pharfalus was fo remarkable for this property, that fhe was called " The juft." It will be impoffible, therefore, to hinder men from forming conjectures, grounded on refemblance [i] and other circumftances, that certain children are their's; and thefe conjectures, though attended with the uneafinefs of anxious doubt, will not prevent the partialities of parental affection. The uncertainty, alfo, will produce many evils in its turn; it will multiply and embitter crimes; raillery and reproach will be converted into irreverence and impiety; love will often degenerate into inceft, and murder into parricide; and when fuch abominations happen, men who are ignorant of the enormity of their crimes, becaufe ignorant that they were committed againft their kindred, will often neglect performing the ceremonies appointed by religion for expiating their unnatural wickednefs [k].

Concord,

[h] The Greek word more commonly means a coufin-german. The Romans faid, " ne fis mihi patruus:" ufing the word uncle metaphorically, for a fevere reprover, and a morofe guardian.

[i] Nicolaus Damafcenus apud Stobæum, ferm. 42. p. 291., mentions a people called Limyrnii, among whom wives were common; and children alfo, until their fixth year; at which age they were affigned, after a public examination, to thofe of the men whom they moft refembled.

[k] See Ethics, l. ix. c. 6.

Concord, doubtless, forms the happiness of states; but this community of wives and children would totally destroy that affection on which concord is founded. As a drop of honey is dissipated and lost in a pail of water, so the sweet affection of love would totally perish through too extensive a diffusion; for two circumstances are requisite to maintain and invigorate this affection, that the objects of it be in themselves lovely, and that they be peculiarly recommended to our love. The community of wives and children, were it in any case to be adopted, might, therefore, be more advantageously established with regard to the peasants, whom Plato has appointed to labour and to obey, than with regard to the military class, whom he has appointed to legislate and to govern. By destroying all affection among the peasants, it would prevent their conspiring against their masters [1].

Chap. 3.

Arguments against the community of goods.

The community of property, depending on different principles, merits a separate consideration. Among some barbarous nations the lands are separately cultivated, but the fruits of them are promiscuously consumed. Among others, the lands are common, and cultivated by the conjunct labour of the community; but each family appropriates its share of their fruits. Where the peasants form a distinct but dependent class, the community of lands will be liberated from several of its inconveniences. The martial lords of the soil, as in that case none of them would have any labour to bestow, could not quarrel

---

[1] Some sentences are omitted in this chapter, either as containing repetitions, or as relating to the subject of Greek love; a perversion of sentiment to which Aristotle, of all the philosophers of his age, shews himself the most decided and most zealous adversary. None of them, indeed, as has been erroneously supposed, patronize such an abominable degeneracy; but Aristotle alone, in his moral and political writings, uniformly treats the subject with that marked reprobation which became a philosopher superior to the prejudices and fashions of his own times.

quarrel with each other about proportioning the fruits of their industry to the quantity of their respective exertions. But should the proprietors themselves cultivate with their own hands their common property, innumerable jealousies would immediately spring up, as fatal experience proves almost always to happen among those connected in too close a communion of life, the partners in a voyage or a journey, who dispute for straws with each other; and as a master is most quarrelsome with those servants who are most frequently in his way, being employed in attendance on his person.

The useful and practical community of goods, a community that will neither engender animosity nor check industry, must result from the salutary discipline of laws, and the skilful application of early and assiduous culture. According to the proverb, "all things are common among friends:" we must imitate, extend, and, if possible, carry to perfection, the plans of those legislators who have in any measure succeeded in producing this desirable effect. At Sparta, the establishment of property does not hinder the free communication of many of the benefits which it confers. The slaves of the Lacedæmonians, their horses, their dogs, their carriages[n], are all at the service of any citizen who has occasion to employ them; goods are appropriated, but their uses are freely communicated; and this double advantage is the natural result of a wise legislation.

Socrates's community of goods would destroy the delightful pleasure which arises from saying "this field is mine." This pleasure,

The useful and practical community of goods.

Contrasted with the fanciful speculations of Plato.

---

[n] ἐφόδια, viatica, things necessary for a journey, which Aretinus translates vehicula, without authority indeed, as to the interpretation of the word, but consistently enough with the sense of the passage. Vid. Xenoph. &c. Republ. Laced. & Plutarch, in Lycurg.

BOOK II.

Marginal notes:
The distinction of property infers its unequal distribution.

The necessity of this illustrated by music.

pleasure, indeed, proceeds from self-love, but a self-love that is natural and just; and as different from selfishness, as a virtuous and proper affection is different from a vicious and blamable excess. Deprived of separate property, we should be deprived of a pleasure belonging to it still more delightful; the pleasure of bestowing it on our friends, on our companions, and even on deserving strangers[n]. Destroy wedlock, and what room will be left for the virtue of chastity? Destroy property, and what room will be left for the virtue of liberality?

Yet the system of Socrates carries with it at first sight a specious shew of humanity, because our attention is withdrawn from its emptiness, and forcibly arrested by the evils actually existing in society; law-suits, perjury, clamorous reproach, and mean adulation, all of which are charged on the unequal distribution of property, but which are all more justly chargeable on human villany. The illusion is supported by a false comparison. We compare the disputes occasioned by separate property, which is of great amount, with those occasioned by common property, which is of little value; not reflecting that the quantities of both ought to be fairly estimated, and that the proportion being thus rightly stated, we should find the evils resulting from common property, to be the greater of the two. A false principle deceived Socrates; he took for granted that the union of his citizens could not be too intimate; whereas, in reality, this union carried beyond certain limits, would prove the destruction of the commonwealth; and the nearer it approximates to its destruction, the commonwealth becomes the worse. Symphony is good, and metre is good; but symphony is destroyed when it changes into sameness

of

[n] ξένοι, foreigners connected with us by the ties of hospitality

of tone, and metre is deſtroyed when it changes into ſame- | BOOK II.
neſs of time°.

Amidſt the innumerable experiments that have been made in matters of government, the ſyſtem of Socrates would undoubtedly have been earlier invented, and ſubmitted with other ſchemes of innovation to a fair trial, had it appeared to be in any degree practicable. If tried by the teſt of experiment, its inſufficiency would manifeſtly ſhew itſelf. The uniting principles in ſtates are,——laws, education, manners, and a congeniality of ſentiments and affections produced by the intercourſe of life, and cemented by mutual good offices ᵖ. But this intercourſe and theſe offices imply the uſual inſtitutions of wards, diſtricts, and common tables; to which, had Socrates confined himſelf, his plan of legiſlation would have wanted novelty; ſince, even in relieving his firſt claſs from the labour and cares of agriculture, he would only have propoſed what the Lacedæmonians had previouſly enacted ᑫ.

The impracticability of Plato's community.

The remaining parts of his plan, Socrates does not clearly explain. We are not informed whether the community of wives and poſſeſſions is to extend to the peaſants. If it does, wherein will they differ from the military? and how can they be kept in obedience, unleſs, like the Cretan ſlaves, they be prohibited the uſe of arms, and forbidden the gymnaſtic exerciſes? Yet, if the peaſants are not comprehended in the new regu-

Imperfectly explained by himſelf.

° This juſt compariſon ſhould have occurred to the fancy of a lively nation, when they were exhorted to embrace the wild deſign of forming a commonwealth from one element.

ᵖ See vol. i. p. 376, & ſeq.

ᑫ ὅπερ καὶ νυν Λακεδαιμονιοι πεινι επιχειρουσι, which the Lacedæmonians are now attempting to do. Ariſtotle ſpeaks as if they had never completely effected their purpoſe. The order of the ſentences is, in this paragraph, ſomewhat altered; and the words ſometimes paraphraſed, the better to expreſs the ſenſe.

regulations, Socrates, who allows them the rank of citizens, will have two republics in the same territory, differing in laws and inftitutions, eternally at variance with each other, and in one of which all thofe diforders will prevail which are found in other ftates. The peafants, individually or collectively, are however to be mafters of the foil, provided they pay to the military a due proportion of its fruits; a degree of independence that would engender infolence, and render them more formidable to the government than the Penefts of Theffaly and the Helots of Sparta[p]. Again, if lands are property, but women common, will the women manage houfes in which they have no feparate intereft, with the fame attention that the men cultivate their own fields? The example of inferior animals does not prove that men and women ought to exercife the fame employments, becaufe no animal but man is acquainted with the benefits refulting from the mutual exchange of the fruits of labour[q]; and the œconomy refulting from appropriate tafks is peculiar to the human race.

Socrates divides his commonwealth into two orders, that of foldiers, and that of peafants; but whether the peafants are occafionally to bear arms, or whether they are ever to be entrufted with any fhare in the government, he does not determine. The wives of the foldiers, that is, the women who are common to this clafs, are to be trained to the gymnaftic exercifes as well as their hufbands; they are not only to participate in the

---

[p] The Penefts (fo called from their poverty) were the defcendants of the neighbouring nations conquered and enflaved by the Theffalians, and moft commonly employed in cultivating the lands of their fevere mafters. In their employments, their numbers, and their continual difpofition to revolt, they agreed with the Lacedæmonian Helots. See Hiftory of Ancient Greece, vol. i. p. 157, & paffim.

[q] See above, p. 38.

the military games of their country, but to sustain the laborious duties and real dangers of the field. Though the military forms a privileged order, yet only a portion of this military is to be invested with the powers of deliberation and final resolution; in other words, a small body of men are to be the sovereigns of the state; and it should seem as if those sovereigns were to reign for life; for Socrates informs us, that the divinity infuses into some men, even at their birth, a portion of intellectual gold; into others, a portion of intellectual silver; but that the third class, the peasants and artificers, are composed of brass and iron. These golden men, therefore, are, according to Socrates, to be perpetual magistrates; but, under such an arrangement, can it be expected that a high-minded people, with arms in their hands, should be restrained from sedition?

Though exempted from this evil, even the governing part of the city, subjected to so many privations and bound to so many hard duties, would not deserve the epithet of happy; and if happiness does not belong to them, can we expect to find it among the peasants and mechanics? Socrates, indeed, says, that it is the business of a legislator to consult, not the good of any particular class of men, but that of the whole state; he forgets that the happiness of a state is to be measured by the common standard of happiness of the individuals composing it; for happiness is not like an *even* number that may be composed of parts which are *odd*.

In his books of laws which were written afterwards, Plato intended to delineate a more practicable scheme of government. Yet even these laws he gradually bends to his favourite system; and except in the articles of the community of wives and possessions,

BOOK II.

unfit for attaining the end of political society.

Chap. 4.

Examination of Plato's books of laws.

possessions, and of the public tables destined for the women, his two republics nearly agree in form, though they differ in magnitude; the first containing one thousand, and the second five thousand men bearing arms. All the discourses of Socrates, doubtless, discover great freedom of thought, and much patience of investigation; they are distinguished by novelty, ingenuity, and elegance; but that all his observations should be just, is more than could be expected from man. Five thousand soldiers confined to the business of war, and cultivating no one kind of productive industry, would, with their due proportion of wives, children, and domestics, require for their comfortable subsistence the plains of Babylon, or some other country equally extensive[q]. Suppositions, though arbitrary, ought not to be impossible.

Socrates

---

[q] The purpose of comfortable subsistence for which commonwealths are instituted, requiring a minute subdivision of labour, Aristotle says, that in this particular view, the more populous is the community, its end will be the more completely attained. But the conveniencies and accommodations, furnished by the mutual exchange of labour and its fruits, are not the only ingredients of comfortable subsistence; education, morals, and other elements, constituting national felicity, set bounds to that populousness which the mere traffic of conveniencies would leave unlimited. It is thus, in general, that the degree in which one political advantage can be attained, is limited by a regard to other advantages which must not be neglected; and to compare and reconcile them with each other, to compensate inequalities and to adjust contrarieties, is the great duty of the statesman. All things considered, he declares in favour of what would be now deemed a very small commonwealth, consisting of 15,000 or 20,000 citizens (which must provide for defence, by confederating with other states formed on a similar plan); and he says, that the third or fourth part of this community could not subsist in arms and idleness, unless the territory was very extensive. Experience justifies this remark. Political writers say, that scarcely one man in a hundred, and certainly not one in fifty, can in modern times be maintained as a soldier without the gradual depopulation of their respective communities. Yet how great is the disproportion between a fourth and a fiftieth? and how scantily are modern soldiers provided for, in comparison with the soldiers of antiquity?

Socrates does not say that his soldiers are to subsist comfortably, but temperately; this is ill expressed, for men may subsist temperately, but wretchedly [1]. He says, that laws ought to be relative to the country, and to the men of that country; he ought to have added, " and to the surrounding nations." The provisions for defensive war, at least [2], ought not to be omitted in any wise plan of legislation.

In his second republic he equalizes estates, but leaves population unlimited; saying, that deaths and barrenness are found by experience to keep the populousness of most countries, at different periods, nearly on the same level. But under ordinary governments, increase of population would only occasion a greater subdivision of landed property; whereas in Plato's republic, the supernumeraries would be altogether destitute of estates; because the lands being already reduced to equal, and, as it were, elementary parts, would be incapable of farther partition. In all countries the just proportion between wealth and populousness ought to be an object of the most serious attention. Neglect in this particular produces that poverty which is the mother of villany and sedition. In the laws of Pheidon of Corinth, one of the most ancient writers on the subject of politics, a regulation is introduced directly the reverse of Plato's; Pheidon limits population, but does not equalize possessions; the relative advantages of either plan we shall afterwards examine.

In Plato's second republic, the characters of men fit for office are very imperfectly described by saying, that in the compo-

His equalization of landed property, imperfect without concomitant regulations.

Imperfection of his constitutional regulations.

---

[1] The author adds, " liberally and luxuriously." The adjuncts, " liberally and soberly" must be united in order to express ζην ευ.

[2] Aristotle, as we shall see hereafter, justifies even offensive war in certain cases.

composition of a commonwealth, the governors should be as different from the governed, as, in the composition of a web, the warp is from the woof. In point of wealth his citizens are divided into four classes, of which the first is to be four times as rich as the last. Having thus permitted the unequal accumulation of personals, why does he so nicely limit the acquisition of landed property? To each family he assigns two houses, a present as inconvenient as it is expensive. The general scheme of his commonwealth is to be neither democratical nor oligarchical, but a mixture of both forms; since all the citizens capable of purchasing heavy armour are to be entitled to a share in the government; a regulation which excludes only the meanest portion of the lowest class. This mixed form of policy is well adapted to common use, but if Plato meant it as the best possible system, next to that of his philosophical commonwealth, he probably rates it too highly; many will prefer to it the government of Sparta, and other systems of policy more strictly formed on the aristocratic model.

Judgment in favour of mixed government.

Some men are of opinion that the best government must be compounded of monarchy, aristocracy, and democracy. On this account they highly commend the institutions of Sparta, which admit of a king, of a senate, and of the democratical power of the Ephori, who are chosen by and from the people. Others regard the power of the Ephori as too arbitrary and tyrannical; and think that whatever is democratical at Sparta, results, not from its political constitution, but from its customs and manners; the common and frugal tables; the public and uniform education; the daily commerce of life, and the habitual interchange of good offices among persons of all ranks.

In

In Plato's second commonwealth there is not any mixture of monarchy, it confifts of democracy and oligarchy, but contains moft of oligarchy; and yet he fays, inconfiftently enough, that the beft government is compofed of democracy and tyranny[1], which two corruptions can hardly be honoured with the name of governments, or if fo called, muft furely be held the very worft of all.

That Plato's second commonwealth inclines moft to oligarchy, is evident from the laws refpecting the appointment of the magiftrates. This appointment is partly by fuffrage, partly by lot; the former of which is conformable to oligarchy, the latter to democracy. This mixed mode of appointment is, therefore,

Particularly with regard to elections.

---

[1] Plato does not fay tyranny, but monarchy. The paffage alluded to is in the Sixth Book of his Laws, p. 858. edit. Ficin. I had often read it without confidering it as liable to the objection ftated in the text, becaufe I never doubted that there was an error of the prefs, viz. μοναρχικη inftead of αριστοκρατικη. In the fenfe in which the paffage is taken by Ariftotle, it is not only inconfiftent with the context, but with the whole tenor of Plato's political writings; decidedly and uniformly hoftile to arbitrary power, whether monarchical or democratical. See his Republic, book i. p. 582. edit. Ficin. The difficulty may, however, be removed without correcting the text, if we fuppofe that Plato confiders monarchy as the limit of ariftocracy, as democracy is of republicanifm. Abfolute monarchy and perfect democracy are two extremes, and good government lies between them. When a republic expands into democracy, it ceafes to be a republic; when an ariftocracy contracts into a monarchy, it ceafes to be an ariftocracy. Republics and ariftocracies, as both Plato and Ariftotle fhew, have refpectively a tendency to this expanfion and contraction, which may be confidered as their ultimate limits; or two contrary extremes, by the due blending of which juft government is produced. In conformity with this, fee what is faid of the twofold juftice and twofold equality; the one confifting in famenefs of meafure, weight, and number, which is eafily recognized; the other hardly difcernible by man, though approved by the judgment of God himfelf; and, as far as it prevails in this lower world, the fcurce of happinefs to individuals and communities. The reafon is given, τῳ μεν γαρ μειζ η πλεω, τῳ δ' ελαττον σμικροτερα νεμει, μετρια εκατερῳ προς την αυτων φυσιν νεμουσα; "for it attributes to the greater more, and to the leffer lefs, affigning to each what is commenfurate to its refpective nature." De Legib. l. vi. p. 859.

therefore, conformable to a mixture of thofe two forms. But that the rich fhould be compelled, under a forfeit, to attend the affemblies for electing magiftrates, and for other public duties, while the attendance of the poor is optional, is a regulation highly favourable to oligarchy. The lower claffes will frequently neglect attendance, and the public affairs will thus devolve exclufively on the more wealthy portion of the community. In conftituting the fenate, candidates are to be named from the four claffes of the citizens at large. But the two lower claffes are not bound to attend at the naming of candidates from men of their own order. From candidates thus named the fenate is, by a new election, to be conftituted; but this fucceffion of elections, in which the magiftrates are chofen from candidates previoufly named, is always a dangerous expedient, fince it expofes the government to be ufurped by a combination of artful men, who need not be very numerous. Such is Plato's fecond republic, a mixture of oligarchy and democracy, as will evidently appear when we have examined more accurately the polity compounded of thofe two forms [1].

Chap. 5. Concerning other fchemes of ideal commonwealths.

Other fchemes of ideal commonwealths have been delineated by philofophers and politicians, and alfo by men entitled to neither appellation; all of which fchemes approach much nearer to fuch governments as have actually prevailed in the world, than do the two republics of Plato. In none of the political models propofed by other writers do we read any thing concerning the community of wives, the community of goods, or common tables deftined for the women. They begin their codes of legiflation by inftitutions more neceffary and more practicable.

To

---

[1] The text is confufed and corrupt. I have given to it the order and the fenfe feemingly moft confiftent with other parts of the work.

To some writers nothing appears of so much consequence as the skilful regulation of property; because it is this much-coveted object that gives birth to most disputes and most seditions. Phaleas of Chalcedon [a] was the first who proposed, as a most salutary institution, the equalizing of wealth among the citizens; a thing, he thinks, easily established in new settlements; and which, he says, might easily be introduced into old countries by one simple law, commanding the rich always to give marriage portions with their daughters, but never to receive any; and the poor always to receive, but never to give them. Plato in his laws, on the contrary, allows the inequality of fortunes within certain limits; permitting, as we before observed, the citizens of the first class to be four times as rich as those of the last. Whoever would regulate the extent of fortunes, must also regulate the increase of families. If children multiply beyond the means of supporting them, the intention of the law will be frustrated, and families will be suddenly reduced from opulence to beggary; a revolution always dangerous to public tranquillity.

That a certain degree of equalization of property tends to strengthen the bands of society, escaped not the sagacity of ancient legislators. In legislating for Athens, Solon acknowledged the

Phaleas's plan for equalizing property.

Its inconveniences.

Other schemes of a similar nature.

---

[a] Neither of this Phaleas, nor of Pheidon mentioned above, have we any notices but those left by Aristotle. Christopher Hendreich (De Repub. Carthagin. p. 166, & p. 239) makes Phaleas a Carthaginian: he was the lawgiver of Chalcedon, a city on the Thracian Bosporus, opposite to Byzantium, or Constantinople, and built seventeen years before it. Chalcedon was called in derision "the city of the blind," because its founders, overlooking the noble situation on which Constantinople now stands, had chosen one greatly inferior to it. Plin. v. 32. Tacitus, xii. 62. A legislator, six centuries before Christ, equalizing fortunes on the eastern coast of the Bosporus— how strange a contrast with the laws now prevalent there!

ARISTOTLE's POLITICS.

BOOK II.

Their futility.

the influence of this principle [x]. The early inftitutions of feveral republics both limit the acquifition, and prohibit, under certain circumftances, the fale, of lands. In Locris a citizen cannot difpofe of his eftate, unlefs he can make it appear that he is reduced to this neceffity by fome unmerited and manifeft calamity. The alienation of ancient inheritances in Leucas prepared the way for a revolution in the government; and offices of magiftracy no longer requiring a fixed qualification in point of fortune, the mixed form of policy gradually degenerated into nearly a fimple democracy. But equality itfelf is not a thing univerfally defirable; for fhares may be all equal, and yet all too great if they fofter floth and luxury; they may be all equal, and yet all too fmall if they engender wretchednefs. Mediocrity, therefore, ought to be the aim of legiflation; but this object will be better attained by moderating paffion than by levelling property.

Phaleas, indeed, propofes not only to equalize poffeffions, but to render education uniform. He does not explain, however, wherein this uniform education is to confift. The citizens may be all educated alike, and all of them ill educated, if care be not taken early to fubdue in them the miferable paffions of avarice and ambition.

The real caufes of civil diforders.

Difcontents arife not merely from the inequality of poffeffions, but from the equality of honours. The multitude complain

---

[x] Solon allowed a brother to marry his fifter on the father's fide, but not his fifter uterine; becaufe by marrying the latter he might have increafed the eftate which defcended to him from his father, by that which came from the firft hufband of his mother; and thus in his own perfon have accummulated two inheritances. Comp. Plutarch. in Themift. p. 128. Petit. Leg. Attic. p. 480. and Montefquieu Efprit de Loix, l. v. c. 5. Several other of Solon's laws breathe the fame fpirit. Conf. Plutarch in Solon, p. 89. Demofth. in Macart. p. 1036. Petit. de Leg. Attic. p. 441—444.

ARISTOTLE's POLITICS.

complain that property is unjuftly, becaufe unequally, diftributed; men of fuperior merit or fuperior pretenfions complain that honours are unjuftly, if equally, diftributed; and that

"The good and worthlefs find their meed the fame [r]."

The bare neceffaries of life, food and fuel, cloaths to cover our nakednefs, and a home to fhelter us from the ftorm, comforts which it is pretended the equalization of property would enable all men to enjoy, are not the only incentives to injuftice. The greateft crimes are committed for none of thofe things, but for obtaining or fecuring the objects of ill-regulated defires, and fenfelefs, becaufe infatiable paffions; and fometimes for acquiring objects of tafte and elegance, from which we expect to derive pleafure unmixed with pain, pure, unfading, and independent enjoyment. It is not to avoid cold or hunger that tyrants cover themfelves with blood; and ftates decree the moft illuftrious rewards, not to him who catches a thief, but to him who kills an ufurper [z]. Phaleas's plan of equalizing property is ufeful, therefore, againft the leaft and moft inconfiderable only of the three evils which difturb fociety; evils, for each of which there is an appropriate remedy; fubfiftence infured by induftry, for the firft; an education infpiring the habit of moderation and felf-command, for the fecond; and for the third, the attractive, rational, and uncloying charms of philofophy; in the ftudy and practice of which men will find a delight, and the only

BOOK II.

Their remedies.

---

[r] Iliad ix. Achilles fpeaks to Ulyffes.

[z] The word τυραννος properly denotes him who has acquired the fovereignty of a ftate formerly free. With whatever moderation he might exercife his power, he was called τυραννος from the manner by which he obtained it. But Ariftotle here means the tyrannical abufer of ufurped power.

BOOK II.

The proper limits of national wealth.

only delight not liable to contingencies, round and complete in itself, and as stable as it is independent.

In delineating the scheme of his republic, Phaleas has confined his attention to matters of domestic policy. He has not inquired, though the inquiry was necessary, how the national force is to be raised or supported. Money, or its equivalents, are essential in war as well as in peace. Phaleas has not endeavoured to ascertain the extent of the national wealth. Yet there are certain limits within which it ought to be confined; its immoderate magnitude might tempt the rapacity or provoke the invasion of greater powers; but it ought to be sufficiently considerable to enable us to meet our equals with confidence; and even to teach our superiors that they may probably lose more by contest than they are likely to gain by victory. When Autaphradates prepared to besiege Atarneus [a], Eubulus, the master of that city, desired him to calculate how much time would be wasted in the siege, and how much money would in that time be expended; observing that for a less sum he would probably be willing to sell the place. Autaphradates calculated, reflected, and desisted from the siege.

Inefficacy and imperfection of laws equalizing wealth.

The equalization of fortunes may have some slight tendency to stifle animosity and to prevent dissension. But its effect is always inconsiderable, and often doubtful; since those who think themselves entitled to superiority will not patiently brook equality. To stand on a level with the multitude is not their

proper

---

[a] See above, p. 7, & p. 11. and Pausanias, b. iv. c. 35. This place had fallen to decay in Pliny's time, though still renowned for precious stones as clear as crystal. " Cepionides in Æolidis Atarne quondam oppido, nunc pago nascuntur." Plin. N. H. v. 30. Conf. xxxvii. 10.

proper place; and to acquire their due elevation, they will conspire together and subvert the commonwealth. The wickedness of man is boundless: it seems at first as if a trifle would content him, but his passions invigorate by gratification; always indulged, always craving, and continually preying on him who feeds them. This evil cannot be remedied by equalizing property, whether lands or moveables, of which last Phaleas has omitted to speak. It can be cured only by that salutary discipline which will make one part of the community delight in doing justice, and by that sound policy which will prevent the remaining part from committing with impunity any serious wrong; for the majority of mankind will always be the sport of their own headstrong passions; and though they ought to be treated with equity and humanity, must be habitually overawed by authority, and seasonably restrained by power. Phaleas's republic will be but a small one if mechanics and artificers be debarred from all share in the government. The institutions of Epidamnus [b] respecting the lower ranks, and those established on the same subject by Diophantus at Athens, are worthy of imitation. Such are the merits and the defects of the republic of Phaleas.

Hippodamus, the son of Euryphon, a Milesian, and by profession an architect, gained celebrity in his own art by constructing the Piræus at Athens, and by improving the method of distributing streets, and planning cities. His love of distinction exposed him to the reproach of vanity; and many ascribed to affectation

BOOK II.

Chap. 6.

The ideal republic of Hippodamus an architect of Miletus.

---

[b] See History of Ancient Greece, vol. i. p. 375. and vol. ii. p. 185. The lower classes in Epidamnus as well as in Athens, though not public slaves as in Laconia and Thessaly, were much employed in what Aristotle considers as servile tasks, because performed by the exertions of mere bodily labour; particularly in building, mining, and other public works.

affectation his magnificent dress, his flowing locks, and the warm mantle which he wore, even during the heat of summer. Hippodamus was ambitious of reaching eminence in all kinds of knowledge, and is the first author who, without any practice in affairs, wrote a treatise concerning the best form of government. His republic consisted of ten thousand men, divided into the three classes of artificers, husbandmen, and soldiers. The territory he likewise divides into three portions; the sacred, destined for the various exigencies of the public worship; the common, to be cultivated for the common benefit of the soldiers; and the private, to be separately appropriated by the husbandmen. His laws also were divided into three kinds, because he thought there were only three sorts of injuries; insults, damages, and death. He instituted a court of appeal, composed of select senators. Sentence, he thought, ought not to be passed by votes or ballot; but that each judge should be furnished with a tablet, on which he should write guilty, if he simply condemned; and which he should leave unwritten, if he simply acquitted; but on which, if he found the defendant in some measure guilty, but not to the full extent of the indictment, he should mark this difference, stating how much the culprit should pay, or what punishment he should suffer. As the law formerly stood, Hippodamus observed, that in all cases requiring this distinction, the judge, who was bound by oath to observe justice in his decisions, must commit perjury whenever he either simply and positively condemned, or simply and positively acquitted. Hippodamus also established a law in favour of those whose inventions tended to improve the constitution of the commonwealth; they were to be distinguished by peculiar honours; and

The new laws.

and the children of thofe who fell in battle were to be maintained and educated at the public expence. This laft regulation, firft introduced by the architect of Miletus, has been adopted by Athens and other cities. According to his plan of policy, the magiftrates were all of them to be elected by the free and impartial fuffrages of their fellow-citizens, confifting of the three claffes of men abovementioned: the concerns of the ftate, the affairs of ftrangers, the care and management of orphans, formed the three important objects entrufted to their adminiftration.

Such are the leading features of the republic of Hippodamus. In examining this republic, the firft difficulty that occurs refpects his divifion of the citizens. The hufbandmen, the artificers, and the foldiers, are all of them to be members of the ftate; but the hufbandmen deftitute of arms, the artificers deftitute of both lands and arms, will maintain a very unequal conflict with the foldiers, if thefe laft fhould be tempted to enflave them. An affociation of men, fo unequally treated by the legiflator, muft continually tend to diffolution. The great executive magiftracies, together with every office of military command, devolve of courfe on the foldiers. Can the two remaining claffes be expected to wifh the continuance of a government, from whofe honours and emoluments they are for ever to be excluded? A revolution, therefore, muft fpeedily take place, unlefs the military be more powerful than both the hufbandmen and the artificers united; and if they actually be fo, of what fignification is it, that thefe degraded claffes are fummoned to give their votes at elections, and mocked with the appellation of citizens? Artificers, fubfifting by the fruits of their own labour, are effential to the exiftence of every city or community. But the clafs of hufbandmen, as regulated by

BOOK II.

Examination of his republic.

ARISTOTLE's POLITICS.

BOOK II.

Hippodamus, by what tie of utility are they linked to the state? The common lands might be cultivated by the military themselves, which would deſtroy the diſtinction between the ſoldiers and the peaſants. They might be cultivated by men deſtitute of private eſtates; and this would form a fourth claſs, diſtinct from the huſbandmen of Hippodamus; who, by a moſt awkward regulation, are to labour one diſtrict, conſiſting of their private eſtates, for their own maintenance; and another, conſiſting of the common lands, for the maintenance of the military; a moſt uſeleſs diſtinction of property, and moſt abſurd partition of employment, by which much valuable time would be loſt, and much unneceſſary expence incurred.

Of his judicial regulations.

The judicial regulations of Hippodamus are not leſs blameable, ſince their direct tendency is to convert judges into arbiters, and thereby to arm them with an arbitrary power of deciſion, which can never be expedient to the parties, unleſs it be ſpecially granted, and voluntarily entruſted. In matters ſubmitted to arbitration, communication of ſentiment and diſcuſſion of opinion is not only allowed but required. In courts of juſtice, moſt legiſlators have ſtrictly prohibited both; commanding each judge ſimply to condemn or ſimply to acquit, as his own reaſon directs. By the innovations of Hippodamus, legal proceedings would be involved in inextricable confuſion. The defendant might be ordered by one judge to pay twenty minæ; by another, more; and by a third, leſs; each might differ from every other; and all from the plaintiff. The ſentence would be thus ſplit into ſuch a multitude of parts as it would be difficult to collect, and impoſſible to unite; and all theſe difficulties would be created and encountered, in order to obviate an imaginary inconvenience; for it is falſe that the

judge

judge is perjured, who fimply acquits a party fued for twenty minæ, although he may believe that he really owes half that fum. The judge would, on the contrary, be perjured, if he did not acquit him; and in all fimilar cafes, the fault lies not in the law or in the judge, but in the libel and in the plaintiff, whofe cafe is not juftly ftated, and whofe action is not fairly brought.

The law in favour of thofe whofe inventions tend to improve the conftitution of the commonwealth, is more fpecious than folid. Bearing beauty on its furface [e], it is fraught with perfecution, innovation, and fedition. It is the opinion of many, that ancient laws, which are good, are preferable to new ones, though better; and that a moderately wife conftitution of government ought never to be altered. Upon this delicate fubject, the following obfervations may deferve attention. The advocates for alteration and improvement obferve, that the gymnaftic exercifes and medicine, as well as all other arts and faculties, have been carried to their actual ftate of perfection by repeated trials and reiterated efforts. If legiflation be a fcience or an art, muft it not partake of the fame nature, and follow the fame progrefs with all other arts and fciences, which being founded on obfervation, have been reared, extended, and perfected by experiment and reflection? That it does partake of the fame progrefs, civil hiftory affords the moft convincing proofs. What can be more rude, what more barbarous, than the

His law in favour of political improvements.

Arguments in favour of political innovation.

---

[e] Ariftotle's expreffion is remarkable; ινεφθαλμον ακουαι: the firft word, denoting what is pleafing to the eye, had come to denote what is agreeable in general; and thence joined with ακουαι, "what is pleafing to hear."

BOOK II. the ancient laws of the Greeks, when they frequented the public places with fwords by their fides; and bought and fold their women like cattle in a market? In thofe ſtates which have adhered too fcrupuloufly to their hereditary ufages, what grofſneſs, iniquity, and cruelty every where prevail? At Cumæ, a man may be convicted and puniſhed as a murderer, on the evidence of the kindred of him who profecutes for the murder. It is not for what is ancient, but for what is ufeful, that men of fenfe ought to contend; and whatever is diftinguifhed by the former quality, cannot be expected to poffefs much of the latter. The ancient inhabitants of the world, whether produced by the genial power of the earth [d], or faved from the ruins of fome dreadful cataftrophe, muſt have been degraded by weakneſs of underſtanding, and difgraced by unruly ſtrength of paſſion. The inſtitutions afcribed to the earth-born giants are not, furely, worthy of being followed with refpectful deference. But innovations, were it defirable to prevent them, are not, however, to be prevented: they are neceſſary and inevitable. Written laws, with whatever comprehenſiveneſs and precifion they may be penned, cannot exprefs all that variety of cafes to which, and which only, they may with juftice be applied. Rights are to be maintained, wrongs to be prevented, and therefore laws are made. Thefe laws are general; exceptions to them occur; new exceptions multiply; and the number and importance of the exceptions at length produce new laws far more equitable than thofe which had previoufly been eſtabliſhed.

Formidable

[d] Ariſtotle is here fpeaking as an advocate; and in ſtating the arguments in favour of innovation, does not, therefore, think it neceſſary to adhere to the eſtabliſhed tenets of his philofophy. See Analyfis, p. 117.

Formidable as these arguments seem, they may be opposed by others of not less weight: arguments which prove that even the rust of government is to be respected, and that its fabric is never to be touched but with a fearful and trembling hand. When the evil of persevering in hereditary institutions is small, it ought always to be endured, because the evil of departing from them is certainly very great. Slight imperfections, therefore, whether in the laws themselves, or in those who administer and execute the laws, ought always to be overlooked, because they cannot be corrected without occasioning a much greater mischief, and tending to weaken that reverence which the safety of all governments requires that the citizens at large should entertain, cultivate, and cherish for the hereditary institutions of their country. The comparison drawn from the improvement of arts, does not apply to the amendment of laws. To change or improve an art, and to alter or amend a law, are things as dissimilar in their operation as different in their tendency: for laws operate as practical principles of moral action [e]; and, like all the rules of morality, derive their force

Stronger arguments against it.

[e] The Stagirite's argument against innovation does not apply to that kind of it proposed by Lord Bacon, namely the imitating that great innovator Time, whose operations are so slow and skilful, that they elude the senses and escape observation, "Novator maximus, tempus; quid ni igitur tempus imitemur?" and again, "Quis novator tempus imitatur, quod novationes ita insinuat, ut sensus fallant?" That great man concludes with Aristotle, "It is improper to try new experiments in the political body, unless the necessity be urgent, or the utility evident. Great care must be taken that the desire of reformation may occasion the change, and not the desire of the change plead for the reformation. Again, let all novelty, though it cannot, perhaps, be rejected, yet be held suspected. And lastly, as the Scripture directs, let us stand upon the old paths, and see and ask for the good way and walk therein." Political Essays, Essay xi. It is worthy of remark, that Bacon lived in the age of reformation in religion, and was himself a great reformer in philosophy. He combated

BOOK II. force and efficacy, as even the name imports, from the cuſtomary repetition of habitual acts, and the flow operation of time. Every alteration of the laws therefore tends to ſubvert that authority on which the perſuaſive energy of all laws is founded; to abridge, weaken, and deſtroy the power of law itſelf [f]. Though innovation in general ſhould not be univerſally

bated ſucceſsfully the pretended philoſophy of Ariſtotle, which was certainly far worſe than no philoſophy at all; but his diſlike to the diſtorted ſhadow made him think, at leaſt ſpeak, too diſreſpectfully of the ſubſtance. Whoever has read only the works of Bacon, is not a competent judge; but whoever has read the works both of Bacon and of Ariſtotle, will be ready to acknowledge that the former is wanting in gratitude to an author whom he is continually arraigning, and continually copying. Yet Lord Bacon is not altogether without excuſe: in his time the pretended authority of Ariſtotle enthralled the human mind. In the preſent age, that illuſtrious modern might, conſiſtently with his *principles*, greatly vary his *conduct*; and exaggerate the merit of the Stagirite, in the ſame ſpirit, and with the ſame views, which made him formerly depreciate his fame.

[f] Notwithſtanding this deciſion of Ariſtotle's, a learned modern writer obſerves; "As to the perpetuating their inſtitutions and rendering them immutable, this entered not into the intention of the old Grecian legiſlation. A ſyſtem of immutable and irrevocable laws might indeed be the barbarous project of eaſtern policy; but the Grecian legiſlators were too well experienced in the nature of mankind, the genius of ſociety, and the ceaſeleſs viciſſitude of human things, ever to dream of ſo ridiculous a deſign." Warburton's Divine Legation of Moſes, b. ii. ſect. 3. This is expreſſed too ſtrongly and too abſolutely. Not to mention the example of Lycurgus, (ſee Hiſtory of Ancient Greece, vol. i. c. 3,) which Warburton indeed admits as an exception, but ſays that Lycurgus was ſingle in the ridiculous attempt of making his laws perpetual; a whole volume might be written to prove Ariſtotle's deciſion conformable to the general voice of poets, orators, hiſtorians, and legiſlators. Διι δὲ και τως νομως τες πατριδος καθαπερ τινας δευτερως θεως συντηρειν. "That we ought to maintain the laws of our country, and reſpect them as certain ſecondary divinities." Stobæus, ſerm. xxxviii. p. 229. Such is the general corollary reſulting from the political writings of Grecian antiquity; a corollary adopted by Cicero [a], their beſt interpreter, De Legibus; and ſuch is the doctrine maintained by Demoſthenes himſelf, when ſpeaking to the Athenians, whoſe decrees, governed by wild demagogues, were as variable as the Euripus. See his Oration

[a] Debet enim conſtituta ſic eſſe civitas, ut æterna ſit. Fragm. de Legibus, l. iii.

fally reprobated, yet various questions would arise, on what occasions it is warrantable. The difference of manners, governments, and of men, by whom alterations are proposed, and by whom they are to be conducted, will produce very complicated and almost innumerable questions; the solution of which we shall defer to a more seasonable opportunity.

In

---

tion against Timocrates, particularly the last pages. In the same Oration (p. 480, ex edit. Wolf) there is a passage worthy of remark. " I am inclined, citizen judges, to explain to you how the Locrians make laws. You will not suffer any detriment by hearing this example; an example of the mode of legislation in a well-regulated state. The Locrians are so firmly persuaded that it is their duty to uphold their ancient laws, and to defend them against the interest or caprice of innovators, that whoever proposes a new law, does it with a halter about his neck. Should the law be approved, the proposer departs unhurt; but should his law be rejected, he is strangled in his own halter. This salutary institution proves an effectual check to innovation; and the Locrians strictly observe their ancient laws; insomuch, that in a great length of time only one single law has been altered. The old law ordained, that whoever struck out the eye of another, should lose one of his own eyes; a punishment which did not admit of any pecuniary commutation, but was to be rigorously inflicted. A man with only one eye, being threatened by his adversary with the loss of the single eye he had, and thinking life insupportable under the calamity of blindness, ventured to propose this alteration of the law; ' That he who struck out the eye of a person who had but one, should be deprived of both his own eyes, so that the punishment might be equal to the crime.' The amendment was approved; and this is said to have been the only alteration in the Locrian law, in the space of more than two hundred years. But your demagogues, citizen judges, make new laws, solely for their own convenience, almost every month: if you do not punish them, the people at large will soon be enslaved by these wild beasts." ηκ αν φθασει το πληθος τυτοι; τοις Οργιοις δηλοιεν. As the law mentioned by Demosthenes is ascribed to Zaleucus (Ζαλευκον ος νομοθετει τα καινα πιστευτα νομοι ερχει πιρικειμενοι, &c. Stobæus, p. 229. serm. xxxviii.) the Locrians here spoken of must be the Locri Epizephyrij; so called from their territory near the promontory Zephyrium, at the southern extremity of Italy. Pindar calls them Zephyrian Locrians, in his short and pithy panegyric:

Νεμει γαρ ατρεκεια πολιν Λοκρων
Ζεφυριων, μελει δε τοισι, Καλλιοπα
Και χαλκεος Αρης.

" Justice

ARISTOTLE's POLITICS.

BOOK II.
Chap. 7.
Obfervations preparatory to an examination of the Spartan, Cretan, and Carthaginian re-

In examining the Spartan, the Cretan, or indeed any fyftem of laws, two queftions ought chiefly to fix our attention. The firft queftion is, Whether thefe laws be calculated to promote the beft interefts of mankind? The fecond, Whether they be calculated to promote thofe interefts which, under particular circumftances, the legiflator takes to be the beft: in other words, whether the inftitutions which we examine be confiftent with the moft defirable and moft perfect model of civil polity; or whether they be confiftent with what the lawgiver, all things confidered, deems the government moft fuitable to thofe for whom he legiflates? In every well-regulated commonwealth, it is agreed that all thofe citizens who have any fhare in the public adminiftration, fhould enjoy leifure for attending to this important concern. But how fuch leifure may beft be obtained, is not eafy to determine. The Penefts have often with arms affailed the Theffalians; and the Helots, the Spartans; and thofe degraded orders of peafants live as it were in continual ambufh, watching the moment to retaliate thofe injuries which they have indignantly fuffered from men whofe leifure refults only from their own toil. The Cretan peafants have never difcovered the fame fpirit of fedition; becaufe the cities of Crete being all of them fupported by the labour of fervile ruftics, it could not be the intereft of any one ftate to teach the flaves

Difficulties in regulating the peafants.

Why they are lefs feditious in Crete than in Theffaly, &c.

"Juftice governs the republic of the Zephyrian Locrians; who cultivate, with equal fuccefs, arts and arms." The law concerning the halter, which Stobæus refers to Zeleucus, is numbered by Diodorus Siculus among the laws of Charondas. But the fame writer tells us, that Charondas borrowed moft of his laws from former codes. Diodor. xii. 79. p. 485. It is probable therefore that the principle of refifting innovation once prevailed at Thurij, as well as in the republic of the Locri Epizephyrij; though hiftory indicates that it was far lefs rigidly adhered to in the former republic, which was difturbed by frequent revolutions. Ephor. apud Strabon. p. 260.

slaves of its neighbours to rebel, since every neighbour, who happened to be hostile, would constantly enjoy an opportunity of retorting the injury. But the Argives, Arcadians, and Messenians, subsisting chiefly by their own labour, and waging eternal wars with Sparta, always endeavoured to divide and divert the enemy's force, by stirring the Helots to rebellion; and the Penests first revolted from the Thessalians, during the wars of the latter with the Acheans, Perræbians, and Magnesians. In the treatment of slaves and peasants, it is difficult to hit the middle point between the extremes of indulgence and harshness; indulgence that is productive of insolence, and harshness that is repaid with hatred. But either extreme is highly inconsistent with the proper management of those lower classes, who form as it were the arms of the community.

Nothing proves more ruinous to a state than the defective education of the women; since wherever the institutions respecting one half of the community are faulty, the corruptions of that half will gradually taint the whole. The undisciplined manners of the Spartan women are inconsistent with every wise plan of legislation, and totally adverse to the principal aim of Lycurgus; who, exacting the most rigid temperance in his men, with a view to harden them to fortitude, has granted every indulgence to his women, and thereby corrupted them with licentiousness. In a nation of soldiers, the errors in female education, and the vicious passions resulting from that fatal source, are doubly prejudicial; for the poet had surveyed life and manners with discernment who first coupled Mars and Venus; all martial nations being immoderately amorous, and therefore particularly obnoxious to the undue influence, or rather the dominion, of women; with the

ARISTOTLE's POLITICS.

BOOK II.

the exception however of the Celts [a], and if there be any other people who openly prefer unnatural love. It is of little confequence whether women rule the ftate, or men, governed by women, rule it in fubfervience to female paffions. During the invafion of the Thebans, the Spartan women [b], inftead of rendering thofe fervices which women on fimilar occafions have often performed, caufed more evil than even the arms of the enemy; and avarice muft always domineer wherever women bear fway.

Whence it arofe.

The incongruous regulations refpecting the two fexes in Sparta proceeded from a natural caufe. The fevere duties of the field had prepared the men for fubmiffion to civil difcipline; but the women, untamed and turbulent, fpurned the yoke of legiflation. The fault, therefore, is chargeable on themfelves, rather than on Lycurgus. But we are not now inquiring who is to blame, but what is blamable?

Faulty regulations refpecting property.

The unequal diftribution of property forms another material defect in the Spartan government. Lycurgus prohibited the acquifition of lands by purchafe, but fet no bounds to their tranfmiffion and accumulation by gifts and teftaments. Landed property therefore has been engroffed by a few; and if the whole territory were divided into five equal portions, not lefs than two of thefe portions would be found vefted in women; fuch is the improvidence of the laws refpecting fucceffion, the enormity of dowers, and the extravagance of marriage fettlements!

Their ill effects.

The natural effect of fuch faulty regulations is to diminifh the populoufnefs of the country, which fcarcely contains the twentieth part of the inhabitants which it is capable of fupplying

[a] Vid. Athenæum, l. xiii. c. 27.
[b] See the Hiftory of Ancient Greece, v. iii. p. 394.

ARISTOTLE's POLITICS.

plying with subsistence, or the twentieth part of the thirty thousand heavy-armed men, and fifteen hundred cavalry, which it was thought able to send into the field. One great evil resulting from this diminution of people was fatally experienced when the single defeat at Leuctra reduced this ancient kingdom to the brink of ruin. It is reported that the kings preceding Lycurgus supplied the waste of the natives in war, by alluring foreigners into the country; and that the Spartans alone amounted to ten thousand men bearing arms. Without examining this report we may affirm, that the strength derived from numbers will be better and more safely promoted by levelling the excessive inequalities of property. Lycurgus, however, certainly wished to increase the strength of the state, when he enacted, that the man who had *three* sons should be exempted from the night watch, and that he who had four should enjoy a complete immunity from all public burdens. But this regulation evidently clashes with the preceding, since, under a faulty distribution of property, an increase of populousness is only an augmentation of misery.

BOOK II.

The popular part of the constitution of Sparta, residing in the Ephori, is liable to many objections; though invested with the most awful powers, the Ephori or inspectors must all of them be chosen indiscriminately from the multitude, and often from those of the lowest and poorest class. The decisions of such men ought not to be arbitrary or final. Their corruption has been shamefully manifest on many former occasions[1]; and in a very recent transaction, their venality, resulting from their poverty, had well nigh ruined the commonwealth. Their authority, too, is exorbitant and tyrannical; even the kings

Advantages and inconveniencies attending the Ephori.

[1] History of Ancient Greece, vol. ii. p. 61.

BOOK II.

kings acknowledge the neceffity of paying court to them; and their undue influence in the government has often expofed the ariftocracy of Sparta to the evils flowing from the moft turbulent democracy. Yet it muft be acknowledged, that this magiftracy of the Ephori, ill regulated as it is, tends to preferve the balance of the conftitution, and has thereby perpetuated its duration. To give ftability to any government, it is neceffary that all orders of the ftate fhould feel their intereft in its fafety. Whether by accident or defign this falutary purpofe has been effected at Sparta. The kings are inflexibly bound to a conftitution which confers on them peculiar honours: the fidelity of the higher ranks of men is fecured by the inftitution of the fenate, an admiffion into which is the exclufive reward of their merit and fervices: the people at large remain content with their condition, when they contemplate the fovereign magiftracy of the five Ephori promifcuoufly elected from the whole; and who ought certainly to be fo elected, though not after the childifh fafhion that now prevails[a]. The indulgences alfo permitted to the Ephori in their ordinary

[a] Ariftotle applies the fame epithet, a few fentences below, to the election of the fenate; but omits telling us wherein this puerility confifted. The defect is fupplied by Plutarch, in the life of Lycurgus; who relates, "That the affembly of the people having convened in the market-place, a certain number of felect perfons were confined in a neighbouring edifice; where, without the poffibility of feeing or being feen by the affembly, they could only hear its fhouts. The candidates for the fenate then marched through the middle of the affembly, one after the other, in the order determined by lot. As each candidate paffed in review, the people teftified their favour by acclamation; while the imprifoned judges marked on tablets the loudnefs and frequency of the fhouts, without knowing to which of the candidates they belonged. He who was honoured by the moft frequent repetition of the loudeft fhouts, was declared fenator." Our author juftly condemns this mode of election as childifh, fince the Lacedæmonians,

ordinary mode of life, are totally inconsistent with the spirit of Lycurgus's legislation. Severity of manners carried to the extremes of harshness and rigour is the prevailing feature of his policy; but while the rest of the citizens snatch only by stealth even the most lawful pleasures, the Ephori are absurdly indulged in the unbounded gratification of all their passions.

BOOK II.

The constitution of the Spartan senate labours under many defects; when the legislator enacted that the members of this council should hold their office for life, he did not consider that the understanding¹ grows old as well as the body. The great and uncontroverted powers vested in the senate might be safely entrusted to consummate wisdom and perfect virtue: but the Spartan senators have been seduced by partiality, and often corrupted by bribes. Their malversations therefore ought to be restrained by the regular operation of a law, compelling them at stated times to give an account of their administration; as their undue exercise of power is but imperfectly checked by being occasionally obnoxious to the wild tyranny of the Ephori. Their mode of election is puerile ᵐ; and that none should be admitted into the senate, but those who canvass for that honour, tends to excite and invigorate that impudence of selfish ambition which occasions half the

Imperfections of the senate.

nians, like children unable to count, contented themselves with probability in a matter where, by telling the votes, absolute certainty might have been attained. This mode of election was also well calculated to gratify the fraudulent designs of the judges; for when they happened to have an undue partiality for any of the candidates, they might guess, from his general character, with what kind of shouts he was likely to be received; and, in opposition to truth, declare the acclamations in his favour the loudest and most frequent. Vid. Thucydid. l. i. p. 58. edit. Francfort, 1594.

¹ See Analysis, p. 50, & seq.   ᵐ See note k.

the wickedness of mankind, and which is imprudently inflamed by the inftitutions of Lycurgus. Whether the office of king be at all ufeful in a republican government, fhall be examined hereafter. In whatever manner that queftion may be determined, it is plain that this office ought to be the reward of tried and approved merit; fince the inftitutions of Sparta have not been found capable of forming men, recommended by the accidental circumftance of birth, worthy of filling a throne. The legiflator, indeed, vifibly defpaired of perfecting his fellow-citizens in virtue, fince he condefcended to derive affiftance from their paffions and their vices. Men at variance with each other are confidered as the fitteft perfons to be joined in the fame important commiffions; and the fafety of the ftate is thought to have no fmall dependence on the diffenfion of the kings.

The Phiditia, or public tables, are ill inftituted, for thofe only can frequent them who are capable of bearing their fair proportion of the expence. At Crete the expence of the public tables is fupplied by the ftate, and even the pooreft citizens may enjoy them; but as managed at Sparta, the Phiditia have weakened the democratical part of the conftitution, which they were intended to ftrengthen and uphold.

The extraordinary powers granted to the high admiral of the republic have been juftly condemned by feveral writers. The two kings are the perpetual and hereditary commanders of the army; but the high admiral is vefted with fuch unbounded authority in naval affairs as renders him a fort of third king in the country, whofe ambition has often fhaken and almoft rent afunder the community.

Plato's

ARISTOTLE's POLITICS.

Plato's obfervation is juft, that the laws of Lycurgus are well adapted to the affairs of war, but to them only; Sparta therefore has been faved by her wars, and ruined by her victories, which fhe knew not how to improve or to enjoy: her citizens thought rightly and wifely, that virtue was better fitted than vice for acquiring conqueft and dominion; they thought erroneoufly and abfurdly, that thefe effects of virtue were more valuable than the caufe.

BOOK II.

Lycurgus's undue prediletion for war.

At Sparta the ftate is poor, and the revenues ill levied, for the wide extent of territory renders the citizens negligent in mutually exacting their reciprocal contributions. The poverty and difintereftednefs of the public thus forms a ftriking contraft with the wealth and avarice of individuals. But enough concerning the Spartan government, of which we have now enumerated the moft material defects.

The irregular collection of the Spartan revenue.

The civil polity of Crete nearly refembles that of Sparta, in fome parts not inferior to it, but in general worfe arranged and lefs polifhed; the Spartan government being later in its formation, and an improvement on the conftitution of Crete, which Lycurgus took for his model. During the travels of that lawgiver, after he ceafed to be guardian to king Charilaus, the ifland of Crete, recommended by its ancient connection with his mother country, chiefly attracted his regard, and long challenged his refidence; for Lyctos was a colony of Lacedæmon, and the fettlers in that diftrict conformed to the laws fubfifting in other parts of the ifland, which have continued to prevail to this day as firft eftablifhed by the elder Minos.

Chap. 8.

The government of Crete.

Crete, rifing in the midft of the Mediterranean fea, projecting towards Peloponnefus on one fide, and on the other advancing towards Rhodes and Triopium on the coaft of Afia, is formed as it were by nature for holding the naval empire of Greece;

Advantageous pofition of that ifland.

which

BOOK II.

Agreement in the Spartan and Cretan institutions.

which is every where a maritime country; Minos industriously availed himself of this advantageous situation, conquered some of the islands, colonized others, and died at Camicus in his unfortunate expedition against Sicily.

There is a striking analogy, we have said, between the Cretan and Spartan institutions: the territory of Laconia is cultivated for the benefit of the public by the subordinate class of Helots; the territory of Crete is cultivated for the same purpose by servile rustics denominated Periæci, because inhabiting the dependent villages scattered over the territory, and surrounding their respective capitals. The institution of common tables prevails in both countries; and these tables, at which the men only assemble, and which are now from their parsimony called Phiditia at Sparta, were anciently called in that country Andria, or tables appropriated to the male sex; a term by which they are still distinguished in Crete, in which island the custom took birth. The senate of Sparta corresponds to the senate in Crete, and the five Ephori in the one country bear a near affinity to the ten Cosmï of the other. The Cretan armies too were originally commanded by kings; but the power of the kings, which consisted, as at Sparta, in their being the hereditary generals of the commonwealth, has devolved on the Cosmï; who, together with the senate, have a negative before debate on the deliberations of the popular assembly, composed of the whole body of the citizens.

The clubs or public tables better regulated at Crete than in Sparta.

The public tables, we have said, are better constituted in Crete than in Sparta; in the latter country each messmate must provide his share of the entertainment, and when he ceases to make this provision, his right of commensality is immediately at an end. At Crete, on the other hand, the corn and cattle, the

the produce of the common lands, and the contributions levied on the Periæci, or peasants, are divided into two great shares; the first of which is appropriated to temples, sacrifices, and other objects appertaining to religion and the public service; the second is destined for the supply of the *Andreia*, or common-tables, and for affording food to persons of either sex and of all ages in the country. The Cretan legislator has some fine speculations on the subject of spare diet and frugality; and employs, for maintaining the due proportion of citizens and subsistence, some extraordinary regulations, the merits of which, we shall take another opportunity to discuss.

The office of the Cosmï at Crete labours under all the inconveniences which were found to result from that of the Ephori at Sparta. There is not any standard of merit by which persons soliciting either of those high offices must, before their election, be examined and tried; and as the Cosmï can only be chosen from a certain number of families, the most illustrious in the island, the honours conferred on them are invidious and dangerous, and have a tendency to excite the greater discontent in the multitude, since those alone who have discharged the office of the Cosmï can be elected into the senate, in which they keep their seats for life, neither controulable in their decisions as judges, nor responsible for their administration as statesmen. That the people have hitherto endured this unequal distribution of power, affords not any argument by which its policy can be defended; for the insular situation of Crete cuts off communication with strangers, and prevents *their* interference by intrigue and bribery, which, whenever it finds room to operate, always proves dangerous to an unjust and partial government. But the remedy

BOOK II.

The bad regulation of the Cosmï and senate.

The evils therefrom resulting.

BOOK II.

The remedy applied worfe than the evil.

remedy employed againſt this evil is ſtill worſe than the evil itſelf; ſince it controls by violence what might be ſubjected to law. The offended citizens conſpire againſt the obnoxious magiſtrate; and ſometimes by themſelves alone, ſometimes with the aſſiſtance of his colleagues, drive him from the community; unleſs he avoids this diſgraceful extremity by ſeaſonably abdicating his office.

The turbulence of the Cretan nobles.

Crete, which is ſometimes ſhaken by the mutinous ſpirit of the people, has been ſtill more fatally convulſed by the turbulence of the nobles, who diſdaining the authority of government, aſſemble their partiſans, levy war againſt the magiſtrates and againſt each other, and for a while rend aſunder all thoſe bands by which communities are upheld and cemented. Men, both willing and able to inflict ſuch dreadful calamities, muſt long ere now have totally ruined their country, had not the ſafety of Crete, as we before ſaid, been wonderfully protected by the ineſtimable advantages of its inſular ſituation; which, by excluding the dangerous interference of ſtrangers, long rendered the fidelity of the Periæci a ſtriking contraſt to the fickleneſs of the Helots. But foreign war having recently invaded the iſland, expoſes the nakedneſs of Crete, and evinces the debility of its government.

Chap. 9.

Excellence of the Carthaginian conſtitution.

The inſtitutions of the Carthaginians have been the ſubject of much commendation; and, when compared with the rudeneſs and coarſeneſs viſible in other ſtates, the refinement of Carthaginian polity, doubtleſs, merits applauſe; particularly thoſe inſtitutions which are analogous to the laws of Lycurgus; for the three conſtitutions of Sparta, Crete, and Carthage bear much reſemblance to each other; they are extremely diſſimilar to all other governments; and all three have adopted many maxims

that

that are wife, and many regulations that are falutary. The excellence of the Carthaginian government is evinced by one fingle reflection. Though its origin remounts to a very ancient date, and though for many centuries it has contained within its bofom a numerous and a free people, yet Carthage has never, to the prefent day, experienced any one fedition worthy of record, nor has it ever endured for a moment the cruel yoke of a tyrant. The common tables at Carthage are analogous to thofe of Crete and Sparta: the council of the Hundred and Four in the firſt mentioned country, refembles the magiſtracy of the Spartan Ephori; except that the Carthaginian Ephori, or infpectors, are chofen with nicer difcrimination: both nations acknowledge the experienced wifdom of fenates; and both fubmit to the authority of kings, limited in peace, fupreme in the field. But the ſtrong claim of merit is preferred to all other confiderations in afcertaining the title to the Carthaginian throne [m]; for weak or worthlefs men intruſted with much power, cannot fail to do much harm; a maxim often exemplified in the kings of Sparta.

The Carthaginian, as well as the Cretan and Spartan governments, whether by fubfequent and unneceffary additions, or in virtue of the primary regulations by which they were refpectively conſtituted, have all of them degenerated from that moſt perfect form of commonwealth, which we call by way of eminence

BOOK II.

The corruptions introduced into the Carthaginian government.

---

[m] The author obferves, that kings, meaning thereby fuch republican magiſtrates as the Suffetes of Carthage and the Kings of Sparta, ought not to be chofen from ordinary families, nor from ordinary individuals of thofe families; and that pre-eminence of perfonal merit fhould take place of feniority. What is faid of ordinary families, μητι τητο το τυχον, bears a reference to the opinion of the Greeks concerning the preeminence of particular races. See the Hiſtory of Ancient Greece, vol. i. c. ii & iii.

BOOK II.

eminence the republic; in which popular and aristocratic powers are harmoniously blended into one equitable system of polity, benefiting all, and doing injury to none. Of the corruptions thus introduced into the Carthaginian government, some have a tendency to relax the republic into a democracy; and others have a tendency to narrow the aristocracy into an oligarchy. To the former kind we may refer that institution which, when the kings and senators do not exactly coincide in opinion, submits every matter of debate to the discussion and final determination of the people; to the latter, we must refer the extraordinary powers of the council of Five, a council self-elected and immortal; and which also elects the Ephori, or supreme magistrates of the people. In the preference of suffrage to lot, and in serving the public without fee or reward, the Carthaginians seem to respect the aristocratic model. But the constitution of the judiciary power is highly oligarchical[n], the whole

[n] Nothing can be more interesting than Aristotle's account of the Carthaginian government; since the misfortunes, which his sagacity foresaw, are described in history; his prophecies being exactly fulfilled. Two centuries after Aristotle's time, Livy observes, "Judicum ordo Carthagine ea tempestate dominabatur; eò maxime quod iidem perpetui judices erant. Res, fama, vitaque omnium in illorum potestate erat. Qui unum ejus ordinis, idem omnes adversos habebat:" "The judiciary order at that time were tyrants in Carthage; and chiefly because their jurisdiction was perpetual. The estate, the character, and the life of each individual was entirely in their hands. Whoever incurred the displeasure of a single judge, had the whole body for his enemies." Lib. xxxiii. c. xlvi. It is here worthy of remark, that Livy's language tends to convey a false notion of the Carthaginian government. There was no judiciary order in Carthage, as in several of the Greek republics, and likewise in Rome, where the judges were appointed, in some ages of the commonwealth, from the senators, and in others from the knights. In Carthage, on the other hand, Aristotle expressly tells us that none but the actual magistrates were allowed to exercise the judiciary function. The political history of Carthage remains still to be written; for the Roman writers universally misrepresent the institutions of that country through ignorance

whole of that power being vested in one court, which tries all kinds of causes, and decides all of them without appeal. Yet that which has principally tended to convert the republic into an oligarchy, is an opinion strongly impressed on the nation at large, that in recommending to office, opulence ought to concur with merit; so that as virtue or merit forms the principle of an aristocracy, and wealth of an oligarchy, the government of Carthage will constitute a third and mixed kind of civil polity; blending in equal proportions the principles of aristocracy and oligarchy, of which it is compounded.

Wealth must be possessed before leisure can be obtained; and until leisure is obtained, office ought not to be courted; since he who is oppressed by private concerns, cannot be expected to manage public affairs, either wisely or faithfully. But the legislator and constitution are in fault, if men eminent for abilities and virtues, whether in public or private stations, be ever disgraced by unseemly poverty, or ever prevented by meaner cares from exercising their powers, and benefiting their country. In the distribution of honours, to prefer wealth to virtue, is to vilify and debase those honours themselves; it is to corrupt and degrade those who wear them. The evil is deep and universal; for such as the heads* of the community are,

ignorance or prejudice; and by bestowing Roman appellations on Carthaginian magistrates, lead the reader to suppose much greater analogy than really subsisted between two states, founded on the most dissimilar principles, and actuated by the most opposite views. But into this extensive and important subject it would be improper here to enter, because I shall have occasion fully to discuss it in my History of the Macedonian Empire; of which I have written the first volume, and collected materials for the second.

* Aristotle says, that whatever seems estimable to the heads of the community, the same will be esteemed by the rest of the citizens. Cicero has admirably translated, generalised,

BOOK II.

are, such must the people at large speedily become. No aristocracy can be safe, which does not prefer personal merit to all other distinctions; for he who by wealth obtains office, will endeavour by office to augment wealth; and if poverty intrusted with authority be liable, even in honest minds, to the suspicion of sacrificing duty to gain, it is absurd to expect that corruption, armed with power, will refuse to repair loss, and to compensate by rapacity the expences of bribery [p].

The dangerous accumulation of office,

The Carthaginian government acts unwisely in accumulating too many offices in the same hands. The example of well-organized generalised, and expanded the reflection. " Nec enim tantum mali est peccare principes (quanquam est magnum hoc per se ipsum malum) quantum illud, quod permulti imitatores principum existunt. Nam licet videre, si velis replicare memoriam temporum, qualescunque summi civitatis viri fuerunt, talem civitatem fuisse; quæcunque mutatio morum in principibus exstiterit, eandem in populo secuturam. Idque haud paulo est verius, quam quod Platoni nostro placet, qui musicorum cantibus ait mutatis, mutari civitatum status. Ego autem nobilium vita vectuque mutato, mores mutari civitatum puto. Quo perniciosius de republica merentur vitiosi principes, quod non solum vitia concipiunt ipsi, sed infundant in civitatem; neque solum obsunt, quod ipsi corrumpuntur, plusque exemplo quam peccato nocent." De Legibus, l. iii. c. xiv. " The vices and crimes of the nobility, though great evils in themselves, are rendered still greater, because they will always be the objects of general imitation. The experience of history teaches, that, in point of morals, such as have been the leading men of a state, such also has been the state itself; and that whatever alteration has taken place in the manners of the great, a similar alteration has followed in those of the people at large. This truth is far better ascertained than the observation of Plato, that the character of a nation changes, by changing the style of its music. But I assert, that it changes by changing the lives and behaviour of the Great. Wherefore profligate princes and profligate leaders are so much the more punishable than other men, because they are not only vitious in themselves, but infuse their vices into the public; and because whatever mischief results from their crimes, still greater results from their example."

[p] Livy speaks as if Aristotle's prophecy had been before his eyes, when he relates the facts by which it was accomplished. " Vectigalia publica prædæ ac divisui principum quibusdam ac magistratibus erant." And again, " Tum vero isti, quos paverat per aliquot annos publicus peculatus, velut bonis ereptis, non furto eorum manibus extorto, infensi & irati, Romanos in Annibalem instigabant." Liv. l. xxxiii. c. xlvi and xlvii.

ganized armies shews the inestimable benefits resulting from the nice partition of duty, and the innumerable gradations of authority. The more minutely labour of every kind is subdivided, the more perfectly, and the more promptly, each man will perform his assigned task; and that government only is firmly supported which associates many deserving citizens to its functions and its honours. The conduct of the Carthaginians is precisely the reverse; and this conduct has produced a deep and permanent disease in the constitution, which the magistrates have hitherto palliated by a temporary and precarious remedy. As the national prosperity of Carthage has long continued in an advancing state, the principal families have been enabled to maintain their odious monopoly of government, by employing those most inclined and most able to subvert it, in the numerous and increasing dependencies of their empire. But the success of this remedy requires the co-operation of fortune; both its cause and effects are barely external. A good constitution should be found within [q]. Such are the excellencies, and such the imperfections, of the governments of Sparta, Crete, and Carthage; which, in comparison with most others, have been justly celebrated.

Of the writers on the subject of politics, some have confined themselves merely to theory; others have illustrated theory by practice, and assisted in their own or in foreign countries, in the administration of those governments which they had devised and established, or of those laws which they had contrived and enacted.

BOOK II.

palliated in Carthage by a temporary and precarious remedy.

Chap. 10.

The constitution of Athens.

[q] These observations are worthy of the most serious attention. When a nation is advancing in wealth and greatness, the most dangerous maladies, existing only in an indolent state, may long lie altogether concealed. The first shock of adversity reveals the fatal secret; but then, perhaps, it is no longer time to attempt the radical cure.

BOOK II.

enacted. The principal doctrines of merely speculative politicians we have already examined; we have likewise described the practical system of Lycurgus; and now proceed to explain the legislation of Solon, who is celebrated as the restorer of the hereditary freedom of Athens, and as the deliverer of the people from the yoke of an intemperate and cruel oligarchy. In the constitution established by Solon, his admirers observe, that the jarring interests of hostile orders are skilfully harmonised into one equitable system, justly formed, and nicely balanced, by the oligarchy of the Areopagus, which is perpetual; the aristocracy of the Archons, who are elective; and the democracy of the courts of judicature, whose members are appointed indiscriminately from all the citizens by lot. Solon, it is probable, did not first introduce, but simply receive and approve, the perpetuity of the Areopagus, and the election of the Archons: but he invented and established the popular constitution of the judiciary power; a constitution, which some writers have branded as introductory to the confusion and tyranny of a wild democracy. Masters of the courts of justice, and consequently of the lives and fortunes of all ranks of men in the state, the people have drained and exhausted every source of authority, not flowing from themselves.

Causes of its degeneracy.

Pericles, with the assistance of Ephialtes, abridged the power of the Areopagus; the same Pericles, by granting fees to the judges and jurymen, and converting a matter of duty into an object of gain, still farther debased the composition, and increased the tyranny, of the Athenian tribunals. What Pericles left imperfect, succeeding demagogues supplied; and one democratical regulation still followed another, until the government assumed its present form, or rather exhibited its present deformity.

deformity. Yet this fatal refult is not imputable to Solon[r], but rather chargeable on fortune. The naval victories of Athens, in the Perfian war, fwelled the infolence of the populace, who, headed by orators more infolent than themfelves, arrogated all authority to their own order, and ufurped the government. Solon juftly intrufted the multitude with the power of electing the magiftrates, and with that of taking an account of their adminiftration; powers which cannot eafily be withheld from the people without degrading them into flaves, or converting them into enemies. But all the executive offices of government were confined to men of the three firft claffes: the *Thetes*, confifting of labourers and mechanics, and forming the moft numerous portion of the community, were totally excluded from every employment requiring either coolnefs of temper or quicknefs of underftanding.

{The legiflations of Zaleucus and Charondas.}

Zaleucus legiflated for the weftern Locrians; and Charondas, a native of Catana in Sicily, gave laws, not only to his own citizens, but to the other Ionic communities fcattered over Sicily and Italy. Some writers trace up to Onomacritus the inftitutions of thofe legiflators, relating that Onomacritus failed to Crete to learn the art of divination; that he became famous as a lawgiver; that Thales was his companion, and Lycurgus the fcholar of Thales, Zaleucus the fcholar of Lycurgus, and Charondas the fcholar of Zaleucus: but this order of fucceffion is not juftified by chronology.

{Of Philolaus.}

Philolaus, a native of Corinth, and defcended from the illuftrious family of the Bacchiadæ, who long governed that city, gave laws to the Thebans. Philolaus was the friend of Diocles,

[r] See the Hiftory of Ancient Greece, paffim. particularly vol. ii. c. xiii.

BOOK II.

Diocles, likewise a Corinthian, who gained the Olympic prize, and who fled from his native city, as detesting the inceſtuous paſſion of his mother Halcyone. Diocles fixed his refidence in Thebes; the affectionate Philolaus foon followed him thither; in that city they lived and died; and there, the monuments of theſe two friends are ſtill ſhewn to ſtrangers, difpofed in ſuch fituations as render them fully confpicuous to each other, that of Philolaus alfo enjoying a view of Corinth, but that of Diocles concealing from the fight both that city and its territory, as if he wiſhed to baniſh from his eyes objects only calculated to recall the ſad memory of his domeſtic calamity. Philolaus having thus fixed his abode in Thebes, propoſed various laws for the benefit of that republic; particularly the law of adoption, contrived for perpetuating the ancient families, and for preferving a due proportion between the number of landholders, and the number of ſhares or lots, into which the territory was divided. Charondas inſtituted a new action² againſt the odious crimes of calumny

---

² The name of this action, as Bentley proves, was ἐπισκηψις, which took place when a man, caſt in a trial by falſe teſtimony, entered his plea to have another trial to prove the witneſſes perjured. It is mentioned by Demoſthenes more than once, and by Lyſias contra Pandionem. See Diſſertation upon Phalaris, p. 368. Bentley ſays, "that Diodorus tells us from his copy of Charondas's laws that he had πολλα ιδια, many things peculiar, and reckons up half a ſcore of them; and yet the ſingle thing obſerved by Ariſtotle does not appear among them." In this Bentley is miſtaken; for the peculiarity of Charondas's law againſt perjured calumniators appears in Diodorus, and makes a great figure there.—His words follow, Τως δ᾽ ἐπι συκοφαντια καταγνωσθεντας προσεταξε περιπατειν ἐστιφανωμενους μυρικῃ, ὁπως ἐν πασι τοις πολιταις πρωτιοι της πονηριας προπεπτωκοιεν· διο και τινας ἐπι τουτῳ τῳ ἐγκλημα καταδικασθεντας, το μεγεθος της ὑβριως ουκ ἐνεγκοντας, ἑκουσιως ἑαυτως ἐκ του ζην μεταστησαι. ἡ συντιλισθεντος, ἐφυγαδευθη πας ἐκ της πολεως ὁ συκοφαντων ἡθως, και το πολιτευμα μακαριον ἐιχε βιον της τοιαυτης κακιας ἀπηλλαγμενον. Diodor. 1. xii. p. 486. "He commanded thoſe convicted of calumny to go about crowned with tamariſk, that they might appear to all the citizens to have attained the laſt ſtage of wickedneſs; therefore ſome of thoſe convicted of this crime, incapable of

ſupporting

calumny and perjury; and his laws furpafs, in elegancy and in accuracy, even the juridical compofitions of the prefent day. Phaleas diftinguifhed himfelf by equalizing property; and Plato by appointing common tables for women; and by propofing among men, the community of wives, children, and goods. His lefs extravagant novelties are, that children fhould be taught to ufe both hands with equal dexterity, and that a perfon bound to the obfervance of perfect fobriety fhould prefide in companies affembled for convivial merriment. The laws of Draco' were remarkable for nothing but their exceffive and undiftinguifhing feverity. Pittacus" did not delineate any new fcheme of policy, but eftablifhed feveral new laws, of which one peculiar to himfelf is, that offences committed by perfons intoxicated, fhould be punifhed with double rigour; a law founded rather on inflexible utility, which confiders how evils may be prevented, than on merciful juftice, which examines what offences ought to be pardoned*. Androgamas, a native

of

---

fupporting the weight of infamy, voluntarily deftroyed themfelves; in confequence of which examples, calumny totally difappeared, and the ftate thenceforth fubfifted happily, being divorced from fuch a mifchief." The word tamarifk is in the original μυρικη, myrice, of which Pliny fays, " Myricen in Italia quam alii tamaricen vocant, cujus infelicia ligna appellamus. Solitaria circum faxa aquofa, qua in domum illata, difficiles partus fieri produnt, mortefque miferas." Plin. Nat. Hift. xii. 21. This unhappy and unaufpicious plant, creeping folitary amidft watery rocks, was a fit decoration for an outcaft of fociety, a wretch fhunned and detefted. To how many expreffive cuftoms of antiquity do we ftill want a key?

' Hiftory of Ancient Greece, vol. ii. p. 105. " Ibid. vol. . p. 225.

* Both Plato and Ariftotle are more indulgent in the article of wine, than the more ancient philofophers and legiflators. A law of Zaleucus is preferred in Athenæus, l. x. p. 226. and commented in Elian, Var. Hift. ii. 37. which treats the drinking of pure

wine

BOOK II. of Rhegium, gave laws to Chalcis in Thrace; his code is most ample on the subjects of heiresses and of murders; but is not distinguished by any peculiarity worthy of record. Let this much suffice concerning plans of policy and laws, which either authority has established, or speculation devised.

wine with Mahommedan severity, ιι τίς ακρατον επιη, μη πραοταξαντος ιατρu θιγαπυας ιuκχ, θxιατος w̃ ἡ ξημια.—" Whoever drinks pure wine, except for the sake of health, and by the prescription of a physician, let him be punished by death."

(125)

ARISTOTLE's POLITICS.

APPENDIX TO BOOK II.

IN my endeavour to illuſtrate various ſubjects treated in this Book, I frequently had occaſion to allude to the Italian republics of the middle age; which exhibited a faint and rude picture of the polities of ancient Greece. Of all theſe republics, there is one, and only one, ſtill ſubſiſting on the ancient model. This ſmall but precious remain of former, and by ſome thought better times, I endeavoured from careful obſervation to delineate upwards of twenty years ago, in an article [a] firſt made public in 1795, and ſince that time frequently reprinted. But the intimate connexion of that juvenile performance with the ſubject of the preſent Book of Ariſtotle's Politics, has ſuggeſted the propriety of giving here an enlarged edition of it, enriched and confirmed by original documents, extracted, through the intereſt of Sir John Cox Hippeſley, from the ſecret archives of the republic, and moſt obligingly communicated to me by Sir John Macpherſon.

"At the diſtance of twelve miles from Rimini and the Hadriatic Sea, we beheld a cloud-capt mountain, ſteep, rugged, and inhoſpitable, yet to Britons, whoſe affection for their own happy

---

[a] Given as an extract from my manuſcript travels in that agreeable work, intitled, "Anecdotes of ſome diſtinguiſhed Perſons chiefly of the preſent and two preceding Centuries."

APPEND. TO BOOK II.

happy ifland cherifhed even the fainteft image of congenial liberty, more attractive and more engaging than all the gay luxuriance of Tufcan [b] plains. A black expanfion of vapour partly concealed from our view the territory of what the Greeks would have called a nation, feldom vifited by ftrangers, though affuredly moft deferving of that honour. Liberty brightens and fertilizes the craggy rocks of St. Marino; and inftead of paradifes inhabited by devils, (for thus the recollection or fuppofition of better times indignantly characterifes the countries through which we had juft travelled,) this little ftate, we were told, would exhibit rugged hills and favage precipices cultivated and adorned by the ftubborn induftry of free men, who labour with alacrity, becaufe they reap with fecurity. We panted at the thoughts of taking a nearer furvey of this political wonder, and were impatient to leave Rimini; but the country adjacent to that city was deluged with rain; the rivers continued to overflow; horfes could not fafely clamber over rocks; and Rimini could not furnifh us with mules. But they are delicate travellers whom fuch puny difficulties could reftrain from vifiting this illuftrious mountain, where Liberty, herfelf a mountain goddefs, has upwards of twelve centuries fixed her rural throne. Carelefs of mules, or horfes, or carriages, to which laft the republic of St. Marino is at all times inacceffible, we adopted

[b] " The epithet Tufcan is juftified by the authority of Polybius, l. ii. c. 14. and c. 17. He defcribes that extenfive plain bounded by the Alps, the Apennines, and the Hadriatic, and alfo the plains about Nola and Capua, called the Phlegræan Fields, as anciently inhabited by the Tufcans. The territory of this people, he fays, formed incomparably the fineft portion of Europe. Before Polybius wrote his Hiftory, the dominion of the Tufcans had contracted to a narrow fpan; and according to the faying of the modern Italians, while the Pope poffeffes the marrow, the Great Duke of Tufcany has now only the bones, of Italy."

adopted a mode of travelling which in a country where pomp is immoderately ftudied, becaufe wealth is too indifcriminately prized, might poffibly have excluded unknown wanderers from the proud manfions of nobles and princes, the palaces of bifhops, and the vineas of cardinals, but which, we rightly conjectured, would recommend us as welcome guefts to the citizens of St. Marino, whofe own manlinefs of character muft approve the congenial hardihood of humble pedeftrians.

"The diftance from Rimini to the Borgo, or fuburbs of St. Marino, for the città, or city, ftands half a mile higher on the hill, is computed at only ten Italian miles. But the badnefs of the weather and of the roads would have increafed the tediouf- nefs of our fatiguing journey, had not our fancies been amufed by the appearance and converfation of feveral perfons whom we occafionally met or overtook, and who, notwithftanding that hardnefs of features which characterifes mountaineers, difplayed in their words and looks a certain candour and fincerity, with an undefcribed mixture of humanity and firmnefs, which we had rarely feen pourtrayed on the face of an Italian. Such virtues, perhaps, many Italians may poffefs; fuch virtues Raphael and Guido probably difcerned in their contemporaries; unlefs it be fuppofed that the *antique* not only ennobled and exalted, but originally infpired their conceptions. Yet whatever might be the pre-eminence of Tranfalpine beauty, during the fplendour of the *cinque cento*, it muft be confeffed of the Italians of our days, that the expreffion indicating virtues of the mild or generous caft, feldom breaks through the dark gloom and fullen cares which contract their brows and cloud their counte- nances. .

APPEND. TO BOOK II.

"At the diſtance of five miles from Rimini, a ſmall rivulet, decorated by a diſproportionably large ſtone bridge, which at another ſeaſon of the year would have exemplified the Spaniſh proverb of a bridge without water, ſeparates the territories of St. Marino from thoſe of the Pope. Proceeding forward, we found the road extremely narrow, much worn by the rain, alternately rough and ſlippery, and always ſo bad, that we congratulated each other on rejecting the uſe of the miſerable rips that were offered to us at Rimini. In the midſt of a heavy ſhower we clambered to the Borgo, ſituate on the ſide of the hill, and diſtant (as already ſaid) half a mile from the città, on its ſummit. The former is deſtined for the habitation of peaſants, artiſans, and ſtrangers; the honour of inhabiting the latter is reſerved for the nobles, the citizens, and thoſe who, in the language of antiquity, would be ſtyled the public gueſts of the commonwealth. In the whole territory there is but one inn; and that of courſe in the Borgo; for lone houſes are rare in all parts of the continent, the Britiſh dominions alone, by their native ſtrength and the excellence of their government, being happily exempted from the terror of banditti in time of peace, and marauders in time of war. We diſcovered the inn at St. Marino, as is uſual in Italy, by the crowd before the door. Having entered, we were civilly received by the landlord, ſeated by the fire-ſide in company with ſeveral other ſtrangers, and ſpeedily preſented with a bottle of ſparkling white wine, the beſt we had taſted in Italy, and reſembling Champagne in the characteriſtic excellencies of that ſprightly liquor.

"We had not remained long in this caravanſera, (for ſuch is the proper name for the place of hoſpitality in which we were received,)

received), when the drefs, manners, and converfation of our fellow-travellers ftrongly excited our attention, and afforded fcope for boundlefs fpeculation. They were the moft favage-looking men that I had ever beheld; covered with thick capottas [c], of coarfe dark brown woollen, lined with black fheep's fkin. Their hats, which they kept on their heads, were of an enormous fize, fwelling to the circumference of an ordinary umbrella. With their drefs and appearance their words and geftures bore too faithful a correfpondence. "*Schioppi*" and "*coltellate*" (gun-fhots and dagger-thrufts) were frequently in their mouths. As the wine went brifkly round, the converfation became ftill more animated, and took a turn more decidedly terrible. They now talked of nothing but fierce encounters, hair-breadth efcapes, and hideous lurking-places. From their whole behaviour, there was reafon to apprehend, that we had unwarily fallen into company with Rinaldo's party: but a few hints that dropped from him who was moft intoxicated finally undeceived us, and difcovered, to our fatisfaction and fhame, that inftead of a band of robbers, we had only met with a party of fmugglers. Their maffy capottas and broad-brimmed hats formed their defenfive armour againft cuftom-houfe officers and *fbirri* [d]; and the narratives which they heard or related with fuch ardor and delight, contained the acts of prowefs by which they had repelled the bravery of the Romans, and the arts of ftratagem by which they had deceived the cunning of the Tufcans. From the intermediate fituation of St. Marino between the dominions of Tufcany and thofe of the Pope, its territory is continually infefted by vifits from thofe unlicenfed traffickers, who being enemies

[c] Great coats. [d] Thofe who execute the orders of civil magiftrates.

APPEND.
TO
BOOK II

enemies by trade to thofe who adminifter the laws and collect the revenues of their country, naturally degenerate into daring and diforderly ruffians, the terror of peaceful men, and both the difgrace and the bane of civilized fociety.

From the company of the fmugglers we longed to feparate, the more becaufe they eagerly folicited our ftay, promifing to conduct us fafely acrofs the mountains, and to defend our perfons and properties againft robbers and affaffins; but we thought it a piece of good fortune, that our moft valuable property, as we fhewed to them, confifted in our fwords and piftols. Having called our St. Marino hoft, we paid him for his wine and his faufage (*profciutto*); and were pleafed to find, that contrary to our univerfal experience of Italian landlords, he was uncommonly thankful for a very moderate gratification, a fingularity which, though it probably proceeded from his being little converfant with Englifh and other opulent travellers, we treafured with delight, as a confpicuous proof of republican [e] virtue, that had efcaped pure and unfullied from the contagion of thofe worthlefs guefts, with whom the nature of his trade condemned him often to affociate.

About two o'clock in the afternoon, we left the Borgo to climb up to the Città, carrying our fwords in our right hands; a precaution which the company we had juft left warranted in this modern republic, but which, as Thucydides informs us in his proem, would have expofed us to be branded with the appellation

[e] According to Machiavelli and Montefquieu, and their mafter Ariftotle, republics require more virtue than monarchies, becaufe in republics the citizens make laws to govern themfelves, whereas in monarchies the fubjects are compelled to obey the laws made by the prince. In republican governments, therefore, the citizens ought, in the words of Ariftotle, and of a ftill higher authority, 'to be a law unto themfelves.' How few nations, therefore, are qualified, in modern times, for living quietly and happily under a republic; and leaft of all, that nation which has fhewn itfelf the leaft virtuous of all.

pellation of barbarians in the republics of Ancient Greece. Before we had reached the summit of the hill, the cloud had dispersed, the sun shone bright, we breathed a purer air, and the clear light, which displayed the city and territory of St. Marino was heightened by contrast with the thick gloom which involved the circumjacent plains. Transported with the contemplation of a landscape which seemed so admirably to accord with the political state of the mountain, a bright gem of liberty amidst the darkness of Italian servitude, we clambered cheerfully over the precipices, never reflecting that as there was not any place of reception for strangers in the Città, we might possibly be exposed to the alternative of sleeping in the streets, or returning to the caravansera, crowded with smugglers, whose intoxication might exasperate their natural ferocity. From all our past remarks, we had concluded that the vice of drunkenness was abominated even by the lowest classes of the Italians. We dreaded their fury and their knives in this unusual state of mind; but amidst all our terrors could not forbear philosophising *f* on what we had seen, and conjecturing, from the tumultuous merriment and drunken debauchery of the smugglers, that the famed sobriety of the Italian nation is an artificial virtue arising from situation and accident, not depending on temperament, or resulting from character. Drinking is the vice of men whose lives are chequered by vicissitudes of toil and ease, of danger and security. It is the vice of soldiers, mariners, and huntsmen;

---

f This word requires an apology; for the sacred name of philosophy has been as shamefully polluted in modern times, by sophists and sceptics, as the word republic by madmen and levellers. The present generation must perhaps pass away, before either of these terms shall resume its pristine and native honours.

APPEND. TO BOOK II.

huntfmen; of thofe who exercife boifterous occupations, or purfue dangerous amufements: and if the modern Italians are lefs addicted to excefs in wine than the Greeks and Romans in ancient, or the Englifh and Germans in modern times, their temperance may fairly be afcribed to the indolent monotony of their liftlefs lives; which, being never exhaufted by fatigue, can never be gladdened by repofe; and being never agitated by the terrors of danger, can never be tranfported by the joys of deliverance.

From thefe airy fpeculations, by which we fancied that we ftripped Italy of what fome travellers have too haftily concluded to be the only virtue which fhe has left, we were awakened by the appearance of a venerable perfon, in a bag wig and fword, cautioufly leading his *bourrique*[a] down the precipice. He returned our falute with an air of courtefy befpeaking fuch affability, that we quickly entered into converfation with him, and difcovered to our furprife and joy, that we were in company with a very refpectable perfonage, and one whom Mr. Addifon has dignified with the appellation of 'the fourth man in the ftate.' The ftipendiary phyfician of St. Marino (for this was the perfon with whom we were converfing) told us, that we might be accommodated with good lodging in the convent of Capuchins; and as we were ftrangers, that he would return, fhew us the houfe, and prefent us to Father Bonelli. We expreffed our unwillingnefs to give him the trouble of again afcending the hill; but of this trouble the deeply-wrinkled mountaineer made light, and we yielded to his propofal with only apparent reluctance; fince, to the indelicacy of introducing ourfelves, we preferred the introduction of a man whom we had even cafually met

[a] Afs.

met with on the road. To the convent we were admitted by a *frate fervente*, or lay friar, and conducted to the *Padre Maestro*, the Prior Bonelli, a man sixty years old, and, as we were told by the physician, descended from one of the noblest families in the commonwealth. Having received and returned such compliments as are held indispensable in this ceremonious country, the prior conducted us above stairs, and shewed us two clean and comfortable chambers, which he said we might command while we deigned to honour the republic (such were his expressions) with the favour of our residence. As to our entertainment, he said we might, as best pleased us, either sup apart by ourselves, or in company with him and his monks. We told him, our happiness would be complete, were we permitted to enjoy the advantage of his company and conversation. My conversation! You shall soon enjoy better than mine; since within half an hour I shall have the honour of conducting you to the house of a charming young lady (so I must call her, though my own kinswoman), whose *conversazione* assembles this evening. During this dialogue a servant arrived, bringing our portmanteau from Rimini, and thereby enabling us with more decency of appearance to pay our respects to the lady, in company with the prior her uncle. The Signora P—— received us politely in an inner apartment, after we had passed through two outer rooms, in each of which there was a servant in waiting. Above a dozen gentlemen, well dressed and polite after the fashion of Italy, with six other ladies, formed this agreeable party. Coffee and sorbettis being served, cards were introduced; and, in quality of strangers, we had the honour of losing a few sequins at ombre with the mistress of the house. The other ladies present took up, each of them, two gentlemen;

APPEND. TO BOOK II. for ombre is the univerfal game, becaufe in Italian affemblies the number of men commonly triples that of women; the latter, when unmarried, feldom going abroad; and when married, being ambitious of appearing to receive company every evening at home. During the intervals of play, we endeavoured to turn the converfation on the hiftory and prefent ftate of St. Marino, but found this fubject to be too grave for the company. In this little ftate, as well as in other parts of Italy, the focial amufements of life confifting chiefly in what are called *converfazioni*, have widely deviated from the *fympofia* of the Greeks and the *convivia* of the Romans. Inftead of philofophical dialogues and epideiktic orations; and inftead of thofe animated rehearfals of approved works of hiftory and poetry, which formed the entertainment and delight of antiquity, the modern Italian *converfazioni* exhibit a very different fcene; a fcene in which play is the bufinefs, gallantry the amufement; and of which avarice, vanity, and mere fenfual pleafure form the fole connecting principle and chief ultimate end. Such infipid and fuch mercenary affemblies are fometimes enlivened by the jokes of the buffoon; the *improvifatore* fometimes difplays in them the powers of his memory rather than the elegance of his fancy; and every entertainment in Italy, whether gay or ferious, is always feafoned with mufic; but chiefly that foft voluptuous mufic which was banifhed by Lycurgus, profcribed by Plato, and prohibited by other legiflators, under fevere penalties, as unfriendly to virtue and deftructive of manhood. The great amufements of life are commonly nothing more than images of its neceffary occupations; and where the latter, therefore, are different, fo alfo muft be the former. Is it becaufe the occupations of the ancients were lefs foftened than

thofe

those of the moderns, that women are found to have acted among different nations such different parts in society? And that the contrast is so striking between the wife of a citizen of St. Marino, surrounded with her card-tables, her music, and her admirers, and the Roman Lucretia, *nocte ferâ deditam lanæ inter lucubrantes ancillas* (Tit. Liv. i. 57.), or the more copious descriptions of female modesty and industry given by Ischomachus in Xenophon's Treatise on Domestic Œconomy? In modern Italy this contrast of manners displays its greatest force. Though less beautiful and less accomplished than the English and French, the Italian women expect superior attention, and exact greater assiduities. To be well with the ladies, is the highest ambition of the men. Upon this principle their manners are formed; by this their behaviour is regulated; and the art of conversation, in its utmost sprightliness and highest perfection, is reduced to that playful wantonness which, touching slightly on what is felt most sensibly, amuses with perpetual shadows of desired realities.

To the honour of St. Marino it must be observed, that neither the Prior Bonelli, nor two *counsellors* who were present, took any considerable part in this too sportive conversation; and the gentlemen at the Signora P―――'s were chiefly Romans and Florentines; men, we were told, whom sometimes misfortune and sometimes inclination, but more frequently extravagance and necessity, drive from their respective countries, and who, having relations or friends in St. Marino, establish themselves in that cheap city, where they subsist on the wreck of their fortunes, and elude the pursuit of their creditors.

Next morning Bonelli having invited several of his fellow-citizens to drink chocolate, we learned from them, that the

morality

APPEND. TO BOOK II.

morality and piety which had long diftinguifhed St. Marino, daily fuffered decline through the contagious influence of thofe profligate intruders, whom good policy ought never to have admitted within the territory, but whom the indulgence of humanity could not be prevailed on to expel.

After breakfaft, our good-natured landlord kindly propofed a walk, that his Englifh guefts might view the city and adjacent country. The main ftreet is well paved, but narrow and fteep. The fimilarity of the houfes indicates a happy mediocrity of fortune. There is a fine ciftern of pure water; and we admired the coolnefs and drynefs of the wine-cellars, ventilated by communications with caverns in the rock. To this circumftance, as much as to the quality of the foil and careful culture of the grape, the wine of St. Marino is indebted for its peculiar excellence.

The whole territory of the republic extends about thirty-five miles in circumference. It is of an irregular oval form, and its mean diameter may be eftimated at fix Englifh miles. The foil naturally craggy and barren, and hardly fit for goats, yet actually maintains (fuch are the attractions of liberty) upwards of feven thoufand perfons; and being everywhere adorned by mulberry-trees, vines, and olives, fupplies the materials of an advantageous trade, particularly in filk, with Rome, Florence, and other cities of Italy.

In extent of territory, St. Marino, inconfiderable as it feems, equals many republics that have performed mighty atchievements and purchafed immortal renown. The independent ftates of Thefpiæ and Platæa were refpectively lefs extenfive; and the boundaries of the modern republic exceed thofe of Ægina and Megara; the former of which was diftinguifhed by its

its commerce and its colonies in Egypt and the East; and the latter, as Lysias and Xenophon inform us, could bring into the field, besides proportional bodies of light troops, 3000 hardy pikemen, who with the service of Mars united that of Ceres and of Bacchus; extracting from bleak hills and rugged mountains rich harvests and teeming vintages.

The remembrance of our beloved republics of Greece, ennobled by the inestimable gifts of unrivalled genius, endeared to us St. Marino, even by its littleness. In this literary enthusiasm, we could willingly have traversed every inch of its diminutive territory: but politeness required that we should not subject Bonelli and his friends to such unnecessary fatigue; and the changeableness of the weather, a continual variation of sunshine and cloudiness, the solemnity of dark magnifying vapours, together with the velocity of drizzly or gleamy showers, produced such unusual accidents of light and shade in this mountain scene, as often suspended the motion of our limbs, and fixed our eyes in astonishment. From the highest top of St. Marino we beheld the bright summit of another and far loftier mountain, towering above, and beyond a dark cloud, which by contrast threw the conical top of the hill to such a distance, that it seemed to rise from another world. The height of St. Marino (we were told) had been accurately measured by Father Boscovich, and found to be nearly half a mile above the level of the neighbouring sea.

Almost immediately after returning from our walk, dinner was served at the convent; for the politeness of Father Bonelli had prolonged his stay abroad far beyond his usual hour of repast. Speedily after dinner we were conducted by the good father to the *converfazione* of another lady, also his relation, where

APPEND. TO BOOK II. where we had the honour of meeting the *capitaneos*, or confuls, the *commiffareo*, or chief judge, and feveral diftinguifhed members of the fenate. Recommended only by our youth and curiofity, we fpent the evening moft agreeably with thofe refpectable magiftrates, who were as communicative in anfwering as inquifitive in afking queftions. The company continually increafing, and Father Bonelli carefully addreffing all newcomers by the titles of their refpective offices, we were furprifed toward the clofe of the evening, and the ufual hour of retirement, that we had not yet feen *Il Signor Dottore* and *Il Pædagogo Publico*, the phyfician and fchoolmafter, reprefented by Mr. Addifon as two of the moft diftinguifhed dignitaries in the commonwealth. A fhort acquaintance is fufficient to infpire confidence between congenial minds. We frankly teftified our furprife to the father. He laughed heartily at our fimplicity, and thought the joke too good not to be communicated to the company. When their vociferous mirth had fubfided, an old gentleman, who had been repeatedly invefted with the higheft honours of his country, obferved, that he well knew Mr. Addifon's account of St. Marino, which had been tranflated more than once into the French and Italian languages. Remote and inconfiderable as they were, his anceftors were highly honoured by the notice of that illuftrious traveller, who, he underftood, was not only a claffic author in Englifh, but an author who had uniformly and moft fuccefsfully employed his pen in the caufe of virtue and liberty. Yet, as muft often happen to travellers, Mr. Addifon, he continued, has, in fpeaking of this little republic, been deceived by firft appearances. Neither our fchoolmafter nor phyfician enjoy any pre-eminence in the ftate. They are maintained indeed by public falaries, as in feveral

other

other cities of Italy; and there is nothing peculiar in their condition here, except that the schoolmaster has more, and the phyſician leſs, to do, than in moſt other places, becauſe our diſeaſes are few, and our children are many. This ſally having been received with approbation by the company, the veteran proceeded to explain the real diſtinction of ranks in St. Marino, conſiſting in the *nobili*, *cittadini*, and *ſtipendiate*, nobles, citizens, and ſtipendiaries. The nobles, he told us, exceeded not twenty families, of which ſeveral enjoyed eſtates without the territory, worth from three to eight hundred pounds ſterling a-year: that, from reſpect to the Holy See, under whoſe protection the republic had long ſubſiſted quietly and happily, many perſons of diſtinction in the Pope's territories had been admitted *cittadini honorati*, honorary citizens of St. Marino, particularly ſeveral illuſtrious houſes of Rimini, and the forty noble families of Bologna. Even of the Venetian nobles themſelves, ancient as they certainly were, and inveſted as they ſtill continued to be with the whole ſovereignty of their country, many diſdained not to be aſſociated to the diminutive honours of St. Marino, and to increaſe the number of its citizens; and that this aggregation of illuſtrious foreigners, far from being conſidered as dangerous to public liberty, was deemed eſſential, in ſo ſmall a commonwealth, to national ſafety.

Leſt the converſation might take another turn, I drew from my pocket Mr. Addiſon's account of St. Marino, which, being exceedingly ſhort, I begged leave to read, that his errors, if he had committed any, might be corrected, and the alterations noted which the country had undergone in the ſpace of ſeventy years, from 1703 to 1773.

APPEND. TO BOOK II.

The proposal being obligingly accepted, I read in Mr. Addison, 'They have at St. Marino five churches, and reckon above five thousand souls in their community.' Instead of which I was desired to say, 'They have in St. Marino ten parishes, ten churches, and reckon above seven thousand souls in their community.' Again Mr. Addison says, 'The Council of Sixty, notwithstanding its name, consists but of forty persons.' That was the case when this illustrious author visited the republic; but the council has since that time been augmented by twenty members, and the number now agrees with the name. These circumstances are important; for from them it appears, that while the neighbouring territory of Rome is impoverished and gloomed by the dominion of ecclesiastics, of which, in the words of Dr. Robertson, 'to squeeze and to amass, not to meliorate, is the object [a];' and while the neighbouring cities of Tuscany are accused of shamefully abandoning their privileges and

---

[a] See Robertson's Charles V. vol. i. sect. iii. p. 157. 'The Doctor adds, ' The patrimony of St. Peter was worse governed than any other part of Europe; and though a generous pontiff might suspend for a little, or counteract the effect of those vices which are peculiar to the government of ecclesiastics, the disease not only remained incurable, but has gone on increasing from age to age, and the decline of the state has kept pace with its progress.' On reading over this passage a doubt arises whether it ought not to be expunged, as unjustly severe. Considered in one view, the dominion of the popes was naturally prejudicial to society; but an evil becomes a good, which prevents evils greater than itself. The authority of popes restrained the alternate tyranny of paramount kings and feudal barons. Religion, in its least perfect form, was a check to headstrong passion, and a restraint on ruffian violence: and should it be admitted, that the temporal government of ecclesiastics had tended to depress the industry and populousness of their immediate dominions, (a position which would require a very complex and elaborate investigation to substantiate,) yet this local depression would be compensated and overbalanced by the distinguished merit of the popes, in the preservation, advancement, and diffusion of learning, civility, and elegant arts; to which Rome, in barbarous ages, offered the only, or the safest, asylum; and of which she still exhibits the most inestimable models.

and their wealth to the Grand Duke, who, parsimonious in the extreme, as to his own person and government, is thought solicitous of seconding by his heavy purse the wild projects of his brother the Emperor Joseph, the little republic of St. Marino, on the contrary, has been increasing its populousness, confirming its strength, and extending the basis of its government. For these advantages it is indebted to its mountainous situation, virtuous manners, and total want of ambition; which last-mentioned qualities, as ancient history teaches us, are far from being characteristics of republican government; though a republic that is without them can neither subsist happily itself, nor allow happiness to its neighbours.

In the republics of Italy, (St. Marino alone excepted,) the people at large are excluded, by the circumstance of their birth, from any principal share in the sovereignty. Instead of one royal master, they are subjects of six hundred[1] petty princes; and their condition is far less eligible than that of the subjects of monarchies; because the latter cannot be collectively degraded by the rank of a monarch, which, excluding comparison, is superior to envy; and are individually entitled to aspire, by their talents and merits, to the exercise of every magistracy, and to the enjoyment of every preferment and every honour which their king and country can bestow. The republic of St. Marino, on the other hand, like several commonwealths of antiquity, and like some lesser Cantons of Switzerland, for the greater are universally moulded after the rigid Italian model,

contains

---

[1] In the shop of an eminent bookseller and publisher of an ancient and celebrated republic of Italy, I was explaining to a young patrician the nature of an English circulating library. 'Why do not you, Pasquali,' said he, turning to the bookseller, 'introduce such an institution?' The other replied, ' *Sono troppo principi!*—We have too many princes.'

APPEND. TO BOOK II. contains what is found by experience to be a due mixture of popular government among so simple a people, and in so small a state. The Council of Sixty is equally compoſed of *nobili* and *cittadini*, patricians and plebeians. This council, which may be called the ſenate, conducts the ordinary branches of public adminiſtration; but the *Arengo*, or aſſembly of the people, containing a repreſentative from every houſe or family, may be ſummoned for the purpoſe of elections and on other important emergencies: it has long uniformly approved the deciſions of the ſenate. In chooſing ſenators and magiſtrates, the reſpect of the citizens for hereditary worth commonly raiſes the ſon to the dignity before held by his father. Indeed moſt profeſſions and employments deſcend in lineal ſucceſſion among this ſimple people; a circumſtance which explains a very extraordinary fact mentioned by Mr. Addiſon, that in two purchaſes made reſpectively in the years 1100 and 1170, the names of the commiſſioners or agents, on the part of the republic, ſhould be the ſame in both tranſactions, though the deeds were executed at the diſtance of ſeventy years from each other.

Notwithſtanding the natural and proper influence of wealth and birth and merit, the liberties and properties of individuals are incomparably more ſafe in St. Marino than they can ever poſſibly be under the capricious tyranny of a levelling democracy; and the people at large have the firmeſt ſecurity that their ſuperiors will not abuſe their juſt pre-eminence, ſince all the plebeians of full age are trained to arms, and commanded by a ſort of military tribune of their own chooſing, whoſe employment is inferior in dignity to that of the *capitaneos*, or conſuls, yet altogether diſtinct from the juriſdiction of thoſe patrician magiſtrates. This important military officer is overlooked by Mr.

Mr. Addison, who has also omitted to mention the treasurer of the republic. The business of the latter consists in collecting and administering the public contributions, and in paying the *stipendiati* or pensionaries, whose salaries, as may be imagined, are extremely moderate; that of the *commissareo*, or chief judge, amounting only to sixty pounds a-year. His income is considerably augmented by the *sportulæ*, or fees paid by the litigant parties; so that his whole appointments fall little short of one hundred pounds *per annum*, a sum which in this primitive commonwealth is found sufficient to support the dignity of a chief justice.

The laws of St. Marino are contained in a thin folio, printed in 1599, at Rimini, intitled, " *Statuta Illustrissimæ Reipublicæ* ;" and the whole history of this happy and truly illustrious, because virtuous and peaceful, community is comprised in the following pages, extracted from the secret archives of the state.

Marino and his companion Leon came from Illyria to Rimini towards the commencement of the fourth century, and exhibited the new phænomenon of Anachorites in the western world. In order to practice their austerities undisturbed, Leon retired to Mount Feretro; and Marino, to Mount Titan; which mountains, distant seven Italian miles from each other, respectively assumed the names of San Leo and San Marino, about the beginning of the ninth century [k].

But

[k] The fame of these Saints appears to have been increased and confirmed by time. Marino, with whom we are concerned, is mentioned in martyrologies and calendars. He is said to have been a Dalmatian by birth, and an architect by profession; and to have come to Rimini, in his youth, towards the commencement of the fourth century. In the annals of Baronius, there is a letter of the year 511, which makes mention of an Anachorite who lived on Mount Titan. Marino, who afforded the first example of this

APPEND.
TO
BOOK II.

But long before this æra, many Italian monks emulating the austere superstition of the Illyrian strangers, had been allured by romantic situations which accorded with the loftiness and solemnity of their own characters; the inhabitants of the neighbouring plains, harassed by the barbarous incursions which prevailed in the fifth and following centuries, occasionally sought refuge among rude and savage mountains, from more rude and more savage invaders. Amidst these ferocious incursions, which were finally repressed by Pepin and Charlemagne, the lay inhabitants of Mount Titan gradually united into a regular commonwealth; and the Anachorites formed themselves into a religious society, under the direction of an abbot. The *republic* early endowed the *convent* with lands amply sufficient for its support; the property of which lands, as appears by a rare manuscript of the year 884, preserved in the secret archives of the republic, was contested by Delton bishop of Rimini against Stephen abbot of Mount Titan. The cause was tried, according to the custom of those times, by the *judices datini* and *scabini*; and decided in favour of the monastery. The same valuable monument which bears testimony to these facts, disproves the fictitious donation of the mountain by King Pepin; of which grant the original has never been produced, but of which there are said to be two copies, one by the Librarian Anastasio, and the other by the Chamberlain Centio.

In this austere mode of life in the west, must have left behind him a strong impression of his piety; since many churches were dedicated to his worship at wide intervals of time and place; among which may be mentioned the Royal Monastery of Pavia, built or restored by Astolphus king of the Lombards; an ancient church with a rich monastery at Rimini; the great parish church in Bologna, as well as the cathedral in the city and island of Arbe in the Adriatic, opposite to the Venetian province of Morlachia.

In the former we read "Serram¹ caſtrum St. Mariani," and in the latter, "Serram caſtrum St. Martini;" inſtead of both which names, St. Marino has been as abſurdly as arbitrarily ſubſtituted; ſince the place now bearing that name retained its original appellation of Mount Titan for more than a century after the date of king Pepin's pretended diploma.

APPEND.
TO
BOOK II.

The firſt inhabitants of the mountain did not eſtabliſh themſelves on the rough and rocky ſummits on which part of the city now ſtands, but occupied the gentle ſlope at a mile's diſtance in the direction of ſouth-weſt, then embraced by deep woods, and ſtill called *Il Luogo Vecchio;* words indicating that it was the ancient ſeat of the republic. In this ſequeſtered wilderneſs the inhabitants of Mount Titan long enjoyed a peaceful obſcurity, undiſturbed by the great powers which ſwayed the politics of Italy; and almoſt unknown to them, until Otho the Great invaded that country in the year 962, to make war on king Berenger. The latter retreated to Mount Feretro, afterwards called San Leo. His fortreſſes there were blocked up two years; he was at length compelled to ſurrender through famine; his queen and himſelf were carried priſoners into Franconia. During this warfare, the diſtrict of Mount Titan, conſpicuous by its vicinity and its loftineſs to the contending parties, was allowed to maintain its neutrality; an indulgence for which it was in part indebted to the jealouſy

ſubſiſting

---

¹ In barbarous Latin and Italian, *ſerra* means a craggy mountain—a word applicable enough, but never really applied in ancient records to Mount Titan, afterwards called "Penne de St. Marino." The name is ſaid, in the manuſcript above cited, to have ariſen from the towers ſhaped like the feathers of an arrow, with which the mountain was crowned.

APPEND. TO BOOK II. subsisting between the emperor Otho and John XII., who then wore the papal crown. The latter laboured by repeated embassies to moderate the ambition of the former, and to restrain the incursions of his troops. The emperor, on the other hand, struck by the singular manners of a people, whose honest simplicity gained his esteem, and whose poverty could not tempt his avarice, frequently visited Mount Titan, while his army was employed in the siege of Feretro; and on one occasion of this fort, confirmed by his Imperial grant the entire liberty and independence which the principal citizens of the republic swore that their ancestors had from time immemorial enjoyed.

During the eleventh century Italy began to be torn by the dissensions of the Guelphs and Ghibellines; the former, partisans of the pope; the latter, of the emperor. This intestine war, which pervaded the whole country, greatly multiplied the towers and bastions by which every province, every district, and the residence of almost every distinguished nobleman long continued to be fortified. Men scarcely felt themselves secure in the most inaccessible situations; and the inhabitants of St. Titan, now denominated St. Marino, removed from the sloping lawn formerly mentioned, to the very summit of the mountain called Rocca di Girone, which natural fastness the jealous republicans farther secured by walls and towers [m].

In the twelfth century they strengthened their security by entering into an intimate connection with the counts of Felori, distinguished ornaments of the Imperial party. This noble family, which afterwards gave dukes to Urbino, condescended to

---

[m] In the principal church of the present city, there is a statue of the supposed founder of the republic, holding a mountain in his hand, crowned with three towers or castles; emblems fitly chosen for the arms of the community.

to become citizens of the republic; and brought to it an acceſſion of ſtrength and wealth, which ſoon diſcovered itſelf in the purchaſe of ſome grounds on the ſouth-weſt, and the extenſion of the city to ſituations more eligible than the Rocca di Girone, where the ſafety of the inhabitants was frequently endangered by the fury of the winds.

During the greater part of the thirteenth century, St. Marino eſcaped moleſtation from the petty, but almoſt continual, hoſtilities which diſtreſſed the neighbouring territories. This happy exemption from the evils incident to war, the republic owed to the wiſdom and moderation of its own councils, and to the friendly protection of the biſhopric of Feretro, which was long hereditary in the family of the counts of Felori of Mount Capiolo. But when that biſhopric fell into the poſſeſſion of the Guelph faction, and eſpecially after the new biſhop treacherouſly ſeized, in 1281, the fortreſs of San Leo belonging to the counts of Felori, the republic had its full ſhare of troubles. Its territories were repeatedly invaded, but the invaders were as often manfully repelled. The danger, however, increaſed when the crafty Malateſta de Verrucchio, who was alſo a warm partiſan of the Guelphs, made himſelf maſter of Rimini towards the cloſe of the thirteenth century; after having expelled from that city the chevalier Percitaule, a powerful Ghibelline, who with much difficulty eſcaped to St. Marino to the houſe of his friend the celebrated Guido Felorio, a man who afterwards inflicted ſignal vengeance on the party of the Guelphs.

From the æra laſt mentioned, the age of perſecution commenced; and the republic was continually haraſſed by the biſhops of Feretro, or by the lords of Rimini, for upwards of a century and a half; until, in the year 1462, the fierce Sigiſmond

APPEND. TO BOOK II.

mond Malatefta, an execrated and excommunicated heretic, as odious by his vices, as eminent for his talents, was totally defeated by Pope Pius II. During this long period of warfare, the republic defended itfelf valiantly, under the counts of Felori and dukes of Urbino, its counfellors, protectors, and generals. About the middle of the fifteenth century, duke Frederic of Felorio procured for it an alliance with Florence; an alliance faithfully maintained on both fides, while that republic continued to fubfift. St. Marino alfo entered into a tranfaction with the king of the two Sicilies in 1459, in virtue of which it acquired the two fouthern diftricts of Fiorentino and Torricella, abounding in rich paftures, embowered in lofty forefts of oak and chefnut trees. At the expence of its perfecutor Sigifmond, it alfo extended its dominions on the north and eaft, by gaining the diftricts Serravalle and Faettano, highly productive in vines and olives; as well as the fertile fields of Mongiardino, which ftill form the granary of the republic.

Thus did this little ftate continue to flourifh amidft perpetual wars, and upheld by the virtue of its citizens, and guided by the paternal care of the family of the Felori. The alliance procured for it with Florence by means of Federico Felorio proved effectual for repelling the incurfions of the pope's armies, which in 1489 befieged Robert Malatefta, the fon of Sigifmond, in Rimini. The Florentines enabled Federic duke of Urbino, to cover the dominions of its ally, and completely to defeat the invaders, who feem to have aimed at nothing lefs than the fubjection of the community. The letters written by the government of Florence in this feafon of danger, are ftill preferved in the fecret archives of St. Marino. They bear teftimony to that fpirit of liberty which had prevailed in Italy from the æra

of

of the famous peace of Conſtance in 1170, when many of the principal cities in that country aſſumed the republican form of government. The Florentines write to their diſtreſſed allies, whom they addreſs by the appellation of "Magnificent lords, our deareſt friends," that they were not more indignant at the inſolence of the pope's troops in making inroads into the poſſeſſions of St. Marino, than if they had carried their incurſions to the gates of Florence itſelf. They obſerve, that they had haſtened to ſend troops and money, and alſo to diſpatch letters to the duke of Urbino, and to the governments of Naples and Milan; that aſſiſtance would ſpeedily arrive; and the remedy, doubtleſs, prove more effecacious than even the greatneſs of the evil required. "Exhortations to you, to be of good comfort, are unneceſſary, eſpecially from us who know the greatneſs of your ſouls, which render you ſo reſpectable a branch of our confederacy. Perſevere in ſhewing your prudence, fidelity, and courage, which, beſides that they will delight and gladden your own ſouls, (ſuch being the nature of virtue,) will greatly oblige us and our allies, who will keep your meritorious exertions in eternal remembrance." Next day the Florentines wrote again, exhorting the citizens of St. Marino "to remain firm and reſolute, to loſe their lives rather than their liberties, ſince it was far better for men accuſtomed to freedom to be dead than enſlaved. God, who favours the cauſe of freedom, will proſper your undertakings; and your intereſts will never be forſaken by us and our friends. You have heard of the ſupplies of men and money already raiſed for your aſſiſtance. More of both will continue to be provided, until you have enough."

From this time forward, until the year 1543, the republic, being unmoleſted by foreign enemies, flouriſhed in peace
and

APPEND. TO BOOK II. and prosperity under the wise guidance of the dukes of Urbino, its counsellors and protectors. But in the year abovementioned, the exile Peter Strozzi, who commanded the French troops cantoned in Mirandola and its confines, where he was busily employed in raising recruits for the service of his master, Francis I. entered into a correspondence with some of the pope's generals in that neighbourhood, for the surprise and conquest of St. Marino. The instrument chosen for effecting this design, was Captain Fabiano of Mount San Savino. The emperor Charles V. had landed at Genoa; and the pope Paul III. had proceeded as far as Bologna, eager to have an interview with the emperor, who was equally solicitous to avoid all intercourse with his Holiness. The movement thereby occasioned in that part of Italy seemed to Strozzi and Fabiano the most favourable moment for executing their treacherous enterprise. Five hundred armed men were sent in small divisions across the ridges of Montagnaola. It was intended that, under the conduct of different guides, they should unite into one body, and assail in the night the unsuspecting republicans. But a thick fog baffled the local knowledge of the guides. The troops could not be in due time assembled: and the inhabitants of the place, being meanwhile apprized of their own imminent danger, immediately flew to arms, and compelled the invaders to retreat with the mortification of committing a fruitless crime, which had redounded as much to their own disgrace as to the honour of their adversaries.

The most memorable circumstance attending this event was the warm interest taken by the Italian powers in the safety of St. Marino. Cosmo di Medici, duke of Florence, in a letter addressed to that government, and dated the 20th June 1543, mentions with how much displeasure he had heard of Captain Fabiano's

Fabiano's undertaking; he requests that he himself might be favoured with a full account of the whole enterprise; its authors, agents, and abettors; assuring the "respectable citizens of St. Marino, his dearest friends, that he will ever be ready to prove, by his utmost exertions, his unalterable attachment to whatever may concern their interest or honour." The marquis of Graffales, then residing at Fano, as ambassador from the emperor to the pope, immediately dispatched a courier to Genoa, to acquaint his Imperial majesty with the transaction. This powerful and renowed prince, whose mind was equal to the greatest affairs, thought not the smallest below his notice. He was no sooner informed of the enterprise against St. Marino, than he sent Bastamenti di Herrera to confer in his name with its magistrates; to congratulate them on their safety, and to assure them that he would always consider their affairs as his own; since, besides his great concern for the tranquillity of Italy in general, he could not but view with the fondest partiality a commonwealth, whose government had ever been so wisely and so regularly administered. The pope, Paul III., did not choose to be behind-hand with other princes in his professions of regard: and in order to ingratiate himself with the emperor, whose favour he then courted, thought fit to order the French troops to quit the neighbourhood of St. Marino, and to keep at an unsuspicious distance from its territory.

This favourable disposition in his Holiness towards them, was cultivated by the republicans with equal assiduity and success. In the year 1548, the pope's treasurer and the officers of his revenue in Romagna endeavoured indeed to subject the commonwealth to the new tax on salt, which had been imposed on all the rest of that province. But Paul himself explicitly

plicitly difavowed this proceeding; and iffued his brief, dated 11th October 1548, declaring the complete independence of St. Marino in temporal affairs; and thus confirming its inhabitants in the enjoyment of their immemorial liberties. The fame equitable conduct towards the republic was purfued by his fucceffors Clement VIII. and Urban VIII.; under the latter of whom, the duchy of Urbino, on the demife of its laft duke in 1623, being united to the dominions of the Holy See, the republic of St. Marino paffed under the protection of the fame power, upon many and well-defined conditions. This political connection with the pope was not thought greatly to intrench on the independence of the commonwealth. It had been ufual with the Italian republics of the middle age to court the patronage of neighbouring princes; and, even in their conftitutional concerns, to have recourfe to noblemen of high rank and fplendid fortune, who might alternately prefide in their tribunals[n], and command their armies. St. Marino had long repofed unbounded yet well-placed confidence in the family of Felori; and what Machiavel fays of Florence is in a great degree applicable to all the other free ftates of Italy, that their affairs were never profperous, unlefs when conducted by the fteady wifdom of fome illuftrious individual.

St. Marino refpected the popes in their civil, and venerated them in their religious character. The warm expreffions of thofe fentiments contented the vicars of St. Peter; but fuch empty acknowledgments would not fatisfy the ambitious and intriguing

[n] St. Marino was diftinguifhed above the neighbouring republics, for the impartiality with which juftice was adminiftered; and was later than moft of them in adopting the "Judice eftero," the jurifdiction of a foreigner, "articolo troppo neceffario per tolgierfi ogni fufpicione nei guidici parfani:" an eftablifhment found neceffary in confequence of the too juft fufpicions againft judges born in the country."

intriguing Alberoni, who, when legate of Romagna in the year 1740, formed a plan for converting refpect into allegiance, and the duty of protection into the right of dominion. A confiderable party of the inhabitants, feduced by his promifes, or gained by his bribes, had confented to betray into his hands the liberties of their country. When the appointed day arrived, Alberoni rode up the mountain, attended by a numerous fuite. He was received by the principal inhabitants at the door of the great church, and conducted by the priefts to a magnificent feat under a canopy. But unfortunately for the execution of his purpofe, the mafs began, as ufual in that republic, with the word "Libertas." This fingle word produced fuch an enthufiafm in the minds of thofe who underftood his defigns, as well as of thofe who only fufpected them, that they rofe with common confent, attacked the cardinal and his attendants, drove them precipitately from the church, and made them defcend the mountain with a degree of difordered trepidation extremely unlike to the flow and pompous folemnity with which they had afcended it. This laft memorable event in the hiftory of St. Marino well correfponds with that firmnefs and courage with which it is fuppofed to have maintained its independence, amidft the hoftile collifions of Imperial and Pontifical power; an independence, however, which appears to have been owing to the penurious circumftances of a people, which could not tempt rapacity, and their virtuous manners which always conciliated the affection of one party, more than they provoked the animofity of another.

From the preceding narrative it is not very eafy to afcertain what fhare Marino, the Dalmatian architect, had in the firft inftitution of the ftate. On the fuppofition that he was its founder

APPEND. TO BOOK II.

founder and lawgiver, Mr. Addison obferves, "that the origin of St. Marino muſt be acknowledged to be far nobler than that of Rome, which was an afylum for robbers and murderers; whereas St. Marino was the refort of perfons eminent for their piety and devotion. This obfervation appears to me to be erroneous in two refpects, decorating with unfair honours the one republic, and heaping unmerited difgrace on the other. If piety founded St. Marino, with this piety much fuperſtition was intermixed; a fuperſtition unfriendly to the beſt principles of fociety, and hoſtile to the favourite ends of nature, preaching celibacy, and exacting mortification, the hideous offspring of ignorance and terror, deteſting men as criminals, and trembling at God as a tyrant. But Rome, according to the only hiſtorian[*] who has circumſtantially and authentically defcribed its early tranfactions, was an expanſion of Alba Longa, itſelf a Grecian colony, which, according to the immemorial and facred cuſtom of its mother-country, diffuſed into new ſettlements the exuberance of a flouriſhing population, produced by the wifeſt and moſt liberal inſtitutions. According to the fame admirable hiſtorian, the manly difcernment of Romulus offered an afylum not merely for robbers and murderers, but for thoſe who were threatened with murder or robbery, who fpurned fubjection, or fled from oppreſſion; for amidſt the lawlefs turbulence of ancient Italy, the weak needed protectors againſt the ſtrong, the few againſt the many; and Rome, at her earlieſt age, already fyſtematically aſſiſted the weakeſt party; thus adopting in her infancy that politic heroifm, that was deſtined by firm and majeſtic ſteps to conduct her manhood and maturity to the fair fovereignty of confenting nations.

Both

[*] Dionyfius of Halicarnaffus.

Both in their origin and in their progress, Rome and St. Marino form the natural objects, not indeed of a comparison, but of a striking contrast; and compressed as is the latter republic between the dominions of the Pope and those of the Grand Duke, to whose subjects St. Marino is now bound to allow a free passage through its territory, its citizens would deserve ridicule or pity, did they affect the character, or imitate the maxims, of those magnanimous senators, who, for the space of more than two centuries, swayed the politics and controlled the revolutions of the world. Convinced that their independence results chiefly from their insignificancy, the senators of St. Marino smiled, when we read in Mr. Addison, ' These republicans would sell their liberties dear to any that attacked them.' We had not the indelicacy to desire them to interpret this smile; or to make ourselves any comment upon it, being persuaded, that, precarious and shadowy as their liberty is, their rational knowledge and their virtues have enabled them to extract from it both substantial and permanent enjoyment, and make them live happier here, amidst rocks and snows, than are their Tuscan and Roman neighbours in rich plains and warm vallies.

To the inhabitants of this little state, the senate, the assembly, the different offices of magistracy, innocent rural labours, and military exercises equally useful and innocent, supply a continual succession of manly engagements. Hopes and fears respecting the safety of their country awaken curiosity and excite inquiry. They read the gazettes of Europe with interest; they study history with improvement; in conversation their questions are pertinent, and their answers satisfactory. Contrary to what has been observed by travellers of other Italians,

APPEND. TO BOOK II.

Italians, the citizens of St. Marino delight in literary converſation; and Mr. Addiſon remarks, that he hardly met with an unlettered man in their republic. In ſpeaking of Beccaria's book on Style, then recently publiſhed, one of the ſenators ſaid, that it was a treatiſe on ſtyle in a very bad ſtyle, abounding in falſe ornaments and epigrammatic galliciſm. Another obſerved, he wiſhed that faſhionable writer, who had been commented on by Voltaire, an author ſtill more faſhionable and more pernicious than himſelf, would confine himſelf to ſuch harmleſs topics as rhetoric and ſtyle; for his book on crimes and puniſhments was calculated to do much ſerious miſchief, at leaſt to prevent much poſitive good; becauſe in that popular work he had declaimed very perſuaſively againſt capital puniſhments, in a country long diſgraced by capital crimes, which were ſcarcely ever capitally puniſhed.

The love of letters which diſtinguiſhes the people of St. Marino makes them regret that they are ſeldom viſited by literary travellers. Of our own countrymen belonging to this deſcription, they mentioned with much reſpect Mr. Addiſon, and Il Signor Giovanni Symonds, now profeſſor of hiſtory in the univerſity of Cambridge. We were proud of being claſſed with ſuch men by the honeſt ſimplicity of theſe virtuous mountaineers, whom we left with regret, moſt heartily wiſhing to them the continuance of their liberties; which, to men of their character, and theirs only, are real and ſolid bleſſings.

For let it never be forgotten, that the ineſtimable gift of civil liberty may often be providentially withheld, becauſe it cannot be ſafely beſtowed, unleſs rational knowledge has been attained, and virtuous habits have been acquired. In the language of the wiſeſt man of Pagan antiquity, a great length of time

time is requisite to the formation of any moderately good government; because that government is always the best, which is the best adapted to the genius and habits of its subjects[r]. The institutions which suit the well-balanced frame of mind of the mountaineers of St. Marino, who, breathing a purer air, seem to have divested themselves of many of the grosser and more earthly affections, might ill accord with the softened tenants of the Capuan plains; since, according to the same penetrating searcher into the secrets of human nature, ' the inhabitants of the Fortunate Islands, if such islands really exist, must either be the most virtuous or the most wretched of men.' Aristotle hardly knew the inhabitants of the British Isles; but let us, who know ourselves and our good fortune, confide in the assurance, that this incompatible author would no longer entertain the above geographical doubt, were he to revive in the eighteenth century, and to visit the British dominions under the government of George III.[s] As we have long been the happiest of nations, let us cherish the hope, that the causes of our happiness are, morally speaking, unalterable. The character of our ancestors, uniting, beyond all people on earth, firmness with humanity, gave to us our government; and the preservation of our government, as it now stands, under a prince who is at once the patron and the model of those virtues on which alone national prosperity can rest, forms the surest pledge for the stability of that character, which has long adorned, and we trust will ever adorn, the envied name of BRITON.

[r] Aristot. Politics, b. ii. p. 6.
[s] About the time this was written, a letter from a foreign prelate, now high in office in a neighbouring country, contained the following memorable words: " Tout ici," meaning England, " est dans un état de prosperité vraiment révoltante."

ARISTOTLE's POLITICS.

BOOK III.

INTRODUCTION.

IN this Third Book, the author, proceeding to inveſtigate the nature and characteriſtic qualities of the different forms of government, begins, according to his uſual method, by analyſing that complex object, a commonwealth, into its conſtituent elements, called citizens. His firſt inquiry, therefore, is, what conſtitutes a citizen? An inquiry that will appear very ſimple to many of thoſe ſimple men who are continually debating particular caſes involved in the ſolution of this general queſtion.

It is worthy of remark that in oppoſition to thoſe ancient, as well as thoſe modern theories, which vainly endeavour to reduce practical matters to metaphyſical preciſion, Ariſtotle maintains that the definition of a citizen which holds good in one ſtate, is often not at all applicable in another. He even beſtows that honourable name on thoſe who, in modern times, are more uſually denominated ſubjects; obſerving, " that as government is properly an arrangement of thoſe who are partners in the benefits of political ſociety, the fitneſs of government muſt, like that of every other arrangement, depend primarily and principally on the nature and differences of the objects that collectively compoſe the ſyſtem. This arrangement, therefore, muſt vary with

BOOK III. with every variation of its parts, materials, or elements; which, in this cafe, are fentient and moral beings, liable to be affected and altered by a wide variety of actuating principles." In enumerating thefe principles, the author obferves, that the diftinctive characters of communities are greatly dependent on the means ufually employed by them for acquiring the neceffaries and accommodations of life. Paftoral, agricultural, and commercial nations are, therefore, feverally marked by ftrong lines of difcrimination. Climate alfo has a confpicuous influence; and innumerable local caufes concurring with the events of time and chance, and co-operating with education and nature fo varioufly mould mankind, that nothing but the blindnefs of ignorance and narrownefs of prejudice could think of extending fimilar plans of policy to nations as differently circumftanced, as they are unlike in the bent of their genius.

But though governments may and muft vary in their form, they ought all to agree in their end, "the good of the governed." Ariftotle ftrenuoufly maintains this doctrine, which will ever found fo harfhly in the ears of political bigots of all defcriptions; and which has ever been as infolently fcorned in the practice of republican demagogues, as it has been fhamelefsly combated in the arguments of court flatterers. By what arrangements the good of the governed is moft likely to be promoted, muft be learned from the experience of hiftory; but, in our author's opinion, that people ought to remain contented with its lot, which is not mocked with fhadows inftead of realities; deluded with tyranny under the femblance of royalty, oligarchy under that of ariftocracy, and democracy under that of a republic. Regardlefs of perfonal danger from tyrants or a tyrannical populace, the philofopher boldly arraigns thofe

bafe

base cheats and vile counterfeits; those unnatural perversions of lawful power, and wicked mimics of legitimate government. It is not easy to discover which of the parties that then divided and tore in pieces their common country, he most heartily abhors. In civil commotions, a man who is called to act, ought publicly to choose his side, though he may often have but a choice of difficulties; but he whose business is speculation will commonly best perform his duty, if, in proportion to the measure of his courage and abilities, he ventures to expose and condemn the excesses of contending factions, and to suggest those reflections that have the most direct tendency to sooth their rage, and to moderate their fury. This task our philosopher skilfully performs, by proving with irresistible evidence that birth, wealth, education, and authority, as well as courage, strength, numbers, and liberty, are all of them essential ingredients in the composition of a well-constituted commonwealth; but that the composition must fall in pieces, when any one of the elements is active beyond its sphere; whether government be engrossed by contemptuous opulence, or usurped by rapacious poverty; oppressed by the unfeeling pride of the few, or disgraced by the malignant passions of the multitude.

The Third Book of the Politics concludes with an enumeration and description of the different kinds of monarchy; a species of government which, according to our author, is not only legitimate, but in many countries necessary. The most extensive survey of history fully justifies the conclusions which the philosopher had drawn from the records of Egypt and the east. The Romans, who in the age of the Scipios had admired " the servile stupidity of the Cappadocians in declaring that they could not live without a king [a]," acknowledged in the age

---

[a] θαυμαζοντες η τοις μεν ετως απηρεσται ωςτε ου δυνασθαι. Strabo, l. xii. p. 540.

BOOK III.

age of Augustus, that their own commonwealth could not happily fu..'t but under the dominion of one prince [b]. The emperor Julian [c] reprefents all the great nations of his own times as governed by the fame political principles, which had been fo uniformly [d] maintained by the Cappadocians. If liberty had been offered to the Thracians, the Myfians, and the Getæ, thofe populous and warlike tribes would, according to Philoftratus [e], have fpurned the unwelcome prefent. The hiftorian Livy acknowledges that the cities fubject to king Eumenes had not any reafon to envy the boafted condition of republicans [f]; and the orator Ifocrates congratulates in ftill warmer language, the felicity of the ftates of Cyprus, which had fubmitted to the dominion of Evagoras [g]. But the ftrongeft argument in favour of monarchy is deducible from the progreffive profperity of moft countries of Europe, during the prefent and two preceding centuries; in which courfe of time the difmembered provinces of the weftern empire have enjoyed under kings a meafure of national felicity unexampled in the hiftory of the world.

As a confiderable part of Ariftole's treatife on monarchy has perifhed, it would be prefumptuous to affign limits to the improvement of which he thought that form of government fufceptible. From a hint in the Sixth Book of his Politics, he appears to have been fully aware of the utility of a revifion of fentences paffed under the influence of popular delufion, or

[b] Seneca de Beneficiis, l. ii. c. 20.   [c] Julian. adverf. Chriftian.

[d] They rejected the republican government when offered to them by their conquerors; and when their own royal line became extinct, called Ariobarzanes to an hereditary throne; and after the extinction alfo of the line of Ariobarzanes in the third generation, cheerfully fubmitted to Archelaus, a ftranger, recommended to them by Mark Anthony. Strabo, l. xii. p. 540.

Philoftrat. in Vit. Apollon.   [f] Liv. l. xlii. c. 5.   [g] Ifocrat. in Evagor.

or extorted through the feverity of legal forms; maintaining that in every well-governed ftate, a difcretionary power of grace and mercy fhould be lodged, not with the fubordinate magiftrate, but with the fupreme executive authority. This doubtlefs, if not the moft fplendid diftinction, is at leaft the moft amiable prerogative of the throne. But there are other diftinctions totally unknown to antiquity, yet calculated to produce both the moft important immediate benefits, and to give to modern monarchy a degree of firmnefs and ftability of which no other form of government can boaft.

We read in Plutarch[h] of the coronation oath adminiftered to the kings of Epirus. Xenophon[i] mentions a fimilar inftitution in Lacedæmon. Both Xenophon and Diodorus Siculus[k] defcribe the conftitutional limitations of the kings of Perfia. The laft-mentioned writer alfo copioufly expatiates on the fingular reftraints impofed on the kings of Egypt during their lives, and relates that thofe of them who had incurred public indignation, were publicly arraigned after their death, and publicly punifhed by the privation of a royal, or even a decent fepulture[l]. Jofephus informs us that this regulation alfo prevailed in Judæa[m]. But all thefe expedients, as well as thofe employed by the Macedonians, the freeft nation of antiquity acknowledging the authority of kings, were coarfe and uncertain contrivances for limiting the regal power; contrivances always fo doubtful, and often fo ineffectual, that by the confenting voice of antiquity, the happinefs of a people was held by the precarious tenure of perfonal merit in the prince. In confequence of this opinion, the

[h] Plut. in Pyrrho.   [i] De Repub. Lacedæm.   [k] L. xvii.
[l] Diodor. l. i. fect. 72.   [m] Jofeph. l. viii. c. 3.

the right of election appeared the most plausible title to a throne; and even in those countries where the royal pre-eminence of particular families was universally acknowledged, there was not any invariable rule for ascertaining among different pretenders the order of succession. This is fully illustrated in the history of the kingdoms formed from the dismemberment of the Macedonian empire, and deserves to be considered as one principal cause of their rapid decline and final extinction. But when the salutary maxims are established "that kings can do no wrong, and that acts of government can be legalised only through the intervention of responsible ministers," the inequalities of personal character in princes become so harmless in practice, that the casual advantages of election totally disappear on comparison with the certain benefit of a fixed and definite rule to which nations may always have recourse for transmitting without bloodshed the inheritance of their crowns.

On this species of monarchy, limited and hereditary, the fruits of genuine republicanism have been successfully engrafted; and are found by experience to flourish there, with a degree of vigour and of beauty which they had never exhibited on their parent plant. This form of government alone completely solves the problem proposed by our author, when he observes, that, "difficult as it is to adjust the true theory of political arrangements, it is still more difficult to keep the component parts in their proper positions." This difficulty, I say, is surmounted by modern monarchy, and by it only; under which also, as will be proved hereafter, that distribution of political functions on which all kinds of good administration so greatly depend, may be most completely established, and most steadily upheld.

BOOK III.

ARGUMENT.

Citizen—How constituted.—Virtues of the man and of the citizen.—Their difference.—Different forms of government.—Their distinctive characters.—Pretensions of democracy—Of oligarchy.—Monarchy.—Its five kinds—Arraigned—Defended.

IN explaining the nature and principle [a] of the different forms of government, which are nothing else than various arrangements of men in society, it is necessary clearly to ascertain what constitutes a state; an object not uniformly conceived, nor accurately defined; since one person often ascribes *that* to the state, which another holds to be an act merely of the king or of the senate, of the tyrant or the oligarchy. A state or commonwealth, then, is a complex object; its component elements are those called citizens; to know therefore what is a commonwealth, we must previously investigate what constitutes a citizen. In different governments, the term citizen denotes different descriptions of persons; in democracies, men in the lowest walks of life are often entitled to this respectable appellation; from which persons of the same class are, in oligarchies, totally

[a] τις ἑκάςη (scil. πολιτεια) και ποια τις. "What each form of government is, and what are its qualities." Its qualities, as we shall see, result from its principle, and this again depends on the materials from which it is composed; for Aristotle did not agree with those audacious political speculatists, who think it allowable to treat men as artificers do wood or metal.

BOOK III.

What constitutes a citizen.

totally excluded. It is not, therefore, the rank in life that conftitutes the rank in a commonwealth °.

The term citizen is fometimes applied to illuftrious foreigners who, for their merit or fervices, have been affociated to the honours and adopted into the bofom of the republic. But fuch honorary citizens form not the fubject of our prefent inquiry. It is plain likewife that the bare circumftance of place, or the habitual refidence in the territory or city, does not conftitute a citizen, fince flaves, and the clafs of men called inhabitants ᵖ, are not diftinguifhed by this appellation. Nor are thofe to be confidered as our fellow-citizens who merely enjoy the protection of our laws, and who are qualified in their own perfons to appear under the characters of plaintiffs and defendants; for ftrangers with whofe countries we have a treaty of commerce, or an intercourfe of hofpitality, are entitled to challenge as their due the protection of our courts of juftice ; although in many cities thofe who are fimply inhabitants cannot profecute or defend in their own name, but in all their legal tranfactions muft have recourfe to their procurator or patron. Minors not yet enrolled at the regifter-office, and perfons fuperannuated, who are honourably difcharged from civil functions, fugitives, outlaws, and men branded by the note of infamy, can none of them be called properly or fimply citizens, fince whenever we apply to them this name, we muft join with it fome epithet or corrective,

---

° For the fake of perfpicuity, I have expanded this paffage conformably to the author's words below, c. iii. and in various parts of his works.

ᵖ μέτοικοι, commonly but improperly tranflated fojourners, fince thefe have a cafual, merely, and unfettled refidence ; whereas the Grecian μέτοικοι refided habitually and fixedly in their refpective ftates, like the clafs called " habitans" in Geneva, and fome Swifs Cantons ; and were, as our author fays in another paffage, fharers in the fame habitation, though not partners in the government.

corrective, without which addition we do not accurately explain our meaning. Who then is simply or properly a citizen? He, and he only, who enjoys a due share in the government of that community of which he is a member.

Of the offices of government, some are limited in point of time; the man who has exercised them once, cannot exercise them again, or at least cannot refume them, till a certain interval has elapsed from the time when he laid them down. Other offices are not thus limited, but may be occasionally exercised by all the citizens, at all times, indifferently. Of this kind is the power of deciding as a judge or juryman in the tribunals, and that of voting as a member in the national assembly. It is true, that jurymen[q] and voters, as their office is common to all the citizens, are not distinguished by any appropriate appellation denoting their indefinite or perpetual powers; they are not even dignified by the name of magistrates; yet if magistracy be something more than an honorary title, it belongs in reality most peculiarly to those who are invested with the highest authority in the state; who direct the national deliberations, who govern the public resolves, and who are the ultimate umpires of reputation, life, and property.

This definition of a citizen cannot, however, be applied in the greater part of governments actually existing in the world, many of which, as will appear hereafter, are nothing better than corruptions

BOOK III.

The share of the government, or magistracy, common to all the citizens is not distinguished by a name.

Though anonymous, the most important of all magistracies.

Under what constitutions the strict definition of a citizen is applicable.

[q] The Grecian tribunals agreed more nearly with our notion of juries than the Roman. The former generally admitted of the citizens at large; whereas the Roman judicature was exercised on ordinary occasions, for near three centuries, by the Patricians exclusively. But that the Romans thought with Aristotle as to the supreme importance of the judicial power, appears from the perpetual struggles on this subject among the orders in the commonwealth; particularly during that most important period which elapsed from the seditions of the Gracchi, to the despotism of the Cæsars.

BOOK III.

corruptions and tyrannies. Neither is it applicable in its full extent in those communities which, though governed with a view to the public good, have substituted the authority of kings or senates to the power of popular assemblies and popular tribunals. In Sparta and at Carthage, as we have before seen, the judiciary power is intrusted to certain magistrates; to the Ephori in civil, to the senate in criminal, trials; and when such magistrates rule by vicarious succession, he may be called a citizen who has a right to govern in his turn. In democracies, this right is extended to the people at large. The definition of a citizen above given is therefore peculiarly applicable to popular governments; and a city or commonwealth is nothing else than a collection of citizens thus described, sufficiently numerous for attaining that purpose of comfortable subsistence, for which civil society was instituted.

Coarse definitions of a citizen.

It is a coarse and unsatisfactory, but sometimes an useful, definition of a citizen, to say that he is one descended from citizens in the male and female line; or one whose ancestors were citizens for two or more generations. The question still recurs, what conferred this character on those ancestors who first founded the state? To them the circumstance of descent cannot possibly apply; and if ancestry alone were sufficient to make citizens, we might inquire, as Gorgias of Leontium, either in doubt or in irony, asked the Thessalians of Larissa, whether as potters make pots¹, there were certain artificers at Larissa for manufacturing Larissæan citizens. It is inquired with better reason, whether those are citizens who have obtained this appellation in consequence of a revolution in the commonwealth? At Athens, Clisthenes, after the expulsion of the tyrants,

Difficulties occasioned thereby.

¹ The original says, " as mortar-makers make mortars."

ARISTOTLE's POLITICS.

tyrants, aggregated many strangers and many slaves to this honourable class [s]. In this case, the question is not whether these are citizens, but whether they became such *justly*. Some, indeed, hold that he who is unjustly a citizen, is a pseudo-citizen, a mere counterfeit. But this cannot be true, if we define a citizen, as above, by the power or magistracy with which he is invested, and acknowledge that many magistrates, and even kings, who have obtained their offices unjustly, still continue nevertheless to govern and to reign. He is justly a citizen who is created such by the act of the commonwealth; but what is an act of the commonwealth may sometimes, as we before observed, be a matter of dispute. When an oligarchy or a tyranny is converted into a democracy, some people are of opinion that the contracts entered into by the magistrates or the tyrant ought not to be fulfilled, because those contracts were the acts not of the commonwealth, but of the government; and of a government too, not founded on public utility, but established by injustice, and supported by force. Yet democracies themselves have often been so established and so supported, and *their* acts, at least, have nevertheless always been considered as the acts of the commonwealth [t].

To

---

[s] Aristotle says, "φυλετικους, distributed among the tribes, many strangers," &c. See above, p. 68.

[t] Therefore, "If the acts of tyrannical democracies are considered as those of the state, in the same manner ought the acts of oligarchies and tyrannies." Hooker had studied Aristotle, and from this *arch philosopher*, as he calls him, (Ecclesiastical Polity, l. i. sect. 10.) he himself borrowed the most solid parts of his excellent, but often misapplied, work. In reference to the subject in the text, he observes, " that in many things assent is given, they that give it not imagining that they do so, because the manner of their assenting is not apparent. As for example, when an absolute monarch commandeth his subjects that which seemeth good in his own discretion, hath

BOOK III.
Chap. 2.
What constitutes the identity of a commonwealth.

To determine what is the act of the body politic often depends on afcertaining the circumftances which conftitute its famenefs or identity; circumftances which are no fooner withdrawn, than its continuity of exiftence is diffolved, and the commonwealth or city [u] no longer remains the fame identical city that it was before. That the famenefs of local fituation does not conftitute this identity, will appear evident to the moft fuperficial obferver. A commonwealth may tranfport itfelf from one place to another, and fome portion of its members may live at a remote diftance from the reft. The Peloponnefus and its feven republics might be inclofed within one wall; but within this wall would be contained not a city or commonwealth, but an aggregate of nations, lefs connected with each other than the inhabitants of Babylon, whofe walls, it is faid, were ftormed and taken upwards of two days before every divifion of the immenfe multitude was apprifed of the public difafter. Concerning the magnitude of ftates we fhall have occafion afterwards to fpeak; and to examine whether they may be compofed of many nations, or ought to confift of one only; an inquiry not mifbecoming a ftatefman. At prefent, let us inquire whether the famenefs of inhabitants, or rather the continuance

hath not this edict the force of a law, whether they difapprove or diflike it? Again, that which hath been received long fince, and is by cuftom now eftablifhed, we keep as a law which we may not tranfgrefs.... And to be commanded we confent, where that fociety, whereof we are part, hath at any time before confented, without revoking the fame after by the like univerfal agreement. Wherefore as any man's deed paft is good as long as he himfelf continueth it, fo the act of a public fociety of men done five hundred years fince ftandeth their's who prefently are of the fame fociety, becaufe corporations are immortal: we were then alive in our predeceffors, and they in their fucceffors do live ftill." Ecclef. Polit. p. 19. edit. 1723.

[u] A city, the author obferves, is one of thofe words which are taken in different acceptations; in the fenfe here meant it is fynonymous with commonwealth.

continuance of the same race of inhabitants, constitutes the identity of a commonwealth, in the same manner as the identity of a fountain or river is ascertained by the flowing of the same kind of water from the same sources, though in perpetually varying streams. Agreeably to this comparison, ought we to say that the commonwealth, while composed of the same race of men, continues the same identical commonwealth? Or rather, ought we not to say that the identity, in this case, is to be ascribed merely to the people or the inhabitants? Every commonwealth, as we have said, forms a sort of partnership or community; and in this community or partnership each individual has his share. This share is determined by the form of the government, which is nothing else than the arrangement of the different individuals in the community; and when this arrangement is altered, the commonwealth, though still composed of the same persons, cannot remain specifically the same. A tragic and a comic chorus may be executed by precisely the same performers; precisely the same notes compose the boldness of the Doric, and the wildness of the Phrygian music. In such cases, though the constituent parts be the same, a difference in their arrangement and disposition produces a totally different result. The identity of a commonwealth depends, therefore, on the continuance of the same form of government; but it is a distinct inquiry, whether, in consequence of a change in the form of government, contracts subsisting before the revolution ought, in justice, to be fulfilled*?

A question

---

* The author does not examine this question, but it is easy to perceive that he would have decided it in a manner little conformable to the prevailing practice of his own times. The Athenians, indeed, gave one illustrious example of their respect for the sanctity of engagements contracted in the name of the public, when they burdened themselves

ARISTOTLE's POLITICS.

BOOK III.

Chap. 3.

Diſtinction between the virtues of the man and of the citizen.

A queſtion naturally follows, whether a good citizen muſt of neceſſity be endowed with the virtues of a good man? This queſtion can only be ſolved by conſidering what are the eſſential qualities of a citizen. A citizen then is, as it were, one of a ſhip's company, and a ſharer with the reſt in one common concern. Different ſailors have different occupations. One ſteers the helm; another is boatſwain; many ply the oars. The accurate and complete definition of each individual muſt, doubtleſs, expreſs his particular employment and his appropriate duty. Yet one general definition is applicable to them all; ſince they are all alike concerned in promoting a proſperous navigation, and all alike intereſted in the ſafety of the common veſſel. The republic is the veſſel in which citizens are embarked; and the ſafety of the republic is, as we proved above, the ſafety of its form of government. To this the virtues of good citizens muſt always be relative; and as civil conſtitutions widely differ, the virtues neceſſary to preſerve them muſt differ as widely. They are virtues not abſolutely, but politically; and bear a reference to an end or purpoſe, independently of which they would not deſerve even the name of virtue. But the virtues of a good man are ultimately deſirable on their own account, as conſtituting in themſelves the perfection and happineſs of his rational and moral nature.

Political virtues relative to rank, age, and ſex.

In no country whatever have the greater part of mankind attained this conſummate excellence; but unleſs the majority in every country were politically virtuous, the commonwealth muſt ſoon periſh, ſince its ſubſiſtence can only be maintained while

themſelves with a loan which had been made to the thirty tyrants. Demoſthen. adverſ. Leptin. & Iſocrat. Areopagit. See alſo my Tranſlation of Iſocrates, p. 495. and Hiſtory of Ancient Greece, vol. iii. p. 125.

while each, or at least the greater part of its members perform their proper offices, or, in other words, exercife their refpective virtues; virtues as different from each other, as are the various exigencies of human life to which they are refpectively adapted. Our comparifon of the chorus is here ftrictly applicable. The office and the virtue of him who leads the band is altogether different from the office and the virtue of any other performer. But of the leader himfelf, of him who directs the chorus of ftate, what are the peculiar excellencies? When he executes his office aright, wifdom and goodnefs are with propriety afcribed to him. There is an education too, that befits men born to command, and them only; leffons of war and horfemanfhip are given to the fons of kings; and Euripides fays in the perfon of a young prince,

BOOK III.

" Teach me not frivolous arts,
" But teach me only how to ferve my country."

There is an education, therefore, becoming a prince, and there are men fit for receiving none other. Jafon *y* of Pheræ declared, without a figure of fpeech, that he was famifhed for want of empire. Power, it feems, was as neceffary to Jafon, as food to other men; and if he had not gained a crown, he muft have ceafed to live. This magnanimous Theffalian had learned, forfooth, only how to command, but a citizen muft alfo learn how to obey; and it is juftly obferved, that, in the equality of free commonwealths, men muft be difciplined by obedience, before they can be fafely intrufted with authority. In proportion, therefore, as the form of government approximates political perfection, the virtues of a good man and of a good citizen will the more nearly coincide. In all fuch governments,
prudence

y See Hiftory of Ancient Greece, vol. iii. pp. 377, 378, & feq.

BOOK III.

Citizens and their virtues different in different forms of government.

prudence in the governors, and right opinion in the governed, are essential and peculiar requisites; other virtues are common to both, but variously modified by age, sex, office, and condition [*].

If virtue, in the strictest sense, be essential to a citizen, by what name shall we call those low mechanics, who are condemned by their indigence to unwholesome and degrading drudgery? They are not slaves, they are not mere inhabitants, their labour is useful to the state, and yet the lives which necessity compels them to lead, contribute not in any degree to the formation of virtue, either intellectual or moral. In ancient times, these mean artisans were sometimes classed with slaves; and as slaves in many cities, they still continue to be considered; for it is worthy of remark, that defining a citizen as above, "one entitled to share the government of his country," we exclude from that rank, women, minors, and children, who are not less essential in a state than mechanics and artisans. But as there are various forms of government, there must also be various kinds of citizens. In democracies, artisans and even day-labourers may enjoy the honours of the state; in aristocracies this is impossible, because office is the reward of virtue; in oligarchies, the labourer never can, but the artisan sometimes may attain the rank of citizen; because in such governments wealth chiefly opens the road to preferment, and industrious and skilful workmen often acquire considerable opulence. A law therefore prevailed at Thebes, excluding every artisan who had not shut shop upwards of ten years, from enjoying any office of magistracy. In times of national calamity, strangers, bastards, persons of half-blood, and even slaves,

[*] I have transposed and compressed this passage, omitting some obscure clauses which are elsewhere more clearly expressed.

slaves, have been associated to the honours of the commonwealth; but this liberality gradually ceased with the public exigency, and an honourable descent, first on the father's side at least, and afterwards on the side also of the mother, was again required for constituting a citizen. Homer introduces Achilles complaining that he is treated like "an unhonoured stranger." A participation in honours and offices is, in fact, essential to the character of him who is truly a citizen; and when the appellation is bestowed on any other, it is to be considered as nothing better than a flattering cheat. It is plain, therefore, that the character of a good man coincides in some governments with that of a good citizen, in others not; but that even in the former, the two characters completely coincide in the case only of those properly qualified to share and to direct the public administration [a].

We now proceed to investigate the number, the nature, and the genius of the different forms of government [b]. Man, we have said, is naturally a herding and political animal; he delights in the company of others, and covets it for no other purpose

Chap. 4.

Of the different forms of government.

---

[a] Hard would be the lot of mankind if those only were fit to live in society who had acquired confirmed habits of virtue. The purpose of comfortable subsistence, for which communities are instituted, does not require in the greater part of the persons composing them such consummate perfection. There is one case, however, pointed out in the text, in which the character of a good citizen necessarily infers that of a good man. This is the case of magistrates or ministers, of those called to direct or conduct the affairs of the community. In political life, the distinction between private and public character was first invented by the most detestable knavery, as it is unhappily perpetuated by the most lamentable credulity.

[b] Aristotle here repeats, that government is the arrangement of men in society, and especially of those men who, by the forms of the constitution, are invested with the sovereignty. He enumerates also some different kinds of republics, as is done by him more fully hereafter in the next chapter.

ARISTOTLE's POLITICS.

BOOK III.

purpose but merely that of enjoyment. But utility soon strengthens the association which nature has collected; for society is recommended to us not only for the purpose of supporting life, a thing so sweet in itself that men are eager to preserve it even under most deplorable circumstances, but for the purpose of living honourably and happily. The comfortable subsistence, therefore, of the whole body collectively, and of each individual separately, ought to be regarded as the end and purpose for which communities have assembled, and the bond by which they are held together. In that most unequal of all associations, the association, if it may be so called, of the master and the slave, we have already proved that there is a strict coincidence of interests; for though the advantage of the master be the thing principally intended, the advantage of the slave (we mean the slave by imbecility of nature) is also a necessary result [c].

That all just government has for its end and object the good of the governed.

In the management of families, the interest of fathers and husbands coincides with that of wives and children; but as every art has for its object the benefit of those on whom it is exercised; physic, the health of the patient; gymnastic, the strength and dexterity of the scholar; so the art of domestic government must have for its object the benefit of the house or family. The benefit of the master is likewise the usual result; for as he who professes the gymnastic may himself sometimes be a wrestler, and as he who directs the vessel must always

---

[c] See above, p. 32. The imperfection of modern language does not enable us to express by one word δεσποτεια, which I have translated the association of master and slave: an association which the author endeavours to prove mutually beneficial to both parties, by observing, as he had before done, that the destruction of the slave would put an end to the δεσποτεια.

always be a paffenger, fo the one fometimes, and the other always, derives perfonal advantage from his refpective art, the direct and effential object of which lies, however, beyond himfelf, and centers in thofe for whofe improvement the leffons of the former are given, and for whofe fafety the fkill of the latter is exercifed. In political partnerfhips, the fame principle holds good; and the art of government, like all other arts, is practifed directly and principally for the benefit of thofe over whom it is exercifed, that is, the good of the governed [d]. This is fo ftrictly true, that in the equality of ancient republics, thofe who performed the tafk and fuftained the burden of magiftracy, and who fubjected themfelves to the painful duties of uninterrupted vigilance and ftrenuous exertion in the fervice of the public, thought it juft that others next in fucceffion fhould perform the fame tafk, fuftain the fame burden, and fubmit to the fame duties; and thus repay the benefit which they had previoufly received, and ferve in their turn as guardians and watchmen of the community [e]. But fees and falaries have corrupted this natural and healthy condition of fociety, and engendered the difeafe of avarice, which is only to be cured by the emolument of perpetual office. The emolument, however, is accidental; the burden effential. Thofe governments, therefore, which confult the good of the public, and thofe only, are right and juft. Thofe which confult the good of the magiftrates alone, are mere perverfions of government, corrupt tyrannies of unworthy mafters

---

[d] Plato, and, before him, the Pythagorean Fragments, forcibly maintain and beautifully illuftrate this doctrine. Vid. Plat. de Repub. l. i. p. 584. edit. Ficin. and Hiftory of Ancient Greece, vol. ii. c. xi. p. 28.

[e] Vid. Plat. de Repub. l. i. p. 584.

BOOK III.
Chap. 5.

Enumeration and definition of the different forms of government.

masters over reluctant slaves: but a commonwealth is the partnership of freedom.

In enumerating and explaining the various forms of government, method requires that we begin with those which are right and just, because these being previously defined, their counterfeits and corruptions will at once become manifest. In every political association, it is necessary that one man, the few, or the many, should bear sway; and whichever of them happens to take place, if the public good be the great rule of administration, the government is right and just, and is called a monarchy when lodged in the hands of one; an aristocracy, when in the hands of the few; and a republic, when in the hands of the many. The word aristocracy denotes the government of the best men, or the government that is best in itself. A republic is the general name of all commonwealths, but is applied particularly to denote a government administered by the people at large, but administered with justice, not oppressive to any class of citizens, but impartially consulting the good of all.

The distinctive characters of governments.

The propriety of these names is justified by the nature of things. That one man, or a few, may be adorned by an accumulation of virtues, is what experience will justify; but that the multitude in any country should be so illustriously distinguished, is inconsistent with experience. The virtue most likely to pervade a whole people, is martial spirit. Citizens, therefore, who are soldiers, naturally bear sway in that form of civil polity which is called by way of distinction *the republic*[f]. The corrupt

[f] The natural connection between republicanism and martial spirit is strongly attested by all the historians of antiquity from Herodotus to Livy. See Herodot. l. v. c. lxxviii. and History of Ancient Greece, vol. i. c. viii. p. 364. and vol. iii. c. xxi. p. 7.

corrupt deviation from monarchy, or rather from royalty, is tyranny; for a tyrant is a monarch who rules with no other view than the benefit of himself and his family. Ariſtocracy degenerates into oligarchy, when the few, who are rich, govern the ſtate as beſt ſuits the intereſts of their avarice and ambition: and a republic degenerates into a democracy, when the many, who are poor, make the gratification of their own paſſions the only rule of their adminiſtration [r]. Wherever wealth alone opens the road to preferment, oligarchy prevails; poverty, on the other hand, is the conſtant attendant of democracy; and the diſtinctive character of thoſe governments conſiſts not in this, that the many or the few bear ſway, but in the one caſe, that rapacious poverty be armed with power, and in the other, that contemptuous opulence be inveſted with authority. But as

BOOK III.

[r] Read in Livy the Hiſtory of Rome after the expulſion of the Tarquins, and the deſtruction of the Decemvirs. But it is worthy of obſervation, that this eſſential connection has been ſometimes overlooked in modern times, and well it might by thoſe who attended only to names; for in ſpeaking of the greateſt battle fought among the Italian ſtates, many of which were called republics, towards the end of the fifteenth century, Machiavel has the following memorable words: " Et fue queſta giornata combattuta con più virtu, che alcun altra che foſſe ſtata fatta in cinquanta anni in Italia; perche vi mori tra l'una parte & l'altra più che mille huomini." Delle Hiſtorie, l. viii. p. 306. " This action was fought with more valour than any other which had happened for fifty years in Italy; ſince on the two ſides, the number of the ſlain exceeded 1000 men."

[s] Ariſtotle makes an apology for ſpeaking ſo freely of oligarchies and democracies, which were in fact the only governments then exiſting in Greece; and into one or other of which all republics have ſo natural and ſo ſtrong a tendency to degenerate. He ſays, that in treating a ſubject philoſophically, and not merely for the purpoſe of practical utility, a juſt theory cannot be educed, unleſs the particulars which enter into the general queſtion be fully enumerated and fairly examined. We are happy in living in a country where the injuſtice and cruelty both of oligarchies and democracies may be unreſervedly expoſed and fearleſsly arraigned.

BOOK III.

Chap. 6.

The unjust pretensions of the partisans of democracy; and

the unjust pretensions of the assertors of oligarchy, or what is now called aristocracy.

as eminence in wealth can only fall to the share of a few, and as *all* may participate the advantages of equal freedom, the partisans of the rich and of the multitude agitate republican states, each faction striving to engross the government.

In the contentions which take place, both parties pretend to have justice on their side; but there is a democratical and an oligarchical justice, which strongly favours of iniquity. Most men are wretched judges in their own cause. Passion narrows their understanding; and in every complicated case they see those circumstances only which are favourable to themselves, and obstinately shut their eyes to whatever favours their adversaries. Justice, the partisans of democracy assert to be nothing but equality; adding, that where men are equal in liberty, they are entitled to an equal enjoyment of all other advantages. Justice, the partisans of oligarchy maintain, and maintain rightly, to consist not in equality, but in proportion [h]; not in this, that the shares of all be equal, but in this, that each man have his due: but as they themselves are superior in wealth, they claim a superiority in all other respects.

Their reasoning would be conclusive, had communities been formed merely for the purposes of preserving and accumulating riches. On that supposition, the proportions of the profit might be exactly ascertained by the shares of the capital. But commonwealths have *not* been instituted for the sake of riches, nor for commerce by which riches are acquired, nor for that sort of justice or convention, by which they are maintained and defended. The Tuscans, Carthaginians, and other maritime nations, are connected by the bonds of mutual traffic; their exports

---

[h] The subject of justice is fully discussed in the Fifth Book of the Ethics, to which the author here refers. See vol. i. p. 257, & seq.

ports and imports are carefully regulated by treaties; they have courts of juftice to which the fubjects of one country may apply when injured by thofe of another; and they have alliances in war ftipulating mutually to enfure to each other their refpective commercial advantages. But here, their reciprocal connections end; they are not fubject, in other matters, to the fame laws, nor governed by the fame magiftrates; they are not united by affection or friendfhip; and provided each party be juft in his dealings, it is totally indifferent to the other what may be his character in all other particulars; an indifference which cannot prevail among thofe who are fellow-citizens in reality, and not merely in name. But fuppofe the connection to be rendered more intimate, and imagine the walls of Corinth to be united with thofe of Megara: fuppofe ftill farther, that the right of intermarriage, a right effential to the exiftence of communities, were eftablifhed; and admit that each individual were protected in his induftry and in his dealings, by laws wifely framed, faithfully adminiftered, and realifing the metaphor of the fophift Lycophron[1], " that law is a furety and a pledge ;" yet nothing of all this, neither the community of refidence, nor the connection of affinity, nor mutual dependence in trade, nor common affociation in war, none of thefe ties, nor all of them together, would be fufficient to confolidate the political edifice, and to conftitute that kind of partnerfhip which is properly called a commonwealth: a partnerfhip aiming not merely at fubfiftence, but at well-being; and fubfervient not merely to the interefts of life, but to the interefts of that kind of life which

is

BOOK III.

Difference between a commonwealth and other affociations.

---

[1] This Lycophron is mentioned by our author in his Sophiftic. Elench. paffim; & Rhetor. l. iii. c. iii.

BOOK III.

is ultimately defirable to man, as the perfection of his focial and moral nature.

This perfection cannot be attained independently of the community of refidence, the connections of affinity, and the long-continued habits of daily and familiar intercourfe. Feftivals, facrifices, common occupations, and common amufements knit mankind into friendfhip, collect families into cantons, and confolidate cantons into commonwealths. By exercifing the energies and operations of the focial principle, the genuine happinefs of human life is improved and perfected: and that man who, by his perfonal excellencies and the lovelinefs of his character, contributes moft to this great end, whatever may be his inferiority to many others in birth or in wealth, ought to be regarded as the principal fharer in the great political partnerfhip [k].

Chap. 7.

Difficulties attending the queftion, in what portion of the ftate the fovereignty ought to refide.

It has been found a matter of difficulty to determine in what portion of the ftate the fovereignty ought to refide. In the majority of the people at large? Then the fovereignty muft be vefted in poverty; and if the poor plunder the rich, who fhall arraign their injuftice? In the few, who are wealthy, or thofe ftill fewer, who are virtuous? Then the public muft be infulted in the one cafe, and difhonoured in the other: for offices of authority are the honours conferred by republics; and fhould the fame men remain always in place, they muft purchafe this pre-eminence by the difgrace of the people at large. Shall we

[k] The author concludes this chapter with a fentence unconnected with the context, namely, "The doubts and difputes concerning governments arife from confidering juftice, which is a complex object, under one only afpect; and thus fubftituting a part of it for the whole." This remark, which was before made, it feemed unneceffary to repeat.

we then eſtabliſh a king? The evil evidently would become the greater, how meritorious ſoever we may ſuppoſe the character of this king to be[1], ſince the ſphere of honour would thus be ſtill more narrowly contracted, and that of diſgrace ſtill more widely expanded. Perhaps the vigour of ſovereign power is incompatible with the imbecility of human paſſion; and, therefore, ought not to be committed to man, but intruſted to law. Yet if the ſpirit of your laws be democratical or oligarchical, wherein will this alteration avail you? The evils complained of, will evidently ſtill prevail.

Great as theſe difficulties ſeem, they are not, however, altogether incapable of ſolution. The people at large, how contemptible ſoever they may appear when taken individually, are yet, when collectively conſidered, not, perhaps, unworthy of ſovereignty[m]. It is a trite obſervation, that thoſe entertainments where each man ſends the diſh moſt agreeable to his own palate, are preferable to thoſe furniſhed by the moſt ſumptuous delicacy of individuals. The people at large are allowed to be the beſt judges of muſic and of poetry. The general taſte is thus acknowledged to be better than that of the few, or of one man,

Solution of theſe difficulties.

---

[1] The author here does not dogmatiſe, but diſcuſs. In purſuing the principle on which he now reaſons, he draws a concluſion againſt royalty: but viewing the ſubject under a different aſpect, he conſiders, in other paſſages, the kingly power as a fit balance between the people and the great; and regards the royal authority as a firm pledge, that the poor ſhall not be oppreſſed, nor the rich plundered.

[m] This is the only queſtion which the author here examines; leaving, as he obſerves, the ſolution of the other difficulties to another opportunity. In the whole of what he ſays, he ſpeaks merely as an advocate; and his arguments, he obſerves, apply not to any people indiſcriminately, but to a people peculiarly circumſtanced (πρς τι πολιτα), who are the only fit materials for what he calls his πολιτεια, or republic; as will be explained more fully hereafter. It is farther worthy of remark, that when Ariſtotle ſpeaks of the people, he here means *populus*, not *plebs*; the people at large, not the lower ranks only.

BOOK III.

man, however skilful. Considered collectively, the people form a complex animal, with many feet, with many hands, with many faculties, with many virtues; each member contributing something, more or less valuable, to the perfection of the whole body. The moral and intellectual excellencies of the multitude thus differ from those of a wise and virtuous man, as the beauty of a fine picture [a] does from the beauty of individuals; of whom some may have eyes, and others may have other features, more perfect and more beautiful than those of the picture; yet the picture, collecting only excellencies, and always avoiding deformities, will be found more beautiful and more perfect than any original in nature, with whom it can be compared. The excellencies, therefore, of that complex entity the public, may sometimes surpass those of the most accomplished prince or most virtuous council. That this commonly holds, I would not, indeed, venture to affirm. It rather seems manifest, that to some bodies of men the argument cannot possibly apply; for if it applied to them, it would extend also to wild beasts, since wherein some multitudes differ from wild beasts it is not easy to discover.

For what functions the people at large are best qualified.

The safety of every free government requires that the major part of the citizens should enjoy a certain weight in the administration. If this does not take place, the majority must be dissatisfied; and where the majority are dissatisfied, the government will soon be subverted. But what sort of magistracy is the humble citizen, the mere unit of the crowd, qualified to exercise? Offices of high personal trust, or of important executive authority, his ignorance would disgrace, or his injustice might

[a] Such was the Helen of Crotona painted by Zeuxis. "Neque enim putavit, omnia, quæ quæreret ad venustatem, uno in corpore se reperire posse," &c. Cicero de Inventione Rhetorica, l. ii. c. i.

might betray. For the performance of extraordinary tasks, extraordinary virtues, as well as extraordinary abilities, are required; and such virtues and abilities are not to be expected in the individuals of a promiscuous multitude. It remains, therefore, that the people at large be intrusted with the deliberative [o] and judicial powers of government, because the members of assemblies, senates, and courts of justice, acting, not individually, but collectively, prove mutually assisting to each other. In such popular tribunals, virtue and passion, reason and sentiment, courage and wisdom, are harmoniously blended into one salutary composition, in which even the grossest ingredients are not without their use; for experience teaches, that the purest nourishment is not always the best, but that fine flour is most wholesome when mixed with the coarse [p].

The exercise of the deliberative and judicial powers.

Guided by this principle, Solon and some other legislators committed to the people at large the power of appointing the magistrates, as well as that of taking an account of their administration. This political arrangement, indeed, is exposed to the following objection. To appoint a physician, or to take an account of his conduct in his profession, seems to belong only to those who are skilled in the art of physic [q]. A geometer must

Objections on this subject proposed and answered.

---

[o] In what sense the word "deliberative" is to be here understood, will be explained presently.

[p] Nam multitudo fere melius quam singuli de rebus omnibus judicat. Singuli enim quasdam habent virtutum particulas, quæ simul collatæ unam excellentem virtutem conficiunt. Quod in medicorum pharmacis, ac in primis in antidoto eo, quod Mithridaticum vocant, perspicue cerni potest. In eo enim pleræque res per se noxiæ, ubi confusæ fuerint, salutare adversas venena remedium afferunt. Buchannanus de Jure Regni apud Scotos, c. xxviii.

[q] Persons thus skilled, the author divides into three classes: δημιεργοι, ερχιτικτονικοι, πεπαιδευμενοι; mere practitioners; men of accurate and profound science; and persons instructed,

BOOK III. muſt be examined by geometricians; and a pilot, by men acquainted with navigation. Wherefore, then, ought the people indiſcriminately to be entitled to judge their magiſtrates, and to appreciate their merit or demerit in employments, which the people indiſcriminately are not qualified to exerciſe? This objection may be anſwered by recurring to the principles already eſtabliſhed, that the people collectively conſidered (unleſs conſiſting of a vile and ſlaviſh populace) are capable of diſcharging functions, of which, in their individual character, they ſeem altogether unworthy. Beſides this, the productions of every art are not beſt appreciated by its profeſſors. The pilot is a better judge of a helm than the ſhip carpenter. A cook is ſeldom conſulted about the merit of the ſupper which he has dreſſed; and he who inhabits a houſe, needs not a jury of architects to aſcertain the degree of praiſe or of blame due to the contrivance of the builder.

There is ſtill another ground on which the arrangement of popular governments is cenſured. That magiſtrates ſhould be elected by, and reſponſible to, the promiſcuous crowd of citizens, convened in aſſemblies and courts of juſtice, ſeems highly unreaſonable, becauſe the upper ranks of men are thus ſubjected to the authority of their inferiors. To be a general or a treaſurer, that is, to command the public force, or to manage the public purſe, or to perform any ſeparate function of executive magiſtracy, it is neceſſary to be endowed with certain pre-eminent qualifications; a mature age, an ample patrimony, an uniformly approved and reſpected character. Ought ſuch dignified perſonages

---

inſtructed, but leſs correctly and deeply, in the healing art. The diſtinction between ὁ ἀρχιτεκτονικοι, or ὁ ιδιωτης and ὁ πεπαιδευμενοι, occurs frequently in other parts of his works, and in reference to other arts and ſciences.   8

personages to be examined, tried, and sometimes prosecuted to punishment, by men of no estimation; of different ages, different characters, and often destitute of fortune? Is not this to commit the greater magistracy to those judged unworthy of holding the lesser? These questions may be satisfactorily answered by observing, that the individuals composing the senate or assembly are not themselves the assembly or senate. They are parts only of those awful tribunals, and the magistrates are tried not by the parts, but by the whole; that is, by the assembly, senate, or courts of justice, which, whatever may be the character and condition of many of the members composing them, are certainly more wealthy and more respectable than any of those magistrates who are held amenable to their jurisdiction. The present difficulty, therefore, may thus be removed; but the doubt which we first started, proves that the laws should always decide whenever their general language (for their language must be general) applies to the case in question; and that judges should then only speak when the laws are silent. But what laws are entitled to the appellation of good, does not yet appear. This only is manifest, that the laws must depend on the nature of the government; just, therefore, under a good government, and unjust under a bad one.

Every science and every art proposes to itself some end or purpose which it considers as absolutely good and ultimately desirable, that is, good and desirable in itself without reference to the attainment of any object beyond it. Of politics, the most comprehensive and the most important of all sciences, the end and aim is the public good of the community, which can only be upheld by justice, which, as we before said, forms the great law of the moral world. To a certain length, the general opinions

Chap. 8.

According to what circumstances political honours and advantages ought to be apportioned and distributed.

BOOK III.

opinions of mankind coincide, refpecting juftice, with the accurate decifions of philofophy. Among equals, juftice is acknowledged to confift in equality; among thofe who are unequal, it is acknowledged to confift in proportion, that is, in giving to each his due. But what, and how many, are the circumftances which ought to regulate this proportion, is not clearly afcertained. Ought a fuperiority in every advantageous quality, when other things are alike, to entitle its poffeffor to a fuperiority of political advantages? Shall men's ftatures or colours be confidered as laying a foundation for the difcrimination of ranks in fociety? In leffer matters, fuch a principle of diftinction is not allowed to operate. At a concert of mufic, the beft inftrument is given, not to the handfomeft man, but to the beft performer. How much foever he may be furpaffed in beauty or nobility, and how much foever the value of beauty and nobility may furpafs that of mufical fkill, yet the beft performer is always honoured with the beft flute. The reafon is plain; the circumftances in which his rivals are fuperior, contribute nothing to the work in hand. They have no manner of relation to mufical performance; and therefore, with regard to it, cannot ftand in competition with the quality in which he excels them. For things fpecifically different, and which admit not of a common meafure, can only be eftimated by confidering how far they refpectively contribute to fome common end. To compare them abftractedly is impoffible or abfurd. A difference in every valuable quality ought not, therefore, to be a fource of political diftinction. Swiftnefs meets with due honour at the Olympic games. But the honours conferred by cities, are apportioned to qualities effential to the exiftence or well-being of the ftate. A community

cannot

ARISTOTLE's POLITICS.

cannot confift of beggars or of flaves. Liberty, therefore, and wealth and birth, naturally contend for pre-eminence; but if thefe things be neceffary to conftitute a commonwealth, juftice and valour are not lefs neceffary to defend and uphold it. In the conteft, therefore, for civil pre-eminence, education and virtue feem fairly entitled to the firft honours; becaufe of all things, education and virtue moft contribute to the perfection of civil fociety. The partifans of wealth allege, that the rich are moft faithful to their engagements; and that thofe who have the greateft fhare in the public ftock, ought to be invefted with the government. The nobles contend, that as flaves are effentially different from citizens, he who is fartheft removed from a fervile extraction, ought to be held a citizen of a fuperior clafs, and therefore to be armed with authority. They ftrengthen this conclufion, by obferving that nobility is nothing elfe but the virtue of the race, hereditary worth, and prefcriptive dignity. But fuch arguments, in their ultimate tendency, would prove, that one man, if more noble and wealthy than the reft, ought to be made king; and even in a virtuous republic, that he who furpaffed his fellow-citizens in virtue, ought to be exalted to regal power. Such is the abfurdity refulting from the fuppofition, that thofe who are fuperior in one particular [r] ought to be entitled to a fuperiority in political fociety; in which mankind have affembled in order to club their refpective advantages, and in order to direct their various but united efforts,

BOOK III.

---

[r] Ariftotle obferves, that nothing is eafier than to eftablifh a democracy, an oligarchy, or a tyranny; becaufe all thofe governments are perfectly fimple in their conftruction; to make them requires no accuracy of comparifon, no power of combination. But he obferves and proves, again and again, that they are all of them mere perverfions and mockeries of juft government.

BOOK III.

efforts, to one falutary end and purpofe; and in which the people at large may always quafh the vain pretenfions of the few, by faying, *we collectively* are richer, wifer, and nobler than you. The beft laws, therefore, are thofe which are framed for the general benefit of the citizens; that is, of men qualified alternately to govern and to obey, differently qualified, indeed, in different governments; but in the beft, qualified and determined to govern and to obey according to the rules which right reafon prefcribes.

Chap. 9.

Virtue beyond compare unfit for fociety.

The exiftence of every commonwealth prefuppofes, however, a certain degree of equality among thofe who are its conftituent members. Should exceffive inequality prevail, efpecially in thofe things which form the power and fplendour of fociety itfelf, the affociation will gradually tend to a diffolution; and, therefore, if one man, or a few, fhould difplay a degree of virtue, by which that of all the reft would be totally eclipfed, fuch men, if too few in number to fubfift by themfelves in a feparate fociety, could not form a part, or be confidered as members, of any community whatever. It is the law of commonwealths, that the citizens compofing them fhould rule by vicarious fucceffion; becaufe thofe who contribute, nearly in equal portions, to the benefit and luftre of the community, are entitled to expect from that community nearly the fame treatment. But the fame treatment, that is, a mere equality of honours and advantages, would be the height of injuftice to confpicuous eminence and incomparable worth. Who is to govern the natural governors of mankind? What laws are made for men who are a law unto themfelves? The attempt to legiflate for fuch men would be expofed to ridicule;

and

and they might anfwer the arguments of thofe foolifh enough to undertake this tafk, as Antifthenes* fays, that the lions, in the affembly of beafts, anfwered the eloquent harangue of the hares on the fubject of equal laws.

BOOK III.

The oftracifm of democracies was invented for levelling that extreme inequality, under which fuch forms of government cannot poffibly fubfift. The affembly banifhes fo a limited time thofe too confpicuoufly diftinguifhed by wealth, popularity, connections, or any other political advantage. For a fimilar reafon, the Argonauts, we are told, rejected the affiftance of Hercules. His virtues too much overtopped thofe of the adventurers with whom he wifhed to be affociated. The counfel, therefore, which Periander gave to Thrafybulus is not blamable, abftractedly and in itfelf, but becaufe that counfel was both given and employed for the purpofe of fupporting a cruel tyranny. Periander, we are told, faid nothing to the queftion of Thrafybulus, "by what means he fhould maintain the fovereignty of Miletus;" but conducting his meffenger into a field of corn, lopped the talleft ftalks, and thus levelled the furface. The meffenger reported what he had feen, and what Thrafybulus appears to have underftood, having fpeedily fet himfelf to cut off the firft men of the city. Both democracies and oligarchies follow the fame policy. The Athenians, in violation of treaties, chaftifed the Samians, Chians, and Lefbians, in order to break the ftubborn pride of thofe fierce iflanders, and to level their afpiring fentiments with thofe of their more fervile allies. The Perfian monarch has often fmit and humbled the Medes and Babylonians, vainly elated by the remembrance of their ancient empire.

Neceffity of the oftracifm.

* Antifthenes was a fcholar of Socrates, who, in imitation of his mafter, mixed facetioufnefs with feverity. See Hiftory of Ancient Greece, vol. iii. c. xxiv. p. 149.

BOOK III.

Illustrated by the example of the arts.

empire[1]. The levelling maxim, therefore, is univerfally applicable in all fuch governments. The fame principle obtains in mufic, in mechanics, in painting, and indeed in every art. A painter would not admit into his performance, any limb or member, however beautiful, exceeding the proportional magnitude of the figure which he delineates. A fhip-builder muft adapt the helm, and every other part, to the fize of the whole veffel; and in a chorus of mufic, an overpowering voice would difturb and deftroy the effect of the fymphony. The oftracifm, therefore, in democracies, and fome analogous inftitution in monarchies, is ufeful for maintaining the harmony of the political concert. It is better, indeed, that the legiflator, at the firft formation of the commonwealth, fhould provide againft the neceffity of ever having recourfe to fuch violent remedies. But if this has not been done originally, he muft, in that cafe, as at fea, tack about, and thus fteer the veffel of the ftate into a fafe harbour.

The grofs abufe of this inflitution.

The oftracifm, however, inftead of being feafonably and ufefully employed, is too often abufed to factious and pernicious purpofes. In corrupt commonwealths, juftice is meafured by the utility of that portion of the ftate, to whofe intereft the public good is, on all occafions, readily facrificed. Such apparent or relative juftice is, indeed, real and abfolute iniquity; but it is the only kind of juftice that, under bad governments, can poffibly prevail. The oftracifm, therefore, will not be properly applied in thofe cafes to which it is folely or chiefly applicable; for it is a matter of doubt, whether this invention

ought

---

[1] The author does not fay that thefe things are right; but he maintains that they are neceffary for the fafety of the government, which being bad in itfelf, can only be preferved by bad means.

ought ever to be employed in a virtuous and well-regulated community. When a man conspicuously overtops his fellow-citizens, I say not in other political advantages, but in virtue itself, what is then to be done? It will not be said, that in a well-regulated state, his superiority in virtue ought to subject him to banishment. Nor will it be said, that such conspicuous superiority, submitting to the law of vicarious succession, ought to command and obey alternately. This would be as absurd as dividing the empire with Jupiter. It remains, therefore, that all men should cheerfully and uniformly obey such rulers, and acknowledge the natural and perpetual sovereignty of their virtues.

This observation naturally leads us to speak of kings. We have formerly numbered monarchy among the just forms of government. But whether is it universally the best form; or useful in some states and hurtful in others? First of all, it is evident that there are various kinds of monarchy. The kings of Sparta, who seem to be of all kings the most limited by law, conduct the military expeditions, and preside in the religious worship, of their country. They are the hereditary generals of the commonwealth. In the heroic ages, kings were not armed with the power of life and death, except by a kind of martial law, limited in its execution to a day of battle. Agamemnon patiently endures reproach and insult in the council; but issuing to the field, he says,

"Who dares inglorious in his ships to stay?
Who dares to tremble on this signal day?
That wretch, too mean to fall by martial power,
The birds shall mangle and the dogs devour,
For death is in my hand ⁎."

This,

⁎ Iliad ii. v. 391. Aristotle quotes Homer, and even Herodotus, from memory;

BOOK III.

This, therefore, is one kind of monarchy, a perpetual generalship, sometimes hereditary, and sometimes elective. Another species of monarchy is that which prevails among the Asiatic barbarians. Their kings exercise a power absolute, unlimited, and almost tyrannical; yet their authority is legal, hereditary, and secure. The genius of the Greeks is, in point of government, different from that of the barbarians; and the genius of the Europeans is different from that of the Asiatics, who of all nations are the most patient of despotism. Their kings, therefore, are guarded, not as tyrants are in Europe, by the arms of foreign mercenaries, but by the servile fidelity of their native troops; and their dominion becomes lawful, because voluntarily endured; insomuch that the guards of European princes are employed against the citizens, and the guards of Asiatic princes consist of the citizens themselves. A third species of monarchy is that of the Æsymnetes in ancient Greece, who were nothing else than *elective tyrants*, sometimes chosen for life, and sometimes appointed for a limited time, or the conclusion of a particular business. The people of Mitylene thus chose Pittacus to conduct the war against the exiles, headed by Antimenides, and the poet Alcæus; who, in one of his convivial songs, arraigns the folly of the multitude, " for appointing, vociferously and tumultuously, the baneful Pittacus to tyrannise a frantic and ill-fated country." The government of the Æsymnetes partook both of tyranny and of royalty; they were despots exercising lawful power, because lawfully granted; but differing from Asiatic monarchs, because their temporary power

so familiar was he with those admired authors. From this circumstance, his citations are not always correct; as in the example before us, where, to the four verses in the text, he adds, from another part of the Iliad, παρ' γαρ ιμοι θανατος—"For death is in my hand."

ARISTOTLE's POLITICS.

power was not congenial to the spirit and usages of their country. A fourth species of monarchy prevailed in the heroic ages, a limited royalty; just, legal, and hereditary. Those who signally benefited mankind in arts or arms, who collected societies, formed settlements, and established colonies, received voluntary submission from public gratitude[x]. They became generals in war, judges in peace, and presided in such acts of religion as were not exclusively attached to particular priesthoods. In deciding the differences of their subjects, they swore to observe the rules of justice; and the form of the oath consisted in elevating the sceptre[y]. In progress of time, these branches of authority were either voluntarily resigned by kings, or forcibly resumed by their people. In most commonwealths, kings have been reduced to the condition of mere presidents in religious ceremonies; and in that country of Greece in which their office best deserves the name of royalty, they are merely hereditary generals.

To these four kinds of monarchy above mentioned, we must still add a fifth and last kind, the most absolute of all. A king may bear to a state the same relation which a master does to a family, having the whole power of the sovereignty concentrated in his own person. The office of such a monarch, and that of

a king

---

[x] See Sarpedon's speech in Homer, Γλαυκε τιη δι ιωι τ.τιμηκισθα μαλιςα, &c. Il. xii. v. 310. and Pope, v. 370—386.

"Such, they may cry, deserve the sovereign state,
Whom those that envy, dare not imitate."

[y] The sceptre was given to kings as the badge of their authority, and entitled them to administer the θεμιςας δικς, Jove's laws; which when they perverted or infringed, the sceptre dropped from their hands. See History of Ancient Greece, vol. i. c. ii. passim.

BOOK III.

CHAP. II.
An eſtimate of the advantages and defects of monarchy.

a king of Sparta, form the two ultimate limits of monarchical power, which cannot be greater than it is in the firſt caſe, nor leſſer than it is in the ſecond. The perpetual generalſhip of Sparta cannot even be ſaid to conſtitute a particular form of government. It is not the conſtitution itſelf, but rather a law of that conſtitution; and a law that may take place under any other conſtitution whatever. We ſhall not, therefore, at preſent examine its advantages or inconveniences; but proceed to conſider thoſe kinds of royalty which contain the ſpecific qualities of kingly government.

In appreciating their merits or defects, we muſt eſtimate the contending pretenſions of good laws and good men [y]. The partiſans of kings obſerve, that laws can only ſpeak a general language; that their applications to particular caſes, which, taken collectively, form the ſum of human tranſactions, is often doubtful, dangerous, or hurtful; that there is not any art of which the practice can be regulated by immutable precept; that even in Egypt, a country ſingularly attached to the formality of rules, phyſicians are allowed, after the third day of the malady, to alter the mode of treatment preſcribed by authority; and even before that time, to alter it at their peril. The advocates for laws aſſert, and aſſert juſtly, that the queſtion partly reſolves itſelf into one more general, "whether ought reaſon or paſſion to bear ſway." Laws, therefore, muſt be eſtabliſhed; but as they cannot completely involve the deciſion of each particular caſe, whether ought one man, or many, to adminiſter and apply them? The arguments in favour of the *judgment* of the many, we have already

[y] In treating of monarchy, Ariſtotle has principally abſolute monarchy in view. He ſtates the objections to it with that fulneſs and force with which he commonly repreſents the arguments of his adverſaries; refuting them afterwards with as much brevity as the ſubject can poſſibly admit.

ARISTOTLE's POLITICS.

already had occasion to explain [a]; and in favour of their *justice*, it may be observed, that the many are less liable to corruption than one man or the few, in the same manner that a large lake is less corruptible than a small pool. If we deal, therefore, impartially with kings, magistrates, and people, regarding them all as composed of the same materials, endowed with similar excellencies, and liable to similar imperfections; it must be acknowledged that in communities consisting of such members, and particularly in the cities of Greece, a republic is better than an aristocracy, and an aristocracy than a monarchy. Kings were originally established by the gratitude of small communities, in which there were but few persons of considerable weight or distinguished merit. But as the number of men deserving the name of peers, or equals, increased, the kingly government was changed for an aristocratical republic. Under this government nations flourished, and riches were accumulated. Riches were followed by luxury, and luxury by rapacity. The wealth of the state became the plunder of individuals. Oligarchies, and then tyrannies, successively prevailed; an usurping faction continually narrowing the basis of its own power, till this power, supported on a single point, was easily overturned by the just resentment of the multitude [b]. Democracy then

BOOK III.

Why introduced, and wherefore abolished.

[a] See above, c. viii. p. 187.

[b] Aristotle's theory of political revolutions is wonderfully confirmed by the ancient History of Italy. In that country limited monarchies first prevailed, which degenerating into tyrannies, made way for aristocracies. Rome, Naples, Capua, Nola, Tusculum, were long governed by senates: but as cities became more populous, an epidemical malady seized the people of persecuting the Patricians. This evil raged during the Carthaginian wars, from which time there was a continual progress towards democracy. Yet in all these republics, whether popular or aristocratical, the supreme power of the state was generally held by distinguished individuals; a Valerius, Camillus, or Fabius, of Rome; a Manilius, chief of the Latins; a Herennius, of the Samnites,

BOOK III.

Inconveniences of hereditary monarchy.

then arofe, and prevailed in its turn; and it is a matter, perhaps, of fome difficulty to eftablifh any other form of government in large cities and populous communities.

Should monarchy be admitted as an ufeful inftitution, a new queftion occurs, whether it ought to be hereditary? Whatever be the character of a young prince, ought he, in default of his father, to affume the government, and to rule for the ruin of his country? But the king, knowing the profligacy of the prince, will provide a more worthy fucceffor. This furely fuppofes a degree of virtue greater than can be expected from man, that, for the good of the public, a father fhould exclude his own fon from a throne. As adminiftrator of the laws, the king muft be entrufted with a military force, fufficient to render them effectual. This force, it is eafy to fee, ought to be fuch as will enable him to coerce refractory individuals, but not to opprefs the community. Such was the proportion of troops anciently committed by the Greeks to their Æfymnetes; and fuch was the rule by which a citizen of Syracufe wifhed to limit the military force entrufted to Dionyfius.

Chap. 12.

Monarchy arraigned.

But fome perfons affert, that it is impoffible to modify kingly power into any thing like reafon and juftice. That the invention is altogether unnatural; and that placing a prince on the throne is nothing elfe than raifing paffion and a wild beaft to the feat of fovereignty. That no man is a fair judge in his own caufe; and that a king, therefore, can never judge fairly between himfelf and his people. That phyficians, when fick, truft not to their own fkill, but require the advice of others; and that mafters of the gymnaftic exercifes pretend not to be
proper

Samnites, &c. all which acted fomething of a fimilar part in the cities of their refpective diftricts, which the Medici did in modern times in Florence, and the Malateftas, Vifcontis, Felorios, &c. in other cities of Italy.

proper judges of their own exhibitions. In all cafes whatever, mankind acknowledge the danger of impaffioned, and therefore partial, decifions, and ought the more earneftly to ftrive againft this danger, in proportion to the importance of the objects that inflame the ardour of defire, and ftrengthen the bias of felfifh- nefs. That the only juft fovereigns, therefore, are God and the laws; efpecially thofe unwritten, moral, and univerfal laws, founded in nature, reared and perfected by education and cuftom. Befides this, were the heart and will of a king not to be diftrufted, his head and his underftanding would be totally unequal to the difcharge of an office not made for humanity. Can one man be fuppofed capable of fuperintending the concerns of a whole people? Let him be ever fo good, two muft ftill be better than one.

" By mutual confidence and mutual aid,
Great deeds are done, and great difcoveries made;
The wife new prudence from the wife acquire,
And one brave hero fans another's fire [b]."

And Agamemnon, fenfible of his own inability to exercife regal power, prayed,

" Oh! would the Gods, in love to Greece, decree
But ten fuch fages as they grant in thee [c]:
Such wifdom foon fhould Priam's force deftroy,
And foon fhould fall the haughty towers of Troy [d]."

That the laws muft be adminiftered, and their general language adapted to particular cafes, by the difcernment of upright judges, affords not any argument in favour of the judge as fuperior to the law. For it is acknowledged, that in every cafe

[b] Pope's Iliad, ii. 224.   [c] Ibid. 370.   [d] Ibid. 443.

BOOK III.

All monarchies resolve themselves into oligarchies, or aristocracies.

Monarchy defended: to what nations it is best adapted.

case to which laws are applicable, they only ought to judge and to govern; and from the law itself men derive those principles that enlighten their reason and direct their decisions. Enured to the discipline of this wise school-mistress, they not only understand the letter, but imbibe the spirit of her instructions; and in continuing habitually subject to the laws, they become duly qualified to explain them, which that man can never be, who is raised above the laws.

Besides, there is an absurdity in supposing that one man with two eyes and two ears can observe as widely, or with two hands and two feet can act as vigorously, as many men with many perceptive and many active powers. Kings themselves bear witness to the law of nature, associating to their government many eyes, many hands, many organs of sense, and many instruments of action. Their *friends*, that is, the friends both of their persons and government, are full partners in power; they would not exert themselves to support a system to which they were unfriendly; and friendship, we have before proved, can only subsist among equals. The government of one, therefore, necessarily terminating in that of many, his peers and equals, it is surely most advisable to form directly and at once, that kind of constitution which must always be circuitously established.

These arguments against royalty are not so conclusive as they seem; because they rest entirely on the fallacy of extending to mankind in general, observations that have been found applicable to some particular communities. Government is nothing else but the arrangement of individuals in a state, and the propriety of every arrangement or composition must depend on the number and nature of its materials. Some societies of men are fitted for living under what we have called a republic,

13 that

ARISTOTLE's POLITICS.

that is, a juft and equal polity, adminiftered by rotation; and no people whatever are fitted for living under a tyranny, whether of one man, of an oligarchical fenate, or of a democratical affembly; all which we have declared bafe perverfions of government, and direct violations of nature. But between thefe extremes, there may be fome nations fo conftituted as fpontaneoufly to obey a lord or defpot, as fervants obey a mafter; and others fo conftituted as voluntarily to obey a king, or even an ariftocratical fenate, as wives and children obey their fathers or hufbands. Thofe who are unequal by nature, cannot be levelled by any contrivance of man; and when authority is juft and ufeful, fubmiffion will be ready and cheerful. Even in republics themfelves, where men are arranged, not according to their wealth, but according to their worth; where the citizens love liberty, which they have arms and courage to defend; yet fhould the illuftrious virtues of one man, or one family, totally eclipfe the merit of the community at large, fuch a man, or fuch a family, muft either be banifhed by the oftracifm or enthroned. So much concerning monarchy, its nature and kinds; what nations it fuits, and for what reafons it fuits them [e].

BOOK III.

[e] The laft chapter is merely a recapitulation; after which the author fays, that it is his intention to proceed to treat of the beft form of government.

ARISTOTLE's POLITICS.

BOOK IV.

INTRODUCTION.

IN the First Book of his Politics, Aristotle examines the origin of society and government, the essential distinction of ranks in a commonwealth, and the best plans of political œconomy. In the Second, he describes the most admired schemes of policy, either delineated by philosophers, or instituted by legislators. In the Third, (of which a considerable part is now lost,) he explained the nature and principle of the various governments existing in Greece and in the ancient world, whether republican or monarchical; bestowing just and liberal praise, where praise seemed to be due; but declaring himself not completely satisfied with any thing that philosophers had devised, legislators prescribed, or that time and chance had produced, he proceeds in the Fourth (commonly published as the Seventh) Book, to exhibit the result of his own reflections concerning the great question, which form of government is the best?

This problem cannot, he observes, be solved abstractedly; because government being an arrangement, the best government must be the best arrangement, and the best arrangement is that which

BOOK IV. which the materials to be arranged, are the beft fitted both to receive and to preferve. The great nations of Egypt and the Eaft had fhewn themfelves incapable of fubfifting under any milder dominion than that of abfolute monarchy, which was not tyranny to them, becaufe voluntarily endured; congenial to their original character, and confirmed by hereditary and prefcriptive ufage. The genius and temper of the Greeks, indeed, were as different from thofe of the Afiatics and Africans, as from thofe of the fierce and undifciplined barbarians in the north and weft of Europe. The queftion therefore comes to be, what is the beft government for the Greeks, or rather for that portion of the Greeks, fufficiently numerous to form a community apart? for Ariftotle thought the whole nation far too bulky to be moulded into one commonwealth, but well adapted by its magnitude to form a powerful confederacy; which by purfuing a line of policy which he marks out, in its foreign as well as domeftic tranfactions, might have greatly accelerated the improvement and eminently heightened the profperity of the furrounding world. The queftion, therefore, ftill returns, How are the firft elements of this confederacy to be produced? What ought to be the conftitution, and what the properties of that political germ, deftined to invigorate into fuch folid ftrength, at the fame time that it expands to fuch flourifhing beauty?

In treating this fubject, Ariftotle proves, with convincing evidence, that the fame energies and habits conftitute the happinefs both of individuals and of nations. Men make governments, not governments them: nor by any fyftem of political arrangement can a happy commonwealth be conftituted from fools or cowards, profligates or knaves. The bricks muft firft be prepared before the edifice can be reared; and to the

fophifts

ARISTOTLE's POLITICS.

sophists of Greece, who maintained, that as men were corrupted by bad governments, so they might be corrected and purified by good ones, the author replies by asking, how a good building can be made from bad materials? To make a government requires great length of time; and to amend a corrupt government, he observes, requires still longer time; because, in this latter case, men have not only to learn what they did not before know, but also to unlearn what they had previously been taught. The happiness of the community at large is the end of all good government; but Aristotle derides the vain opinion that this happiness, which is often destroyed by the injustice and cruelty of magistrates, is only to be recovered and restored through the operation of popular assemblies. The majority of the people are poor, their justice will therefore be rapacity; the majority of the people are ignorant, their policy therefore will be folly; the majority of the people are themselves domineered by headstrong and impetuous passions, their dominion therefore will be anarchy, oppression, and cruelty; and to intrust government, even for a moment, to such clumsy and artless hands, will, instead of having any tendency to reform it, be the likeliest means to prevent the possibility of any thing like rational reform from ever being effected.

Virtue, in a political sense, is defined the love of the constitution; but under the best constitution possible, virtue simply, and political virtue, perfectly coincide. How virtue, simple and unqualified, that is, virtue in the strict philosophical sense, may be rendered the actuating principle of government, Aristotle proceeds with great accuracy to explain; and the aristocracy which he thus establishes, while it maintains the just pre-eminence of the few, will invariably promote the

BOOK IV.

best

BOOK IV. best interests of all; containing in itself a perennial spring of gradual but sure improvement; and raising to higher benefits all descriptions of men, (not excepting slaves themselves,) exactly in proportion to their capacities for enjoying them.

Readers of reflection will peruse with pleasure his judicious observations concerning the extent and populousness of his commonwealth; the most advantageous soil and climate, the best situation of the country and of the capital; their necessary accommodations, and most desirable embellishments. Such particulars as these sufficiently explain themselves; but the three following points, two of which relate to domestic, and one to foreign policy, are not unworthy of illustration.

For cementing his citizens into friendship, and for maintaining, unimpaired, the true spirit of any thing like a free and a good constitution, Aristotle, both in this and other Books, ascribes singular efficacy to those convivial meetings, called by the Greeks *syssities*, and by the English *clubs*. In the Greek sense of the word, clubs long formed the prevailing characteristic and peculiar delight of one modern nation. Our neighbours neither had the name nor the thing: and an Englishman who had inhabited the capital, whatever inducements might lead him to foreign lands, always sighed with regret (and that in a degree proportional to his good sense) for those precious hours unincumbered by care and unfettered by ceremony, where franknefs chastised by decency, and ardour fraught with knowledge, flowed in full and free streams of unguarded conversation. Before hastily condemning Aristotle for ascribing great and momentous effects to slight and trivial causes, it may be worth while to pause, and carefully to consider how much this singularity in our own manners contributed to form that character,

racter, and especially that temper, which is best calculated for enjoying, without abuse, the inestimable benefits of a free government.

A second point on which Aristotle rests the chief support of his commonwealth, is the distribution of public functions among its citizens, according to their respective ages. That a city or commonwealth may subsist comfortably, as to matters of bodily accommodation, it must be provided with peasants, mechanics, and merchants; that it may subsist happily, securely, and respectably, it must be provided with magistrates, priests, and soldiers. Aristotle endeavours to prove, both by experience and arguments, that the classes of men habitually employed as instruments of productive industry, ought to be all of them strictly confined, each to his assigned task; and that the more minutely their tasks are subdivided, and the more rigidly each through life adheres to his own, the more promptly and the more perfectly will the work of all be performed. But does the same reasoning apply to those public and political functions which constitute the duty and dignity of a citizen? As the trade of a weaver ought never to be conjoined with that of a smith or a carpenter; in the same manner ought the military profession never to be exercised at the same time, and by the same persons who perform the offices of priests and magistrates. Aristotle maintains, that those functions ought to be performed by the same persons, not however simultaneously, but at different periods of their lives. Young men in the bloom of their health, strength, and courage, make the best soldiers; the matured vigour of understanding is necessary to the due exercise of deliberative and judicial powers; whereas the honourable functions of the priesthood, not requiring any painful or

ary

BOOK IV.

any strenuous exertion either of the body or of the mind, ought to be reserved for the occupation and the reward of declining years.

Aristotle would have easily perceived the incompatibility of such regulations with the condition of modern times. The civil law of Athens, and of every other republic of Greece, was a science still more simple than the civil law of Rome, of which Cicero boasts, that amidst all his variety of occupations he could make himself master in the course of a few weeks. In the Christian kingdoms of Europe, priests are not only the performers of religious ceremonies, but the great moral instructors of mankind; and the preparations requisite for the profession either of the law or of the church are sufficient to employ and exhaust the diligence of that portion of life which, according to Aristotle's plan, ought to be dedicated to far different pursuits. It is thus that the arrangements in political society must always depend on the materials to be arranged; and that institutions seemingly the most natural and most salutary will, under given circumstances, be found the most absurd and most destructive. The study of abstract politics is, therefore, of all sciences the most liable to abuse, though of them all the most useful, when confined within its proper sphere. By determining those arrangements which, independently of local and temporary circumstances, are most conformable to the essential structure and essential ends of society, it supplies the conductors of public affairs with a political limit or model of perfection, to which, without ever reaching, they may continually strive to approximate; thereby counteracting that tendency from bad to worse, of which the superficial as well as the deep observers of human life have at all times and in all countries so justly and so universally

versally complained. In moral and intellectual endowments, one man is scarcely ever more different from another, than the same man is different from himself at different periods of his life. The distinctions of age are the most natural, the most palpable, and the least invidious of all distinctions; and wretched must be that commonwealth, in which the prerogatives of virtuous old age are not both honourably sustained and cheerfully acknowledged!

The just and natural prerogatives of age ought, however, to be carefully distinguished from the absolute and unnatural dominion of fathers over their children, which was established by law in ancient Persia, and in ancient Rome. With respect to the former country, Aristotle says, that its regulations concerning the *patria potestas* were barbarous and tyrannical[a]. At Rome, fathers were not punishable for selling their children, or even for putting them to death; and a son, while his father lived, could not, unless emancipated, legally enjoy any separate property. Extraordinary as those powers seem, they were not, however, rashly given to fathers by the founders of the Roman state, the deepest of all politicians, " since they were induced to confer them, by considering the natural pre-eminence of fathers, the innumerable labours which they sustain for the sake of their children, the necessity of keeping the latter under a watchful authority; which they knew, from the instinctive affection of parents for their offspring, would be mildly exercised." Such are the sentiments of Simplicius[b]; but Aristotle holds, that parents, as to the treatment of their children, and masters, as to the treatment of their slaves, ought

[a] Ethic. Nichom. viii. 12.   [b] Ad Epictet. Encheirid.

ought to be amenable to the laws, and accountable to the magiftrates; fince power without refponfibilty is not made for man.

The third point in the prefent Book requiring illuftration, relates to the moft important branch of foreign policy. According to the theory at leaft, though not the practice, both of the Greeks and Romans, war could be warrantably undertaken only for the purpofes of felf-defence, of making reprifals, and of revenging injuries[c]. But the mild and manly fpirit of Chriftianity, reprobating, as an unjuftifiable caufe of action, every fpecies and every degree of revenge, is thought to have altered and improved the law of nations refpecting war and peace; and to have reftricted the right of hoftility fimply to refiftance. Even this law of refiftance or defence has been rejected by the fcruples of fome of the aufterer fects: but their arguments, founded on the literal fenfe of particular texts, have been anfwered by proving, that thefe texts enjoin forbearance only in the cafe of flight and trivial injuries, and are to be regarded as general recommendations of Chriftian patience, not as particular commands for abandoning to unjuft violence our perfons, our families, our friends, and our country. Had Chriftianity purpofed the complete abolition of war on all grounds whatever, fuch an innovation muft have been announced in language fpecific and peremptory. The new and extraordinary law would not have been left to be collected by inference; it would have been exprefsly declared and folemnly promulgated. By the power, indeed, of moral motives, and the force of rational arguments, Chriftianity renders odious or contemptible, ambition, avarice, uncharitablenefs, and all thofe felfifh

[c] Omnia quæ defendi, repetique et ulcifci fas fit. Liv. l. v. c. xlix.

selfish passions which are the principal and ordinary causes of aggression. Were its divine doctrines universally respected, wars would from that moment universally cease, because none could meditate future wrong; and the party who had already committed injuries would be solicitous amply to repair them. But until this happy revolution be effected in human manners, violence may be repelled by force; crimes may be punished for the sake of amendment and example; and incorrigible offenders, whether individuals or communities, may be utterly cut off, when their destruction appears essentially requisite to the public safety. Besides those plain and palpable grounds of war, which have always been avowed in the practice at least of all Christian nations, Aristotle maintains, that individuals or communities, qualified for command, may assert by arms an authority justifiable, because useful, to those who are its subjects; an authority moderate and political over freemen, absolute and despotic over slaves. For extenuating the harshness of this decision, it may be observed, that by metaphors familiar to most languages, we speak of the infancy of society, indicating that many human beings, who have attained the age of manhood, are nearly as incapable as children of governing their own conduct. To such full-grown children, it would surely be a piece of good fortune to fall under the direction of a wise and virtuous father. We speak of other communities of men as servile, barbarous, savage, and even brutal; it would, assuredly, be highly advantageous to such nations to meet with wise and virtuous masters. Barbarous and savage nations, therefore, may be rightfully attacked in war, if, without being conquered, the former could not be civilised, nor the latter be tamed.

BOOK IV.

This specious maxim is liable indeed to be frequently abused, because it must be explained and applied by human reason, dark in itself, and often clouded by passion. But does the principle of self-defence, which Grotius would substitute in its stead, delineate an unerring rule of action? According to the uniform current of modern history, has not the approved right of self-defence been constituted by an apprehension of remote and improbable contingencies? In the practice, at least, of nations, does it not include whatever our avarice, our ambition, in one word, our selfishness, supposes essential to our well-being, the increase of our wealth or power, the superiority of our military or naval force, the preservation of our hereditary advantages, and the insurance of our future prospects? One nation is too strong—our safety requires that it should be weakened; another, by its situation, may be tempted to extend its borders—our own frontier is to be fortified by new acquisitions of territory, and defended by new bulwarks; by territory to be gained by invasion, and bulwarks which inspire more real terror than that by which they were raised. It would be endless to recite the incongruities resulting from the interpretation of a law, which tends to set the practice of nations at continual variance with their principles; a law too refined for the coarseness, and too limited for the variety of human transactions; which, in our present imperfect state, require that the exercise of the right of war, like all other deliberate acts, should be governed by the fallible dictates of human prudence, adjusting, as well as may be, the measures of coercion to the salutary ends of public expediency, including the best interests both of the victors and of the vanquished.

It

It may be worthy of remark, in concluding this introduction to Ariftotle's ideal commonwealth, that his great political as well as philofophical adverfary was employed, in 1663, to delineate a plan of government for Carolina. He gave the whole authority, legiflative and executive, to the eight proprietors. The great Milton propofed a plan of government for England [d]. The fovereignty was to refide in a grand council, not only fupreme but perpetual. Compared with Ariftotle's commonwealth, that of Locke will appear no better than a diet of *ftarofts*; and that of Milton, an oligarchy of *decemvirs*.

[d] See his "Ready and eafy Way to eftablifh a Free Commonwealth."

BOOK IV.*

ARGUMENT.

Different views of national happiness.—Fair estimate thereof.—The best commonwealth.—Extent and nature of its territory—Commerce -- Naval power — Climate—Constituent members—Health—Marriage—Children.

RIGHTLY to investigate the best form of government, it is necessary previously to ascertain what is the best kind of life; since the latter of these remaining undetermined, the former also must continue to be unknown. Those men (barring improbable accidents) are the happiest, who live under the best government of which their circumstances admit. We must begin, therefore, by examining what kind of life is most eligible for mankind in general; and secondly, whether the well-being of individuals and of communities results from the same causes, and is to be estimated by the same standard. The former of these topics has been sufficiently discussed in our popular discourses; where we made use of a division that appears to be indisputably accurate; namely, that the happiness of men depends on their external prosperity, on the frame and habit of their bodies, on the state and condition of their minds. He surely would be unworthy to be called happy, who possessed not the smallest particle of fortitude, of temperance, of justice, or of prudence; since the wretch totaliy destitute of these

BOOK IV.
Chap. 1.
The foundation of public happiness.

* Commonly published as Book VII.

BOOK IV.

these virtues respectively, would be frightened at the buzzing of a fly; would wallow unrestrained in the most beastly sensuality; would not hesitate, for the smallest gain, to destroy his best benefactor; and in point of intellectual operations, would betray either childish imbecility or frantic absurdity. That a certain portion of virtue is essential to the well-being of a human creature, cannot, therefore, be a matter of dispute; but to what this portion ought to amount, occasions much diversity of opinion. In general, mankind are satisfied with their respective shares of virtue, how scanty soever they may be, but extremely dissatisfied with their shares of all other advantages; for their measure of virtue, however inconsiderable it may appear to others, rarely appearing deficient to themselves, they seek not to augment it; while their estates and money, their fame and their power, cannot possibly, in their own opinion, be too widely enlarged, or too highly accumulated. But *we* say to them, that such vulgar illusions, even vulgar observation may suffice to dispel. The external advantages of power and fortune are acquired and maintained by virtue, not virtue by them; and whether we consider the virtuous energies themselves, or the fruits which they unceasingly produce, the sovereign good of life must evidently be found in moral and intellectual excellence, moderately supplied with external accommodations, rather than in the greatest accumulation of external advantages, unimproved and unadorned by virtue. External prosperity is indeed instrumental in producing happiness, and therefore, like every other instrument, must have its assigned limits; beyond which it is inconvenient or hurtful. But to mental excellence no limit can be assigned: the farther it extends, the more *useful* it becomes, if the epithet of *useful* need ever to be superadded to that of *honourable*. Besides this, the relative importance of qualities is best estimated by that of their respective subjects. But the mind, both in itself and in reference to man, is far better than the body, or than property. The excellencies of the mind, therefore, are in the same proportion to be preferred to the highest perfection of the body, and the best disposition of external circumstances. The two last are of a far inferior, and merely a subservient nature; since no man of sense covets or pursues them, but for the sake of the mind, with a view to promote its genuine improvement, and to heighten its native joys. Let this great truth then be acknowledged; a truth evinced by the Deity himself, who is happy, not from any external cause, but through the inherent attributes of his divine nature.

Prosperity and happiness, then, are things altogether different. Chance or fortune may bestow the former, but they cannot produce the energies of virtue, which are the essential source of the latter. These energies are precisely the same, whether exercised by individuals or by communities; neither altering their inward form, nor changing their external effects. Public and private happiness, therefore, must rest on precisely the same foundation, a conclusion justified even by universal consent; since those who place the happiness of the individual in riches, are solicitous chiefly about preserving and augmenting national wealth; and those who place the happiness of the individual in power, are solicitous chiefly about preserving or augmenting national dominion. A similar inference is drawn by the admirer of virtue: He who regards it as the supreme felicity of the individual, also considers it as the main source of national happiness.

Chap. 2.

The same with that of individuals.

But

BOOK IV.
Chap. 3.

The best schemes of national happiness.

But since virtue is twofold, speculative and practical, and that men ambitious of excellence respectively dedicate themselves to the pursuit of philosophy or that of politics; it is worth while to consider which of the two kinds of life, a life of strenuous action or of peaceful contemplation, is most deserving of being imitated by states; since it is the office of wisdom to teach nations as well as individuals to prefer the best ends, and skilfully to pursue them. The advocates for peaceful repose and contemplative tranquillity observe, that for a nation to govern its neighbour despotically is the height of injustice, and therefore the most consummate folly; and that to govern them moderately and carefully, though not liable to such palpable objections, is however a work of great difficulty, and fraught with much trouble and much anxiety. Other reasoners, though they condemn every kind of injustice and despotism, maintain that the contentious agitations of war and government form the happiness and glory of nations, since they afford the best and noblest field for the public exhibition of illustrious abilities, and of pre-eminent virtues. A third class, and this is the most numerous, boldly patronise ambition and tyranny, and assert that the main business of nations consists in extending their power and aggrandising their empire.

The practice of most great nations shews that they placed it in valour and conquest.

In Sparta and in Crete, the public education, as well as the laws, are contrived merely as means for attaining this favourite end. The same remark applies to the Scythians, the Persians, the Thracians, and the Celts; and, indeed, to all those great nations whose valour or populousness have enabled them to assert their pretensions, or encouraged them to display their ambition. In Carthage, a soldier is entitled to wear as many rings as he has served campaigns. There was an old law in Macedon,

ARISTOTLE's POLITICS.

Macedon, that the man who had not slain an enemy in the field of battle, should be girt, not with an ornamental belt, but with a halter. The Scythians, in their public festivals, never presented the circling cup to hands guiltless of blood. The Iberians, a martial people, adorn the tombs of their deceased warriors with obelisks or pillars, equal in number to the enemies whom they have respectively slain [e]. Similar institutions prevail in other countries, either enacted by law, or established by custom; and yet nothing can appear more absurd to men capable of reflection, than to believe it the business of government to hold either nations or individuals in reluctant subjection. Who ever heard that it was the duty of a physician to compel, or even to persuade his patients to be cured, or the duty of a pilot to compel, or even to persuade the ship's company to be saved? The science of government, like that of physic and of navigation,

---

[e] The institutions of Rome had not acquired that celebrity, which entitled them to be cited as examples in the time of Aristotle, who flourished towards the beginning of the fifth century from the building of the city. Yet, even at this early period, the Romans were distinguished above all nations in the world, by the nice gradation, as well as by the general diffusion, of military honours. From the time of the Publilian law, "ut plebiscita omnes Quirites tenerent," U. C. 416. which was a confirmation of the Valerian, U. C. 506.; and which was itself confirmed by the Hortensian, U. C. 467.[*], the people at large enjoyed an ascendancy in the government; and the military ambition of the commonwealth thereby acquired that degree of vigour and activity, which (external circumstances permitting) has always most conspicuously appeared under such a political arrangement. In modern times, military distinctions, as well as the martial spirit, have prevailed most in monarchies. This was not the case anciently, but completely the reverse: and it may be observed, that external circumstances being the same, the ambition of conquest diffused through the general mass of a society, must be a more ardent as well as a more firm and steady principle of action, than when confined within the breasts of a few individuals, whose passions are not, like those of communities, immortal.

[*] Conf. T. Liv. iii. 55. vii. 42. Plin. Nat. Hist. xvi. 10. & Pompon. de Origin. ii. 8. Aul. Gell. xv. 27.

navigation, is invented for the public benefit; and men will allow themselves to be benefited, without perſuaſion and without compulſion.

Their eſtimate proved to be erroneous.

The conduct of nations has perplexed this ſubject, becauſe the conduct of nations has been diſtorted by paſſion. They have impoſed laws on their neighbours, which they themſelves would have indignantly rejected. Behaving moderately and equitably at home, they have acted tyrannically abroad, confounding the limits of politic and deſpotic government, although, as we have already proved, to enſlave freemen, is not leſs abſurd and contrary to nature, than to hunt and eat them. A ſtate may be ſo circumſtanced as to exiſt happily without conqueſt and without war; and how ſplendid ſoever military glory may be deemed, it is valuable merely as the means of obtaining a ſtill more valuable end. This end cannot ſurely conſiſt in gratifying the luſt of ambition, for no pleaſure is more contemptible than that of commanding ſlaves, and to reduce freemen into ſervitude is an unnatural gratification, equally dangerous and deceitful. The happineſs of communities, as well as of individuals, conſiſts, doubtleſs, in action; but to the external action of a ſtate, a wide field lies often in the diverſity of genius and character of the ſurrounding nations, each of which, to be treated juſtly, muſt perhaps be treated differently. Beſides this, there are many internal relations which the conſtituent parts of a commonwealth bear to each other, and many reſulting duties to be habitually and daily performed[f]. But were nothing of this kind to be performed, nor

---

[f] Ariſtotle here dwells on what is often repeated in other parts of this work, the injuſtice of any kind of authority not derived from nature; the differences between the power or juriſdiction of maſters, fathers, and huſbands, and the evils reſulting from confounding the limits of governments ſpecifically different.

ARISTOTLE's POLITICS.

nor any external effect to be produced, action would not, therefore, cease; nor the purpose of happiness be defeated. The pleasure of intellectual action is the more perfect, in proportion as such action terminates in itself. The geometer who solves his problem, the philosopher who pursues his speculation[g], respectively exercise energies immediately delightful in themselves, independently of any distant end, or any external effect. What can be external to God and the universe? Yet the action of the universe is not therefore suspended; and the Deity[h], who sustains

BOOK IV.

---

[g] τῆς τῆς διανοίας ἀρχιτεκτονικῆς. The word architect in Greek was extended to signify a contriver in general, the man who planned with his head, what others were to execute with their hands. In this sense it is used in the text; of which I have endeavoured to convey the full meaning without adhering literally to the words. How, indeed, can we translate clearly, yet literally, πολὺ μᾶλλον τῆς αὐτοτελοῦς... ἡ γὰρ εὐπραξία τέλος, ὥστι καὶ πρᾶξίς τις. Cicero, in many of the finest passages of his works, expands and adorns Aristotle's thoughts. " Si nobis, cum ex hac vita migraverimus, in beatorum insulis, immortale ævum, ut fabulæ ferunt, degere liceret, quid opus esset eloquentia, cum judicia nulla fierent? aut ipsis etiam virtutibus? nec enim fortitudinis indigeremus, nullo proposito aut labore aut periculo; nec justitia, cum esset nihil, quod appeteretur alieni; nec temperantia, quæ regeret eas, quæ nullæ essent libidines: ne prudentia quidem egeremus, nullo dilectu proposito bonorum et malorum. Una igitur essemus beati cognitione naturæ, et scientia, qua sola etiam deorum est vita laudanda. Ex quo intelligi potest, cetera necessitatis; unum hoc voluptatis." Cicero Fragment. Philosoph. sive Hortensius.

[h] This is conformable to a sublime theological passage in the Treatise de Cœlo, L. ii. c. xiii. p. 465. in which Aristotle, after explaining the Pythagorean system of astronomy, is endeavouring to refute one of its principal doctrines. The Pythagoreans held the element of fire to be more precious than that of earth, and therefore assigned to it the more honourable place, and considered it as the center of the celestial motions. This center being the post of greatest importance in the universe, and requiring the most vigilant watch, they called the fire occupying this post Διὸς φυλακήν, the watch of Jupiter. In opposition to these hypotheses, Aristotle, constantly guided in his conclusions by observation and analogy, takes notice that the center or middle is certainly that which is most important and principal in any system, when it is that by which the system is connected and sustained. But this middle, or rather this principle of

connection,

BOOK IV.

sustains the whole, enjoys the perfection of felicity in exercising his divine energies. By such sublime comparisons we are taught, that the happiness of men, considered collectively or individually, is still to be found within themselves; and that the same kind of life which is the best for each citizen apart, is also the best for the whole community.

Chap. 4.

Transition to the examination of what is absolutely the best commonwealth.

This short preface seemed a necessary prelude to our treatise concerning the best form of government, for it was proper to begin with that which is the most important of all, to which all other things are relative and subservient, and *without* which they are not, all of them taken collectively, of any, the smallest value: we now proceed to examine those external advantages and outward accommodations, which serve as the materials from which the best commonwealths are composed, and as foundations on which the best constitutions are constructed.

That such a commonwealth has limits in point of populousness.

In explaining this subject our suppositions, doubtless, are arbitrary; but good sense requires that they be not impracticable. The statesman, like the shipbuilder or the weaver, requires a due provision of materials; and the better those materials are, the more perfect will be the fruit of his political labour. The materials of the statesman or legislator, are the number and character of his people, the extent and quality of his country. The

connection, will not be found to coincide with what is the middle in point of magnitude, or with what is called the center of gravity. In animals, the connecting and sustaining principle resides not in the middle of their bodies; neither is there good reason for supposing it to be so situated in the universe. Philosophers need not, therefore, give themselves trouble about the safety of the universe, setting a watch at the center of its space or magnitude, but rather to investigate its connecting and sustaining principle, where and of what kind it is. The rest is mere matter; this is the soul of the system: ὃ ποια της ουσιας, "that which gives the system its characteristic form, makes it subsist, and be what it is."

The excellence of a commonwealth, however, is not to be estimated by its populoufnefs or extent, but by its fitnefs for performing its proper functions. Hippocrates was a greater phyfician than many phyficians twice his fize. Slaves, fojourners, and ftrangers render a city populous, but do not make it *great*; neither can this epithet be beftowed, where there are many mechanics and manufacturers, but few citizens completely armed and fkilfully difciplined. The experience of hiftory proves, that ftates of unlimited populoufnefs have never been well regulated. How is it poffible that they fhould, if law be nothing elfe than an arrangement, and if *that* be incapable of arrangement which is indefinite in number or quantity? To harmonife immenfity into fyftem, is the work only of that Divine Power which comprehends the univerfe. Beauty commonly refults from the proportion of quantity; and that which exceeds, as well as that which falls fhort of the due proportion, cannot be called beautiful, either literally or figuratively. There is a limit, therefore, to the magnitude of every whole or fyftem, whether it be the work of nature or of art. A fhip of two furlongs in length, is as unfit for the purpofe of navigation as one of two fpans; and although a community may contain a greater number of individuals than are requifite for thofe purpofes of felf-fufficiency and comfortable fubfiftence, for which commonwealths are inftituted, yet this excefs is not unlimited; fince, when carried beyond certain bounds, it would difqualify the body-politic for its proper functions; rendering it incapable both of prudent command and of prompt obedience. An army reinforced by continual acceffions, would finally ceafe to be an army; for were Stentor fit to be its herald, who would prefume

BOOK IV.

What thefe limits are.

to be its general? What human fkill would undertake to combine its operations, and to harmonife its movements? The fovereign functions of a ftate confift in appointing magiftrates, and in deciding differences. But it is impoffible that magiftrates fhould be judicioufly appointed, or differences fkilfully decided, unlefs the characters and abilities of the citizens be carefully obferved and accurately afcertained: and thefe precautions will not be eafily taken in countries of unbounded populoufnefs; in which, alfo, there is this inconvenience, that ftrangers and fojourners will have an opportunity, through the difficulty of detection, of clandeftinely ufurping the rank of citizens. The magnitude of a commonwealth, though variable, has, therefore, on either fide, its fixed boundaries. It muft be all-fufficient in itfelf for the purpofes of comfortable fubfiftence, and for the reciprocal fupply of mutual wants. But its inhabitants muft not be too numerous to be comprehended at one glance of the ftatefman's eye, and to be conducted in all their actions by the vigilant operation of political difcipline.

Chap. 5.

Concerning the extent and nature of the territory.

Upon fimilar principles we muft decide concerning the extent and nature of the territory. That which is moft fertile in the greateft variety of productions feems entitled to a juft preference, provided this fertility be not fo luxuriant as to encourage indolence or engender voluptuoufnefs [1]. Military men will tell us what makes a country eafy of egrefs yet difficult of invafion.

---

[1] The author here promifes to examine more accurately hereafter, what ought to be the limits of national wealth; but in the work as it now ftands, this promife is not fulfilled. Several other queftions are ftarted by Ariftotle in his Politics, which are not any where anfwered; which proves that performance to have come down to us in an imperfect ftate.

ARISTOTLE's POLITICS.

tion. The territory should also be compactly situate; that it may easily fall within the superintending eye of the statesman or general, that its parts may be able mutually to assist each other, and that the whole may be readily defended.

The maritime position of the capital will greatly contribute to this last purpose; for its inhabitants may speedily embark, and sail to the defence of any part of their possessions that happens to be attacked; and they may attack the enemy in those parts that are most vulnerable. It is also of great importance to commerce, and especially to the transportation of wood and other bulky articles, that the capital be conveniently situate with regard both to the sea, and to the circumjacent land. Yet, in other respects, the vicinity of the sea [k] is attended with dangerous consequences. Men will generally entertain a higher veneration for their hereditary institutions, in proportion as they less communicate with strangers; and the promiscuous crowd of sailors and foreigners, which traffic naturally collects, can scarcely fail to injure the morals of well-educated citizens.

BOOK IV.

Chap. 6.

Whether the capital ought to be situated near the sea.

If

[k] Maritime power was so grossly abused by the ancient republics, that it is continually branded by moralists as producing vile and versatile manners, *ηθη ποικιλα και φαυλα*, Plato de Leg. sub. init. The surprising of defenceless cities, the desolating of unguarded coasts, attacks without glory, and retreats without shame, were represented as operations not less inconsistent with true courage, than incompatible with humanity and justice. Isocrat. Orat. de Pace, & Plato ubi supra. The ancient republics entrusted arms to those only who had a property to defend. Their soldiers were levied from the first classes, or privileged orders, of society. But sailors were taken from the promiscuous crowd, and generally from the meanest populace. This practice, which prevailed equally in Greece and Rome, was founded on sound policy. The exertions of sailors, being naturally directed against foreign enemies, are less likely to prove dangerous to the internal stability of government.

VOL. II.   G G

BOOK IV.
How far commerce ought to be cultivated, and how its inconveniences may be remedied.

If we cultivate commerce, it must be for accommodation only, not for gain: our citizens are not to degrade themselves into brokers and carriers, nor to squander away in the arts of luxury that labour which may be far more profitably as well as more honourably employed, in the cultivation of the soil and in the production of necessaries; the occupation which is of all others the best adapted to the bulk of mankind, the most favourable to the health of their minds and bodies, and therefore the best fitted to promote national prosperity. Our commerce must be limited to the purpose of supplying our domestic wants; and in order to attain this purpose without endangering the purity of our domestic manners, we may imitate the example of those cities and countries which have their decks and harbours enclosed by walls and fortifications, and separated at a due distance from the capital; thus permitting the importation of foreign commodities, but intercepting the contagion of foreign vices.

Concerning naval power.

Naval power is peculiarly useful for the purposes of intimidating our enemies and protecting our allies; but its extent ought to be commensurate with the rank which a state aspires to hold in the political system. A people ambitious of command must be provided with a strong navy; and this may be equipped without raising the naval crowd to the condition of citizens. Even on shipboard, those who brandish the spear must maintain their superiority over those who handle the oar; and the latter, in whatever number they may be wanted, will easily be raised from the mass of the peasants and labourers. Such is the practice of several wise states, particularly of that of Heraclæa, which maintains a numerous fleet of gallies, yet preserves its citizens untainted by the contagious profligacy of mariners. Thus

Thus much may suffice concerning the extent of the city and territory, and concerning the magnitude of the naval force. We formerly assigned due limits to the number of the citizens, and now proceed to consider what ought to be their genius and character; a question that will be best solved by passing in review, and examining, those nations of Greece, and of the world in general, which appear to be most worthy of our esteem.

The inhabitants of Europe, and of most cold countries, abound in strength and courage; but their intellectual powers are feeble or defective. They enjoy liberty, but are unacquainted with good polity; and though capable of maintaining their independence, are unworthy of aspiring to empire. The inhabitants of Asia, on the contrary, are artful and ingenious, but mean-spirited and dastardly. They have, therefore, always been, and continue to this day, either subjects or slaves. But the intermediate situation of the Greeks seems to have happily blended in their character the virtues of courage and prudence, and to have formed them for thinking calmly, yet feeling strongly. They enjoy, therefore, the double advantage of liberty and laws; and are qualified for ruling the world, were they happily confederate under one form of government[1]. The Greeks, however, are not all equally conspicuous for this happy

BOOK IV.

Chap. 7.

Of the character resulting from a cold climate; from a warm climate; from a temperate climate;

---

[1] Aristotle maintained in a former chapter that a commonwealth had its limits in point of populousness; and endeavoured to point out with sufficient accuracy for all practical purposes what these limits were. In the passage before us he says, γενος δυναμενον αρχειν παντων, μιας τυγχανον πολιτειας. "That the Greeks would be able to command all nations, if they had the same form of government." In fact, the extreme difference in the forms of government in Greece, was the great obstacle to their national union in one political confederacy; which is the thing here intended by Aristotle, since, according to the principles above explained, Greece was far too populous to be happily united in one commonwealth.

ARISTOTLE's POLITICS.

BOOK IV.

The best moral materials for legiſlation.

happy temperament, and the manly policy which is its natural reſult. In ſome nations the character is rude and ſhapeleſs; one quality being deficient, while another is redundant: but in whatever people ardent courage moſt naturally harmoniſes with cool combination, and dignity of ſentiment with energy of intellect, that people muſt be conſidered as the beſt materials for legiſlation, and the fitteſt to be moulded into a virtuous commonwealth. It is ſaid by ſome writers, that the military guardians of ſtates ought, like faithful dogs, to ſhew themſelves mild towards thoſe whom they know, but fierce towards ſtrangers. Yet true magnanimity is incapable of ferocity, and is never moved even to aſperity, but in reſentment of injuſtice or inſult. When theſe provocations proceed from friends and acquaintances, our anger is enhanced by this circumſtance. "Waſt thou not tormented by thy friends?" ſays Archilochus, to whet his ſatire; and it is reaſonable that men ſhould be doubly offended when they meet with injury and neglect, where they had a right to expect friendſhip and regard. Hence the proverbs, "cruel are the wars of brothers;" and "thoſe who are incapable of anger and reſentment, muſt alſo be incapable of friendſhip and gratitude;" and indeed all thoſe affections originate in one and the ſame ſource[1]. Thus much may ſuffice concerning the qualities moſt uſeful towards the formation of good citizens; for in practical matters, ſcientific accuracy is neither attainable nor requiſite.

Chap. 8.

Diſtinction between the integral parts of a ſtate, and

Every whole or ſyſtem, whether it be the work of nature or of art, may require many things for its ſubſiſtence which are not to be numbered among its conſtituent parts. Food is neceſſary for ſupporting animal life, but is not a part of thoſe animals who conſume it. Land and other objects of property, whether

[1] See vol. i. b. vi. c. ii. p. 288. & ſeq.

ARISTOTLE's POLITICS.

whether inanimate or endued with life, are neceſſary for upholding ſtates, yet none of theſe poſſeſſions or inſtruments form any part of the commonwealth; which, as defined above, is the aſſociation of equals for the purpoſe of living happily, that is, of living virtuouſly, for happineſs has been proved to conſiſt in the exerciſe of virtuous energies; though men, indeed, ſeek to find it in very different purſuits, hunting vain ſhadows, which diverſify without correcting their purpoſes of life, and vary without improving their forms of government.

the things neceſſary for its ſubſiſtence.

The things eſſential to every ſtate, whether as conſtituent parts or as concomitants ᵐ, may be reduced to the ſix following heads. 1. Food, the great want of mankind. 2. Arts, becauſe to effect the comfort of life is a work requiring many inſtruments. 3. Arms, for citizens muſt be armed to prevent domeſtic diſorders, and ward off foreign violence. 4. Money, as the medium of exchange, and meaſure of value, and neceſſary in the exigences of war as well as in the operations of commerce. 5. An eſtabliſhment for the functions of religion ⁿ, which are of all functions the firſt in dignity. 6. Councils of deliberation, and courts of juſtice, which are of all eſtabliſhments the moſt neceſſary. Any of theſe objects being wanting, the commonwealth is imperfect, or incapable of anſwering its end. In every commonwealth, therefore, there muſt be huſbandmen, artiſans, ſoldiers, merchants, prieſts, and judges °.

Enumeration of the things neceſſary for the ſubſiſtence of a commonwealth.

A queſtion

ᵐ The author dwells here on this diſtinction, which is fully explained elſewhere.

ⁿ If we except the French republic, the Chineſe are the only great nation who, according to recent accounts, ever diſſented from Ariſtotle in this particular. See Staunton's Embaſſy to China, vol. ii. p. 101.

° Under the name of judges he means to comprehend, as in the following chapter, το βελουμενον περι των συμφερόντων, as well as το κρινον περι των δικαιων, "thoſe who deliberate and determine in queſtions of public expediency," as well as "thoſe who examine into and adjuſt the controverſies between individuals."

BOOK IV.
Chap. 9.

In the best commonwealth, those employed in mean and mercenary labour not to rank as citizens.

A queſtion ariſes, whether in that moſt perfect community of which human nature is ſuſceptible, the citizens ſhould aſſume indifferently, and as their occaſions may require, all thoſe various characters; or whether certain employments be not inconſiſtent with the habitual exerciſe of thoſe virtuous energies, which we have proved to be the principal end and aim of every political partnerſhip. It appears at firſt ſight, that a life of mechanical drudgery, or a life of haggling commerce, is totally incompatible with that dignified life which it is our wiſh that our citizens ſhould lead, and totally adverſe to that generous elevation of mind with which it is our ambition to inſpire them. The mere trade of huſbandry, the aſſiduous labour and minute attentions which it requires, would be deſtructive of that ſecure leiſure which is eſſential to the formation of their characters; and ſuch ſordid cares would impede and obſtruct the generous and manly exertions by which virtue is diſplayed and confirmed. Men, habitually addicted to the lowly purſuits of providing neceſſaries and accumulating gain, are unfit members of our republic, becauſe they are incapable of reliſhing thoſe enjoyments in which we have ſuppoſed its chief happineſs to conſiſt. They are to be claſſed with things neceſſary to the commonwealth, but not to be ranked with its citizens; for the beſt and moſt perfect commonwealth muſt provide for the happineſs of all its members, and a commonwealth founded on virtue cannot provide for the happineſs of men who are but feebly touched by her charms. Such men, therefore, though neceſſary to a commonwealth, are not parts of the commonwealth, any more than food, though neceſſary to an animal, is part of an animal; or than the inſtruments employed in producing any work, are themſelves parts of that work. The productive labour of

peaſants

ARISTOTLE's POLITICS.

peasants and artisans, how necessary soever to the purposes of outward accommodation and comfortable subsistence, is not, therefore, to be confounded nor classed with the high political functions of soldiers, priests, and magistrates[o].

It remains, therefore, to examine, whether arms, religion, and magistracy ought to be regarded as things specifically different, and of which the offices ought to be separately exercised by distinct professions. In every good government the military ought, doubtless, to depend on the civil power; but will men bearing arms be contented with a condition of unalterable dependence? Or will those who feel their ability to change the constitution at pleasure, submit for ever to a political arrangement disgraceful to themselves? Such patient resignation cannot reasonably be expected, nor can that which is contrary to reason be requisite to good government. The capacity for exercising military and civil functions depends on qualities that are variable, because they result from a variable cause, the changeable powers of man in the different periods of human life. Strength, agility, and courage attain their highest perfection at that period of youth when the body reaches its prime; foresight, temper, and wisdom do not acquire their full maturity, but with the acme and perfection of the mind. The *same* persons, therefore, but at *different* periods of their lives, must exercise military and civil functions; and thus each class of citizens will perform that office for which it is best qualified, and to which it is best entitled. It remains only to speak of the priesthood. This solemn function must, doubtless, be exercised by men of

BOOK IV.

What are the proper employments of citizens.

That their employments ought to be distributed according to the different periods of human life.

the

[o] In this passage I have changed the order of the sentences, the better to prepare the modern reader for a decision, which to him must appear harsh in the extreme, though it could not be viewed in that light by the readers of antiquity.

the moſt reſpectable claſs. But to perform with decency and dignity the rites of religion, requires not any violent exertion of body or mind. Such honourable duties, therefore, ought to be reſerved for the occupation and the reward of declining years; and thoſe who have ſpent their youth and their manhood in more active and ſtrenuous cares, ought to dedicate their old age to the calm ceremonies of religion, and finally to repoſe in the peaceful ſanctuaries of the gods.

Chap. 10.

That the wiſeſt nations of antiquity acknowledged the diſtinction between citizens on the one hand, and peaſants and artiſans on the other.

The diſtinction between the conſtituent parts of a commonwealth, and things merely neceſſary for its ſubſiſtence, remounts to the higheſt antiquity. Both in Egypt and in Crete [p], the ſoldiers have long been, what they continue to this day, a claſs altogether diſtinct from the peaſants. Seſoſtris is ſaid to have eſtabliſhed this arrangement in Egypt; and Minos, in Crete. The *ſyſſitia* or public tables, in that iſland, are thought to have been inſtituted as early as the time of Minos; and ſimilar eſtabliſhments are ſaid to have taken place in Italy at a ſtill earlier date. For the hiſtorians of that country inform us, that Œnotria received the name of Italy from king Italus; a name comprehending the coaſt between the Scyllatine and Lametine gulphs; which are oppoſite to each other, and diſtant by land only half a day's journey [q]. Italus is ſaid to have changed the Œnotrians from ſhepherds into huſbandmen, and to have given them other laws relative to their new mode of life, and particularly thoſe regulating the public tables; which remain in force among his deſcendants to this day. For northwards, from the country firſt called Italy, the Opici and Auſonians

---

[p] This chapter may be conſidered as an illuſtration of the principles eſtabliſhed in the preceding, from the hiſtory of thoſe nations who diffuſed religion, laws, and civility over the ancient world.

[q] Vid. Cluverii Ital. Antiq. p. 1290. & ſeq.

Aufonians extend themfelves, on one hand, towards the Tufcan fea; but on the other hand, the Chaonians, an Œnotrian tribe, have ftretched towards the Ionian fea and Iapygia. Among them the eftablifhment of *fyffitia* firft prevailed, and from them it was adopted by other nations. But the feparation of citizens and peafants prevailed much earlier; for the age of Sefoftris long preceded that of Minos. It is probable that political, like all other inventions, have been often difcovered and often loft; and that many inftitutions have been laid afide and revived, times without number. Men having acquired neceffaries, naturally feek accommodations; and having provided for the ftrength and fupport of their political edifices, they fet themfelves to improve and embellifh them. The ftyle of fuperfluous ornaments varies with the caprice by which they are produced; but there are ornaments connected with ufe, which ought to be found in every well-regulated commonwealth; and why we take the *fyffitia* to be of this kind will be afterwards explained.

We are now to fpeak of the diftribution and character of the peafants and artifans, which, according to our principles, muft be partly the property of the public and partly the property of particular citizens; for although our republic rejects the community of goods as repreffive to exertion, and even deftructive of virtue, yet wifhing poffeffions to be ftrictly appropriated, we wifh that their ufes be freely communicated; that according to the proverb all things may be common among friends; and that no one of the citizens may long continue in want of any object with which another can conveniently fupply him. The citizens, therefore, are to be maintained at public tables,

Of the diftribution and character of the peafants and artifans, and that liberty ought to be propofed as the reward of all flaves worthy to enjoy it.

the expences of which, as well as those of the sacrifices and religious festivals, are to be supplied from the lands laboured in common by the public slaves; for men of small incomes could not contribute sufficiently for these purposes, and at the same time support easily the charges of their private families. The territory, therefore, ought to consist partly of common, and partly of private property; and each of these ought to be again subdivided, since the common is destined to answer two purposes, and to supply the expences of religion and those of the *syssitia*; and since the lands of each citizen ought to lie partly in the vicinity of the capital, and partly on the frontier, or, if united in one mass, ought to have some situation nearly equidistant from those extremes. Both justice and expediency require such a distribution; for advantages and inconveniences will thus be more fairly balanced among the private citizens, and the state itself will be thus rendered more unanimous in public deliberations and military enterprises. As possessions are now arranged, one portion of the community is commonly too much, and another too little, alarmed at the prospect of a foreign war; wherefore some states have enacted that landholders living on the frontier should not be allowed to vote in questions concerning war and peace, because such persons are likely to sacrifice to private interest the advantage and honour of their country. Such ought to be the distribution of the territory, and those who cultivate it ought (if we can have them to our wish) to be slaves of various extractions, different in manners and endowments, but all destitute of courage. But if this cannot be obtained, let them be the barbarians in our neighbourhood, of strong bodies and servile minds. How slaves are to be treated we shall afterwards explain; and also assign our reasons why liberty ought to be the reward of all slaves universally ' who approve themselves worthy of obtaining and capable of enjoying it.

We have explained what is the best situation of the capital, both with respect to the sea and to the contiguous territory. But its situation ought also to be relative to health, which depends chiefly on good air and good water; and calculated for the enjoyment of peace, and for safety in war. The circumstances, therefore, that ought to determine the position of our capital are these four, air, water, comfort, and security. In Greece, cities open to the east are deemed the most healthful; and next to that, a northern aspect is preferred, chiefly for the sake of coolness. A capital situate to our wish, ought to abound in salubrious fountains; and if that advantage cannot be obtained, preparations should be made for receiving the rain water

BOOK IV.

Chap. 11.

The situation of the capital ought to be determined by the circumstances most conducive to wealth, comfort, and security.

The circumstances most conducive to health;

' The most solid objection to slavery is that of its perpetuity; that a human being, whatever may be his acquirements and his merits, should never be the director of his own conduct; and how well qualified soever he may become to govern himself, should be perpetually and unalterably subjected to the authority of another. This objection forcibly struck Aristotle at a time when the lower classes of men in all countries and under all forms of government universally subsisted in the condition of servitude. It is to be regretted that we have not his reasons at length why emancipation, the practice of which was so common in the ancient world, should not depend on the will of individual masters, but should result from the general will of the community, granting on certain conditions, and after a certain time, liberty to slaves. It may be objected indeed, that a cruel or unjust master would be ready to impose a double task on those who were likely soon to escape from his hands. But this is answered by saying, that according to Aristotle's principles such a man was not qualified, and therefore not entitled to be a master; and that slaves in the ancient republics at least were under the protection of the laws, which restrained or punished the cruelty or injustice of masters. See above, b. i. c. iii. p. 33.

BOOK IV.

water in copious refervoirs; and the purest fprings fhould be fet apart for the fuftenance of human life, under ftrict prohibitions of employing them for any lefs important purpofe. This law ought not to be regarded as frivolous: for good health depends chiefly on the quality of thofe things of which we make the moft frequent ufe; and fuch manifeftly are air and water.

to comfort and fecurity.

The nature of fortifications and fortreffes is relative to the nature of government, and ought to vary with the alteration of its forms. Lofty and impregnable citadels beft fuit monarchies and oligarchies. The equal defence of walls, guarding with impartial juftice the fafety of the people at large, is beft adapted to republics and democracies; and the authority of ariftocratical nobles will be moft fecurely maintained, neither by walls nor citadels, but by a number of well-fortified caftles. With regard to the form and diftribution of manfions and ftreets, the modern ftyle of building, introduced by the architect Hippodamus[s], is moft favourable to health and pleafure, and moft convenient for all the occupations and purpofes of civil life. But his ftraight lines and fpacious openings impair ftrength while they embellifh beauty, and render his cities eafily pervious to an invading enemy. For the purpofes of war, ftreets ought to be winding and intricate, obftructed by impediments and entangled by perplexities. But that cities may anfwer the ends both of war and peace, they fhould be at once ftrong and elegant; and this complex object will be beft effected by imitating the labours of the gardener in planting his quincunx, where refiftance combines with arrangement, and where perplexity refults from uniformity itfelf. There is more folly than magnanimity in the opinion, that cities ought not to be walled. True

[s] See b. ii. c. vi. p. 95. & feq.

True courage will not reject the affistance of art under manifest inequality of strength; and as missile weapons and battering engines have been perfected by the ingenuity of the present age, the safety of cities requires that the science of defence should keep pace with that of attack. The Lacedæmonians and others who have disdained walls as the refuge of cowardice, have dearly paid for their temerity.

By good regulations, fortified cities may enjoy all the advantages of those that are open to the country on every side; and the bulwarks and battlements may be converted into agreeable ornaments, scenes of pleasing recreation to the citizens, but of threatening aspect to hostile neighbours. The guard rooms may serve as halls for the syssitia or common tables; near to which may be worshipped, in one edifice, those Gods whose temples neither laws or oracles command to be separated, at a certain distance from all other buildings. This edifice, erected in honour of religion in general, ought to be as lofty and conspicuous as its purpose is useful and dignified, of awful magnificence and commanding strength. Around this temple a forum ought to be formed and inclosed, similar to that of Thessaly, called the liberal rendezvous. This spacious inclosure is not to be encumbered by the shops of artificers, nor polluted by the tricks of traffic. Neither peasant nor mechanic is ever to enter its pure precincts, unless summoned by the magistrate; for it is consecrated as the scene of liberal converse and manly exercise; where persons, classed by their ages, are to invigorate and confirm their powers by emulous contention; and where youth is to be trained to modesty and manliness, under the vigilant superintendence of virtuous old age. The square employed for the market-place, is to be totally distinct; it ought to

BOOK IV.

Chap. 12.

The ornaments of the capital.

The liberal rendezvous.

The market-place, and courts of justice.

ARISTOTLE's POLITICS.

BOOK IV.

The districts and townships.

to be easily accessible to imports by sea, and transportations by land; the officers of police and the courts of justice are to assemble in its neighbourhood; it is destined for business and necessity, as the liberal forum is destined for exercise and enjoyment. The districts and townships are to be regulated after the model of the capital; but on this subject it is not necessary to enlarge: to contrive good arrangements is easy; the difficulty lies in reducing them to practice. Good intentions are sufficient for the first; the second requires the co-operation of good fortune.

Chap. 13.

Transition to the character of the citizens of the best commonwealth.

Having thus explained the external accommodations of our commonwealth, we next proceed to examine what ought to be the genius and character of its citizens; and to explain what are the means most likely to inspire that genius, and impress that character, which will best qualify them for enjoying political happiness. The perfection of human felicity requires that we should choose the best ends, and employ the best means for attaining them. These objects sometimes harmonise, and are sometimes discordant; the means being bad while the ends are good, or the ends being bad while the means are good; and sometimes neither the one nor the other are worthy of approbation; which happens when the means are not likely to attain the end proposed, and when this end itself, though attained, is not likely to promote the great ultimate purpose of good or happiness. This takes place in physic, when the physician errs both in ascertaining that habit of body which is most conducive to the health of his patient, and in appreciating that mode of life, that diet, and exercise which are fitted to superinduce the habit which he has erroneously preferred. But the felicity of men depends not entirely on human efforts; for

nature

nature or fortune muſt alſo contribute their ſhare. Yet to minds confirmed in virtue, few accommodations are requiſite; while ſuch is the depravity of ſome characters, that the moſt favourable circumſtances only heighten their wretchedneſs; and to think with the vulgar, that external advantages alone can produce happineſs, is not leſs abſurd than to call the lyre a muſician, and to aſcribe *that* to the inſtrument which ought to be referred to the artiſt. A good man will, on every occaſion, act handſomely; and perform his duty under poverty and diſeaſe, as well as in health and proſperity. A juſt judge will condemn guilt as well as reward merit. Yet the happineſs of a good man and the juſt judge is connected with the latter circumſtances rather than with the former; becauſe in the latter no painful conflict is required, but the mind is left to the free exerciſe of virtuous energies, unclogged by difficulties [1] and unretarded by obſtacles. In forming our republic, we may, therefore, ſuppoſe the work of fortune to be done to our hands; our buſineſs is to teach the legiſlator how to perform his duty; or, in other words, how to render his commonwealth virtuous and happy.

BOOK IV.

What this character ought to be.

Happineſs depends on virtue; and virtue depends on nature, cuſtom, and reaſon. That we are formed capable of virtue, and ſuſceptible of certain qualities of mind and body, is the bounty of Nature, which has made us of the human kind. But habit can improve or pervert theſe natural advantages. Other animals

Chap. 14.

Analyſis of education.

---

[1] This doctrine is more fully explained in thoſe paſſages of the Ethics which treat of happineſs. What the author calls in the text the χρησις αρετης τελεια, and the χρησις ἁπλωσεως; " abſolute and conditional virtue;" is ſufficiently explained by the examples given in the tranſlation. Happineſs conſiſts rather in ſuch actions as are virtuous *ſimply and abſolutely*, than in ſuch as neceſſarily imply ſome pre-exiſting evil, which they are exerted to remedy.

BOOK IV.

animals march uniformly in the tract of nature; some few are guided also by custom; but man only is disciplined by reason; and may be persuaded even to change bad habits, by the influence of example and the conviction of argument. From these two united, the power of education results; that forming and preserving power without which the best political fabrics would soon crumble into dust; and which we now proceed to explain, having formerly described what ought to be the natural dispositions of those most susceptible of its benefits.

That education ought to be public and uniform.

First of all, this education ought, according to our principles, to be uniform; for it is our aim to render the citizens at large virtuous and happy, and to qualify all of them for the offices of government as well as for the duties of obedience. Were one portion of the community as far distinguished above the rest, as we believe the gods and heroes to be exalted above men, or as Scylax says, "that the kings of India are superior to their subjects, in the virtues of mind and body," it would be proper that these dignified races or families should be invested with hereditary and unalterable authority; and, for this purpose, trained and educated in a manner peculiar to themselves, and relative to that pre-eminent rank which they were for ever destined to hold. But since such races or families are no where to be found in these parts of the world, justice concurs with good policy, in requiring that the citizens should rule by vicarious succession; and how this ought to be done, nature herself sufficiently indicates. According to the order of Nature, some men are young while others are old. This distinction of age is the least invidious of all distinctions; and it is well observed, that those only are qualified to command, who have been skilfully trained to obey. Of the command exercised by

despots

despots we do not here speak; *their* government is useful only to themselves, to their families and favourites; but the government of a commonwealth is instituted for the benefit of the governed; who in youth will cheerfully submit to many talks and many services, which would be disgraceful if performed merely for the sake of others, but which are ennobled by their tendency to promote the improvement of those on whom they are imposed.

BOOK IV.

Since the education of the citizens ought then to be uniform, and since we formerly proved that the virtues and happiness of the citizen coincide with those of the man, we have next to inquire wherein the perfection of the individual consists. In the human soul there are two distinct parts, one of which is endowed with reason, and the other, though not possessing reason in itself, is framed capable of listening to, and obeying its dictates. On the disposition of these two parts, the virtues and excellencies of human nature depend; but in which of the two the ultimate end or chief happiness of man is placed, will not be difficult for those acquainted with our philosophy to decide. From the works of art and nature submitted to our observation, it it easy to remark that things which are worse are always made for the sake of those that are better; that this order is never on any occasion reversed; but how long soever may be the series of means and ends, that all the intermediate ends finally terminate and center in some one great and ultimate purpose. But that part of the soul which is endowed with reason, is manifestly better than that which is merely capable of obeying its dictates; the operations of the one, therefore, must be proportionably better than those of the other; and the exercise of the latter must be considered as merely preparatory to the

What are the ends at which it ought to aim.

energies of the former. The energies of reason or intellect may either be employed in comtemplation, or applied to the practice of life. It is, therefore, theoretical or practical; the former engaged in the pursuit and contemplation of truth and beauty, the latter occupied in the acquisition of things necessary or useful to ourselves or others. Human life is thus divided between war and peace, business and leisure, the occupations imposed by necessity, and the enjoyments attending that refined pleasure which accompanies and completes our intellectual energies. In his system of education, the legislator ought to have respect, doubtless, to all these objects; yet never to forget that war is undertaken for the sake of peace, and business for the sake of leisure; and that the occupations of utility and necessity ultimately terminate in the pursuit of beauty and truth.

That these ends have been mistaken by Lycurgus and other legislators.

But in opposition to these unalterable maxims, the most famed legislators of Greece have illiberally perferred things useful to things honourable, and have been illiberally and absurdly praised by Thibro, and other writers, for this preposterous preference of means to ends. Lycurgus is celebrated for forming a nation of conquerors; his laws were in force when the Lacedæmonians were defeated and subdued. Yet had his design been successful, it would not have been either commendable or profitable, since the unjust dominion exercised by Sparta over her neighbours and allies would have taught some second, but more lucky Pausanias[r], to render himself the tyrant of his country. Absolute power over equals is desirable neither for individuals nor states; nor ought war ever to be waged in order to obtain it. Yet the military virtues will be cultivated by

[r] See History of Ancient Greece, vol. ii. c. xii. p. 56. & seq.

by every wife republic; firft, for its own defence; fecondly, for acquiring a dominion juft and lawful, becaufe advantageous even to the vanquifhed; and thirdly, for reducing into flavery nations incapable of living fafely under any more honourable condition. Experience juftifies thefe affertions. Moft ambitious nations have been faved for a while by war, but finally ruined by conqueft. Their characters rufted like iron, and in peace loft their fplendor. Their misfortunes are chargeable on a faulty legiflation, which had not taught them to enjoy leifure.

But, according to the proverb, leifure is not made for flaves. This beft bleffing muft be acquired and preferved by ardent enterprife and unbending fortitude; fince a community deftitute of courage and impatient of fuffering, muft fpeedily fall under the yoke of fome more warlike neighbour. The active and ftubborn virtues of war are neceffary, therefore, as remote means towards enjoying the happinefs of peace; but they are neceffary barely as means, for the enjoyment itfelf muft be fought in wifdom. The virtues of juftice and temperance are neceffary under all circumftances, but chiefly in peace and profperity; for the hardfhips of war are a fchool of difcipline, whereas the indulgences of peace naturally engender infolence; fo that were the fable of the Fortunate Iflands to be realifed, their inhabitants would of all men moft require the affiftance of wifdom, juftice, and temperance; fince, deftitute of thofe virtues, they would be of all men the moft wretched. Our commonwealth, therefore, is not to be moulded after the narrow Lacedæmonian model, nor are our citizens to be great only in war; they are to be chiefly illuftrious in peace; and to render them fuch, muft be the work of early and affiduous culture.

BOOK IV.

Chap. 15.

Our commonwealth to be formed on a more extenfive plan; great in war, but chiefly illuftrious in peace.

BOOK IV.

This must be the work of education. The order in which it is to be conducted.

In explaining how this culture ought to be conducted, we must again observe, that man being compounded of soul and body, the soul itself is composed of a rational and irrational part; and that those parts of our complex frame which are first in their origin, are last in dignity. The body is made before the soul, and the desires and passions of the soul, constituting its irrational part, appear in young children and infants long before the age of reason. Yet the rational part is that which properly constitutes the man, being the end and perfection of his nature. With reference to this end, therefore, culture should begin early to operate, by means of custom and habit, on the appetites and passions; so that when reason first dawns, these subordinate powers may already be disposed to acknowledge her authority, and to mingle with her in due time, in the sweetest harmony. Such then is the order in which education must be conducted. The body is first to be formed, and that for the sake of the soul; and then the irrational part of the soul is to be disciplined, and that for the sake of the rational.

Chap. 16.

Importance of the question respecting the age fittest for entering into wedlock.

According to this system of arrangement, the first care of the legislator ought to consist in ascertaining the age and qualities of persons fit to be joined in wedlock. Persons so united, ought to descend together into the vale of years; and their powers of producing beings like themselves ought together to co-exist, uniformly to decay, and nearly at the same time to cease: the contrary of which seldom fails to occasion much domestic uneasiness. Respect also should be had to the succession of children, who ought neither to be too remotely distant, nor too closely to tread on the heels of their parents. When the former takes place, parents can expect to derive but little

little benefit from their children; and when the latter is the case, children will seldom entertain much reverence for their parents, who, being nearly their equals in age, will be considered as on a foot of equality in all other respects; and with whom, therefore, they will be often ready to differ in matters of opinion, or to quarrel about matters of interest. It happens most fortunately that all these ends and purposes may be attained and answered by precisely the same means, the coupling parties in wedlock at the proper and seasonable age.

About the age of seventy, men commonly cease to be husbands; and after the age of fifty, women seldom become mothers. The times of entering into marriage for the different sexes ought to be respectively regulated by these extreme limits; which will reduce the fittest marriageable age of women to eighteen, and of men to thirty-seven, a little more or less; for the propriety of practical matters consists not in an indivisible point. In consequence of this regulation, the contracting parties, in that which forms one main object of their union, will enjoy the happiest correspondence, their powers will simultaniously flourish, and simultaniously decay. Premature conjunctions produce imperfect offspring, females rather than males, and those feeble in make, and short in stature. That this happens in the human race as well as in other animals, is visible in the puny inhabitants of countries where early marriages prevail. But to the female sex premature wedlock is peculiarly dangerous, since in consequence of anticipating the commands of nature, many of them suffer greatly in childbirth, and many of them die. The evil reaches the mind itself, for early habitudes make the most indelible impressions; and the germ of voluptuousness too speedily expanded, will penetrate the whole frame, and for ever vitiate the character. In males, premature

BOOK IV.

premature venery feems to ftunt the growth: the animal ought to be itfelf perfect before it is duly qualified to propagate its kind. Let the fexes, therefore, contract marriage at the periods above determined. They will be then refpectively in the acme and full bloom of their age. The correfpondence of their powers will render their defires harmonious, and their lives happy. They will grow old together; and, as fuch feafonable marriages will for the moft part be foon productive of progeny, the fon will be advancing to perfect manhood when the father is verging to the extremity of old age.

The fitteft feafon and beft habit for the purpofe of wedlock.

Winter is the fitteft feafon for confummating marriage; and, as naturalifts tell us, when the wind blows from the north[a]. The ftate of body moft likely to fupply the commonwealth with good children, is neither the artificial brawninefs of prizefighters, nor a frame emaciated and worn out by abftemioufnefs or fatigue; but a conftitution equally remote from thefe vitious extremes, invigorated by fuch exercifes as the life of a free citizen requires; not exceffive, but frequent; various, not violent.

Attention due to pregnant women for the fake of their minds and of their offspring.

Thefe obfervations are applicable to both fexes; but of women in pregnancy particular care is to be taken that they do not indulge themfelves in indolence, nor enfeeble their offspring by ufing too thin a diet. For the prevention of both evils, (fince exercife will ftrengthen appetite,) the legiflator fhould enjoin his countrywomen, when pregnant, to walk daily to the temples, and pay their devotions to the powers prefiding over childbirth. At the fame time the female mind, in this delicate fituation, fhould be diligently attended to, neither foured by neglect

[a] This explains why the governors of the winds were invoked by the Greeks wifhing to have children: a thing which archbifhop Potter thinks extraordinary and unaccountable: " What bufinefs the winds have in generation is difficult to imagine." Potter's Antiq. vol. ii. c. xiv. p. 318.

neglect nor ruffled by paſſion, but amuſed by images of pleaſure, and ſoothed into unalterable ſerenity; for plants do not more certainly indicate the ſoil from which they ſpring, than children receive and reflect the temper of their parents.

Concerning the expoſition of children, let it be enacted that nothing that has life ſhall be deſtroyed unleſs it be defective in its members, or grofsly deformed in its ſhape. Yet means muſt be taken to prevent exceſſive population¹; and, as one period of life is unripe, ſo another is too far decayed for the purpoſes of wedlock. Thoſe who diſtribute the epochs of life into periods of ſeven years, aſſign fifty for the acmè of the mind. Four or five years after fifty, a man, therefore, ſhould abſtain from the rites of love merely for the ſake of offspring, which would probably enjoy neither vigour of mind nor health of body. Let the rites of the marriage-bed be at all times equally reſpected by the huſband and by the wife; but ſhould the huſband, during the period limited for giving children to the republic, be convicted of a breach of chaſtity, let him be puniſhed with public infamy, and thoſe evils which follow in its train.

The nouriſhment of children is bountifully ſupplied by nature in the copious exuberance of milk, which the example of warlike nations, and even of wild animals, proves to be of all kinds of food the moſt congenial to the body, and the moſt favourable

Concerning the expoſition of children and chaſtity.

Chap. 17.

Concerning the nouriſhment of children, their exerciſes and treatment.

¹ το δι ὅτιν και το μη, διωρισμινοι τη αισθησει και το ζην ιςαι. Ariſtotle would have the exuberance of population to be reſtrained, yet nothing that has life to be deſtroyed, unleſs marked or depraved by exceſſive deformity. In the career of his ſtern deciſions he ſtops ſhort of the unrelenting Chineſe: "among whom habit ſeems to have familiariſed a notion that life only becomes truly precious, and inattention to it criminal, after it has continued long enough to be endowed with a mind and ſentiment; but that mere dawning exiſtence may be ſuffered to be loſt without ſcruple, though it cannot without reluctance." Staunton's Embaſſy to China, v. ii. p. 153.

BOOK IV.

favourable to its growth and strength. Wine, doubtless, gives spirits and vigour, but the use of wine in children might be productive of disease. All young animals delight in freely exerting their natural motions; and this instinctive propensity is equally strong and equally salutary to infants. Care, however, must be taken that their delicate members be not distorted through too eager a contention: in this view various mechanical contrivances have been invented, and proved by experience to be of important use. Infants should be early accustomed to bear cold; which will invigorate their strength, and gradually prepare their bodies for resisting the hardships of war. Some barbarous nations plunge their new-born infants into rivers. The Celts expose their children in thin coverings to the northern blast; and whatever is to be effected by custom, should be begun early, and carried on gradually. In the present case, the first experiments will not be attended with danger, for the natural heat of children fits them for surmounting the impressions of cold. Such are the attentions required by our first years.

In the following age, and until children have completed their fifth year, no painful task should be imposed, and no violent exertion required from the mind or body, lest health might be injured, and growth obstructed. All that utility demands, is to keep their faculties awake, and to prevent them from contracting any habits of sloth; which will be best effected by such plays and sports as are neither illiberal, nor fatiguing, nor sedentary. The tales and fables which are told them, ought to be written, at least examined, by the magistrate who presides over education; and their playful amusements ought, in general, to be imitations of those serious transactions in which they will be concerned when called to the business of life. Laws and contrivances

trivances have been devised and framed for preventing those compressions of the breath and those exertions of the voice which are frequent with young children; but all such attempts to counteract the designs of nature, we totally disapprove. The contentions of the breath and spirits are known by experience to invigorate the exertions of men; and the crying of children, which occasions similar intensions and remissions of their organs, is equally salutary to them, promoting their growth and augmenting their strength.

Until the age of seven complete, the school for children ought to be the father's house; but during this early period, they must be strictly guarded against the infectious communication of slaves; no illiberal gesture is to be presented to their sight; no illiberal image is to be suggested to their fancy. Lewd indecency of language ought to be reprobated and punished in every well-regulated city; for, from using filthy expressions without shame, there is an easy transition to the practising of filthy actions without disgust. Obscene statues or pictures are never to be seen but in the temples of those divinities, whom the law enjoins to be worshipped under such emblems, by fathers, in behalf of their wives and families; nor ought children to be spectators of comedy or farce, before the age of admission to the public tables, when education, if well directed, will have confirmed their morals. Theodorus, the celebrated tragic actor, made it a rule never to allow any player, how inferior soever might be his talents, to occupy the stage before him; observing, that mankind were always governed by first impressions. If that be the case, how much care should be taken to render the first impressions of children favourable to virtue, and to make them regard as strange and monstrous what-

BOOK IV.

ever might fow the feeds of malice, cruelty, or turpitude? Let them behold in their tender years, thofe honourable occupations, and thofe martial exercifes, which they are deftined in due time carefully to learn, and fkilfully to practice. Above all, let thofe important periods of life preceding and following puberty, be the objects of moft affiduous vigilance; but as this depends not entirely on age, we are lefs to regard the fanciful diftinctions of numbers, than to watch the folid differences of nature; of which it is the fole bufinefs of education to fecond the views, and to fupply the defects.

ARISTOTLE's POLITICS.

BOOK V.*

INTRODUCTION.

IN the Fourth Book Ariſtotle deſcribes the beſt form of government; and in the Fifth, he explains that ſyſtem of education by which this government will be beſt upheld. Plutarch and other approved authors, ancient and modern, who have expreſsly written on education, do little more that expand and illuſtrate the pregnant ſenſe which uniformly pervades this Book; omitting ſome remarks, which, being peculiar to Ariſtotle, will be found by moſt modern readers equally new and important.

Muſic, conſidered under a certain aſpect, was the claſſic learning of antiquity, and regarded as intimately, almoſt inſeparably, connected with morality, as well as poetry. The author, therefore, as might be expected, expatiates on the ſubject of muſic; which he claſſes with thoſe ſciences that terminate completely in themſelves, and which, independently of profit or utility, merit cultivation merely for the ſake of pleaſure; forming at once the higheſt embelliſhment and happieſt exerciſe of the mind.

Having

* Commonly publiſhed as Book VIII.

BOOK V. Having repeatedly remarked, that education ought to be relative to the nature of the government, he maintains as a confequence of this maxim, that the cuftoms prevalent in his own age ought to be totally reverſed; and that the people in democracies ought to be trained to modefty and refpect for their fuperiors, while the nobles in ariftocracies ought to be habituated to moderation and affability towards their inferiors. In conformity with this doctrine, he thinks that education ought to be public; and I believe that the experience of modern as well as of ancient times will juftify and confirm his concluſion; having had an opportunity to remark during a long refidence in a great variety of different countries, that the inhabitants were better educated almoft exactly in proportion to the degree in which public education prevailed among them.

BOOK V.

ARGUMENT.

Education.—Its different branches.—How far to be cultivated.— Grammar—Drawing—Gymnastic—Music.—Exercises adapted to different ages.—Doubts concerning music.—Its different kinds. —Purgation of the passions.

THAT the education of youth ought to form a principal object of the legislator's attention cannot be a matter of doubt; since it is education that first moulds, and that afterwards sustains the various modes of government; a democratical education alone suiting a democracy, an oligarchical an oligarchy; and the better and more perfect are the different systems of education, the better and more perfect will be those plans of government which they are respectively calculated to introduce and uphold. Preparation and exercise are necessary for the acquisition of every art; and not least for the attainment of the great art of political life. In this important object fellow-citizens are all equally and all deeply concerned; and as they are all united in one common work for one common purpose, their education ought to be uniform and public, and regulated by general consent; not abandoned, as at present, to the blind decision of chance, or the idle caprice of parents. For the children of citizens belong to the commonwealth, of which they are destined to be members; and, like every member or part, must be formed and fashioned in subserviency to the

ARISTOTLE's POLITICS.

BOOK V.

Chap. 2.

Wherein political education confists.

Its different branches.

To what extent each branch ought to be cultivated.

the good of that whole, or fyftem, to which they collectively appertain. Such are the maxims of the Spartans, which cannot in this particular be too highly extolled. Of all men they are the moft attentive to education, and their education is public.

But wherein ought political education to confift ; what are its different branches, and in what manner, or to what extent, ought each branch to be cultivated ? The difcordant practice of nations has involved thefe queftions in much perplexity. Different fyftems of legiflation have different fcopes and tendencies, and even when they agree in the fame end, they employ different means for its attainment. Is education to be chiefly directed to things of common and vulgar ufe, fubfervient to bodily accommodation and productive of external profperity ? Or ought its main bufinefs to confift in fharpening, fortifying, and ennobling the mind ? If the mind and virtue be juftly preferred to the body and fortune, yet by what principles are we to arrange the virtues themfelves ? With which of them ought our culture to begin, and in which of them ought it to terminate ? Firft of all, it is evident that children ought to be inftructed in things fubfervient to the purpofe of external accommodation, in proportion to their neceffity or utility, provided fuch things be not illiberal and fordid, tending to diftort or enervate the body, to narrow or debafe the foul, to chill the fancy or encumber the intellect. From fuch mean and mercenary drudgery, which would difqualify them for the exercife of virtue, and unfit them for the offices of freemen, our citizens muft totally abftain. Even to thofe arts dignified by the epithet of liberal, their application ought not to be directed without due felection and prudent referve. In many accomplifhments, mediocrity is preferable to excellence ; for an ambition gratified by what is frivolous will

be

be incapable of aspiring to what is great. In ascertaining the doubtful nature of those frivolous but agreeable talents, much depends on the end or purpose for which they are acquired and cultivated. To display them for vanity or gain, is worthy of none but slaves; but they will not misbecome a citizen, if he exercises them for his own amusement, or the gratification of his friends; as relaxations from severer studies, or preparations for higher pursuits.

Education is most commonly reduced to four heads, grammar[a], gymnastic, music, and drawing. Letters are the elements of calculation, as well as of grammar or composition, and are essentially requisite in innumerable purposes of daily occurrence. The same may be observed of drawing, which teaches the knowledge of forms, about which so many indispensable occupations are continually conversant. The gymnastic is subservient to strength and courage, invigorating the body and fortifying the mind. Music, indeed, is now degraded into a playful pastime, but was introduced into education, by our wiser ancestors, because youth ought to be taught, not only how to pursue business, but how to enjoy leisure; an enjoyment which is the end of business itself, and the limit in which all our active pursuits finally terminate. This enjoyment is of a nature too noble and too elevated to consist in plays and pastimes, which it would be absurd to consider as the main end and final purpose of life, and which are chiefly useful in the intervals of toilsome exertion, as salutary recreations of the mind, and seasonable unbendings from contentious activity.

Leisure is in itself pleasurable; and on its own account, desirable: whereas business is never undertaken and pursued merely

BOOK V.

Chap. 3.

Grammar or letters, their use.

Drawing, its use.

Gymnastic, its use.

Music, its use.

The example of music proves that there is an

[a] Conf. Diodor. Sicul. vol. i. p. 486.

BOOK V.

education requisite to the enjoyment of liberal leisure.

merely for its own sake, but for the sake of something beyond it; a something as variable as the opinions of men are manifold, and their habits diffimilar; some placing happiness in one kind of enjoyment, and others in another; but those who are best formed and most skilfully educated, placing it in such enjoyments only as are honourable and laudable. An education, therefore, is requisite to make us delight in those things which are best calculated to afford genuine satisfaction; and the arts and studies from which this satisfaction results, are not to be degraded by the epithets *useful* or *necessary*, since they relate to nothing external, but terminate in themselves, and are on their own account and ultimately the objects of desire, as the immediate causes of rational and honest pleasure. In this view the ancients considered music, and gave it a distinguished rank in their scholastic system; not as a thing useful, for to what purpose does it serve? Not as necessary in the way that letters are necessary in accounts, in œconomy, in literature or science, and a thousand political purposes, both civil and military; or as drawing is useful in teaching the knowledge of forms, in appreciating works of art, and in preventing deception in the purchase of instruments and utensils, the implements of trade, or the articles of furniture. It remains, therefore, that music should be acquired and cultivated as a thing desirable in itself, for the agreeable occupation of liberal leisure, and the elegant embellishment of life. Therefore Homer says, "Let sweet Thalia decorate the feast;" and again, "The bard is called to ravish every ear." And Ulysses thus paints the best enjoyments of peace and prosperity,

"How sweet the products of a peaceful reign,
The Heaven-taught poet and enchanting strain [b]."

The

[b] Odyss. ix. v. 213.

The example of mufic, as taught by the ancients, juftifies us, therefore, in afferting, that our fons ought to be inftructed not only in things ufeful or neceffary, but in things liberal and honourable. How many, and what thefe things are, and by what means the tafte for them may be beft infpired, and the knowledge of them beft communicated, we fhall examine hereafter. At prefent it is fufficient to have proved by the authority of the ancients, that fuch things exift, and ought to be objects of our care. This is plain in the cafe of mufic; and a little attention will fhew that it holds true in other ftudies. The knowledge of letters is ufeful in the bufinefs of life, in reading and accounts, and innumerable other purpofes. But the ftudy of them is not bounded by this vulgar utility. They are preparations for higher branches of fcience. Drawing alfo is ufeful for the ordinary and coarfe purpofes above fpecified; it is, therefore, admitted into the general courfe of common education. But the ftudy of drawing leads to fomething beyond thefe vulgar ufes; and by familiarifing us with the nature and variety of forms, carries us to the contemplation of *beauty*, as letters, which are the elements of calculation and compofition, terminate in the contemplation of *truth*. Thofe men reft fatisfied with a condition far fhort of the perfection of their nature, whofe minds have never opened to fuch fublime pleafures. To be always feeking what is ufeful, is unworthy of a liberal, and inconfiftent with an elevated, character.

We have before obferved, that moral education ought to precede the intellectual, and that the culture of the body ought to precede that of the mind. The nations moft attentive to the formation of the body, ftrive to give to it an athletic habit, which injures the beauty of the fhape, and ftunts the growth.

Chap. 4.

How the body is to be hardened by exercife without injury to the city of character.

The Lacedæmonians avoid this error; but by imposing excessive labours on the body, they engender ferocity in the mind, thinking this conducive to martial spirit. But, as we before observed, education ought not to be confined to any one object, nor chiefly directed to such objects as military valour; and if this excellence were our principal concern, it would not be inspired by the Spartan discipline. For neither in men nor in animals does valour accompany sullen ferocity, but is rather found in mild, generous, and lion-like natures. There are many nations who delight in carnage, that are destitute of courage. The Achaei and Heniochi of Pontus, cowardly as they are, feel neither horror in shedding, nor disgust in tasting human blood; some inland nations of Asia equal or surpass this brutal savageness; they are cruel beasts of prey, not warlike men. Even the obstinate fierceness of Sparta could not maintain her pre-eminence. She has been excelled by her neighbours in the virtues of war as well as of peace. While the Lacedæmonians alone cultivated arms, they acquired an easy ascendancy over undisciplined troops. But since their neighbours have been trained to martial exercises, they have approved themselves superior in war to the Spartans. Neither a wolf nor any other such bloody savage, but only a brave man, is truly qualified to maintain an honourable conflict. For mere warlike courage, taken separately by itself, is a doubtful and defective quality; and cultivated too assiduously by the hardening discipline of toils and struggles, will degrade and debase the man, blunt his faculties, narrow his soul, and render him as bad a soldier as he is a contemptible citizen.

Of the exercises best adapted to The gymnastic, therefore, must be taught and exercised in subserviency to nobler pursuits. Till the age of puberty, the

lighter

lighter exercises only should be enjoined and practised: athletic exertions and a forced diet ought to be proscribed and prohibited; for such artificial violence would marr the work of nature, disfigure the shape, stunt the growth, and for ever prevent the attainment of manly strength. That this must be its effect, experience evinces. In the long list of Olympic victors, scarcely two or three have gained the prize, both when they were boys and after they became men. Their capacities were checked, and their powers exhausted by premature exertions and an unseasonable regimen. During the three years immediately following puberty, the application of youth should be directed to those branches of education which form and invigorate the mind. They will then, at the age of seventeen, be capable of submitting to a regulated diet, and of sustaining the fatigue of athletic exercises. For laborious contention of the mind and of the body ought not to take place at the same age; the exertions of the body obstructing those of the mind, and the exertions of the mind relaxing the vigour of the body.

BOOK V.

the respective ages.

In a former chapter, some difficulties occurred respecting music, and some doubts were started concerning its power and its end. Is it merely a soothing recreation, like the two *care-killing* powers of sleep and wine? Thus they are characterised by Euripides; and it must be acknowledged that, by many, music, sleep, and wine, are arranged in the same class, and used for the same purpose; to which, dancing, also, is by some thought to contribute. Or is music not merely a recreative pastime, but an essential branch of discipline, capable of moulding and fashioning the mind, not less than the gymnastic moulds and fashions the body? Or is the efficacy of this noble art limited by neither of these uses, and music to be regarded

Chap. 5.

Doubts concerning music.
Is it merely a footing recreation?

or an essential branch of discipline?

BOOK V.

or an enjoyment complete in itself?

Difficulties attending these questions.

garded neither as a recreation from past labours, nor a preparation for future exertions, but as an enjoyment complete and perfect in itself, analagous to the pleasure essential to moral and intellectual energies, which, forming the perfection of man, are desirable on their own account, independently of any thing that has preceded, or of any thing that is to follow them?

That music, considered as a branch of education, is not merely for recreation or sport, is deducible from this, that every effort of attention, and therefore the learning of music, is, in children, attended rather with pain than pleasure. It is equally evident, that children are not instructed in music as the agreeable employment of their liberal leisure; for such perfect enjoyments could not be relished by their imperfect faculties, nor the most complete fruits of life gathered from their crude immaturity. But, perhaps, children are taught music that it may contribute in their riper years to their recreation, their improvement, or their enjoyment. Yet these purposes may be better attained without learning the art, or ever touching the lyre. The Persian and Median kings attain them completely, when they enjoy the correct execution of the best musical performers; the Lacedæmonians, without learning music, boast that they can readily distinguish between manly and effeminate airs; between melodies that contribute to moral discipline, and those that vitiate the mind, or dissipate themselves in empty sound. To distinguish and relish good victuals, is it necessary to be a cook? Which of the poets ever introduced Jupiter singing and harping? Such occupations are universally ascribed to inferior divinities; and among men, we know that they belong to mercenary practitioners, whose undivided application to music has given them great proficiency in this art,

but

but has debased their souls and narrowed their faculties; whereas by truly liberal and ingenious minds, music is seldom considered as a serious engagement, and is rarely practised, but as a recreative pastime, or a natural expansion of jovial merriment. Such are the doubts attending the accurate arrangement and proper use of music; and such the difficulties in ascertaining the place which this agreeable art ought to hold, and the function which it is calculated to perform, in the important system of political discipline.

Yet let it be considered whether this refined art, though it cannot be accurately and exclusively referred to any one of the ends above specified, may not in some measure comprehend them all. Play is introduced for the sake of recreation; and affords no small degree of pleasure, merely as a repose from the pain of labour, of which it is the natural remedy. But the liberal exercise of our best energies is sweetened by pleasure as well as ennobled by dignity; for happiness, which consists in this exercise, certainly includes both these elements. Now music, whether simple or accompanied by poetry, is acknowledged and felt to be one of the most delightful of pleasures; wherefore Musæus says,

"Of human joys, the sweetest is to sing."

On this account, its power is summoned to gladden our festivities, to brighten and exalt the enjoyments of peace and prosperity. Our children, therefore, ought to be instructed in music, because every innocent pleasure is not only useful as a salutary and seasonable recreation, but desirable in itself as one of the best enjoyments of life. But as the lives of most men are a continual variation of toil and repose, they are apt to confound the light and temporary pleasure of recreation, with those more permanent

BOOK V.

The efficacy of music in moral discipline.

The cause of this efficacy explained.

nent and more ferious joys, which conflitute the perfection of human happinefs; efpecially fince there is this refemblance between them, that neither of them have reference to futurity, our nobleft and moft delightful energies *terminating* in *themfelves*, and our lighteft and moft frivolous paftimes, being the medicine of *paſt* labours, and relative to nothing that is future.

Yet it is worthy of confideration, whether recreation and enjoyment be not both of them, in this cafe, mere acceſſaries; and whether mufic, if properly directed, may not effect a more important purpofe, promote moral improvement, refine the fentiments, and exalt the character. Mufic will be acknowledged to have this tendency, fhould it appear capable of affecting the paffions and changing the manners; and that it really does this, manifeftly appears from various examples, and particularly from the melodies of Olympus, which cannot be liftened to without infpiring enthufiafm, which is plainly a moral affection. Independently of meafure or melody, even the fimple cries of nature, when faithfully imitated, powerfully excite our fympathy, and difpofe us to joy or to grief. Mufic is naturally pleafant, and the main object of moral education is to teach us to be pleafed or offended as propriety requires, to love what is truly amiable, and to hate what is truly deteftable. Nothing, therefore, is of more importance than to learn this art, and by cuftom to confirm our approbation of thofe rythmical fucceſſions of melodious founds, which are expreffive of decent and dignified manners, of manly and honourable actions. Ingenuous and well-difciplined natures find in the varieties of melody and rhythm, ftriking refemblances of anger and meeknefs, of manlinefs and temperance, and of all fuch moral affections, as well as of their contraries. This is proved by the effect of mufical performance; which, while we liften to it,

changes

changes the form and quality of the foul, melts it to tenderness, or hardens it to fortitude; and the habit of being thus powerfully affected by the resemblances of manners, is nearly related to that of being affected still more powerfully by their realities; since, were we highly delighted with looking on a portrait, for no other reason than its beautiful form, it would follow of necessity, that we should also be still more delighted with beholding its original. Of all the objects of our senses, sounds are the most striking resemblances of manners. The objects of our touch and of our taste have no moral resemblance whatever: and even in the objects of our sight, shapes, and colours, the resemblance is faint and imperfect, because calm and motionless, and rather a mere sign of manners than their natural imitation, since manners can only be exhibited by actions, and therefore only represented by motions, by which alone actions are forcibly expressed. Yet even the mere signs of manners are not to be rejected as things useless in education; and our youth ought, doubtless, rather to contemplate the works of Polygnotus, and such artists as skilfully employ those signs or marks, than stare on the unmeaning productions of Pauson. But if the mere signs be useful, how much more efficacious must be the resemblances. And such resemblances evidently prevail in the *melodies*; each of which having its distinctive character, produces its peculiar effect; so that our affection changes with each change of the music; and in hearing one melody we are agitated with quite different emotions from those with which we were affected at hearing another. At the will of a skilful composer, the mind expands into joy, or contracts into grief; some airs melt us into softness, while the Dorian mode confirms our fortitude, and the Phrygian inspires us with enthusiasm. These

BOOK V.

remarks have been well illustrated by the writers on music, who take experience for their guide; from which it appears that the efficacy of time, that is of rhythm or measure, is not less than the efficacy of tune, that is of the modes and melodies. Some movements are brisk and lively, others grave and sedate; some vulgar, and expressive of irregular passions; others liberal, and expressive of well-governed affections. But music consists in the skilful combination of time and tune, from which its power appears manifestly; and, therefore, the propriety of teaching it to youth, especially as music is naturally pleasant, and the attention of that early age is difficultly detained in any exercise or employment in which pleasure is not an ingredient. It appears also that there is an affinity between measures and melodies, and that both have a near relation to the soul; from which some have inferred that the soul is harmony, and others that harmony is one of its essential attributes.

Chap. 6.

That children should be taught to perform music.

We now proceed to examine whether children should be taught, not only to understand and relish, but to practise and perform music. This question must be answered in the affirmative, for it is impossible, at least exceedingly difficult, to be a good judge of performances which we are ourselves unable to execute; and whatever affections or qualities music may excite or produce, its efficacy will be the stronger when it is the work of our own hands. Besides this, children require some employment to occupy and exhaust their restless activity; for which reason Archytas's rattle is no contemptible invention, since while shaking this noisy plaything, their activity is agreeably and harmlessly employed. Education, well directed, is the rattle of boys; and at this age they may be taught arts, which it would misbecome them afterwards to exercise, but

of

of which the practice in youth will enable them in manhood to relish works of art the better, and to appreciate them the more skilfully. The objection to music as illiberal, may be easily removed, if we distinguish between that taste and skill in the art, which would disqualify a man from performing the offices of a citizen, and that taste and skill which would be attended with no such pernicious effect. If the music that we study, enervates or debases the soul, or the instruments on which we practise, distort or enfeeble the body, or if the mind is narrowed by the intense application to one secondary pursuit, it is plain that this ingenious art will occasion much mischief, and both incapacitate the young for learning their political duties, and disqualify the old from performing them honourably. The artificial and complicated music, therefore, which has little other merit than the difficulty of execution, and little other effect than to astonish the gaping multitude, but which has engrossed and degraded our public exhibitions, ought never to have been introduced into education, whose best purposes it is only calculated to pervert [b].

Musical performance may be cultivated, and manual dexterity acquired; but the degree in which they are desirable, is limited by that proficiency requisite for enabling us to relish liberal rhythms and manly melodies, not to practise those vulgar sleights and musical trifles which delight children, slaves, and even some brute animals. It is plain, therefore, that the simplest instruments deserve the preference, as fittest for the purpose of education. The flute, the harp, and others of that kind are to be rejected as too artificial and complex, and requiring

[b] For better understanding what follows concerning music, the reader may consult History of Ancient Greece, v. ii. c. . . p 238, & seq.

BOOK V. quiring more attention and practice than liberal minds can spare from more important pursuits. The flute is, besides, better fitted to excite enthusiasm than to regulate the affections, and is therefore better adapted to purgation than to instruction; to operate as a violent remedy under violent disorders of the mind, than to serve in usual health for salutary nourishment. In playing the flute it is impossible to use the voice, on which account our ancestors finally rejected this instrument, which they had introduced into education with innumerable other novelties, amidst the intoxication of their Persian victories. After the repulse of Xerxes, a Lacedæmonian exhibiting at his own expence a chorus of music, himself played on the flute; and there was then scarcely an Athenian citizen totally unacquainted with this instrument, as appears by the picture dedicated by Thrasyppus of the musical exhibition, which he defrayed and directed. But on mature reflection, the flute was proscribed in education, and its use forbidden to freemen; and the same may be said of the dulcimer and various other instruments of different shapes and names, which are fitly employed for amusing the vulgar, by their admitting wonderful displays of manual dexterity. It is an ancient and well-contrived fable, which says, that Minerva after inventing the flute rejected its use. The reason why she did so, is not a bad one; namely, that she was angry at seeing how much the blowing of the flute distorted her countenance. Yet it is far more probable, that Minerva, who is believed to preside over learning and science, disdained an instrument which contributed nothing to mental improvement; which neither fortified discipline, nor sharpened intellect, nor elevated sentiment. All complex and difficult instruments are, therefore, to be banished from the pure region of education,

and

and to be consigned to the sordid displays of mercenary practitioners, who cultivate music, not for any salutary purpose, but for the low gratification of an illiberal audience; whom such things only can please as nourish their corrupt passions, by a mean compliance with which, the musical performers in our days disqualify themselves in mind and body, from performing the duties of good citizens.

In music two things are to be considered, tune and time, the varieties of the former constituting the different modes and melodies, the varieties of the latter constituting the different measures and rhythms. Are all these gradations and all these proportions of sound to be used indifferently, or ought due selection to be made? Ought this selection to be invariably the same, or ought it to be modified by the different ends and purposes of musical performance? And in music, which is the principal, time or tune? For minute and circumstantial solutions of these questions, we refer to the philosophical writers on music, meaning to touch but slightly on the subject, and as far as seems requisite in a work on legislation. We approve the general division of music into moral, practical, and rapturous; according as it is fitted to regulate our affections, to excite us to action, or to inspire us with enthusiasm. Experience proves that different melodies and rhythms are respectively adapted to these different purposes; so that as moral strains are to be employed for mental discipline and liberal pleasure, the enthusiastic, and sometimes the practical, may be listened to for the purpose of what, by a natural metaphor, is called purgation ᵉ which shall be more fully

BOOK V.

Chap. 7.

Analysis of music.

Its division into moral, practical, and rapturous.

ᵉ Plutarch de Auditione, p. 42. edit. Paris, quotes a saying of the philosopher Ariston, that neither a bath nor a discourse did any good unless they cleansed and purified; using the verb from which the substantive here translated purgation is derived.

BOOK V.

What is meant by purgation of the paſſions by muſic.

fully explained in our treatiſe on Poetry. Let it ſuffice at preſent to obſerve, that thoſe paſſions (ſuch is the uniſon of minds) by which one perſon is ſtrongly affected, are felt in a certain degree by all around him[c]; and, therefore, when ſkilfully expreſſed by the muſician, they will be powerfully communicated, eſpecially to thoſe who, by their natural conſtitution, are peculiarly expoſed to their influence; and whoſe extreme ſenſibility will thus be excited and agitated, and thereby purified and refined[d], and

rived. In the following ſentence, by a bold mixture of metaphors, he ſays, λογῳ δριμει την διανοιαν αχλυος πολλης και αμβλυτητος γεμουσαν εκκαθαιρ̣ε. "That we ought to be thankful to philoſophers, who, by the ſeverity of their exhortations, purge our underſtanding from the thick darkneſs and bluntneſs with which they are filled."

[c] Compare above, c. v. ακροωμενοι των μιμησεων, γιγνονται παντες συμπαθεις.

[d] This obſcure ſentence is beſt explained by a collateral paſſage in Plato de Republica, p. 625. edit. Ficini. He is treating of the neceſſity of combining in a well-directed education, muſic with the gymnaſtic; becauſe men who apply only to muſic, will ſoften into effeminacy; and thoſe who apply only to the gymnaſtic, will harden into brutality. In expanding and illuſtrating this obſervation, he ſays that ſtrength is increaſed and courage confirmed by the gymnaſtic, but what will happen if a youth is trained to the gymnaſtic only? ουκ, αν τι οντ' αυτω φιλομαθης εν τη ψυχῃ, ατι ουτε μαθηματος γευομενου μηδενος, ου ζητηματος, ουτε λογου μετισχοι, ουτε της αλλης μουσικης, αςθενης τε κακωφος και τυφλος γιγνεται, ατι ουκ εγειρομενος, ουδι τρεφομενος, ουδι διακαθαιρομενων των αισθησεων αυτω. "In this caſe, even ſhould he naturally be endowed with an ingenuous and inquiſitive mind, yet having never taſted the pleaſures neither of ſcience, nor inveſtigation, nor reaſon, *nor the other muſic*, his condition as a man will be that of blindneſs, deafneſs, and debility, his faculties having never been *nouriſhed, excited, agitated, and purged*." What Plato means by ſaying *the other muſic*, may be underſtood by the words of Strabo in the admirable mythological digreſſion in his Tenth Book, where he remounts to the root and ſource of myſticiſm in the human heart, and examines the fabulous traditions and religious arcana of his country, with that liberal criticiſm which became an hiſtorian, that was a traveller and a philoſopher. ου μεν γαρ ερχεται και τουτε, της ανθρωπω; τοτι μαλιστα μιμεισθαι της θιοις, οταν ευεργετωσιν· αμεινον δ'αν λιγοι τις, οταν ευδαιμονωσι· τοιαυτα δε τε χαιρειν και το ιορταζειν και το φιλοςοφειν και μουσικης απτεσθαι· μη γαρ ει τις εκπτωσει; προς το χειρον γινεται των μουσικων εις δυσπαθειας τρεποντων τας τεχνας εν τοις συμποσιοις, και θυμιλαις και σκηναις; και αλλοις τοιουτοις διαβαλλισθω το πραγμα· αλλα η φυσις η των παιδευματων εξεταζεσθω την αρχην ενθενδε εχουσα.

and (*as melancholy is purged by tears*ᶜ) difburdened and lightened with a pleafurable relief. Thus it is that, at the celebration of Orgic rites, enthufiafm vents itfelf and evaporates in thofe facred melodies, during the performance of which the mind undergoes a kind of purgation, and is thereby cured of its frenzy. The fame thing happens in all other violent affections, whofe exceffes cure themfelves; and of which, in proportion as the preceding agitation has been the greater, the fubfequent relief proves the more delightful.

To this purpofe theatrical mufic might be happily directed; but as the fpectators at theatres confift, not merely of the liberal and enlightened, but of the vulgar and illiterate; of mechanics, manufacturers, fervants, and flaves; such perfons require paftimes suitable

The different kinds of mufic; their nature and effects.

ιγνοκ. Και δια τυτο μυσικην εκαλισιν ὁ πλατων, και ετι προτερον οἱ πυθαγορειοι, την φιλοσοφιαν, και κατα ἡρμενιαν τον κοσμον συνεστάναι, παν το μυσικον θεων εργον ὑπολαμβανοντες. Ουτω δε και αἱ Μουσαι θεαι και Απολλων Μουσαγετης, και ἡ ποιητικη πασα ἱμνητικη ουσα· ὡσαυτως δε και την των ἠθων κατασκευην τη μουσικη προσιεμενοι ὡς παν το ινανερθωτικον τη ιν τοις θεοις εγγυς ον.

" It has been well faid, that a man moft imitates the gods, when he does good; but it would be better faid, when he is happy; that is, when he enjoys merriment and feftivity chaftifed by the decent charms of mufic and philofophy. For though mufic is often degraded in our theatres, in our ftreets, and at our entertainments, into the pander of fenfual paffions, yet the art itfelf ought not, therefore, to be arraigned, but rather the merit of that difcipline fairly eftimated, of which mufic is the principle and the fource." On this ground Plato, and the Pythagoreans before him, called philofophy, mufic, maintained that the world fubfifted by harmony, and that mufic in its largeft fenfe, meaning arrangement and proportion, fhone in every work of the gods. The mufes themfelves are goddeffes; Apollo is the leader of the mufes; and poetry, which originally confifted in hymns, was invented to fing the praifes of the divinity. To mufic the ancients alfo referred moral philofophy, or ethics, confidering as the gift of Heaven whatever tended to exalt and purify the mind ¹.

ᶜ Plato de Republ. l. III.

¹ Literally, " confidering as near to the gods whatever is corrective of the mind." If every work of the gods partook of mufic, then moral philofophy, as corrective of the mind and a gift of Heaven, might be referred to mufic as the fpecies is to its genus. But this will not neceffarily follow, if we tranflate with Cafaubon, " that all mufic is the w rk of the gods."

BOOK V.

suitable to their taste; and their perverse minds can relish none but perverse music; a music overstrained by the vehemence of contention, and disfigured by a crowd of motley embellishments. But that which is a fit amusement for slaves and men of servile characters, would be of all things the most improper for the liberal discipline of youth. To the purpose of education, the manly Doric, and other congenial moral melodies, are found to be the best adapted. Socrates in Plato's Republic admits no other modes of music but the Dorian and Phrygian; but there is an inconsistency in admitting the latter after he had excluded the use of the flute, for the Phrygian is among melodies what the flute is among instruments, a pathetic enthusiastic strain; and so peculiarly adapted to dithyrambics, that when Philoxenus attempted to set these rapturous hymns to Doric music, he found the thing impossible, and naturally reverted to the Phrygian mode. The Dorian is to be preferred for its firmness, gravity, and stability, as holding the middle place between two excesses, that of fury on the one hand, and that of effeminacy on the other.

The different kinds of music respectively adapted to different periods of human life.

In education we ought never to lose sight of possibility and propriety; and propriety generally lies in the middle between two vicious extremes. Propriety, therefore, is mediocrity; but this mediocrity, in practical matters, does not consist in an indivisible point, but admits of considerable latitude, and is to be modified in different cases by different circumstances; and in the case of music, chiefly by the circumstance of age. Strong sounds and rapid movements accord not with the debility of declining years. The writers on this subject, therefore, justly blame Socrates for banishing the gentle languor of soft music, as producing the noxious consequences of wine, when the ardour

ardour of intoxication has given place to painful laffitude or
liftlefs torpor. But men meafure every thing by their own
ftandard; and that may be approved by old age, which feems
feeble or languid to the prime of life. Youth, alfo, has a mufic
peculiarly adapted to it. This is the Lydian, which unites
grace with ftrength, and while it regulates the affections, has no
fmall tendency alfo to embellifh the manners. It is plain then,
that poffibility, mediocrity, and propriety are views and boundaries, of which, in education, we ought never to lofe fight.

(273)

ARISTOTLE's POLITICS.

BOOK VI.*

INTRODUCTION.

IN this Book Ariſtotle approves himſelf, as even Locke acknowledges, "a maſter in politics;" ſurpaſſing in perſpicuity and preciſion every writer ancient or modern in explaining how " civil ſociety is formed into different models of government, and the ſeveral ſpecies of it ª." His writings on this ſubject are eminently diſtinguiſhed from thoſe of his rivals and detractors. As he ſtands on a loftier ground, his ſight has a wider range; and while his ſituation is more commanding, his eye is alſo more piercing. A great part of his life was employed in doing for moral and political philoſophy, that which, with regard to modern geometry, Vieta and Deſcartes began; Barrow and Leibnitz and Newton ſo wonderfully carried on and improved; and that which Waring and a few others of our contemporaries are ſtriving ſtill further to extend and perfect. The extraordinary elevation which that noble ſcience has attained, is owing chiefly to obſtinate and patient induſtry in improving and perfecting the ſigns by which our notions of

magnitude

---

* Commonly publiſhed as Book IV.   ª See Locke's Letter to King.

BOOK VI.

magnitude are compared; and the refults of our comparifons furely drawn, and clearly expreffed. The Stagirite was equally fuccefsful with thofe great men, in the ftill more important tafk of fimplifying and improving the figns or expreffions by which comparifons are made, involving the civil happinefs of mankind and the beft interefts of fociety. His diftinction between the effential members of a commonwealth and its barely ornamental concomitants; his divifions and definitions of the different forms of government, with the important principle by which the form is diftinguifhed from the fubftance; the mutual relations between government and laws; and the relations between both thefe and the variable moral nature of man, which make thofe inftitutions and arrangements, that are juft and falutary in one country, unjuft and pernicious in another; thefe and other collateral points are explained in the prefent Book, with a copioufnefs that affords fatisfaction, and a clearnefs that defies contradiction.

In treating of the *fovereignty* in a ftate, our author analyfes this complex object into deliberative, appointing or elective, and judicial, powers. To juftify his divifion in comparifon with that which modern writers have fubftituted in its ftead; namely, powers legiflative, executive, and judicial; it may be obferved 'that in every community the fovereignty, whether refiding in one, the few, or the many, muft neceffarily be employed in deliberating concerning public meafures; in electing or appointing magiftrates; or in diftributing juftice, and deciding differences. But the work of legiflation, when once complete, ought never afterwards, according to our author, to be touched but with a cautious and trembling hand [b]; and to fay that the actual fovereign, whether king, nobles, or commons, or all three collectively, are invefted with

[b] See above, b. ii. c. vi. p. 101.

with the plenitude of legiflative authority, is in his opinion to grant to them a power, which, in its full extent, they cannot ever rightfully exercife, unlefs it could be fuppofed that one generation of men might be fairly entitled to intercept from pofterity the improvement made, and the light accumulated in the long courfe of preceding ages. To do this, is a ftretch of authority to which the moft defpotic princes of Afia have never yet laid claim. In the abfolute monarchies of Europe, while unjuft wars were undertaken, exorbitant taxes impofed, and temporary regulations refpecting every public meafure capricioufly made, and capricioufly abolifhed, the fundamental laws of their refpective kingdoms were acknowledged and refpected by thofe branded as the wildeft and moft furious defpots. In matters of policy that cannot be juft or fit, which never can be ufeful; and our author endeavours to prove that it never can be ufeful for a nation completely and fuddenly to depart from its hereditary inftitutions: a departure which, deftroying that principle on which the efficacy of all laws is founded, would deftroy government itfelf[c]; that illuftrious work of nature, which mere human powers, as they could not originally eftablifh it, cannot have a right to purfue thofe meafures by which it is likely to be eventually overturned[d].

The branch of government now denominated the executive, Ariftotle calls the appointing power, when it refides in one; the electing power, when it refides in many. His language is more accurate than our's. To give orders, and to appoint or elect thofe empowered to carry them into execution, is doubtlefs a branch of the fovereignty; but the part merely executive belongs

[c] See above, b. ii. c. vi. p. 102.   [d] Ibid. b. i. c. ii. p. 22, & feq.

BOOK VI.

belongs to low inftruments; and all the intermediate functions, between the firft order or appointment, and the final execution or effect, fall within the department of dependent and refponfible minifters.

After thus analyfing the fovereignty, the author proceeds to examine how its different elements are diftributed in the different forms of government, and how they ought to be placed in a well-conftituted commonwealth; holding the juft mean between the vicious extremes of domineering oligarchy and furious democracy. Nothing can be added to the copioufnefs and perfpicuity with which he explains under what circumftances democratical and oligarchical laws are to be alternately felected; and on what occafions neither the one nor the other ought to be entirely and exclufively adopted, but rather both to be blended into one truly political and falutary inftitution. The perfection of practical matters, as he often obferves, lies not in a fixed and indivifible point; it varies with the indefinite variation of circumftances; but the beft practical tefts of good government, he holds to be univerfally the two following: firft, when men of the middle ranks abound more than either the infolent rich or the rapacious poor; and fecondly, when there is a difficulty in determining to which of the fimple forms of government the conftitution moft inclines, and ought moft properly to be referred. There is a pleafure not to be expreffed, but which every friend to his country muft warmly feel, in reflecting that Ariftotle's two tefts are more applicable to the government eftablifhed in this ifland, than to any other which hiftory exhibits.

The praifes which the author beftows on the fuperior happinefs of the middle claffes in fociety, tends to reconcile the people at large with their refpective lots, and to fhew that the condition to

which

which every man by an ordinary degree of prudence and good fortune may attain, is precisely the best in which he could be placed. The miseries of individuals, as well as the convulsions of nations, originate in that most prevalent and widely-diffused error of considering rather their relative than their absolute advantages[*]. To the blessings of health and competency with security and a good conscience, what slender additions can be made by the most extensive power and most unbounded opulence? The lowest situation in civilised society is preferable to the highest among barbarians. But instead of contemplating with grateful complacence the real enjoyments within its reach, discontent broods over its comparative inferiority; and each thinking too highly of himself, even the more fortunate individuals will scarcely allow that full justice is done to their merit; while they depreciate the prodigious sum common to all, and magnify the minute differences by which the shares are distinguished.

[*] Suique ipsam, *malo arbitrio*, quo a proximis quisque minime anteiri vult, penituisse. T. Liv. l. vi. c. xxxiv.

BOOK VI.

ARGUMENT.

Governments—Their classification.—Democracy—Its four kinds.—Constitutions—One thing by law—Another in fact.—Materials respectively fitted for different governments.—Mixed governments.—Tests of good government.—How governments may be meliorated.—Sleights by which the nobles deceive the people—And the people the nobles.—Analysis of the sovereignty—Constitution of its different branches—Agreeably to the different spirit of different governments.

IT is the business of every science, and every inquiry that bears a reference to any whole class of objects, to consider not only the powers or capacities belonging to the best and most perfect individuals comprehended under that class; but those which belong to the class in general, or rather to the most considerable portion of it; and also those which belong to such individuals of the class as are peculiarly circumstanced. The master of exercises, the physician, and every other artist pays due attention to this threefold division. The teachers of the gymnastic art, for example, well know that of the youths committed to their care and discipline, few are capable of attaining the most athletic habit, or likely to carry off the first prizes either of strength or agility. Yet it is the duty of their profession to improve the natural powers of their disciples, and to exercise each of them in such accomplishments as are most suitable to their respective views and particular constitutions.

Chap. 1.
Politics as a science, how it ought to be treated.

tions. It is not enough, therefore, for the speculative politician, if he would render his speculations practically useful, to consider what arrangements best suit men provided with a complete accumulation of external and internal advantages. He must consider also, what are the arrangements best adapted to the particular circumstances in which communities are placed; and most likely to promote that particular scheme of national happiness which the founders of the commonwealth have thought fit to prefer; though neither the most desirable absolutely in itself, nor the best even in relation to the means and materials which nature or fortune had supplied. Above all, the political philosopher ought most diligently to investigate that form of government adapted to mankind in general, circumstanced as they are most commonly found to be; from the neglect of which inquiry, authors who have written well, have not written usefully. In all matters of practice, possibility is to be considered as well as perfection; and things easily accomplished are preferable to those barely possible. In opposition to these maxims, projectors in politics content themselves with devising arrangements adapted only to men formed and circumstanced agreeably to their mind and wish, the mere creations of their own fancy; or if they condescend to take lessons from history, they are satisfied with extolling and recommending the Lacedæmonian or some other approved government, without stopping to reflect whether the ordinary circumstances in which nations are placed, will ever allow them to imitate such admired models. For it is not an easier task to regenerate a constitution, than originally to establish it; since in working this reformation, it is necessary that men

should

should not only learn what they did not formerly know, but unlearn many things which they had previously been taught[r].

To treat the science of politics completely and usefully, we must not be contented with the general division of governments into monarchies, aristocracies, and republics; and their respective corruptions, tyrannies, oligarchies, and democracies. It is necessary still farther to examine wherein one government, or one corruption of government, differs from another bearing the same name. We shall then more easily discern for what materials each political structure is best adapted; what are the changes which it is most likely to undergo; and what are the laws and regulations by which it may be preserved, subverted, or amended.

The cause of the wide variety in governments must be sought for in the wonderful diversity of their constituent parts; for a state is a very complex object, composed of individuals and families; some rich, others poor; some subsisting by agriculture and pasturage, others by manufactures and commerce; and some provided with arms, while others are altogether defenceless. The higher classes of men are also variously distinguished by their abilities, their virtues, their birth, or merely by their wealth; which last, when considerable, enables them to rear and train horses, a circumstance which alone has been sufficient to decide the nature of the government. For in ancient times, wherever the national force consisted in cavalry, oligarchy was prevalent; as among the Chalcideans, the Eretrians, the Magnesians situate on the banks of the Meander, and

BOOK VI.

Chap. 2.

How governments are to be divided and classed.

Chap. 3.

General division.

[r] In the first chapters of this book there is much derangement, and much repetition. I have endeavoured to express the author's sense in fewer words, and with greater perspicuity.

BOOK VI.

and many other wealthy communities of Afiatic Greece[r]. It is plain, therefore, that governments vary according to the differences of thofe conftituent parts of the ftate, which either engrofs or fhare the fovereignty. The moft palpable, and alfo the moft fpecific difference (as will appear hereafter) is the diftinction of riches and poverty: wherefore, all governments have been divided into oligarchies and democracies, as the winds are divided into the north and the fouth, the former comprehending the weft, and the latter the eaft; and as melodies are divided into the Dorian and Phrygian, all other kinds of mufic, in proportion to their refpective proximities, being afcribed to the one or the other of thofe very different fcales. But the general divifion, above given in this work, appears more fatisfactory and more ufeful: namely, that certain polities are wifely combined and juftly tempered, as certain harmonies are fkilfully compofed and properly blended; that other polities, as well as other harmonies, are vitious deviations and bafe corruptions, whether they be ftrung into defpotifm, or relaxed into democracy.

Chap. 4.
Particular divifion.

The more minute fubdivifions of governments muft be obtained by the fame means, by which other objects of fcience are compared and claffed. In zoology[h], we begin by confidering what are the conftituent parts of animals, or, in other words, the parts effentially neceffary to their exiftence. Thefe are fome one of the fenfes[i], with an inftrument for feizing, and another for receiving food, together with fome inftrument or member by which the motions belonging to the animal may conveniently be performed. But all thefe parts or organs are fufceptible

---

[r] Hiftory of Ancient Greece, vol. i. c. vii.   [h] See Analyfis, p. 125.
[i] ἵνα τῳν αἰσθητηριων. See Analyfis, &c. p. 41.

susceptible of great variety in their respective structures, since, in some animals, one member is very differently formed from an *analogous* member in other animals; that is, from a member answering a similar purpose. But if our enumeration of the parts or organs be correct, and if we have carefully distinguished the differences in the structure of each organ, we must obtain the whole number of kinds or classes by multiplying the number expressing the differences in one constituent part, into the product of the numbers expressing the differences in all the other constituent parts.

The same principle applies to the classification of commonwealths, those complex moral entities, consisting of many parts or members, differently constructed, and variously combined. An essential ingredient in every commonwealth is, that great portion of the people employed in providing food, which may be variously supplied by the different modes of industry and accumulation above specified. A second indispensable ingredient consists of those employed in arts and manufactures, whether necessary for subsistence, or useful for accommodation. A third class of the people are those conversant about exchange or traffic, foreign as well as domestic. The soldiers form a fourth class, not less necessary than any of the preceding; since communities are collected for all-sufficiency, and cannot have attained their end, if continually exposed to destruction or servitude. Judges, to administer justice, and persons qualified by their abilities to deliberate and decide concerning public concerns, are the fifth and sixth classes: for if a soul be necessary to constitute an animal, not less than a body, justice, valour, and political wisdom, are not less essential to a state, than those

The constituent parts of commonwealths.

BOOK VI.

exertions of bodily labour by which daily wants are supplied[*]. The seventh and eighth classes consist in those who perpetually, or interchangeably, exercise the various duties of executive magistracy; and those who, by their seasonable contributions, supply the occasional exigencies of the public service. Of those various offices or functions, some indeed may be united in the same person. The same individual may alternately decide as a judge, and deliberate as a senator; the same hands may alternately hold the plough and brandish the spear. But as opulence and poverty cannot in any country be ascribed to the same person at once, the most distinct classes of every state are the poor and the rich; and the evident differences in government must result from these distinctions: from power engrossed by wealth, or power usurped by indigence. Kings, they say, are chosen in Æthiopia on account of their beauty and stature. If the same rule prevailed in electing republican magistrates, the principle of election would be highly oligarchical, because the tall and beautiful are always the smaller number. The rich also are commonly the few: and the poor the many; but to constitute an oligarchy, the few, who are masters of the government, must be rich; and to constitute a democracy, the many, who are masters of the government, must be poor; for it is only when both circumstances concur in those governments, that their respective characters are strongly impressed, and their opposite genius fully displayed. At Apollonia, near the Ionian sea, and in the isle of Thera, the descendants of the first settlers retained the whole government in their hands, notwith-

---

[*] The author here, as elsewhere, blames Plato for considering in his " Republic" soldiers as mere supplements, while he places husbandmen, weavers, &c. among essential parts or members.

notwithstanding powerful accessions of new inhabitants. But the government was not a democracy, because the rulers were inconsiderable in number when compared with the subjects over whom their power was exercised. At Colophon, on the other hand, the many were masters of the government; yet they did not constitute a democracy, because, before the Lydian war, the far greater proportion of the inhabitants of that commercial city were possessed of considerable opulence.

- The nature of oligarchies and democracies must vary in consequence of variations in their parts or elements. When the notables, or nobles, are distinguished by their education and virtue, there will result a very different kind of oligarchy from that in which the sovereigns of the state are characterised merely by their birth or their wealth. The differences in the people at large are occasioned chiefly by the different occupations which they pursue. Some live by agriculture; others by manufactures and commerce; and many cities and islands subsist chiefly by the sea. Their vessels are employed in war, commerce, fishing, and carriage. In some places, almost the whole shipping is destined for one single use; as the fishing boats of Byzantium and Tarentum, the gallies of Athens, the merchantmen of Ægina and Chios, and the transports of Tenedos. In the commonalty of a country, there may also be a variety in the proportion of mere populace, persons destitute of property, condemned through poverty to the meanest drudgery, and participating, on one side at least, of a foreign or even servile extraction. Such are the differences in the parts or elements, from which such a variety of dispositions, habits, manners, and characters must necessarily flow, as will render

those

Democracy, its four kinds.

BOOK VI. those arrangements which suit the genius of one people altogether unsuitable to that of another. The first kind of democracy requires that all men should be treated alike; that the rich and the poor should indifferently share the government, and enjoy an authority in its deliberations and measures exactly proportional to their numbers. Liberty, the partisans of this government assert, is chiefly to be found in democracies; and when all men are placed on a foot of equality, then, and then only, this liberty will be complete. The second kind of democracy requires a small qualification in point of fortune, in those entitled to offices of government. The third kind excludes from those offices persons branded by any note of infamy, or chargeable with any public delinquency. The kind first mentioned does not make these distinctions, but admits to magistracy without exception, the citizens at large. Yet all these democracies are governed by general and fixed laws, which it is the duty of magistrates and assemblies to administer and apply, without ever interposing their own authority, unless the law be silent or its voice uncertain. But there is a fourth species of democracy, differing from the others just mentioned, in this important particular, that it is governed not by permanent laws, but by occasional decrees. This happens through the dangerous artifices of demagogues, a description of men for which there is not any room in countries subject to law; but where law is set aside, the authority of wise and good men is overturned, and that of demagogues established on its ruins; the people in the assemblies assuming the form of one complex monarch; tyrants not individually, but collectively. The authority of the many is reprobated by Homer, in what sense is uncertain.

uncertain [1]. In such a democracy, then, the people knowing itself to be an absolute monarch, assumes all his pretensions, and exercises all his prerogatives; setting every principle of order at defiance; rewarding and honouring none but the basest flatterers; and exhibiting in all its transactions the same contrast to a well-constituted republic, which a tyrannical usurpation exhibits to a legal monarchy. Of the real individual tyrant, and of this tyrannical corporation, the manners are precisely the same. The decrees of the one are as despotical as the edicts and ordinances of the other. Both prove the bane of human society, the oppressors of virtue, the munificent rewarders of vice. The court flatterer flourishes under the tyranny of one man; the demagogue, under the tyranny of the multitude; and the flatterer and demagogue are equally solicitous to extend that unlawful domination on which their own influence depends. The demagogue persuades the multitude to disregard the authority of precedent, and to trample under foot every law of the constitution, that full scope may be given to the authority of occasional decrees, well knowing that while the passions of the multitude govern, he who can manage those passions must be master of the state. The multitude listen with delight to one who seems to have nothing at heart but to promote their interest, or gratify their pleasure; and cheerfully accept his invitation of taking the public concerns entirely into their own hands;: so that every established magistracy, and every regular function of political power is enfeebled, suspended, or utterly abolished. The author, therefore, who arraigns such a democracy

---

[1] εκ αγαθη πολυκοιραιη, Iliad, ii. v. 204. Aristotle says, it is uncertain whether Homer meant to brand the complex tyranny of the multitude, or the authority of many individually. Pope prefers the former meaning, "That worst of tyrants, an usurping crowd." Iliad ii. v. 242.

ARISTOTLE's POLITICS.

BOOK VI.

cracy as unworthy of the name of government, seems to reason juftly; for what government can fubfift without laws? If we admit, therefore, democracy to be a form of government, it is plain that a ftate continually fubject to the caprice of occafional decrees, cannot properly be claffed even under the name of democracy [m].

Chap. 5.

Oligarchy, and its four kinds.

Of oligarchy as well as of democracy, there are various kinds. The firft kind is that in which all political power belongs to men of a certain cenfus or fortune, and in which this cenfus is fo high, that the great body of the people are totally excluded from every fhare in the adminiftration. The fecond kind is that in which the pecuniary qualification for office is not fo high as totally to exclude the majority of the citizens, but in which the various councils and magiftracies fupply by election the vacancies that happen among their own members: if they elect from the citizens at large, they act conformably to the principle of an ariftocracy; if they confine their choice to men of a certain cenfus only, they act conformably to the principle of an oligarchy. A third kind of oligarchy takes place, when offices are hereditary; and a fourth, when in addition to this circumftance, the magiftrates govern by their own will and pleafure, and not by eftablifhed laws. This laft and worft kind is called in Greece a dynafty. It bears the fame relation to oligarchy that tyranny does to monarchy, and that the turbulence of the democracy laft defcribed bears to the fair equality of popular government.

Such

[m] This worft fpecies of democracy is what Polybius calls an ochlocracy.—It takes place, he obferves, wherever the will of the majority prevails; one cafe only excepted, that of a people among whom it it habitual and hereditary to venerate religion, law, virtue, and old age. Comp. Polybius, l. vi. c. iv. & c. ix. This ochlocracy, he obferves, neceffarily terminates in the tyranny of one defpot. Ibid.

Such then are the various kinds of oligarchies and democracies. But it ought not to escape the notice of a diligent inquirer into politics, that a constitution may be of one kind by law, and of another in fact. Some states are governed democratically, of which the fundamental laws are not democratical; and others are governed oligarchically, of which the fundamental laws are not oligarchical. In such commonwealths the practice of the government is at variance with its theory; and this most frequently happens in consequence of a silent, gradual, and, therefore, unperceived revolution. In operating this revolution, there is sometimes a long conflict between laws and manners.—Manners finally prevail. The law remains only as a dead letter; while the men who have effected the change, become masters of the commonwealth.

BOOK VI.

A constitution sometimes one thing by law and another in fact.

How this happens.

The forms of oligarchy and democracy, which we have hitherto examined abstractedly, have each of them suitable materials with which they naturally incorporate. A people subsisting chiefly by agriculture, and possessed, as is usual with such a people, of very moderate fortunes, naturally arrange themselves into a legal and well-constituted democracy. They may subsist comfortably by labour, they would be soon ruined by idleness; they contrive a government, therefore, which requires as little expence of time as possible; and employ on all occasions, when it is practicable, the great machine of law to save the labour of man. Their assemblies convene but rarely, because they never convene unnecessarily. A certain census is requisite for enjoying a share in the government; but this census is so moderate that it may be acquired by every industrious citizen, without greater exertions of labour than are necessary to make provision for his family. Among such a people,

Chap. 6,

Of the people qualified for enjoying the best and cheapest form of democracy.

BOOK VI.

people, government is carried on without salaries, without revenues, and without taxes. The affairs of the community, therefore, are left to assume their natural order; since men have no undue motive to engage them to abandon their own profitable concerns, in order to employ themselves in matters which will be much better managed without their unseasonable interference[1].

Of the profit only for the worst and most extravagant democracy.

Between this simple and frugal democracy, and that which naturally establishes itself in consequence of wealth acquired by commerce or conquest, there are two intermediate gradations; one, in which without requiring any qualification in point of fortune, all those who are not of a servile or foreign extraction, are held partners in the government; and another, in which without any regard even to descent or birth, all those who are freemen enjoy the rights of citizens. Yet as under both those gradations, salaries and fees of office are unknown, there will not be any unseasonable interference in matters of administration; and the regularity of law will prevail over the caprice of human affection. The fourth kind of democracy arises the last in point of time, because it cannot take place till cities have acquired a certain measure of population and of wealth. A great population, and that condensed in cities, makes the multitude feel, and enables them to exert their strength. All men indiscriminately claim a share in the government; and as most people cannot, without reducing themselves to beggary, afford time for exercising the functions of the citizen or statesman, their public services must be paid by the commonwealth, and the revenues of the state must supply the deficiencies of their private fortunes. By such an expedient the poorer citizens obtain a greater command of leisure than even the rich themselves. The

[1] This meaning is naturally suggested by what immediately follows.

The former have nothing to care for, their wants being supplied by the public; the latter are encumbered with the weight of their private affairs; and on every occasion so much outvoted, that they often cease to attend any assemblies whatever, either deliberative or judicial, thus abandoning their country to the licentious and lawless multitude.

The first kind of oligarchy naturally takes place, when there is a considerable but not an excessive disproportion among the estates of individuals; and when the census requisite for sharing the government, excludes the majority of the people, yet comprehends, however, such a considerable number of men, that motives of personal interest are outweighed by considerations of public good. Excessive wealth and excessive poverty are equally productive of that restless temper which subverts laws and ruins states. When the members of a democracy are not so poor that they must subsist at the public expence, and the members of an oligarchy not so rich that they disdain the management of their private estates, neither the one nor the other will be easily persuaded unseasonably to interfere in matters of government; and their own interest and convenience will naturally lead them to prefer the authority of laws to that of men. But when the wealth of an oligarchy increases as the number of its members diminishes, then ambition will take possession of every breast; and the *oligarchy* will be exactly the more vicious, in proportion as it approaches to *tyranny*. While diffident of its own strength, it will content itself with commanding elections, and raising to office its creatures and dependents. It will then proceed to govern by itself without the instrumentality of others, and advancing from one step to another in its ambitious career, will render its power

Chap. 7.

Of the people fit for living under the different kinds of oligarchy.

first

first absolute, and then hereditary; thus succeffively degenerating into what has been called a lawlefs and tyrannical dynafty [m].

Befides monarchy, democracy, and oligarchy, there are two other kinds of government ; that which is commonly called an ariftocracy, and that which we have named by the general appellation of all commonwealths, a republic ; a form of political arrangement which, as it rarely occurs, has been omitted by Plato and other writers. In ftrictnefs of language, an ariftocracy is that form of polity in which the pre-eminence of birth, wealth, and every fuch political advantage totally difappears and vanifhes in comparifon of that which is infinitely greater than them all ; a government in which civil honours are diftributed or apportioned by no other rule or ftandard but that of virtue alone ; and in which the duties of a good man perfectly coincide with the duties of a good citizen. But the ariftocracies which commonly prevail, are formed on a coarfer model ; and as they differ from oligarchies on the one hand, fo they differ from this perfect republic on the other. In fuch ariftocracies, refpect is had, not merely to wealth, not merely to virtue, not merely to ftrength and numbers ; but all thofe political advantages claim their refpective fhares of political confideration ; and, combined with each other, form the rule or principle according to which honours and offices are diftributed and conferred. Such is the political arrangement of the ariftocracy of Carthage. Virtue, pure and unmixed, is not the governing principle of that ftate. Yet virtue ftill enjoys a certain fhare of influence ; maintaining in the political conflict, an honourable ftruggle againft wealth and numbers ; equal to either of them fingly, though inferior

[m] Ariftotle here repeats that this kind of oligarchy correfponds with the fourth fpecies of democracy.

inferior to their united strength. In Sparta, virtue and numbers long divided the field; and the reciprocal shocks of those contending principles maintained the pre-eminence of the few, and the freedom of all. There are then various kinds of aristocracies, besides that which is the best and most perfect; and to those already mentioned, we may add every form of mixed government in which the balance of power visibly inclines to the side of the few.

It remains now to treat of this mixed government and of tyranny; which last we throw into the background, as being of all others the least deserving the name of polity. The nature of a mixed government, or what for distinction sake we call a republic, will evidently appear by considering the elements of which it is composed. These are, oligarchy and democracy; though such mixed governments as incline most to the side of democracy are commonly called republics, while those which incline most to the side of oligarchy are commonly called aristocracies; because birth and education seem to have a natural connection with wealth; the rich being already in possession of that very object for the acquisition of which men are most frequently stimulated to injustice. In vulgar language, therefore, a rich man is confounded with a good one; and as there are only three distinct principles which contend for political authority, virtue, wealth, and numbers, (for birth may always be analysed into hereditary virtue or hereditary wealth,) it is plain that if we comprehend under the name of aristocracy, all those governments in which virtue forms a constituent element, we must define a republic, strictly so called, to be that in which wealth and numbers, that is, the prerogatives of the few, and the rights and liberties of the many, are duly respected and impartially maintained. The laws, therefore, adapted to a republic, must be formed by properly blending those

BOOK VI.

Chap. 9.

Of a republic, strictly so called, or mixed government:

its definition.

BOOK VI.

By what nice principles establish-ed, and regulated;

Illustrated by examples.

which prevail in democracies and oligarchies. When, with regard to any one object, the respective laws of these distinct forms of polity are not incompatible with each other, both are to be employed; when they are totally inconsistent, neither of them is to be employed, but a new law is to be framed holding a due middle between them; and when the oligarchic and democratic laws regulating any object, are both of them complex, and consist of many articles or clauses, some clauses are to be copied from the one, and some from the other. In oligarchies, for example, the service of the rich as jurymen, is compelled by a fine; but that of the poor is not rewarded by a fee. In democracies, on the contrary, the attendance of the poor is rewarded, but the non-attendance of the rich is not punished. A law, truly politic and republican, must unite both those partial regulations, by punishing the non-attendance of the rich, and paying the attendance of the poor. Again, in oligarchies a high qualification, in point of fortune, is necessary to constitute the right of voting in the national assembly; in democracies this qualification is often reduced to a mere trifle. A good political law will adopt neither of these extremes, but prefer and establish what is the just middle between them. Again, appointment to office by suffrage is most suitable to the nature of an oligarchy, and appointment to office by lot is most suitable to the nature of democracy; in the former government a high census is required in the candidates; in the latter a small census only, or none. A well-constituted republic, therefore, will borrow the clause respecting the mode of appointment to office from oligarchies, and the clause respecting the pecuniary qualification of the candidates, from democracies. It will *elect* its magistrates, but without paying undue regard to their opulence.

The

The strongest proof that a republic is well composed and happily blended results from this, that the terms oligarchy and democracy may be applied to it with equal, though not exact propriety. Such a republic seems to comprehend both extremes, because it contains a due mixture of opposite principles, nicely poised and accurately adjusted. Of this kind is Sparta, which many call a democracy, because the children of the poor enjoy a similar education with those of the rich; because, in their advancement to manhood, the same institutions and modes of life still embrace both ranks; in their dress and diet there is not any distinction; they eat at common tables, and the clothes of the most wealthy are such as even the poorest can afford to wear. Of the two highest magistracies, the citizens elect the one, and may be themselves elected to the other. The senators are chosen by the assembled multitude, and every one of the people may be chosen to fill a place in the council of the Ephori. On the other hand, many call Sparta an oligarchy, because all offices are conferred by suffrage, none bestowed by lot; and because the power of life and death resides in the breasts of a few. A well-mixed republic, then, must participate of oligarchy and democracy; it must seem to be both, and neither; and it must subsist by internal vigour, not by foreign influence. Any form of commonwealth, good or bad, may be kept together by the impression of external force; but that form is good which flourishes by its native energy; for this can only take place, when each component part feels its own benefit intimately connected with the safety of the whole.

We now proceed to speak of tyranny, rather for the sake of method, than that such an institution is at all worthy of consideration. In treating of monarchy, we formerly examined whether kings were, in general, useful in a commonwealth; and

BOOK VI.

Rule by which it may be known whether a republic be well constituted.

Chap. 10.

Of tyranny, and its different kinds.

BOOK VI. and under what particular circumstances royal government might with propriety be established. We likewise mentioned two kinds of tyranny, both of which bear a resemblance to royalty; the first is, that which generally prevails among barbarians, and which is consonant to their genius and character; the second is, that which occasionally prevailed in some countries of Greece, the government of the Æsymnetes. Both the Barbarian monarchs and the Grecian Æsymnetes, were unquestionably tyrants, since they exercised unlimited and absolute power. But they resembled kings in this, that their power was voluntarily conferred, cheerfully submitted to, and, therefore, lawfully established. But there is a third kind of tyranny, which most properly deserves that odious name, and which stands in direct opposition to royalty; it takes place when one man, the worst, perhaps, and basest in the country, governs a kingdom with no other view than the advantage of himself and his family: a government, which it cannot be supposed, that those who know what freedom is, should voluntarily endure.

Chap. 11.

Principles by which it may be determined, what is practically the best form of government.

We proceed now to investigate what is practically the best sort of commonwealth: not such a commonwealth as requires for its construction any extraordinary combination of virtues and talents, embellished by an accumulation of external advantages; the union of all which ought to form the object rather of our prayers, than of our hopes; but such a commonwealth as is adapted to the ordinary condition of society, and of which most men are qualified to be members. The aristocracies which we formerly described, are either too refined for the coarseness of practice, or approach so nearly to what we have called a republic, that they may be examined by the same principles, and estimated by the same standard; and, indeed, the maxims which we formerly established in our treatise of Ethics, will enable us to appreciate the practical

9 value

value of all governments whatever. The best and happiest life, we proved in that treatise, to be a life of virtue, unobstructed in its exertions by external impediments; and virtue itself, we proved by an accurate and full analysis, to consist in mediocrity. What the best kind of life, therefore, is to an individual, the best government is to a state; for the government I mean (as above specified, not the government constituted by law, but the government existing in fact) is the life of the state. The perfection, therefore, of this political and incorporated life, must be found within the same limits or boundaries which comprehend that condition of external circumstances, and that inward frame of mind, constituting the happiness of those individuals of whom communities are composed.

With regard to external circumstances, communities are composed of three classes of men: men encumbered by wealth, men oppressed by poverty, and men enjoying a happy mediocrity of fortune. Excess of wealth, like superiority in strength or in beauty, disdains the dictates of propriety, and spurns the authority of reason: extreme poverty, like weakness and deformity, sours the temper and debases the character. The former excesses produce insolence; the latter engender baseness: and these, together, form the ordinary sources of all human turpitude; the one spreading into every species of audacious guilt, the other sinking into every kind of cowardly fraud and mean mischief. Under great inequality of external circumstances, a city therefore must be filled, not with men, but with despots and slaves, of those unfit for exercising legal authority, and those unfit for yielding liberal obedience; while friendship, the bond of social life, is broken, destroyed, or corrupted into contempt on the one side, and into envy on the other. A certain mediocrity is necessary to equality, equality to friendliness, and friendliness to security. Under all governments, the happiness

BOOK VI.

Illustration of these principles; and the praise of mediocrity.

BOOK VI.

pineſs of thoſe men is moſt ſecure, whoſe condition is above committing, and below provoking, an injury. Therefore, Phocylides[n] ſaid, and prayed,

"How happy is the middle walk of life,
"O! may it be my portion in the ſtate!"

It is plain, therefore, that the beſt commonwealth is that in which middling men moſt abound; and prove, if not more powerful than both, at leaſt, ſuperior to either of the extremes. When this does not take place, the commonwealth neceſſarily degenerates either into oligarchy or into democracy; both which forms of government are much more likely than a republic abounding in the middle ranks to fall under the tyranny of one man; as ſhall be explained more clearly hereafter, in treating the ſubject of political revolutions. Such a republic is not only leſs liable to be ſubverted: it ſubſiſts unagitated by ſedition; the great intermediate maſs reſtraining the activity of the two hoſtile extremes; for this reaſon, democracies are found to be more durable than oligarchies, becauſe in the former, the middling claſs is more numerous than in the latter; and large communities enjoy more tranquillity than ſmall ones, which, from the paucity of their members, have few citizens of an intermediate condition between riches and poverty. It is this intermediate claſs, however, that alone balances and keeps ſteady the veſſel of the republic; when this claſs is deſtroyed or removed, an outrageous democracy takes place, which is ſpeedily overwhelmed in its own fury.

The

[n] A gnomic or moral poet of Miletus, who flouriſhed five hundred years before Chriſt, the contemporary of Theognis, of Megara; which two, together with old Heſiod, Iſocrates conſiders as the beſt maſters of life and manners. Orat. ad Nicocl. The remains aſcribed to Phocylides do not contain the words in the text; but although. they amount to only 215 verſes, they thrice repeat the ſentiment. See vv. 12, 52, 65.

8

ARISTOTLE's POLITICS.

BOOK VI.

The best legislators have, in point of rank and fortune, been men of an ordinary level. As to himself, Solon attests this in his poetry. The same is to be said of Charondas, and of almost all others. Lycurgus was not the king, but the legislator of Sparta. A republic founded on the salutary principles of mediocrity and just equality is, indeed, a rare phænomenon. Of all those invested with power, one man alone[o], as far as history informs us, could be prevailed on to establish such a political arrangement; most other leaders, whether of the nobles or of the people, never contenting themselves with equality, but always aspiring to superiority, and alternately abusing their advantages for giving an undue preponderancy to their respective factions. In this fatal ambition they have been encouraged and confirmed by the leading states of Greece, which have always been solicitous to mould every neighbouring republic after their own model. Blinded by passion, contending parties have been unable, or unwilling, to perceive any thing between the miserable alternative of commanding with insolence, or obeying with servility; and substantial happiness has therefore been almost constantly sacrificed to silly pride. Having thus examined what is practically the best commonwealth, it will be easy to appreciate the merit of all others, by their degrees of approximation to this model of perfection; a model, which the legislator ought always to keep in view under every condition of society, but which the wide variety of materials, on which he has to operate, will enable him to imitate under different circumstances with more or less exactness, and more or less facility.

The passions of individuals, and of states, resist the establishment of the best government;

which is a limit and model of perfection, to which legislators ought continually to approximate.

In

[o] Aristotle perhaps means Clisthenes, the Athenian, whom he praises in other parts of this work, particularly l. vi. c. 4. See the History of Ancient Greece, v. ii. c. xviii. p. 118. Clisthenes restored the institutions of Solon. This was his chief merit. I rather think, therefore, that Aristotle means Solon himself.

BOOK VI.
Chap. 12.

The legislator and state-man ought always to strengthen the middling class, and to render it more powerful than either extreme.

ARISTOTLE's POLITICS.

In every community whatever, the stability of government requires, that those who desire its continuance should be more powerful than those who desire its dissolution. The political arrangement, therefore, of every state, must always depend on the prevailing inclination of that party which is preponderant; and this preponderancy again must consist either in quantity or quality; quantity, denoting mere superiority in number; and quality, the distinguishing excellencies of the upper ranks, birth, wealth, education, the love of glory and of the republic. Quantity and quality often acting in opposite directions, their relative forces must be estimated, and a proportion instituted for discovering which principle will prevail in the conflict. If one party surpasses in quality more than it is surpassed in quantity, it is plain that the balance must incline to the side of the few, and different kinds of oligarchies must necessarily be established. If, on the contrary, the popular party exceed more in quantity, than they are excelled in quality, democracy must prevail: the first and best kind of democracy, if the majority of the people be husbandmen; the last and worst, if tradesmen and manufacturers: and, in proportion to the ingredients composing them, the intermediate kinds, more or less faulty. But, in all those cases, a wise legislator will constantly endeavour to comprehend, in his scheme of polity, men of the middle rank, and to render them, if not more powerful than both the extremes, at least superior to either; because, when this takes place, the government is likely to prove durable. There is not any reason to apprehend, that the rich and the poor should lay aside their natural animosities, and conspire against this class which is comparatively on good terms with both, and the natural mediator between them. The contending parties cannot, therefore, weaken or diminish its influence,

ence, without proportionally strengthening the power of their respective adversaries. But those who establish oligarchies neglect this consideration; and by aspiring to an imaginary good, incur a real evil: for the preposterous ambition of the great proves ruinous to more states than even the unjust violence of the multitude.

The great, in order to disguise their ambition, and the multitude, in order to palliate their injustice, have recourse to many juggling artifices, by which they endeavour mutually to deceive each other. These devices regard the five following objects; the assembly, the courts of justice, the magistracies, the militia, and the gymnastic exercises. To engross all power in the assembly, the rich and noble easily delude the people into a law, exacting a severe fine for non-attendance from men of a certain census. Such men, therefore, will be careful to attend; while the poor, who are not liable to any penalty, will for the most part desert their duty, and thus abandon their share in the government. A similar contrivance succeeds with regard to the courts of justice, and the duty of serving as jurymen. By a law of Charondas[p], a fine was in this case imposed even on the poor; but so small, that it served no other purpose than that of saving appearances; for when one trick is discovered, another is substituted in its stead. Thus, all who have inscribed their names in the public register, are entitled to exercise the functions of deliberative and judiciary power; but if, after this, they neglect to exercise them, they subject themselves to a severe penalty; the poor, therefore, avoid enrolling their names, lest they should incur the penalty. With regard to burdensome offices, they are permitted to excuse themselves from holding them, without other proof than that of their own oaths; they are not compelled, under heavy fines, to provide

[p] See above, b. ii. c. x. p. 121.

BOOK VI.

Those by which the democratical party deceive the great,

Rule by which the the census ought to be established.

Rule by which the military force ought to be established;

provide themselves with arms, nor to acquire skill in the gymnastic exercises; and all those exemptions, which they are taught to regard as indulgences, effectually diminish their consideration in the state.

The lower classes of men sometimes endeavour, in their turn, to encounter the artifices of the great with similar addres. The non-attendance of the rich in the assembly, or courts of justice, is not punished; but their own attendance is rewarded; and this fee or reward, which is to them a mighty matter, is far too small to operate as a motive on their superiors. A well-constituted republic ought, as we observed before, to fee the poor, and fine the rich; by which means, both parties would be rendered diligent in the discharge of their political functions, and neither side be enabled to engross power, and usurp the commonwealth.

Wealth is a thing relative and indefinite; and the census, therefore, in each state, must vary with the circumstances of the community. It ought never to be so high, as to leave that portion of the citizens which is excluded from office, more considerable than that which is admitted: otherwise, the government cannot be expected to prove durable. The mere populace will easily submit to exclusion, but they will not tolerate injustice, or brook insult. They will even fight boldly, if they are fed abundantly; and the patient submission of the people may generally be ensured by the prudent moderation of their superiors.

The census, we have said, is a thing comparative and indefinite: but the right of bearing arms has its precise limit. It must be bestowed on citizens, and them only; for to disarm men is little less than to enslave them. In some states, as the republic of Malea, all those who have ever borne arms, exercised the

deliberative

deliberative and judiciary powers; but offices of executive magistracy belonged to those only who were actually enrolled as soldiers. After the subversion of royalty, the first governments in Greece were entirely in the hands of military men, and those wholly horsemen; for before the invention of tactics, the strength of states consisted merely in cavalry. But as populousness increased, and tactics were improved, the sphere of political consideration was extended, and the people at large became sharers in the great partnership of government. What is now regarded as an aristocratical republic was, therefore, anciently *called* a democracy, but had, in *fact*, a strong tendency to oligarchy, or even to royalty. The intermediate ranks were then few in number, and destitute of strength; and therefore they, as well as their inferiors, easily submitted to the authority of the same men in peace whom they had been accustomed to follow and obey as their leaders in war.

Having thus examined states in relation to the materials of which they are composed, and shewn how many, and what kinds of compositions result from the various combinations of the same simple elements, we must proceed to analyse and explain what is properly called the sovereignty. This complex object comprehends the deliberative, executive, and judicial powers[a]; powers, which must be differently regulated and distributed in relation to the nature and plan of each particular constitution; but which, in all constitutions, ought to be regulated and distributed agreeably to public utility, the great end of all legal governments. The deliberative power is generally supposed to include the right of determining concerning war and

---

[a] I have here expressed Aristotle's sense in modern language. In this chapter he treats concerning that part of the sovereignty which he calls, το βυλιυομενον, translated the deliberative;—in chapter xv. concerning that part which he calls το περι τας αρχας, translated the executive;—in chapter xvi. concerning that part which he calls το δικαστικον, translated the judicial.

BOOK VI.

The various modes in which it may be regulated in democracies;

and peace; concerning laws, treaties, alliances, death, banishment, and confiscation; as well as the right of calling the magistrates to account for malversation in office. These important matters must be entrusted either to the people at large, or to a certain description of the people constituting one or more distinct councils: or some of those great questions must be decided by the popular assembly, and others committed to distinct tribunals, or particular magistrates. That all matters of deliberation should be decided by all the people, which is consonant to the nature of democracy, is susceptible of many variations; for all the people may be entitled to deliberate and decide, either collectively, or successively; which latter obtains in the republic of Telecles the Milesian. In some republics, the different magistrates form a supreme council, which directs the ordinary business of government; but magistracy is exercised by men drawn promiscuously from tribes, wards, districts, and the minutest subdivisions of the people, until it passes successively through the whole body. Yet the citizens at large never convene in the popular assembly, except for the purpose of making new laws; of regulating the constitution; or of hearing, on any important emergency, the resolves of the magistrates. In other republics, the assembly convenes not only for those purposes, but for the purpose of elections, for deciding war and peace, and for examining the conduct of men in office, who, on all ordinary occasions, direct, as well as carry on, the business of government, acting for the people at large[r], from whom

[r] In modern language, representing the people at large. We shall soon find deliberative and elective assemblies, composed of a part of the citizens, acting for, or representing the people at large; which Aristotle sometimes considers as the best form of democracy, and sometimes qualifies with the title of πολιτεια. ιδι δι ἱ τροτοι τα παντας πλιυες' ι.ς μη, το κατα μερος, αλλα μη παντας αθροες. This is said with regard to deliberative assemblies, c. xiv. and with regard to elective assemblies, he says, c. xv. το δι, μη παντας αμα μη καθιςαναι, ιξ απαιτων δι, ::: πολιτικον.

whom they are appointed by lot, or elected by suffrage. Another mode of constituting the deliberative power is, that the national assembly convene, to appoint the magistrates, to take an account of their administration, and to decree war or peace; but that all other matters be determined, as well as conducted, by distinct magistrates or ministers appointed by lot, when ordinary talents and plain honesty are sufficient for the proper discharge of their duty, and elected by suffrage when, in addition to these qualities, experience and skill appear requisite for the due execution of their office. The last and worst mode of constituting the deliberative power, is that of lodging it on all occasions with the great body of the people, convened in the public assembly, and rendering the magistrates, as to matters of volition, mere passive instruments for executing the pleasure of the multitude. This preposterous distribution prevails only in that kind of democracy, which we have proved to be analogous to oligarchic dynasty and monarchic tyranny.

All the modes of regulating the deliberative power, above explained, are consonant with the nature of democracy; but when this power is always lodged with a part of the community, or with a particular description of men, to the perpetual exclusion of all others, an oligarchy necessarily takes place. Yet, when this description includes men of moderate fortunes, and when all who acquire such fortunes are of course summoned to the council, and when there are certain fundamental laws, which even this supreme council does not think itself empowered to abrogate or alter, the moderation of such an oligarchy approaches nearly to the arrangements of what we have called a well-constituted republic. That also may be called a moderate oligarchy, in which men of a certain census elect a council entrusted with the deliberative power, but bound

BOOK VI.

to exercife this power agreeably to eftablifhed laws. The oligarchy degenerates into a tyrannical dynafty, when the deliberative body fupplies, by its own authority, the vacancies among its members; or, what is ftill worfe, when prudence in deliberation is fuppofed an hereditary virtue, and the right of deciding abfolutely for the community at large is vefted in certain families, and defcends from fathers to their children [r].

in mixed governments.
When fome matters of deliberation are entrufted to the magiftrates, and others committed to the people at large, particularly the alternative of war and peace, and the impeachment of men in office, fuch an arrangement may be called ariftocratical; particularly when the magiftrates are appointed by election, or by a mixture of choice and chance, that is, appointed by lot from perfons whofe characters have been previoufly examined, and generally approved. The mixture of lot and fuffrage, and the appointment to fome deliberative functions in the one way, and to other deliberative functions in the other, is confonant to the nature of what we call a republic. Such then are the modes of diftributing this portion of the fovereignty, conformably to the nature of different governments.

How democracies and oligarchies may be improved into better governments.
It would be highly conducive to the improvement of what is now called democracy, were that oligarchic regulation to be introduced which fines the rich for non-attendance. By this means, the affembly would be better compofed, and its deliberations more moderate and more falutary, the paffions and interefts of different orders mutually repreffing that violence to which all of them, unchecked, are liable. It would, alfo, prove greatly advantageous, that in each tribe or diftrict, certain deliberative functions fhould be conferred by fuffrage, and others

[r] See above, p. 288. with which compare Polybius, vi. 8. vol. ii. p. 471. edit, Sweigh.

others decided by lot; and if the populace be extremely numerous, that only certain divisions of them should be entitled successively to receive fees, or allowed successively to try their chance in the appointment by lot. In oligarchies, on the other hand, the people at large might be rendered less hostile, nay friendly, to the government, were certain deliberative functions entrusted to men chosen from the whole promiscuously, or were an institution to be introduced similar to what prevails in some republics, called the Council of Preadvisers, who prepare and impartially examine those public questions, which the nobles or citizens are afterwards entitled to decide. Nay, the nobles or magistrates might assume the office of preadvisers, which would give them a negative, before debate, on all popular decrees; or they might submit public measures to the free discussion of the people, reserving to themselves the right of ultimate decision. In republics, the people convened in the national assembly ought to have the power of acquittal, but not of condemnation; the latter, in the last resort, ought always to rest with the magistrates and the law. The reverse of this prevails; the power of acquittal depends on the few, that of condemnation is lodged with the many. So much with regard to the deliberative power, which constitutes the foundation and root of the sovereignty.

The executive power of government must necessarily be entrusted to magistrates, in whose appointment, regulation, and distribution, there is a great variety of cases. How many magistrates ought there to be? with what functions ought they to be entrusted? how long ought each office to last? a year, six months, longer than the former period, or shorter than the latter? Ought any offices to be for life, and ought the same

offices

BOOK VI.

offices to be held more than once by the same person? Still farther, who ought to elect or appoint the magistrates? from whom ought they to be chosen or appointed? and in what manner ought the appointment to be made? A philosophical statesman ought clearly to comprehend all those varieties, and to be capable of solving each question in all the ways that are particularly adapted to the nature and end of the different forms of government.

Wherein the executive power consists.

First of all, it is not perhaps clearly ascertained what properly constitutes a magistracy. A state requires many assistants and many superintendants—priests; ambassadors; sacred heralds; exhibitioners, at their own expence, of public amusements; all of whom, if not necessary for its mere subsistence, are yet essential to its well-being and happiness. None of these, however, are called magistrates, though they be appointed, as all magistrates are, by suffrage or lot; neither do we call magistrates those destined to functions merely subservient to œconomy, as corn-meters; nor those employed in offices rather menial than magisterial; offices, which in states moderately wealthy, are commonly consigned to slaves. He then is a magistrate who, in his own person, or associated with colleagues, is in certain matters entrusted by the public with the power of deliberating, of judging, above all of commanding; and to define the word more nicely, is not necessary for our present purpose.

The discrimination of offices in relation to the magnitude of the community, and the various forms of government.

To return then from words to things, we observe that the division of labour greatly facilitates all pursuits, and that each kind of work is best performed, when each is allotted to a separate workman. To the complicated affairs of government, this observation is particularly applicable; but it is not always possible that it should be practically applied. Small communities require

quire nearly the same diſtinct offices of magiſtracy, that are neceſſary in large ones; but they do not require, that the duties of any one office ſhould be ſo often exerciſed, or that the magiſtrates ſhould ſo often perform preciſely the ſame functions. Small communities therefore may, without much inconvenience, admit of pluralities; and this is a fortunate circumſtance, ſince it would not be eaſy, in ſuch communities, to find a ſucceſſion of men willing and well qualified to exerciſe all public offices ſeparately. It is neceſſary, therefore, to have recourſe to an accumulation of employment, and to make the ſame individual anſwer ſeveral purpoſes; competently, though not perfectly; like thoſe complex contrivances, the *cbeliſcolychnia*, which, in the houſes of the poor, ſerve alternately as ſpits and candleſticks. Some offices muſt be ſeparated, on account of the different places in which they are exerciſed; and others, on account of the different objects or perſons to whom they relate. Can the ſame magiſtrate, who preſides over the police in the market-place, direct that important object elſewhere? Ought he, who ſuperintends the modeſty of boys, to have the additional burden of guarding that of women? Under different forms of government, there muſt be different magiſtrates, and thoſe, inveſted with different degrees of power, and appointed from different deſcriptions of perſons. The office of ſenator is conſonant to the nature of democracy; but that of preadviſer, which was above deſcribed, is peculiarly applicable to oligarchy. In ſome democracies, indeed, the authority of the ſenate is inconſiderable; but this happens only in that laſt and worſt kind of democracy, where the people, corrupted by fees, forſake their private affairs, to carry on the lucrative trade of government. The cenſor of manners, is a magiſtrate adapted only to an ariſtocracy. What ſhould he do in a democracy!

BOOK VI.

The various ways of appointing magiftrates.

Is it poffible, under fuch a government, to keep the wives of the poor in their houfes! and his remonftrances would be fuperfluous in an oligarchy, where women, efpecially the wives of the magiftrates, are diffolved in luxury.

We now proceed to the important fubject of the appointment of magiftrates; a fubject included within three terms, each of which admits of three variations. The three terms are, thofe who may appoint, thofe who may be appointed, and the manner of the appointment. Thofe who appoint, may confift either of all the citizens, or of a part only; or, in fome offices, they may confift of all; in others, of a part. Thofe who may be appointed, may confift either of all the citizens, or of a part only; or, in fome offices, of all; in others, of a part. The manner of appointment is alfo threefold, by election; by fuffrage; in fome offices by election, in others by fuffrage. There are, therefore, in all, nine variations or differences; and it comes to be confidered in how many ways thofe nine differences may be combined with each other; the appointers, the appointed, and the mode of appointment entering into each combination. The three variations or differences, in the appointers, combined with the fame number of variations or differences in the appointed, will give, it is plain, nine combinations of two terms; and each of thefe nine may be repeated three times, fince the appointment may be made in three ways. There are, therefore, in all twenty-feven combinations, or twenty-feven varieties in the appointment of magiftrates; of which varieties, fome are confonant to the nature of one kind of government, and others to that of another. That *all* the citizens fhould be capable of appointing, or capable of being appointed, is confonant to the nature of democracy; but more efpecially when the word *all* is taken to denote the whole body

of

ARISTOTLE's POLITICS.

of the citizens collectively. It also denotes the several tribes and minuter divisions of the citizens, which, united, compose the whole. In this latter sense, all the citizens are capable of appointing successively, or of being successively appointed; each division enjoying those advantages in its turn; which regulation, while it prevents the tumult incident to numerous assemblies, ensures the benefits of equality and freedom[s]. We have shewn that each of the three terms concerned in the appointment of magistrates, admits of three varieties. If two of the terms, namely, the appointers and appointed, be limited to two varieties only, and consist in all elections either of the whole or a part of the citizens, without coupling together the whole and the part in the manner above specified, then all the varieties in constituting magistrates will be reduced to twelve[t]. For the whole citizens may appoint from the whole, by suffrage; by lot; in some offices by suffrage, in others by lot: or the whole may appoint from a part by suffrage; by lot; and sometimes by suffrage, sometimes by lot. This, then, affords six varieties; and there must be the same number precisely when a part only appoints. For this part may appoint from the whole by vote, by lot; or sometimes by vote, sometimes by lot; and likewise from a part, by the same three modes of appointment, that is by vote, by lot; and sometimes in the one way, sometimes in the other. There will,

[s] Such, according to Aristotle, was once the plan of the republic of Mantinæa, so justly celebrated; and such was the republic of Teleclcs the Milesian. Polyb. l. vi. c. xliii. Ælian Var. Hist. l. ii. c. xxii. Maximus Tyrius, Dissert. vi. The last mentioned author calls Mantinæa an aristocracy, which the learned Schweighæuser, Annot. ad Polyb. t. v. p. 384. says, agrees with Aristotle, Polit. l. vi. c. iv. This, however, is not true; for Aristotle calls it a democracy.

[t] When there are three varieties in each of the three terms, then $3 \times 3 = 9 \times 3 = 27$; but when two of the terms are supposed to vary only in two ways, then $2 \times 2 = 4$. & $4 \times 3 = 12$. The text is corrupt; and it seems scarcely possible to give any clear explanation of it, that will not be liable to philological objections.

BOOK VI.

adjusted to the different forms of government.

will, therefore, be twelve combinations, without coupling together the whole and the part, either in the appointers or the appointed; that is, without reckoning the combinations resulting from the whole appointing in some cafes, and a part in others, and from the capacity of the whole to be appointed in some cafes, and that of a part only in others. A simple democracy requires that the whole collectively should appoint from the whole by vote; by lot; or in some offices by vote, in others by lot. A well-ordered republic requires that the whole not collectively, but separately by divisions, should appoint from the whole, or from a part; by suffrage, by lot, or by a due mixture of both. An oligarchy requires that a part only should be invested with the right of appointing, either by vote or by lot; or in some cafes by vote, in others by lot; and this last mode, as it is most satisfactory to the people at large, is most favourable to the stability of the government. In aristocracies, all the citizens may be invested with the right of electing, but the elected must be persons of a certain description. In oligarchies, the sphere of the candidates, as well as that of the electors, must be narrowed and confined to persons of a certain cenfus. Such then are the principal modes of constituting magistrates, which are respectively adapted to different governments; but when different modes are equally well adapted to the frame of the government, the propriety of preferring the one to the other will depend on the duties and functions of the office or magistracy itself. Under the same form of government there may be good reasons for appointing a general in one way, and a judge in another.

Chap. 16.

Of the judiciary power.

Of the three portions of the sovereignty above mentioned, the legislative, the executive, and the judiciary, the last only remains to be treated. The varieties of courts of justice are limited by the different modes in which they may be constituted;

tuted; the qualities of the members of whom they may be composed; and the various kinds of causes which they are empowered to determine. Judges may, like other magistrates, be appointed by suffrage, or by lot; from all the citizens indiscriminately, or from persons of a certain description only; but the different nature of the causes which they are empowered to determine, forms the specific distinction among courts of justice. These causes may all be reduced to the eight following classes: 1. The responsibility of magistrates; for in every government not arbitrary, there must be a court of impeachment. 2. Acts of injustice respecting the property of the community, whether committed by magistrates or private persons. 3. All acts, by whomever committed, which have a tendency to subvert or change the constitution. 4. All matters relating to fines and amercements. 5. Disputes concerning contracts of a certain importance, or concerning objects exceeding a certain value. 6. All causes concerning homicide, including under that general name, malice propense, chance-medley, and all the various cases in which the life of a man is acknowledged to have been taken away, but the criminality of the act is the matter in question. The court of Phreattæ in Athens tries persons who, having fled for murder, have returned to their country; which causes, however, cannot prove so numerous as to require a separate jurisdiction, even in large communities. 7. The causes of strangers, whether among themselves or between strangers and citizens, form the seventh class. 8. The eighth includes pecuniary questions of small amount, five drachmas, or a little more, which must indeed be determined, but which ought not to occupy the attention of a numerous tribunal.

BOOK VI.

Judicial proceedings reduced to eight kinds.

BOOK VI.

How inferior courts are formed, is not always a matter of the most essential importance; but unless those supreme judicatures be well regulated, which decide great political questions, and ascertain men's rights in society, confusion and sedition will ensue.

The various ways in which courts of judicature may be constituted.

Such courts may be constituted from the citizens at large, appointed by lot or suffrage, to judge of all political or public causes; or the judges in some causes may be appointed by lot, and in others by suffrage; or in trying the same causes, or causes of the same nature, the same court may be constituted partly by suffrage, and partly by lot. There are, therefore, four ways in which the judges may be appointed from all the citizens collectively; and there are precisely as many when courts are constituted from all the citizens, not collectively, but successively; that is, when each division of the people enjoys in its turn the privilege of supplying the country with judges. Again, if the judges are to be appointed from men of a certain description only, courts may, on this supposition also, be constituted in four ways. For men of this decription, distinguished by wealth, birth, or merit, may be appointed by lot or suffrage to try all political or public causes; or the judges in some causes may be appointed by lot, in others by suffrage; or in trying the same causes, or causes of the same nature, the same court may be constituted partly by lot and partly by suffrage. There appears, therefore, to be in all twelve modes of forming judiciary assemblies, without coupling together the whole and the part; that is, without supposing that some courts are formed from the whole citizens collectively or successively, and others composed of men of a certain description only; or that the numbers

numbers of the same courts are chosen partly from the citizens at large, and partly from men of diſtinction.

That all political or public cauſes ſhould be determined by judges choſen from the people at large, is agreeable to the nature of democracy; that all ſuch cauſes ſhould be determined by men of a certain deſcription, is agreeable to the nature of oligarchy; but that ſome courts ſhould be formed from the citizens at large, and others from a diſtinguiſhed portion of the citizens; or that the members of the ſame court ſhould be appointed, ſome of them from the whole body of the people, and others from a diſtinguiſhed part of the people; ſome of them by lot, and others by ſuffrage; all theſe mixtures and combinations are agreeable to the nature of a juſtly conſtituted and fairly balanced republic.

(317)

ARISTOTLE's POLITICS.

BOOK VII.*

INTRODUCTION.

THIS Seventh Book treats of political revolutions, whether flow and gradual, or rapid and violent; whether originating in the nature of civil society itself, or refulting from the form and principle of different conftitutions of government. Had the author written with the exprefs defign of benefiting the prefent age, this part of his work could not be more ufeful or more feafonable. Even a more ferious attention is due to it, than to any thing which the prefent times could poffibly produce; fince at this momentous æra, when the nations which have overturned their own governments, are continually exhorting and encouraging neighbouring ftates to imitate their example, we here find the opinions of the wifeft man of antiquity on the great and awful queftions which now agitate the world: the opinions of an author remote from our concerns, unmoved by our paffions, unaffected by our interefts. On this ferious fubject, therefore, which now more than at any other period in modern hiftory, comes home to the bufinefs and bofoms of individuals, I need not be greatly apprehenfive of tiring the reader, when I endeavour to place in a clear and
ftrong

* Commonly publifhed as Book V.

BOOK VII.

strong light, those observations of the Stagirite which seem best calculated to answer the immediate purpose of public and present utility.

From the nature of society, which, as above explained, is not a mere mass but a system, implying a distinction and subordination of parts; and still more palpably, though not more necessarily, from the nature of property, the creature of society; which in its very essence implies inequality, there must grow up and co-exist, with every community of men, whatever be the form of the commonwealth, a popular and an aristocratical interest [a]; and thence, not indeed a perpetual conflict, but a perpetual tendency to conflict, between the rights and privileges of the many, and the pre-eminences and prerogatives of the few. This fermenting discontent may be hindered from blazing into sedition, either by force or by art. All ranks may be levelled by the cruel hand of despotism; they may all be confounded by the wild rage of democracy. But these are remedies which cure the evil only by killing the patient. The important question is, how this tendency to dissension may be repressed, without destroying that degree of independence or security which is essential to happiness, or that degree of power and authority which is essential to humanity itself; since indispensably necessary in rearing and holding together the fabric of political society, in which all the perfections of humanity originate, and in which only their energies can be unfolded and displayed [b].

The

[a] In some of the Italian republics of the middle age, the people destroyed the nobles; but the distinction immediately sprang up between "il popolo grasso & il popolo minuto;" and faction, instead of being softened, was thereby exasperated. Machiavel, Nerli, Malavolti, passim.

[b] See above, p. 21, & seq.

The propofed queftion Ariftotle endeavours to anfwer. He BOOK
obferves that the evil moft threatening to fociety, may be leffened VII.
by fkilful political arrangement, nicely adapting to each other the
principles and fprings of government; but that it never can be
eradicated unlefs one portion of mankind are fo trained and
educated that they will difdain to commit injuftice, and think
themfelves more degraded by offering an infult, than even by
receiving it; while thofe of an inferior ftamp, how much inclined foever many of them may be to do wrong, are convinced
that it cannot be done with impunity, and that they cannot
hurt their fuperiors, without thereby more materially hurting
their families and themfelves[c]. In an age expofed like the
prefent to the conflict of oppofite and unrelenting factions, the
Stagirite, therefore, maintained that oligarchies, ariftocracies,
and every defcription of government vefted in the few, can
only be upheld by moderation in language as well as in behaviour; and that a fingle word of contumely had fometimes
fhaken the proudeft *dynaflies*[d]. He maintained that popular
governments on the other hand, could reft fecurely on no other
foundation than that of political juftice; which confifts in
diftributing to each individual his due, and in affigning to
wealth and birth as well as to talents and virtues, their legitimate diftinctions and fair honours. While he thus endeavours
to moderate the hoftility of contending extremes, and to
fmooth their mutual afperities, he ftrenuoufly exerts himfelf to make the middle claffes of men love and cherifh their
condition as the very beft and happieft in which they poffibly
could be placed; and, therefore, to reject and repel every attempt that might difturb or deftroy it, as a daring invafion of
their

[c] Book ii. c. vii. paffim.   [d] See above, p. 283.

their dearest interests. Governments are good and nations happy, in proportion to the preponderancy of the middle ranks, and their ability to defy the pride and oppression of the great, as well as to resist the rapacity and malignity of the vulgar. Where this grand test of national felicity is found, the citizens or subjects ought to regard as matters of little moment, and even to consider with distrust, any proposed additions to their political advantages; which it will be always easier for vice and folly to destroy or diminish, than for the most enlarged wisdom to meliorate or extend [e].

Governments must always have their imperfections, while conducted by such imperfect creatures as men, whose nature it is to bestow an undue preference on the present above the future, and on a slight immediate benefit resulting to themselves above a far greater, more extensive, and more permanent advantage accruing to the public. All governments, therefore, that ever were established or devised, have contained, on the slightest examination, innumerable inconveniences; which when deeply and intimately mingled in the nature of the constitution itself, ought rather to be patiently endured than violently corrected [f], because they are as much more tolerable than would be the evils of anarchy and sedition, as a state of civilization in which men lie under many oppressive restraints, is preferable to that of savage ferocity in which they are continually tearing to pieces each other; a melancholy spectacle which history never fails to exhibit, when government is for a moment suspended, or its powers to a certain degree enfeebled. The inherent vices of man, his pride, avarice, ambition, and selfishness, render it necessary that power should somewhere be exercised, lest injury should every where be committed; and the fewer and

[e] See above, Book iv. c xi. [f] See above, Book ii. c. vi. p. 101, & seq.

and feebler those vices are, the government will naturally be the milder and more moderate. All plans of policy which suppose a complete reformation in the manners of mankind, are chimerical; but reformation to a certain point, salutary discipline will gradually produce; and exactly in proportion to the effect of this discipline, governments may be meliorated, and one system of policy be rendered more gentle and more desireable than another [c]. For this reason our author observes, that the more society is improved and education perfected, the more equality will prevail, and the farther will liberty be extended.

But even this political equality or liberty has, according to the Stagirite, its fixed and unalterable limits; since no political advantage, except the equal protection of just laws, can be carried to its utmost height, without becoming inconsistent with other advantages, collectively more important. Men in one sense are born equal; they are all equal as to their visible powers or *energies*, because they are all at their birth devoid of *any* that can be of the least public utility; but they are even then, extremely unequal as to their latent endowments or *capacities*; since, with precisely the same treatment and the same education, different individuals will attain very different measures of courage and wisdom, as well as of strength and agility. This original inequality is confirmed and strengthened by the exigencies and necessities of society, under all its possible forms; which, the more perfect it is, the more perfectly it will concur with the views and intentions of nature in promoting the benefit and happiness of the human race; purposes that can only be promoted

by

[c] αιτι δι το βελτιον ηθος, βελτιονος αιτιον πολιτειας. Polit. l. viii. c. i.

ARISTOTLE's POLITICS.

BOOK VII.

by the fubordination of paffion and ignorance to reafon and wifdom. This is the great and paramount law of political fociety by which all men are bound from infancy to old age, and from their birth to their death [d]. Society then is a fyftem, having the good and perfection of humanity for its end, and requiring for the fpecific purpofes for which the fyftem is ordained, an interchange of action, a reciprocity of aid, a diftinction and fubordination of parts; heads to contrive, and hands to execute. For this reafon, the inferior ranks of men, thofe habitually employed in perfonal fervice or productive induftry, were debarred in moft Grecian republics from high political functions; functions deemed incompatible with thofe mean and mercenary employments, that have a tendency to narrow or debafe the faculties; to obftruct liberal thought, and reftrain manly exertion. What is properly called the populace in contradiftinction to the people at large, then confifted almoft entirely of flaves; a palpable and odious deformity in the ancient republics; fince a great proportion of mankind was thus fubjected to a government, not of law; but of arbitrary will [e]. Yet perfect equality and univerfal fuffrage are arrangements not lefs blameable or lefs dangerous; fince, as our author perpetually inculcates, thefe wild projects would totally fubvert the principles on which fociety is built, and overturn

[d] " A natural ariftocracy is diffufed by God through the whole body of mankind." Harrington's Oceana, p. 14. edit. 1656. " An army may as well confift of foldiers without officers, as a commonwealth confift of a people without a gentry." Ibid. Yet Harrington, furely, was not a man of a flavifh mind. How far have the profeffed followers of Locke, the Roufſeaus, the Turgots, the Prices, &c. outdone the enlightened friends of liberty in former ages!

[e] See above, b. i. c. iv. p. 32. The Grecian inftitutions, as I have there fhewn, tended to palliate, but certainly did not cure the evil.

overturn the great fundamental law on which only it can rest.

Innumerable examples might be given of the same kind, all conspiring to prove that an ambition to reach perfection in one point of advantage, is destructive of other advantages not less essential. An experiment has been made in our own times of forming a simple legislature; or, in other words, of confiding what is called by Greek writers the deliberative power of government to one single assembly. This experiment stands in direct opposition to the recorded wisdom of antiquity, which maintained that two deliberative assemblies were essentially necessary in every well-regulated state, because absurd and ruinous resolutions were much less likely to be taken by two different bodies of men deliberating concerning the same object, than by one body of men only; whether a senate of the nobles, or an assembly of the people. If we suppose it to be ten to one, that such an extraordinary combination of circumstances should occur, as might extort from one of those courts or assemblies a decree ruinous to the state, or to any part of it, the rules of calculation will teach us, that it is not twenty, but an hundred to one, that the same decree should at the same time be confirmed by the second court or assembly, differently composed, and differently constituted. For the safety of the public, therefore, two deliberative bodies are always better than one; and according to the same principle of reasoning, three would be still better than two, and four better than three. But it is easy to perceive that though the purpose of mature deliberation would thus be more perfectly secured by the multiplication of courts and assemblies, the great end of seasonable and wise decision would not thereby the more probably be attained; but on the contrary, through

BOOK VII.

delays and diffenfions, would commonly be entirely defeated. From this plain and palpable example, we may learn to perceive with our author that, in matters of far more difficulty and delicacy, political wifdom confifts in avoiding extremes. He continually inculcates and repeats, that the propriety of practical things lies not in an indivifible point, but in a broad middle; that in them nice accuracy is not to be aimed at; but that we muft be contented in politics with fuch a degree of perfection as fuits the coarfenefs of the fubject; nor prepofteroufly forego, by over-refinement in one point of advantage, other advantages ftill more folid; relinquifh certainty for hope; or incur the danger of real evil for the fake of imaginary improvement.

Of all political errors (an error long prevalent in the practice as as well as in the theory of the Greek republics) the greateft is that of thinking that the inftitutions of one people may be fafely communicated to another, differently endowed and differently circumftanced. Men are no where to be found unwritten tablets. Their minds are deeply impreffed by education and habit, as well as by the events of time and chance, which giving to each nation its diftinctive character, peculiarly adapt it to that form of political arrangement into which it has been gradually moulded. The eftablifhing of governments is the work of time; and to new-model them fuccefsfully and happily, requires ftill more time than originally to eftablifh them; becaufe laws operate as practical principles of moral conduct, and old principles muft be obliterated by time and cuftom, before the new can by the fame means be communicated and impreffed. Men deftitute of principles are the moft odious and moft abominable of favages; and practical principles are to be acquired by practice only; they are

the

the refult of repeated acts, fortified by time and familiarifed by cuftom. Yet in direct oppofition to thefe maxims of reafon, confirmed by univerfal experience, we have feen the revolutionary doctrines which prevailed in the worft times of Greece, revived in the prefent age; and a fingle nation propofing in a tone of authority the inftitutions, which fhe herfelf has thought fit to adopt, to all the countries around her; and, in her eagernefs not only to diffufe her political principles as extenfively as the world, but to reduce them every where to practice, ftriving, with the cruel tyranny of Procruftes, to fit the body of each captive traveller to her murderous and torturing bed.

When Ariftotle oppofes innovation, however, it is not on coarfe popular arguments: he does not appeal merely to our feelings; he does not addrefs our *prejudices*; he does not attempt to excite a fuperftitious veneration for antiquity. To prefer what is ancient, merely becaufe it is ancient, and to deduce the expediency of our laws and cuftoms merely from the practice of our remote anceftors, he well knew, was to appeal to the imagination and paffions, in a cafe that ought to be decided by the fole authority of reafon. In various parts of his works, and not leaft in his book on political revolutions, he powerfully interefts the heart; but he always endeavours to reach it by the road of the underftanding: nor did it ever occur to his difcernment, that any thing could be prudently faid to the feelings of the former, which might not bear to be examined by the light of the latter. With him, mere feeling was but a part of the low animal nature, a part which in brutes is directed to its proper ends by an intelligence not their own; but which in man muft, according to the ordinance of Deity itfelf, be directed and difciplined by reafon and cuftom, that it may thus be strengthened into habit and exalted into virtue; for, in the language of ancient philosophy, virtue, as the attribute of a man, is synonymous with habit. In every well-regulated state, early institution is the great forming and vivifying power of government; and that which education begins, the law carries on and perfects[f]. They are both practical principles, and right

[f] Aristotle places the stability of government chiefly in the three following points: first, the respect due to age and experience; secondly, the distribution of honours and offices according to evident and approved merit; thirdly, an education accurately adapted to the pattern of the commonwealth. Were we to examine the history of all the governments on earth, we should perceive that they have been upheld by an adherence to those grand principles, and subverted by a departure from them. I shall select, for the sake of illustration, the examples of China and France; the former of which is rendered familiar to the reader's mind by a recent publication, and the latter is impressed by the momentous events and unexampled calamities which mark the present times. In China, the paternal authority is the main pillar of the political edifice; all offices are bestowed, according to the proficiency of the candidates in useful knowledge, by comparative trials, similar to those by which academic honours were formerly conferred in Europe; and the education of youth is so accurately fitted to the plan of the government, that the education in China exactly suits that country, and it only. The consequence of all this is plainly attested in history: the constitution of China has been, and continues, the most invariably stable of any known in the world. The constitution of France, on the other hand, has been completely subverted in the course of a few years. What are the causes? The veneration for aged experience had ceased; intrigue supplied the place of merit; and the principles instilled into youth, and into the public at large, directly counteracted the spirit of the government. The ministers of Louis XV. are known to have set the first example in France of bestowing the highest dignities of the church on young gentlemen of family; thus degrading those sacred honours which Aristotle maintains ought to be the exclusive reward of venerable age; from which chiefly they derive their awful influence over the minds of men. Their ambition, and that of their successors under a new reign, rendered them the armed abettors of American independence. Reasons were to be found for justifying a measure in direct opposition to the laws of nations and the faith of treaties. These reasons were only to be deduced from that principle, fruitful in monsters, the unalienable sovereignty of the people; which was, therefore, now first adopted in France; cherished, invigorated, and propagated with a degree of zeal and activity which established

right only, when originating in a right practice; by means of which, combined with example and exercife, they operate an early and wonderful change on the paffions and appetites; fo that as reafon fortifies and improves, thefe fubordinate powers of our nature are continually more difpofed to acknowledge her authority, and to mingle with her, in due time, in the fweeteft harmony. To alter laws and political inftitutions without the moft evident neceffity, is, therefore, wantonly to tamper with the fpring of moral action; to weaken or deftroy that principle in man, on which the perfuafive efficacy of all laws is founded; from which governments derive their ftrength; and individuals, their fecurity.

In oppofition to the tenets which have been fo induftriously propagated in fome modern nations, Ariftotle, while he inhabited the freeft and moft democratical republic of all antiquity, maintained that, from a due mixture of ariftocratic elements, the fabric of political fociety derives both its folidity and its fplendour. The very popular doctrine, therefore, which maintains that all power is derived from the people [f], to the majority

of

---

blifhed a democracy in the public mind, even during the exiftence of the monarchy. The diforders of the finances were the immediate occafion, not the ultimate caufe, of the revolution. The notables, and afterwards the ftates general, had only to affemble in order to prove by their conduct that opinion governs the world.

[f] According to Dr. Price, liberty is "The power of a civil fociety to govern itfelf by its own difcretion, or by laws of its own making, by the majority, in a collective body, or by fair reprefentation. In every free ftate every man is his own legiflator." Price on Civil Liberty. This definition contains the effence of Locke on government, and of its French tranfcript, the "Contrat Social." Locke, I firmly believe, was a religious man, and a good fubject; yet, by a ftrange combination of circumftances, the philofophical opinions of this great adverfary of Ariftotle, have had no fmall tendency to promote fcepticifm, and his political principles to encourage rebellion.

of whom it unalienably belongs, and by whom it may always lawfully be refumed, muft have appeared to him not lefs wicked than it is weak, not lefs deteftable than it is extravagant; efpecially, could he have forefeen that many of the authors who fupported this wild affertion, fhould have exerted themfelves moft ftrenuoufly to deftroy all reverence for thofe inftitutions, which, while they enlarge the wifdom and exalt the affections of the few, have the moft direct tendency to reftrain the vices and to moderate the paffions of the multitude. What renders Rouffeau of Geneva, and other writers of that ftamp, fo hoftile to Chriftianity? They tell us that it commands fubmiffion to the higher powers; and is, therefore, a religion fit only for flaves[h]. But an author, not inferior to Rouffeau in vigour of fancy, incomparably his fuperior in point of learning and judgment, and a far better advocate in the caufe of true liberty, had long before proved that the pretended flavifhnefs of Chriftianity amounts to nothing more than lending its awful fanction to fupport eftablifhed magiftracy, and uphold lawful authority[i]. In this particular, Chriftianity commands what philofophy had uniformly prefcribed; maintaining that obedience to authority is effential to humanity, fince the powers of human nature cannot be unfolded but in a ftate of fociety; and fince, without government, fociety could not for a moment be fecurely preferved, any more than it could, without government, have been originally eftablifhed. Upon this foundation, the Stagirite afferts that birth and wealth, as well as talents, morals, and experience, ought to have their due weight in every community which has the good of the whole for its main object, and that every principle

[h] Contrat Social, l. iv. c. viii.
[i] Buchannanus de Jure Regni apud Scotos, c. lxiii. lxiv. & lxv.

ciple which tends to maintain a reasonable and moderate aristocracy, ought to be improved and cherished, in order to counteract that dangerous propensity to sedition and anarchy, which, wherever they prevail, render the habitations of men more bloody and more abominable than the dens of wild beasts[k].

As a due proportion of aristocratic elements is essential to the very existence of a commonwealth, it is a question of the utmost importance how that aristocracy ought to be constituted? When superiority in wealth is accompanied by superiority in worth, which will naturally happen when the higher ranks are more watchfully and more liberally educated, in proportion to the extent of their fortunes, the plain and palpable distinction of opulence will then, doubtless, be entitled to a certain degree of political pre-eminence. The evil is, when the respect either for wealth, or for birth, which is recommended chiefly as hereditary wealth, gives to such distinctions, independently of the education and manners with which they ought to be accompanied, too decided and too overbearing a superiority; and when the aristocracy is thereby so much narrowed, that its interests are detached and separated from those of the community at large. The worst species of aristocracy degenerates into what Aristotle calls a *dynasty*; the absolute power of fierce and arbitrary chieftains over timid and servile vassals. When power is not an appendage of the person or the individual, but belongs to the whole body of nobles, who serve mutually to check

---

[k] απειρος γαρ η της επιθυμιας φυσις, ης προς την αναπληρωσιν οι πολλοι ζωσι. "How is this universal evil, the senseless desires and dangerous propensities of the multitude, to be controlled?" ας πττυς τι ωσι, και μη αδικωνται. "By the weight of authority, and the equity with which it is administered." Polit. l. ii. c. vii. p. 324.

BOOK VII.

check and controul each other, the government, by a proper degree of moderation in the magiſtrate, may be rendered ſafe and ſalutary, and the object even of affection to the ſubject[1]. But the beſt adjuſtment of thoſe ariſtocratical elements is that by which they are rendered ſubſervient to the intereſts of the community at large; productive of its proſperity, and conducive to its ſtability. Ariſtotle has endeavoured to ſhew how theſe deſirable ends were attained in ſome governments of antiquity. But the moſt illuſtrious example of this kind which the hiſtory of the world ever exhibited, is the ariſtocratical arrangement in the conſtitution of Great Britain. The nobles of this country are not inveſted individually with any degree of pre-eminence or authority that can be at all dangerous to the meaneſt of the people, ſince all executive power flows ſolely from the crown, and is exerciſed by reſponſible miniſters; a king of Great Britain being conſtitutionally, in the words of the Stagirite, " a public guardian; and his high office, a pledge and ſecurity that the nobles ſhall not be ſubjected to injuſtice, nor the people to inſult[m]." The peers, taken collectively, form a ſecond deliberative

[1] This obſervation is ſtrongly confirmed by the hiſtory of the two ariſtocracies of Venice and Bern, the former (till its late deſtruction) comprehending the moſt beautiful and beſt cultivated territory in the north of Italy, and the latter extending over the third part of Switzerland. Under both theſe governments, the ſubjects have long enjoyed an enviable condition of peace and proſperity; happy in themſelves, and therefore contented with their maſters. But it would be an error to believe that thoſe republican inſtitutions which ſuit a certain mediocrity of circumſtances, might be ſafely adopted by great nations.

[m] Polit. l. v. c. x. p. 403. That the majeſty of the throne is the beſt ſafeguard of equal laws and public liberty, is a truth perpetually atteſted in the annals of modern Europe. The people at large, whenever they had an opportunity of declaring their ſentiments freely and fully, uniformly maintained the authority of their kings againſt the arrogant pretenſions of prieſts and nobles, and the daring invaſion of upſtart factions.

ARISTOTLE's POLITICS.

berative affembly, which was formerly proved to be an inftitution effentially requifite in every well-regulated ftate. They conftitute alfo the propereft tribunal that could poffibly be devifed for trying perfons impeached by the Commons. A feat in the Houfe of Peers is naturally and not unfrequently the reward of important fervices and illuftrious merit; and muft, therefore, continue to operate in the commonwealth as a perpetual incentive to emulation, and an unceafing fpring of energy. With all the privileges and advantages peculiar to that order, the peers are entitled even to refpect only when they exhibit characters fuitable to their rank. They dare not opprefs; they dare not injure; they cannot infult with impunity the meaneft of their fellow-fubjects. They are intimately united in their moft effential interefts with the other branches of the conftitution. They cannot, confiftently with their own fafety, co-operate

BOOK VII.

factions. The nations of the north and of the fouth on every occafion difcovered the fame difpofition, and preferred even the abfolute power of a prince to the more dreaded exertions of a divided authority. To the deputies of the people at large, affembled not as ufual at Odenfee, but in the midft of the populace of Copenhagen, the kings of Denmark owe the prerogatives which they have enjoyed fince 1660. The crown of Sweden, which had been trampled on by the nobles in 1756, was reftored to its ancient fplendour by the co-operation of the burghers and peafants in 1772. If we examine the hiftory of the cortes of Spain, the ftates general of France, the diets of Germany, we fhall fee in all thofe affemblies alike, that the Tiers Etat, the deputies of the people, were the moft ftedfaft adherents to the fovereignty of kings *; and in England, when monarchy was overthrown by a combination of knavery and fanaticifm, it was re-eftablifhed with more general confent than was, perhaps, ever given to any public act by fo great and populous a nation.

* In the tumultuary ftates of 1614, the deputies of the people defended againft the nobles and clergy the authority of an undivided executive. "Que l'autorité du roi foit et demeure abfolue fur tous fes fujets de quelque profeffion qu'ils foient; & foit ce tenu pour loi fondamentale du royaume que la perfonne du roi eft fainte et inviolable, auquel eft due toute obeiffance et fidelité, fans qu'il foit loifible à aucun de fes fujets, de quelque qualité et condition qu'il foit, acclefiaftique ou feculier, de s'en exempter."

U U 2

operate with thofe leaders of the people who might be inclined to inftitute a republic; becaufe their own honours and preeminences originating in the monarchy, can only be upheld by its ftability; they could not abet the meafures of thofe courtiers or minifters (were it poffible to find any of fuch confummate folly) who might be inclined to render the crown abfolute; becaufe they would thereby not only furrender the birthrights of their own children, but totally degrade and debafe themfelves. Their lives, and liberties, and properties, are maintained by the fame falutary inftitutions, which guard thofe of the people at large. Compared with this ineftimable benefit of juft and equal laws, how light in the balance are their pre-eminences, their diftinctions, and their titles? The conftitution of England has taken for its model Nature herfelf; and in afferting the exclufive privileges of the few, offers to the enjoyment of all, great and abfolute benefits, before the fplendour of which perfonal and relative advantages fade away and vanifh.

BOOK VII.

ARGUMENT.

Causes of seditions.—Insolence and rapacity of men in power.— Secret combination of obscure factions, &c.—Particular causes in each form of government respectively.—How governments are to be preserved—By strengthening the middle ranks, &c.— Of laws relative to Democracy—Oligarchy—Monarchy—Tyranny.

HAVING considered almost all the other questions that formed the object of this inquiry, we proceed to examine the important subject of political revolutions; their nature and number; their causes and their consequences: an examination which will enable us to determine by what regulations and expedients, government in general, as well as each form of government in particular, may be strengthened and upheld. Justice, the great law of the moral world, is acknowledged in all communities; but dissentions, and thence revolutions, take place, because the rules of justice are often estimated by very different standards. The citizens at large, because they are all equal in freedom, think themselves entitled equally to participate in all other advantages; the distinguished portion of the community, because they are superior in some particulars, think themselves entitled to claim pre-eminence in all other respects;

BOOK VII.
Chap. I.

Of the primary causes, or fountains, of sedition.

BOOK VII.

respects; and as it is difficult for any system of government to gratify the expectations of the rich or noble, on the one hand, and those of the people at large on the other; the seeds of discontent lurk in the bosom of every community, and require but a favourable season to ferment into sedition. Birth, wealth, strength, and every such political element, strives to extend its influence, and to enlarge its dominion; and when checked in its ambitious purposes, is prepared to convulse the state. Virtue alone remains contented with the place allotted to it in the general arrangement, and though contributing more to the happiness of civil life than all its other elements united, yet virtue never emblazons its titles, nor exaggerates its prerogatives; it neither plans conspiracies, nor foments factions; and in this forbearance, it shews as much wisdom as goodness, for the virtuous are comparatively so few in number, that should they imprudently enter the political lists, their party would be foiled in every conflict.

The general object and aim of revolutions.

Such then are the principles, and, as it were, the fountains of sedition; of which the object may be, either to subvert established government, or to acquire the principal share in administration; to change monarchy or aristocracy, into a republic or a democracy; or to incline the balance of power, more than the constitution warrants, to the side of the prince, of the nobles, or of the people; to alter or abolish some particular magistracy, as Lysander, at Sparta, endeavoured to destroy the office of king; and Pausanias, in the same republic, strove to abolish the authority of the Ephori. At Epidamnus^a, the power

---

^a Epidamnus, an Illyrian city, and one of the most considerable sea-ports on the coast of the Hadriatic. See History of Antient Greece, vol. ii. p. 185.

power belonging to the heads of tribes was transferred to a senate. The government was thus partially altered °.

In all political conflicts, the contending factions alternately appeal to juftice; but the one party, as we obferved before, meafures juftice by an arithmetical, and the other by a geometrical ftandard^p; whereas, in fact, it ought to be regulated by both; and fuch governments as equitably combine arithmetical and geometrical proportion into one compound political ratio, can alone expect to be profperous or ftable. Regard ought, therefore, to be had to pre-eminent advantages peculiar to the few; regard ought, alfo, to be had to ordinary but ufeful qualities, common to all; yet, in the great partnerfhip of a commonwealth, if men's fhares are to be apportioned by one fingle ratio only, that of equality, in point of fafety, is preferable^q; for in democracies, there is but one principle of difcord, the jarring interefts of the many and of the few; but in oligarchies, the few not only maintain a perpetual conflict with the many, but frequently quarrel with each other; whereas, the diffentions of the people, among themfelves, are comparatively flight and inconfiderable. Befides, a democracy is nearer to what we have called a republic, or government refiding chiefly in men of the middle rank; which, of all popular conftitutions, is the beft and fafeft.

In examining the nature of political revolutions, we have to confider the fituation of mind or difpofition of thofe who are diffatisfied

BOOK VII.

The beft means of preventing them.

Chap. 2.

In political revolutions three things to be confidered.

° The next fentences have a reference to fimilar changes in Athens; but the text is imperfect and corrupt.
^p See what is above faid of arithmetical and geometrical proportion, vol. i. B. v. c. vii. p. 264.
^q The author here prefers democracy to an oligarchic dynafty, as explained above, B. vi. c. vii. p. 291. But every people are not fit for living under the former government, " fince, wherein fome favage multitudes differ from wild beafts, is not eafy to point out." See above, B. iii, c. vii. p. 184.

BOOK VII.

Of the causes of discontent incident to all governments.

dissatisfied with the existing government; the causes which excite this dissatisfaction; and the various selfish passions of which the meanest, when fully roused, is sufficient to inflame discontent into sedition. Men who think themselves worthy of being treated as equals, will not contentedly submit to be treated as inferiors; and men who think themselves entitled to pre-eminence, will not contentedly brook equality. The situation of men's minds, therefore, which fits them for attempting revolutions, is a conception, well or ill founded, that they are deprived of their due rank in the commonwealth. This rank is a complex object, and resolves itself into profit and honour. Men, therefore, are tempted to sedition by a desire to increase these objects, and to diminish their contraries; to increase their profits and honours; or, on the other hand, to prevent loss and avoid disgrace. They are tempted to sedition, not merely that they may enrich or aggrandise themselves, but because they see other men unjustly enriched, and unjustly aggrandised; and, oftentimes, the most solid merit offends by the glare of too conspicuous a prosperity. The ordinary sources of sedition then are, insolence, contempt, fear, disproportionate increase, and immoderate elevation. Impelled by such causes, men fly to arms, and suddenly subvert the government. The same event happens as surely, but more slowly, through the combination of obscure factions'; through negligence in the magistrates, particularly in disregarding the effect of small alterations; and

' Of this there is a striking example in the following passage of Livy, l. ix. c. 46. " Eodem anno (scil. U. C. 449.) Cn. Flavius Cn. filius, scriba, patre libertino, humili fortuna ortus, ceterùm callidus vir et facundus, ædilis curulis fuit. Ceterùm Flavium dixerat ædilem forensis factio, Appii Claudii censura vires nacta'; qui senatum primus, libertinorum filiis lectis, inquinaverat: et postquam eam lectionem nemo ratam habuit, nec in curia adeptus erat quas petierat, opes urbanas, humilibus per omnes tribus divisis, forum et campum corrupit. Ex eo tempore in duas partes discessit

and through a variety of differences and incongruities, particularly a moral diffimilitude in the citizens.

That the infolence, the rapacity, and the invidious honours of men in power, are, all of them, caufes of fedition, is too obvious to require illuftration. Refentment is eafily transferred from perfons to things. In odious hands, authority itfelf becomes hateful: and the feelings of mankind confpire with their reafon, to deftroy a government pregnant only with mifchief, difgraced by private injuftice, or deformed by public peculation. The undue influence of one man, or of a few, and their elevation towering too high above the level of the community, converts free governments fometimes into monarchies, and fometimes into *dynafties*, the worft fpecies of oligarchy. To prevent fuch fatal revolutions, the Argives and Athenians have recourfe to the oftracifm. But it is better to reprefs the firft fymptoms of immoderate elevation, than to counteract its tendency by a remedy as cruel as it is violent; a political amputation, which fevers from the commonwealth thofe qualified to form its beft defence and higheft ornament.

Fear operates in two ways as a caufe of fedition; fince thofe who dread to fuffer wrong, will attempt to difarm the oppreffor;

BOOK VII.

Chap. 3.

The infolence and rapacity of men in power.

Fear, its twofold operation as a caufe of fedition.

difceffit civitas: aliud, integer populus, fautor et cultor bonorum, aliud, forenfis factio tenebat." This unfortunate divifion of the city, fomented by Appius, a proud ariftocrat, and by Flavius, a plebeian notary, gave to the rabble of the Forum a decided advantage over the found and refpectable part of the community. The former party fupplied by experience and trick, their grofs defects in point of fortune, morals, and liberal education. Their triumph, however, was not lafting. The illuftrious Q. Fabius, who, from this atchievement, acquired the name of Maximus, purged the commonwealth from this excrement, which he threw into "four city tribes." Omnem forenfem turbam excretam in quatuor tribus conjecit, urbanafque eas apellavit. Tit. Liv. ubi fupra.

BOOK VII.

Contempt, its operation illuſtrated by examples.

oppreſſor; and thoſe who have committed wrong, will attempt to anticipate the hand of vengeance. Contempt converts oligarchies into democracies, when the ſtrength of the many is brought into compariſon with the weakneſs of the few; and the ſame paſſion ſubverts democracies, when the concerted wiſdom of the few is contraſted with the folly and anarchy of the multitude. The tumultuous democracy of Megara was deſtroyed by its own violence. The ſame cauſe overturned the popular government of Thebes, after the famous battle in the vineyards. Anarchy ſubjected Syracuſe to the tyranny of Gelon; and the diſorderly behaviour of the Rhodians enabled an ariſtocratical conſpiracy to ſeize the government.

The diſproportionate increaſe of any of the conſtituent parts of the commonwealth.

The diſproportionate increaſe of any of the conſtituent parts, is not leſs fatal to the political, than to the natural body; and when any of theſe parts is changed, not only in quantity or bulk, but in organization or form, new governments muſt reſult, ſpecifically different from the old. Such alterations happen ſometimes gradually and imperceptibly; at other times, ſuddenly and palpably. Soon after the Perſian invaſion of Greece, the flower of the Tarentine nobility was cut off in a battle againſt the barbarous Iapygians; and this diſaſter, diminiſhing, by a ſudden jerk, the weight of the ariſtocracy, enabled the people to change the *mixt polity* of Tarentum into a ſimple democracy. The overthrow of the Argives by Cleomenes, king of Sparta, compelled them to aſſociate their peaſants to the honours of government. In the Lacedæmonian war, the Athenians were ſummoned to take the field in the order of the muſter-roll; and the moſt diſtinguiſhed portion of the citizens thus ſuffered a great and ſpeedy diminution; which operated the ſame effect

on

on the form of government, as would have been produced by a sudden and disproportionate increase of the populace.

Marginal note: BOOK VII.

Governments change gradually through the secret combination of obscure individuals. At Heraea, the aristocratical mode of appointment to office was changed for one more popular, because a combination of mean mechanics determined to vote for none but persons of their own level. The higher ranks of men, therefore, preferred the capricious decision by lot, to the certain partiality of election.

Marginal note: The secret combination of obscure factions.

Governments are changed through negligence, when high offices of state are entrusted to persons unfriendly to the constitution. The oligarchy of Oreum¹ was thus subverted by Heracleodorus, a partisan of democracy. Great revolutions sometimes arise from slight neglects. At Ambracia¹, the census requisite for a citizen was small. It was imprudently reduced to nothing; and the country soon fell into the hands of a houseless rabble.

Marginal note: Negligence.

Nothing is more unfriendly to public tranquillity than dissimilitude of character in the citizens. A heterogeneous assemblage of mixed tribes, cannot speedily coalesce into a nation; and communities, which have grown populous by sudden accessions, are generally torn by sedition. The Achæans and Træzenians", united in colonising Sybaris; but the Achæans, reinforced by new colonies from home, expelled the Træzenians. The

Marginal note: Dissimilitude of manners and character;

Marginal note: its effect in producing revolutions illustrated by examples.

---

* Formerly, Hiſtiæa, a city in the iſle of Eubœa. See Hiſtory of Ancient Greece, vol. i. p. 389.

' A Corinthian colony in the Ambracian gulph, which derived its name from Ambrax, the grandſon of Lacaon. The capital was ſituate on the doubtful confines of Theſprotia and Moloſſia. Comp. Stephan. Byzant Pauſan. Eliac. p. 437. & Tit. Liv. l. xxxviii. c. 4.

" Træzené, a city in the territory of Argos.

BOOK VII.

The Sybarites who colonifed Thurii, experienced a fimilar misfortune; and claiming fuperiority over their fellow-planters, in virtue of their prior poffeffion of the country, they were driven into banifhment. The new inhabitants of Byzantium were difcovered confpiring againft the old; attacked, defeated, and expelled. The Antiffæans firft received with hofpitality, but afterwards ejected by arms, the Chian exiles; and the exiles of Samos ejected the Zanclæans*, by whom they had been hofpitably received. Apollonia, on the Euxine, was deformed by domeftic difcord, from the moment that its populoufnefs was increafed by a new colony. After the expulfion of their tyrants, the Syracufans enrolled as citizens, mercenaries and foreigners. Diffenfions and battles enfued. Amphipolis admitted a colony from Chalcis ʸ: moft of the original inhabitants were driven into banifhment. So true it is, that every promifcuous multitude cannot be fafhioned into a commonwealth, the formation of which requires materials fkilfully prepared, and muft be the work of time; for the caufes of diffenfion are innumerable. Even the diverfities of local fituations engender parties, and foment faction. At Athens, the inhabitants of the Piræus are diftinguifhed from thofe of the upper city, by their fond admiration for democracy. In the city of Clazomené, the inhabitants of the main land were commonly at variance with

* Zanclé, the ancient name of Meffana, now Meffina, derived from the Sicilian word ζαγκλον, a fcythe or fickle. Steph. Byzant.

ʸ The Chalcis in Thrace, which gave name to the Chalcidicé. Hiftory of Ancient Greece, vol. ii, c. xv. p. 196. The Thracian Chalcis was fo called from its metropolis, the principal city in the ifle of Eubæa, fituate at the narroweft part of the Euripus, where Eubæa is fuppofed by Pliny to have joined the continent of Bœotia. Plin. l. iv. c. 12. This city colonifed the eaftern fhore of Sicily, and was the mother of a new Chalcis, of Naxos, Catana, Leontium, and other Sicilian republics. See Hiftory of Ancient Greece, vol. ii. pp. 12, & feq.

with those in the island. Localities, equally unimportant, distracted into parties the citizens of Colophon and of Notium[a]. In war, the smallest ditch or rivulet disorders the ranks, and breaks the phalanx. In politics, every distinction forms a ground of separation, and opens a source of hostility; and the slightest differences may occasion the most important revolutions, when they happen to arise among persons of weight in the state. Syracuse was anciently divided into two exasperated factions, in consequence of a frivolous love-quarrel between two young men, who happened to be both in the magistracy. In the absence of the one, the other corrupted his mistress[b]; the injured man retaliated, by seducing his colleague's wife; and the whole state took part with one side or the other. The difference, slight in itself, had this extensive consequence, because it arose between persons in the magistracy, and thus affected the source and principle of the government itself; and the principle, or beginning, by the trite but just proverb, is counted " the half of every thing;" so that a small deviation from rectitude at the first outset, diverges into a great and even indefinite distance at the further extremity. Shortly after the Persian invasion of Greece, the dispute of two brothers, men of note, concerning their father's inheritance, involved Hestiæa in a civil war. The rich sided with the fortunate brother; and the poor took party with him who complained of being deprived of his patrimony; and of the concealment of a large treasure which, he said, had been found by his father. An ancient quarrel about a marriage occasioned all the seditions that have happened at Delphi to the present hour. A bridegroom,

BOOK VII.

Chap. 4.

Even the frivolous quarrels of the great.

Their baneful effects illustrated by example.

---

[a] Notium derived its name from νότος, the south, being situate a few miles to the south of Colophon. History of Ancient Greece, vol. i. p. 292.

[b] τον ερωμενον

BOOK VII.

groom, terrified by some unlucky omen, rejected the bride; whose relations, enraged at this injury, conveyed into his pocket, while he was sacrificing, a quantity of the sacred money, and then slew him as guilty of sacrilege. At Mitylenè, two young women, heirefses, occasioned all the misfortunes of that republic, and the war with the Athenians, in which Paches took the city. The young women were the daughters of Timophanes; Doxander sought them in marriage for his two sons; his demand was slighted; he meditated vengeance, began to cabal at home, and applied to the Athenians, with whom he was allied by hospitality, and stimulated them to a war, which proved ruinous to his country. An incident nearly similar occasioned the sacred war at Phocis. An heirefs was concerned; the authors of the sedition were Mnasias, the father of Mneson, and Euthycrates, the son of Onomarchus. A contract of marriage changed the government of Epidamnus. The father of a young woman betrothed, happening to be archon, had occasion to exercise his authority as magistrate, in fining his intended son-in-law; the latter, thinking himself not only injured but affronted, conspired with those diffatisfied with the government, and effected a revolution.

Governments overturned by an alteration of the relative importance of their constituent parts.

Governments are changed, when the relative importance of their constituent parts is altered. During the Persian war, the council of the Areopagus, by the wisdom and firmness of its measures, acquired just renown; and the merit of this tribunal, composed of the principal citizens, tended to invigorate the aristocracy; but soon afterwards, the Athenian seamen, consisting of the lowest rabble [b], having gained the battle of Salamis, and thereby raised their country to the sovereignty of the sea, increased the weight of democracy in a far greater proportion.

Examples thereof.

The credit gained by the Argive nobles in the battle of Mantinæa,

[b] See above, B. iv. c. vi. p. 225.

tinæa, and the defeat of the Lacedæmonians, occafioned the attempt to deftroy the popular government at Argos. The Syracufan mariners, having conquered the Athenians, changed, on the other hand, the mixed republic of Syracufe into a fimple democracy. The merit of the people of Chalcis, in affifting the nobility of that city to deftroy Phoxos, the tyrant, procured for them a fhare in the government. A circumftance exactly fimilar converted the oligarchy of Ambracia, after the expulfion of the tyrant Periander, into a democracy. And the obfervation univerfally holds, that whenever any portion of the ftate, magiftrates, nobles, or people, has procured for the public fome fignal advantage, a foundation will be thereby laid for political commotions, which often terminate in revolutions. For the honours beftowed on thofe public benefactors excite jealoufy, and embitter envy; and the benefactors themfelves, elated by their newly-acquired importance, difdain to reft fatiffied with their hereditary rank and prefcriptive advantages.

Governments, alfo, are univerfally liable to be fhaken, when parties, animated by principles of mutual hoftility[c], are nearly equal in ftrength; when the natural influence of wealth, or of nobility, is refifted, for inftance, by the weight of numbers and the independence of induftry; for fhould either the rich or the poor be incomparably more powerful than their adverfaries, the weaker party abandons the ftruggle in defpair. For this reafon, virtue, though the principal element in public happinefs, and therefore juftly entitled to political pre-eminence, feldom however comes forward to affert its pretenfions, and to claim its well-earned reward. Virtuous men know how inconfiderable their own party is; they

BOOK VII.

General theorem on this fubject.

Governments difturbed in confequence of the near equality of hoftile parties.

[c] Parties are thus animated when there is not a middling clafs between the great and the vulgar to hold the balance between them. See above, B. vi. c. ii. p. 298.

BOOK VII.

All revolutions effected by force, or by fraud, or by a mixture of both.

they feel and acknowledge the irrefiftible ftrength of their opponents.

Such then is the general nature of political revolutions. They are produced either by violence, or by fraud, or by the union of both; for, fometimes, what is begun by fraud is ended by force. It was thus that the tyranny of the four hundred was eftablifhed at Athens. The people were firft cheated out of their liberties, by the delufive hope of Perfian fubfidies; and when the deceit was difcovered, the four hundred had recourfe to arms. In this cafe, force was employed as an auxiliary to fraud; but fraud is often fufficient to do the work alone.

Chap. 5.

General caufes of revolutions modified by the nature of each government in particular.

Democracies ruined by the impudence of demagogues.

The caufes of fedition, hitherto enumerated and explained, apply univerfally to all governments; but thefe general caufes are varioufly fubdivided and modified by the nature and form of each government in particular. The impudence of demagogues is the ordinary bane of democracies. By private calumny, and public impeachment, thefe incendiaries exafperate the poor againft the rich; and compel the rich, through their common fears, to unite into an exafperated faction, actuated by oppofite interefts to thofe of the community at large. The refentment of men of property, provoked by the wickednefs of demagogues, overturned the democracy of Cos. In Rhodes, the demagogues profecuted and defrauded the Trierarchs, in order to corrupt the foldiery; the troops, raifed from the promifcuous multitude, were thus feduced and bribed at the expence of thofe who generoufly equipped and maintained the guardian navy of that maritime republic. But the indignation of the Trierarchs mutinied againft this complication of ingratitude and injuftice, deftroyed the demagogues, and overturned the

the democracy. Heraclæa, foon after its populoufnefs was augmented by an Athenian colony, fell a prey to fedition. The perfecution of demagogues drove moft families of diftinction from the place; but the emigrants returned with an armed force, and eftablifhed an oligarchy. Revolutions, proceeding from fimilar caufes, and exactly fimilar in their iffue, happened at Cumæ and at Megara: And it may be regarded as a general theorem in politics, that demagogues are the pefts of democracies, ruin liberty under pretence of preferving or augmenting it, corrupting the multitude by indulgence, and exafperating the rich by agrarian laws and the weight of public burdens, till neceffity compels the latter to refift oppreffion by force, and to fight in their own defence with courage heightened by defpair.

BOOK VII.

In ancient times, when the talents of the ftatefman and the general were often cultivated by the fame man, democracies often ended in tyrannies. The demagogues, equally fkilled in war and in eloquence, fupported their arguments by arms, and eked out fraud by force. But fince rhetoric has become a fcience of fuch extent, that none can acquire it in diftinguifhed perfection, but thofe who cultivate it with undivided attention, demagogues have been contented with deceiving the people, and have feldom attempted to enflave them. Tyrannies, befides, were of old more frequent than now, becaufe it was then ufual to entruft particular magiftrates with more extenfive difcretionary powers, (witnefs the Prytanes of Miletus,) and becaufe, while men lived fcattered in the country, diligently employed in their hufbandry, cities were lefs populous than at prefent, and therefore lefs capable of refifting with concert and activity, the eloquence and artifices of their demagogues, efpecially when reinforced by military fkill and martial fpirit.

Why democracies in ancient times terminated differently from the manner in which they terminate at prefent.

The

ARISTOTLE's POLITICS.

BOOK VII.

How demagogues deceive the people, and by what means their machinations might be defeated.

The confidence of the multitude, however, was the great engine by which these military politicians and politic generals assailed the freedom of their country; and the pledge of this confidence was their hatred and persecution of opulence and nobility. It was by persecuting the wealthy Pediaci, that Pisistratus enslaved Athens: Theogenes pursued the same plan at Megara, and there met with similar success. Dionysius, by the impeachment of Daphnæus and other rich men, raised himself to the throne of Syracuse. Democracies sink into the lowest degeneracy, when the national assembly is persuaded to supplant the authority of laws by the caprice of occasional decrees: This generally happens through the seduction of those, whose ambition to obtain office is too extravagant to yield to any civil duty, and too violent to be checked by any moral obstacle; and who avail themselves of the confusion and tumult incident to crowded assemblies, to precipitate the heedless multitude into the most ruinous measures. To prevent or diminish this evil, it will be expedient to alter the mode of election to magistracy, and to entrust this power not to the people collectively, but to the various parts or tribes into which the community happens to be divided [a].

Chap. 6.

Causes of the revolutions in oligarchies. Insolence or injustice of the magistrates.

There are two most manifest causes of revolutions in oligarchies. When the people at large are grossly injured by men in power, they willingly hearken to and follow any leader of sedition; but this leader is more especially dangerous, if he happens to be one of the magistrates. This was the case in Naxos, where Lygdamis, jealous of his colleagues, overturned the oligarchy, and afterwards made himself king [b]. When an oligarchy, the name of which denotes that the few govern

[a] See above, B. vi. c. xv. p. 312. [b] Athenæus, l. viii. p. 348.

govern the many, is still further narrowed, so that magistracy, instead of extending by rotation among the general mass of wealthy and eminent citizens, is confined within the circle of a few families, opulence and eminence will not patiently brook an absolute exclusion from authority, but will rather convulse the state than submit to be debarred from civil honours. In the concentrated oligarchies of Marseilles, Ister, and Heraclea, the political edifice was overthrown in consequence of the narrowness of its base. The wealthy citizens of Marseilles never ceased plotting against the government, till all men of a certain census were declared capable of holding offices, not indeed simultaneously, but, as in some other countries, alternately or successively; that is, first, the eldest brother of a family, and then the younger, or if more in number, each in his order. The rigour of oligarchy was thus mitigated at Marseilles. In Ister, the oligarchy was changed into a democracy: And at Heraclæa, the power which had formerly been lodged in few hands, was communicated to six hundred citizens. The dissensions of the Cnidian nobles, respecting the limitation of candidates for office, encouraged the people, headed by one of the better sort, to attack and overthrow the oligarchy. In ancient times Erythræ [c] was well and wisely governed by the family of Basilides, of which the individuals lived in perfect harmony with each other: yet the people disdained to remain subject to their authority, and to permit those honours and offices, which they considered as the public stock, to continue the patrimony of a family.

BOOK VII.

Oligarchies overturned by narrowing their base.

Examples thereof.

Oligarchies

[c] There were cities of this name in Bœotia, Locris, Libya, and Ionia. That in Ionia was one of the twelve Ionic cities, and founded by Neleus, son of Codrus. It is now reduced to a miserable village, but still called Erethri. See Hist. of Ancient Greece, vol. i. c. iii. pp. 101, & seq.

BOOK VII.

Oligarchies destroyed by the flattery of sycophants.

Examples thereof.

Oligarchies overturned by spendthrifts, by mercenaries, and by the arrogance of the magistrates.

Oligarchies not only perish by external violence but suffer, and sometimes sink, under internal diforders; they are not exempted from the pest of demagogues, flattering partifans of tyranny, as the demagogues in democracies are of licentiousness, and who, to promote their own views, seduce, inflame, and betray that party in the state to whose interests they affect to be most entirely devoted. At Athens, Charicles was the demagogue of the thirty tyrants; and Phrynichus was the demagogue of the arbitrary faction of the four hundred. When persons by their census capable of office are dependent on the people for their elections, like the state guardians of Larissa and Abydus, those who covet preferment frequently have recourse to the dishonest arts of seduction and flattery. The same consequence happens, when the judiciary power is in the hands of the people at large; the nobles are ruined in the courts of justice, and the oligarchy is thus overturned: this was the fate of the government of Heraclæa [d] on the Euxine. Sometimes an oligarchy is narrowed into a junto; and the party illegally excluded from office, is compelled in its own defence to appeal to the people.

Spendthrifts are always promoters of innovation: in oligarchies they strive to usurp tyranny for themselves, or to procure it for one who will reward their labours. At Syracuse the spendthrift Hipparinus warmly seconded the views of Dionysius. The profligate Cleotimus, by the assistance of a colony from Chalcis, raised an insurrection in Amphipolis. In Ægina, a man of ruined fortune, distinguished by his well-known transaction with Chares, attempted to change the government. Ambition and rapacity often set the members of oligarchies at variance with each other; and when

---

[d] One of the Greek cities on the southern coast of the Euxine, of which Sinopé was the mother and the queen. See Hist. of Ancient Greece, vol. iii. c. xxvi. p. 224.

when divided among themselves, they are eafily fubdued by the people. This happened at Apollonia on the Euxine: but where perfect harmony prevails, an oligarchy is not eafily fubverted; witnefs that of Pharfalus. The oligarchy of Elis was narrowed into a cabal of ninety fenators, whofe authority was arbitrary, and whofe office was perpetual [e]. In war, oligarchies are ruined for want of confidence between the nobles and the people: the former hire mercenaries for the public defence, and the leader of the mercenaries often becomes mafter of the ftate. It was thus that Timophanes made himfelf tyrant of Corinth. When there are different bodies of mercenaries under different leaders, thefe will fometimes combine their ftrength, and form themfelves into what is called a dynafty, the worft fpecies of oligarchy. To prevent thefe evils, the nobles, when they have occafion to ufe the fervice of the people in war, fometimes voluntarily admit them to a fhare of the government. In peace, oligarchies are fubverted when the nobles and the people are mutually fo diftruftful of each other that they commit the fafety of the ftate to a garrifon of foreign mercenaries, whofe commander, inftead of continuing the mediator between the two parties, makes himfelf the mafter of both: this happened both at Lariffa and at Abydus. The overbearing infolence of individuals, quarrels about marriages and law-fuits, fometimes occafion public commotions which terminate in revolutions. Diagoras's difappointment in marriage overturned the oligarchy of the knights or horfemen of Eretria [f]. Seditions arofe in Thebes and in Heraclæa

[e] Ariftotle fays their election refembled that which prevailed in electing fenators in Sparta. The text is corrupt. See above, B. ii. c. vii. p. 109.

[f] A flourifhing fea-port of Eubœa before the Trojan war, oppofite to Delphinium in Attica. Strabo, p. 687. It was demolifhed by the Perfians in their invafion, but its ruins were to be feen in the time of the above-mentioned geographer. Ibid.

Heraclæa in confequence of the degrading fentences paffed on Archias and on Eurytion, that they fhould ftand (the former for adultery) in the pillory in the market-place. The defpotic arrogance of the magiftrates fubverted the oligarchies of Chios and Cnidos.

In confequence of the events of time and chance.

Revolutions fometimes happen in confequence of the events of time and chance, independently of human defign or human forefight. In oligarchies, and in what we have called republics in oppofition to wild democracies, a certain cenfus is requifite for holding civil offices; all whofe fortunes fall fhort of this ftandard are excluded; fo that the majority of the people are excluded in oligarchies, and thofe who in point of fortune are confiderably below the middling clafs, are excluded in republics: but in confequence of a long peace, or other fortunate events, the value of lands may be fo greatly enhanced, that the poffeffions of the pooreft man fhall exceed the regulated cenfus: and this, whether it happens flowly or fuddenly, will occafion a political revolution. Governments change not only from one form into a contrary, but from one fort of democracy or of oligarchy into another that is different; as from governments acknowledging the authority of laws to democracies ruled by the caprice of the multitude, or oligarchies confifting of a junto of tyrants.

Chap. 7.

Caufes of the revolutions in ariftocracies.

The fupreme authority may center in a few men of wealth and credit, or may refide in a few perfons of diftinguifhed virtue: in the latter cafe the government is called an ariftocracy, and is expofed to revolutions from the paucity of thofe who engrofs power. From a coincidence in this circumftance, an ariftocracy is liable to be confounded with an oligarchy,

Their fimilarity to oligarchies.

which a high-minded people muft always be defirous to overthrow. The Parthenia, fprung from the beft blood of Sparta,

Sparta, but degraded by the illegitimacy of their birth, and debarred from public honours, were caught confpiring againft their country, and fent to colonife Tarentum. The lofty virtue of Lyfander difdained to acknowledge a fuperior even in a king: the ftubborn audacity of Cinadon [f] confpired to deftroy every Lacedæmonian of a rank fuperior to his own. Ariftocracies are alfo liable to convulfions in confequence of the great inequality of private fortunes, efpecially when, by an invading enemy, any confiderable part of the country has been ravaged, and the inhabitants reduced to beggary: this happened to Sparta in the Meffenian war, when the people infifted on an equal divifion of lands, as we learn from a poem of Tyrtæus, called the *Eunomia*, by which he appeafed the fedition.

BOOK VII. which a high-minded people will not brook.

As the accumulated honours even of good men are apt to excite envy and jealoufy, fo the moderate and defined honours of bad men prove incentives to the luft of dominion, and encourage them to attempt rendering their power arbitrary and their honours unbounded: this fatal project was at Carthage adopted by Hanno; and in Sparta by king Paufanias, who repelled the invafion of the Medes.

The magiftrates corrupted by their honours.

An error in the original ftructure of government often proves ruinous to republics and ariftocracies. When the ingredients of virtue, wealth, and numbers (efpecially the two latter) are unequally combined, or improperly blended, the compofition has a tendency to feparate with noife and violence into its conftituent elements: when the balance inclines to the fide of numbers, a republic, that does not degenerate into a fimple democracy, retains its original and fpecific name; but when the balance inclines to the fide of wealth, it is frequently, though improperly, called an ariftocracy. Of thofe two

Revolutions in republics, or mixed governments.

[f] For all thefe events confult the Hiftory of Ancient Greece.

two forts of republics, that verging to democracy is the moft fecure and the moft permanent, becaufe the majority are mafters of the ftate, and the people at large, as before obferved, are lefs liable to the temptations of a felfifh ambition: yet wherever the political forces of wealth and of numbers are not duly adjufted, that is, when they are not proportioned to each other with as much accuracy as matters of practice require or admit, the fabric of the conftitution is always liable to overfet. Sometimes it falls on that fide to which it formerly inclined. A republic thus relaxes into a perfect democracy; and what is called an ariftocratic government is ftrung into a tyrannical and cruel oligarchy: but this does not invariably take place; for when the prevailing powers are guilty of grofs injuftice, the ftrenuous efforts of their oppreffed antagonifts to recover their due weight in the ftate, fometimes changes the conftitution into its direct contrary; the refentment of the poor changing an ariftocratic republic into a democracy, or the indignation of the rich converting a popular republic into an oligarchy. The former event happened at Thurii; the balance of political power being on the fide of the nobles, or rather on that of property, they yielded to the temptation of injuftice, and engroffed, contrary to law, almoft the whole lands of the country: provoked at their rapacity, the people, who were warlike, flew to arms, expelled the mercenary garrifon, and divefted the nobles of their overgrown and unjuftly acquired eftates.

An ariftocratical government, in proportion as it partakes of the nature of an oligarchy, has a tendency to foment infolence on the one hand, and to excite refentment on the other. By committing too much authority to the nobles, it enables them to promote what they take to be their private or domeftic mestic interests, at the expence of what is the interest of the community at large. The connection formed by marriage, between a family of distinction at Locris and Dionysius the tyrant, ruined that state; and such a connection would not certainly have been permitted either in a democracy, or in a well-balanced aristocratical republic.

BOOK VII.
Example.

The neglecting of little matters, as altogether immaterial, was formerly said to be a general cause of political innovation. Nothing, however little, should be regarded as unimportant, which touches the spring of the government; since by changing the form of the smallest part, the beauty of the whole system may be destroyed. It was the custom at Thurii, that those who had been officers in the army should not be re-elected to military command till after an interval of five years. Some spirited young men, whose martial ardour had acquired for them great popularity among the troops, endeavoured to procure a law for enabling them to retain their rank: a committee of the senate appointed for examining this business, at first resisted, but finally yielded to the project of innovation; thinking, that being gratified in this one point, the officers would not proceed farther, but allow the constitution in general to remain unaltered; but in this they were miserably disappointed. New alterations were proposed, which the magistrates, now overawed by an armed force, durst not venture to oppose; their authority was thus overturned; and the government fell into the hands of those who had been gratified in their first dangerous demand.

Neglect in little matters.

Example.

Such are the internal sources of the dissolution of governments. They may also be destroyed by external violence. To this evil they are particularly exposed, when a neighbouring state is governed on principles directly opposite: or when this

External causes of revolutions in republics.

354 ARISTOTLE's POLITICS.

BOOK VII.

oppofite fyftem prevails in a ftate more remote but alfo more powerful, with which the governments in queftion are connected by the ties of commerce and confanguinity, or by the relations of war or alliance, of war undertaken or meditated, of alliance enjoyed or coveted. It was thus that the Athenians and Lacedæmonians, as their fortune alternately rofe and funk in the fcale of Greece, refpectively deftroyed, the former oligarchies, and the latter democracies; becaufe each of thofe domineering republics afpired to mould the political edifices of their neighbours or allies after their own model.

Example.

Chap. 8.

How good governments are preferved:

We now proceed to examine how governments in general, and each form of government in particular, are to be upheld and perpetuated. Firft of all, it is evident, that if we clearly comprehend the caufes which deftroy governments, we may eafily difcover thofe which are beft fitted to preferve them; for deftruction and prefervation being things in their nature contrary, contrary means will be fuccefsfully employed to produce thofe contrary effects. In well-balanced republics, then, all deviations from eftablifhed laws are to be carefully avoided, efpecially in matters, which becaufe they are little, are apt to appear infignificant: it is by fmall expences that the greateft eftates are brought to ruin, becaufe the occafions of fuch expences are fo numerous, that they may be confidered as infinite and unlimited; and becaufe men are always liable to be deceived by the vulgar fophifm, that one grain makes not an heap; and therefore that a trifling expence may fafely be incurred, or a trifling alteration may be harmlefsly made.

by avoiding fmall, and feemingly infignificant alterations:

by counteracting political fleights.

The next rule of importance for upholding the ftability of well-mixed governments, is, that the nobles and the people be mutually on their guard againft the political artifices or juggling fleights,

ARISTOTLE's POLITICS.

fleights, formerly enumerated and defcribed [f], by which the one party endeavours to difguife its ambition, and the other to palliate its injuftice.

Some republics have been long preferved, not by the excellence of their ftructure, but through the folid virtues of thofe who governed them: though appointed from men of a privileged order, the magiftrates, while they lived with their colleagues and equals in fraternal harmony, were careful never to infult, never to injure their inferiors; they were careful never to provoke the proud by contempt, nor to exafperate the poor by rapacity; and the leaders of the multitude moft diftinguifhed for their merit, whatever might be the circumftances of their birth, were feafonably exalted to a higher clafs, and thus affociated to the honours of government [g]. When the nobles are extremely numerous, they form a fort of democracy among themfelves, and ought therefore, in managing the affairs of their own order, to adopt the inftitutions beft calculated for preferving that form of government. It will be ufeful, for inftance, to infift on a frequent rotation of office; and in fome cafes to enact that magiftracies fhall be held only for the term of fix months; for as democracies have their demagogues, fo oligarchies and ariftocracies have their talebearers and fycophants, mean and malicious flatterers of men in power; who, in proportion to the extent and duration of that power, will be more likely to degenerate into tyrants.

Governments are fometimes preferved, not by the remotenefs, but by the proximity of danger. The terror hanging over them

Marginalia: BOOK VII. Governments, defective in their ftructure, preferved by the virtues of the magiftrates: by the proximity of danger:

[f] See above, B. vi. c. xii. p. 301, & feq.

[g] The reader's own fagacity will apply thefe obfervations to the effects refulting from the different conftitution of the privileged orders, as they have been called, in the different countries of modern Europe.

them keeps men continually on their guard. This salutary vigilance may be excited by imaginary causes, when real ones are wanting; by approximating diſtance, and anticipating futurity. The dangerous animoſities of the great are to be diligently watched, and, if poſſible, ſpeedily appeaſed; and much care is to be applied that thoſe who ſtill remain diſpaſſionate and impartial, be not whirled within the vortex of either of the contending parties: diſcord between men diſtinguiſhed by rank, fortune, and office, may produce the moſt baneful effects, becauſe its operation is exerted on the firſt principle or moving power of government; and to perceive and obviate errors in their principle or beginning, which might ſwell to much greater evils, is the work of no ordinary ſtateſman. To prevent ſuch revolutions as gradually proceed from the augmentation or diminution of private fortunes, it will be neceſſary to have recourſe to the cenſus. In ſmaller ſtates, which are liable to more frequent concuſſions, the cenſus may be taken annually; in larger republics, every third or fifth year; and the qualifications for office muſt be heightened or lowered in proportion to the increaſe or diminution of eſtates.

It is dangerous under every form of government, whether ſimple or mixed, whether democracy, oligarchy, or monarchy, to allow ſuch diſproportionate exaltation of particular men, or particular families, as greatly overtops that of perſons and families of their own order. Honours to be laſting muſt be moderate; and there are but few minds of ſuch a firm and perfect texture as to bear with impunity the infectious aſſaults of ſudden and ſignal proſperity. Yet if any honoured individual has been greatly exalted by an accumulation of dignities, it is not adviſable to reduce him at once to the ordinary level; his

his too luxuriant honours must be lopped gradually; and above all, it ought to be the aim of a wise legislation, in the first place, to prevent, if possible, any individual from attaining too conspicuous a superiority in power, in wealth, or in the number and strength of his adherents; or, if the evil has not been prevented, to remove him from his vantageground at home, under pretence of employment in honourable commissions abroad.

BOOK VII.

Since manners have so powerful an influence on government that many are found willing to overset the constitution for no other reason but that in future they may be at liberty to live as they list; it is useful in every commonwealth to have a particular magistracy to superintend the manners of the citizens, and to check or discourage every deviation from that mode of life which is best adapted to the nature and principle of each form of government.

by the censorial power.

The events of time and chance will often give to some one of the constituent parts of a state, or to some particular magistracy, more than their due importance and their proper weight. This alteration must be carefully watched, and whereever the balance inclines, whether on the side of the rich, the noble, or the populace, care must be taken to correct the preponderancy; and by the distribution of honours and offices to equalise the contending factions, and to strengthen that intermediate portion of the people which is always more stedfastly attached to the public welfare, than either those who are elated by wealth, or those who are depressed by poverty [h].

by strengthening the middle ranks:

Every principle of law, and every maxim of government, ought to be skilfully and steadily directed against the peculation of men in office. Oligarchies, especially, ought never to lose sight of this object; for the people at large will be greatly incensed when

by preventing peculation:

[h] See above, B. vi. c. ii. p. 297.

BOOK VII.

when they are not only excluded from offices and honours, but robbed by thofe who adminifter the one and engrofs the other; whereas the firft hardſhip, taken feparately by itfelf, will be greatly foftened by the confideration, that an exclufion from public employments operates as an advantageous exemption; and allows thofe who enjoy the immunity, to apply with undivided attention to the improvement of their private fortunes [1].

by paying the magiſtrates with honour, not with fees and falaries:

A republic, in which the various offices of ftate fhould be paid merely by honour, but rewarded by no emolument whatever, might unite the advantages both of ariftocracy and democracy, without incurring the inconveniences of either. The people at large might be entitled to every employment; but the poorer fort would certainly wave their claim to unprofitable pofts, that they might ply their profitable trades. They would relinquifh public concerns to thofe who had more time to fpare than themfelves. The better fort of the citizens, therefore, would thus efcape the grievance to which they are fubjected in democracies, of being frequently governed by perfons greatly their inferiors; and the poorer and lower claſſes of men would efcape the grievance, to which they are fubjected in ariftocracies and oligarchies, of being legally and perpetually excluded from all public preferments. The abolition of fees and falaries will not, however, be alone fufficient to enfure the benefits of this falutary regulation. The revenues of the ftate muft be publicly

by exactly infpecting

[1] Such maxims were purfued for many centuries by the ariftocracy of Venice, where all honourable offices were proportionably expenfive. The policy of the ariftocracy of Bern was directly the reverſe. A man's fortune might be often ruined by holding thoſe offices which belonged exclufively to noble Venetians; his fortune is always benefited by holding thoſe which belong exclufively to the citizens of Bern.

ARISTOTLE's POLITICS.

publicly received, and publicly deposited; and separate accounts of them must be kept in the halls of the various tribes, wards, and fraternities into which the republic may happen to be divided.

To preserve the stability of democracies, the leaders of the populace must cease to harass the rich and noble by agrarian laws. The old proprietors must not only retain their hereditary lands, but also enjoy, unmolested, their annual fruits; which, as matters are now managed, are often indirectly and imperceptibly wasted for purposes the most useless and the most frivolous. Shows, dances, vain illuminations, and pompous processions, are unprofitable to those who behold, and ruinous to those who exhibit, them. A reasonable people, instead of condemning their richer fellow-citizens to such grievous expences, would turn with disdain from the childish gratifications for which they are incurred [k].

To preserve the stability of aristocracies or oligarchies, great regard must be had to those classes of the people who are excluded from a share in the sovereignty. Injuries committed against them, especially when accompanied with insult, must be punished with more severity by the magistrate than those committed against persons of his own rank or his own order. Such subordinate employments as are attended with fees or perquisites should be granted in preference to the poorer sort of citizens; and to promote equality, as much as is consistent with the nature of the government, it will be proper to restrain the

Marginalia: BOOK VII. The administration of the public revenues. The demagogues in democracies must not harass the rich by agrarian laws, and the demand of expensive exhibitions. In oligarchies, peculiar indulgencies should be granted to those classes of the people who are excluded from a share in the sovereignty.

[k] It appears from the History of Greece, that this was indeed most salutary, but with respect to him who proposed it, very dangerous advice. By a law of the demagogue Eubulus, it was made capital at Athens, to propose diverting the theatric funds to any other purpose than that of the public amusement. History of Ancient Greece, vol. iii. c. xxxii. p. 475.

BOOK VII.

A similar rule applicable in all governments.

the freedom of donations and marriage contracts, and thereby to limit or prevent the accumulation of too many estates in one family. It is of essential use in preserving all governments, that those who are the least sharers in the sovereignty, be treated with great equity, and even peculiar indulgence, in all other respects. In oligarchies, the people, in democracies, the wealthy, ought respectively to enjoy every advantage and every preference that is not incompatible with the nature of the government. The superiority given to them in matters of little moment, will dispose them patiently to brook their inferiority in solid power.

Chap. 9.

The requisites for holding supreme magistracies.—Patriotism. Capacity. Virtue.

To partake of this power, or of what in every state forms the sovereignty, three qualifications are essentially requisite. The supreme magistrates must be animated with the warmest love for that constitution, the government of which they are called to administer. They must be endowed with the capacities and powers necessary to the discharge of their high functions. They must, in the third place, possess that particular species of virtue, and especially of justice, which, in each form of government, is best fitted to ensure the stability of that particular constitution; for as justice is measured by different standards in oligarchies and democracies, it is plain that, in a political sense, the virtue of justice is itself variable, and that what is right in one government, may be wrong in another. When the three requisites above mentioned do not concur in the same person, an important question will arise, to which of them is the preference due? In the appointment, for instance, of a general, a man presents himself possessed indeed of great military talents, but not remarkably distinguished by his justice or his patriotism. Another is eminent for those virtues, but has never exhibited

When these requisites do not all concur, by what rule the preference among them is to be decided.

any

any signal proof of his genius for war, and his capacity for command. By what rule ought the preference to be decided? We answer, there is a middle portion of talent, as well as of virtue, that is the ordinary lot of humanity. Whatever exceeds this middle portion can fall to the share of a few only. Many men possess enough of justice and enough of patriotism to make good generals; but there are few endowed with that degree of skill and experience which is requisite for the honourable discharge of high military trust. This degree of skill and experience is, therefore, chiefly to be regarded in the choice of a general. Were we to appoint a public treasurer, we must still reason on the same principle, and because we reason on the same principle, we must in this case vary our decision; and give the preference to moral, rather than to intellectual, accomplishments. The skill, experience, and capacity requisite in a magistrate of this description, are such as the greater part of mankind may be supposed to possess. But his justice and integrity ought to rise above the common level; and it will be the best recommendation to his office, that those virtues shine in his character with more than ordinary lustre.

But as to a proper discharge of public offices in general, it may be asked, why I have said that there are *three* essential requisites? Let us suppose a man endowed with a sufficient capacity for his employment, and animated by a warm love for his country; will not those qualifications alone render him an upright and useful servant of the public? I answer, they will not; and affirm that, in addition to them, and in order to complete the character of a good magistrate or minister, a third ingredient must necessarily enter into the composition. He must possess, at least in a certain degree, the practical habit of all

ARISTOTLE's POLITICS.

BOOK VII.

all the virtues, without which, how much foever he may love his country, and how well foever he may underftand its interefts, he will often be hindered by floth, diffipation, intemperance, or cowardice from rendering it any effential fervice; nay, he may be tempted by thofe, though oftener by contrary vices, to do his country much pofitive mifchief. Men are generally clearfighted enough in perceiving their own intereft; and they cannot be fufpected of not loving themfelves with an affection fufficiently fincere; yet how many, through a defect of moral attainment, daily plunge themfelves into inextricable diftrefs? Can it be expected that they fhould treat their country better than they treat themfelves?

In what manner laws are relative to different governments,

Laws, we have faid, are things relative, and therefore variable; and in order to be good, they muft be adapted to the circumftances of the people for whom they are promulgated. Whatever law is well adapted to the conftitution, will facilitate its motions, invigorate its health, and thereby confirm its ftability; and efpecially if the law, pregnant with that which we have often mentioned as the great and principal element of political fafety, confpires to convince the people at large, or at leaft that portion of the community which is moft numerous or moft powerful, that their intereft and happinefs are intimately connected with the prefervation and permanence of the conftituted authorities. Befides this, the fafety of ftates requires that the legiflature fhould never lofe fight of that golden mean, which is univerfally overlooked or defpifed in corrupt republics. Many inftitutions, feemingly favourable to democracy, have proved its ruin; and many inftitutions, feemingly favourable to oligarchy, have totally deftroyed that form of government. Demagogues and fycophants, the partifans of the multitude, and the flatterers of the great, regard that plan

particularly to democracies and oligarchies.

of policy which they refpectively efpoufe, as the confummate pattern of perfect excellence, and therefore think, or affect to think, that they cannot poffibly do too much for promoting the interefts of democracy on the one hand, or of oligarchy on the other. In this, however, they err egregioufly; and fet themfelves in oppofition to the firft principles of fociety, and to the whole analogy of nature. The limb of an animal may be elegant without being ftraight; and the nofe, that characteriftic feature, may deferve in a certain degree the epithets of depreffed or aquiline, and yet this fmall deviation from ftraightnefs into curvature may heighten and embellifh beauty. But if you increafe too much its fwell or its depreffion, you will thereby disfigure the whole countenance. There is not any reafon whatever, why the fame obfervation fhould not apply to forms of government. The popular and ariftocratical powers, acting in nearly oppofite directions, will, if nicely adjufted, keep the motion of government ftraight and uniform. This right line, however, may, by a fmall variation in the relative force of the generating powers, deviate a little into either of the oppofite curvatures, without affecting the beauty of the fyftem. But if you vary this force or celerity too much, if you render the democracy too democratical, or the ariftocracy too ariftocratical, you will firft of all enfeeble, then fhake, and finally fubvert the government. The nature of democracy requires that the fupreme authority of government fhould refide, not in the diftinguifhed few, but in the great body of the people; the nature of oligarchy or ariftocracy, requires that the fupreme authority of government fhould refide, not in the people at large, but in the few diftinguifhed by wealth or virtue. Both oligarchies and democracies, therefore,

fore, imply the exiſtence of thoſe oppoſite deſcriptions of perſons, the rich and the poor, the few and the many. Theſe deſcriptions are the elements of which ſuch governments are compoſed; and in proportion as you diminiſh or deſtroy either of the conſtituent elements, you muſt impair or demoliſh the whole fabric of the conſtitution. How abſurdly, therefore, do thoſe demagogues and thoſe ſycophants reaſon; who, the former in democracies, would plunder and haraſs the nobility; and the latter, in oligarchies, would oppreſs and perſecute the people? How weak as well as wicked are thoſe oaths which are taken in ſome oligarchical governments, " I will reſiſt the populace with all my might; I will bear them eternal ill-will, and never ceaſe to inflict on them every injury in my power?" Did theſe haughty but contemptible nobles conſult their own intereſt and honour, they would ſwear the direct contrary; "I will never injure the people, I will always treat them with kindneſs."

The citizens muſt be taught to ſhape their lives by the pattern of the commonwealth.

But the main ſource of political ſafety conſiſts in an expedient now univerſally neglected by ſtates, though it has more efficacy alone, than all other contrivances combined. How wiſely ſoever laws may be framed, and with whatever preciſion they may be penned, they will prove impotent and uſeleſs, unleſs thoſe who are deſtined to adminiſter them, be carefully trained to ſhape their lives agreeably to the pattern of the commonwealth. The conſtitution of a ſtate, as well as that of an individual, may be ruined by intemperance; and the danger of intemperance can only be prevented by early and aſſiduous culture. If the government, therefore, is a democracy, the education muſt be democratical; if it is an oligarchy, the education muſt be oligarchical.

garchical. But an education properly adapted to either of these forms of government, must not be such as will excite their respective magistrates to indulge their political propensities, and to gratify their selfish or factious passions, but such as will give to their public conduct that firmness and moderation, which the safety of the state requires, and without which it will be impossible for the popular party long to defend the democracy against the nobles; or for the partisans of the Few, long to defend the oligarchy against the people. Education, when properly directed, is the preserving and vivifying principle of all good policy; but as it is now conducted, it becomes the cause of instability, and produces frequent revolutions. Under every species of oligarchy, the children of the great are brought up delicately, and often indulged criminally. The children of the poor are hardened in their bodies by exercise, and fortified in their minds by discipline. Can it be expected that weakness should long continue to prevail over strength; or that men softened by sloth, should long continue to command men invigorated by exertion? In democracies, on the contrary, where justice is defined by equality, and where it is thought sufficient, that all be treated alike, without considering whether each will thus have his due, liberty too naturally degenerates into licentiousness, and the citizens, instead of submitting cheerfully to the salutary restraints of discipline, think themselves entitled, as Euripides says,

"Each man to live as perverse will directs:"

because otherwise, forsooth, their liberty would be abridged. But this is absurd in the extreme. To be obliged to shape our lives to the pattern of the commonwealth, is not slavery but safety.

Such

BOOK VII.

Chap. 10.

Of revolutions in monarchies.

The origin of royalty.

Of tyranny.

Such then are the caufes and contingencies which, in republics, promote or prevent revolutions; we now proceed to explain thofe caufes and contingencies which have been found to overturn or to uphold monarchies.

Monarchies, whether limited or abfolute, are liable to nearly the fame changes and accidents which befal republics; for royalty is analogous to ariftocracy; and tyranny is compofed of rigid oligarchy and the worft fpecies of democracy, and is, therefore, moft ruinous to its fubjects, as containing the evils and deformities of two peftilent mifchiefs. The two kinds of monarchy are different in their origin. Royalty is produced from the weight and influence of the nobles concentrated in one diftinguifhed and illuftrious character, in order the more firmly to refift the dangerous encroachments of the populace. Tyranny, on the other hand, is generated by the combined ftrength of the populace, who think they can never enough exalt the leader who undertakes to defend the popular caufe, and to repel oligarchic oppreffion. Moft tyrants, therefore, have fprung out of demagogues, who had captivated the affections of the people, by traducing and perfecuting their fuperiors. This, I fay, has happened in large ftates; for in ancient times, and before the aggrandizement of cities, kings would often tranfgrefs the limits of their lawful power; and magiftrates, availing themfelves of the duration and importance of their civil and religious offices, which then lafted much longer than they do now, would often by theft or robbery ufurp a throne. The tyranny of Pheidon of Argos was nothing but an undue extenfion of his royal authority. The fame may be faid of the other tyrannies which about that time prevailed in Greece. Phalaris of Agrigentum, and the tyrants of Ionia, were originally republican magiftrates,

who

who abused the authority of their elective functions for obtaining unlimited power. But Panætius of Leontium, Cypfelus of Corinth, Peififtratus of Athens, and Dionyfius of Syracufe, all thefe and many others acquired tyranny by flattery; they firft captivated the *affections* of the people, before they enflaved their *perfons*.

Royalty, we faid, is analogous to ariftocracy. It may, in fact, be analyfed into the fame elements; fince kings are created for their perfonal or hereditary worth, and for the benefits which they feem capable of conferring, or which they have actually conferred on their nation. Codrus, who defended the Athenians in war; Cyrus, who delivered Perfia from bondage; the martial leaders of the Lacedæmonians, Macedonians, and Moloffians, whofe fuccefsful valour acquired lands for their refpective followers, and maintained them in quiet poffeffion of their important conquefts; thefe and fuch illuftrious men received the honours of royalty from the admiring gratitude of the public, and adorned the throne by the fame virtues through which they were enabled to afcend it.

A king, in his nature and end, is a public guardian. His office is a pledge, that the nobles fhall not be fubjected to injuftice, nor the people to infult. A tyrant, as we have faid and repeated, is not effentially governed by any public-fpirited motive; and if ever he confults the intereft of his country, it is merely as that intereft happens accidentally to affect his own. To enjoy pleafure, the meaneft pleafure, is the only reafonable aim of a tyrant; to acquire glory, the brighteft glory, is the aim of a king. A tyrant, therefore, delights in wealth, as furnifhing means to his end; a king delights in honour, juftly obtained and hardly earned. A tyrant is guarded by mercenary foreigners; a king, by the affection of his people.

The

BOOK VII.

Analysis of tyranny; the inherent evils of its constituent elements.

The mischief of that complex thing a tyranny, will manifestly appear by considering the inherent evils of its constituent elements. It is composed, we said, of rigid oligarchy and of lawless democracy. From the former it borrows that rapacity for wealth, (the proper end of oligarchy,) without which the tyrant can neither purchase criminal pleasure, nor pay his mercenary attendants. In imitation of oligarchic magistrates, the tyrant will distrust and disarm his subjects, plunder and banish them, as fear or avarice directs; and, disregarding every domestic and every social tie, transplant them, as suits his conveniency, from one district to another, and thus tear asunder their affections, and render them strangers in their native country. From democracy, on the other hand, tyrants will borrow their animosity to the nobles, and lose no opportunity of destroying them, secretly or openly; of banishing them from their country, and of inflicting on them every calamity, that either vengeance can dictate, or that fear may suggest. For tyrants never forget that the most distinguished portion of the community must ever be the most hostile to their government, and the most able as well as the most willing to subvert it; because of such men, some will be ambitious of dominion, and all of them must be impatient of subjection. Tyrants, therefore, regarding them as hindrances in the way of their power, and obstacles to the unbounded gratification of their passions, will never lose sight of the advice of Periander to Thrasybulus, "that in order to reap the full harvest of their government, it is necessary to cut off the tallest stalks, and to level the political field."

Causes of the revolutions in tyrannies.

From these observations, it is plain that both the causes which precede, and the consequences which follow revolutions, must be nearly the same in monarchies and in republics. The immediate

immediate and impelling caufes of innovation, are injuſtice, fuf- **BOOK VII.**
fered or apprehended, fear, contempt, and efpecially fuch acts of
injuſtice as are accompanied with infult. The ends in view Infult.
are to ſtrip the tyrant of his ill-gotten wealth, and to diveſt
him of his ufurped power, in order to apply the former to the
exigencies of the community, and to divide the latter among
lawful magiſtrates. Confpirators fometimes ſtrike at the tyranny, fometimes at the perfon of the tyrant. The latter takes
place in the cafe of infult; for perfons infulted commonly
feek not advantage, but vengeance. It was thus that Harmodius Examples.
and Ariſtogeiton overturned the tyranny of the Peifiſtratidæ.
The infult offered to his fiſter, animated the hand of Harmodius; the infult offered to his beloved Harmodius, ſharpened
the ſteel of Ariſtogeiton. Periander of Ambracia provoked the
vengeance even of his pathics by the infolent obfcenity of his
language. Philip of Macedon was ſlain by Paufanias, becaufe
he made light of the difgrace which that young nobleman had
fuffered from the audacious impurity of Attalus. The indignant
manhood of Derdas puniſhed by death the brutal affaults of Amyn-
tas, furnamed the Little [i]. The refentment of blows and ſtripes
has often threatened the fafety of men in power, and often
proved fatal to them: witnefs the Penthalidæ at Mitylené, and
alfo Penthilus himfelf, the former of whom were deſtroyed by
Megacles, the latter by Smerdes; witnefs alfo, the aſſaſſination
of Archelaus king of Macedon, effected at the inſtigation of
Decamnichus, whom that prince had caufed to be whipped, in
compliance with the defire of Euripides the poet [k]; who was
provoked at being taunted by Decamnichus for his ſtinking
breath.

[i] A few fentences are omitted, the fubject being as impure as the text is corrupt.
[k] Hiſtory of Ancient Greece, vol. iv. c. xxxiii. p. 5.

breath¹. Innumerable inftances might be given of kings and tyrants who, through fuch caufes, have been at once deprived of their power and of their lives; efpecially when the indulgence of their unbridled paffions has been accompanied by an open defiance of the fentiments of mankind, and when injury has been heightened by mockery and infult.

Fear, contempt, &c. with examples.

The fear or the contempt of fubjects often proves ruinous to kings. Xerxes commanded Artabanus, the captain of his guard, to kill Darius. Artabanus did not obey the order, thinking the king himfelf might forget, or be willing to revoke it, as the command was given in his cups. But the officious envy of courtiers failed not to refresh the king's memory; and Artabanus, alarmed for his own fafety, confpired and flew his mafter. The mean effeminacy of Sardanapalus, who, if the ftory told of him may be credited, was found weaving and fpinning with his women, excited that contemptuous indignation which tumbled him from the throne. The drunkennefs of the younger Dionyfius, which rendered him defpicable to his fubjects, animated the republican patriotifm of Dion, and enabled him to rid Syracufe of a tyrant. This paffion of contempt is moft likely to operate on two claffes of men; on the friends of the monarch, who, becaufe they enjoy his confidence, think it will be eafy for them to deceive and to deftroy him; and on the minifters of his power, becaufe they think it will not be difficult for them to ufurp his dominion. Cyrus was only the general of a provincial army; but he became mafter of the Eaft, becaufe he defpifed the luxury of Aftyages, and the flothful effeminacy of his

¹ This paffage is fomewhat abridged. Compare Diodorus Siculus, b. xiv. fect. 37.

his guards. Seuthes, the Thracian general, confpired againft his mafter Amadocus, and feated himfelf on his throne. Sometimes avarice, and fometimes ambition, combines with contempt, and accelerates revolutions. The love of money made Mithridates dethrone Ariobarzanes. Ambition often fprings up in men of courageous natures invefted by monarchs with high military command; for courage becomes enterprife, when armed with power. Ambition alfo, in another view, is productive of revolutions; an ambition, not to gain power, but to obtain glory. Confpirators, animated by this principle, are few in number; for they muft difregard what moft men highly value, perfonal fafety; and like the high-minded Dion, muft be carelefs how far they proceed in their enterprife, but think, that while invading the power of a tyrant, the firft ground they gain will be an honourable grave.

Monarchies, like other forms of government, perifh through external violence. An interference of interefts renders them obnoxious to democracies: for as potters, according to Hefiod, envy potters, fo is a fingle tyrant expofed to the hatred and vengeance of a tyrannical populace. An oppofition of principle and fyftem renders tyrannies odious to royalties and ariftocracies. The ariftocracy of Sparta, therefore, deftroyed many tyrannies; as did alfo the republic of Syracufe, while wifely governed. In deftroying monarchies, external violence is often affifted by domeftic difcord. This happened in the cafe of Gelon; and recently in that of the younger Dionyfius. Thrafybulus, Hieron's brother, playing the demagogue, corrupted by pleafures and profligacy the heir-apparent of Gelon's monarchy, that he himfelf might be king. A confpiracy was formed to deftroy Thrafybulus while the tyranny remained fafe, but a part of the conspirators seized the opportunity of divesting the whole family, at once, of honours which no individual of it seemed worthy to wear. The family of Dionysius was divided against itself; for Dion was his kinsman. By the assistance of the people he expelled the tyrant; but through the unjust suspicions of the same people, he was afterwards himself most unworthily slain.

Different operation of hatred, contempt, and anger.

Of the two causes which destroy tyrannies, hatred and contempt, the first is inherent in the very nature of tyranny, since that man cannot fail to be odious, who is invested with arbitrary power. Contempt, though not essential to tyranny itself, is, however, a more frequent cause of its destruction. Experience justifies this remark. Those who were the first to mount a despotic throne, have for the most part been able to preserve it; they were odious, but not contemptible; but their successors, naturally becoming contemptible as well as odious, have universally been divested of their unlawful power; and as shamefully disgraced as they were unworthily exalted. Anger may be regarded as a species of hatred; it differs however in this, that as its proceedings are destitute of reflection, it is always more prompt, and sometimes more efficacious; but hatred, as it acts under the direction of reason, though more slow, is commonly more dangerous and more fatal. The arbitrary government of the individual perishes (to speak in general) through the same causes which destroy rigid oligarchies and lawless democracies; both of which are nothing else but complex tyrannies.

Of revolutions in limited monarchies.

Royalty is not easily demolished by external violence; and this form of government often lasts long, since honours are naturally durable in proportion as they are moderate. Royalty perishes, however, through the internal discord of men in office, and through the preposterous ambition of kings to make them-

themselves absolute. At present, states are seldom erected into royalties; for amidst the great equality of mankind, few are thought worthy of unrivalled pre-eminence, or deemed capable of sustaining with dignity a lawful and voluntary sceptre; and a king, whose authority must be supported by force or by fraud, immediately degenerates into a tyrant. To the causes, therefore, already mentioned of the destruction of monarchy, we must add one peculiar to hereditary monarchy; the contemptible characters of youths born in the purple, and their proneness to offensive insolence. The authority of such youths cannot be *voluntarily* endured; and thus, the government, if a royalty, is effectually destroyed, and a tyranny, probably of short duration, substituted in its stead. These and other such causes produce revolutions in monarchies.

The means of their preservation, it is plain, must in general be directly contrary to the causes of their destruction. As to limited monarchy, or royalty, the more it is limited, the longer it is likely to last. Moderation, therefore, is the great preservative of this form of government. Princes, the farther they recede from despotism, and the nearer they approximate to equality of right with their subjects, are the less exposed to hatred, envy, and all that train, or all those complications of passions, which so often prove ruinous to their power. Moderation long upheld the monarchy of the Molossians. The royalty of Lacedæmon, which has proved so permanent, was, from the beginning, moderated by division between two kings; and farther attempered, under Theopompus, by a due mixture of popular and democratic powers. When that wise prince instituted the office of the Ephori, he abridged the power of royalty, but increased its stability. The short-sighted pride of his queen

asked

BOOK VII.

The worthlessness of youths born in the purple.

Chap. 11.

Limited monarchy preserved by moderation.

BOOK VII.

Absolute monarchy preserved by the two contrary modes of intension and remission. The former mode explained with an enumeration of tyrannic maxims.

asked him, whether he was not ashamed to transmit to his posterity a sceptre less splendid than that which he had received from his ancestors? " No, surely," he replied ; " I shall transmit to them a throne more stedfast and more durable."

Absolute monarchy, or tyranny, is preserved by the two contrary modes of intension and remission. The first mode consists in tightening the reins of power, by vigilance and severity; it is usual and hereditary among tyrants. The suspicious and stern Periander exercised it in all its bitterness at Corinth. The cruel institutions of the Persian monarchs are stamped with the same character; and the maxims which we formerly mentioned, of mowing the tallest stalks; of prohibiting, under severe penalties, convivial meetings of clubs and assemblies ; of destroying public schools; and of subverting every establishment that may have a tendency to engender mutual confidence, or to create a national spirit; all these precautions, and others of the same kind, would, if any thing could, render tyranny secure. It will tend to the same purpose, that persons of distinction frequent the halls, or crowd the gates, of the palace; their machinations against the government will thus be easily discovered and speedily suppressed; and their minds, degraded and debased by the servility of court attendance, will finally become incapable of forming any generous resolution. These, and such like, are Persian, Barbarian, and Tyrannic maxims, directly tending to destroy that freedom of communication which is as essential to mutual confidence, as mutual confidence is essential to boldness of enterprise. Spies, accusers, insidious listeners, like the Syracusan tale-bearers, are instruments useful to tyrants, whose interest it is to set their subjects at variance, instigating the people against the nobles,

and

and the rich and noble against each other. Above all, the poverty of the subjects is the best pledge of the permanence of tyranny; for people impoverished have neither the leisure to contrive, nor the means to effect, revolutions. The pyramids of Egypt, the magnificent dedications of the Cypselidæ, the rebuilding of the Olympian temple by the sons of Peisistratus, the sumptuous works of Polycrates of Samos; these were the productions of toil and misery, monuments as useful for the power of monarchs, as ruinous for the prosperity of their subjects. Enormous contributions in money, and enormous contributions in labour, have precisely the same tendency. By both alike the people are reduced to poverty and wretchedness; their *time* is enslaved; they must be beggars or drudges; and men robbed of leisure are not likely to recover liberty. Under the tyrannical government of Dionysius, the subjects of Syracuse returned, in the space of every five years, the amount of their whole property into the exchequer. Still faithful to his principle, the tyrant delights in war; extorting not only the wealth, but the blood of his people; especially since military expeditions are calculated to engross their whole attention, and to confirm their habitual submission. The safety of a king lies in his friends; but a tyrant distrusts *his friends* beyond all others; knowing that all others are willing, but that his friends only are always able to destroy him. The institutions adapted to lawless democracy, equally suit tyranny. The unbridled licence of slaves and of women, forms the reproach of both these governments. The order of society is inverted; in families, slaves are disobedient, and women are imperious; they are spies and accusers of their masters and husbands; and cherished by the single, as well as the complex tyrant, for those odious

BOOK VII.

Examples.

BOOK VII.

odious purposes, they become abettors of unjust domination, which they strive to perpetuate and extend. None but the worst or meanest of mankind can have credit in democracies and tyrannies. The furious sanguinary demagogue is all-powerful in the first; the cruel unfeeling courtier is alone regarded in the second; for the licentious multitude and the tyrant are governed by their passions; and as their passions are criminal, wicked instruments alone are qualified to gratify them. Tyrants, sensible of their own worthlessness, stand in perpetual need of flattery, without which anodyne, the internal smart of their crimes would render them intolerable to themselves. But men of elevated minds are totally incapable of every species of adulation. Tyrants, therefore, cannot endure any such men; their liberal spirit and conscious dignity are regarded as insolent usurpations of the imperial prerogative. None, therefore, can associate with tyrants, but those who will comply with their humours; and in admission to their table and familiarity, foreigners, as less dangerous, will always be preferred to their native subjects. Such are the expedients by which tyranny is upheld; expedients wicked in the extreme, and indefinite in number, but which are all contrived for the three following purposes: First, to debase the souls of their people; for it is not the part of low-minded persons to become political reformers. Secondly, to destroy all mutual confidence, for without confidence in each other, it is impossible for any set of men to effect a revolution; tyrants, therefore, are necessarily enemies to honesty, not only because men of integrity are naturally hostile to their government, but because such men alone, by the confidence which their characters inspire, are capable of subverting it. Thirdly, tyrants will strive to reduce their people to indigence and debility;

Tyrannic maxims all reduced to three.

lity; and thus deter them from all thoughts of sedition, by making them sensible of their total inability to effect any salutary revolution.

This, then, is the first mode of preserving a tyranny; the second is directly the reverse. We may perceive wherein it consists, by reflecting on what was above said concerning the destruction of royalty. As royalty is destroyed by rendering it tyrannical or absolute, so tyranny may be preserved by rendering it royal or moderate; with this condition, however, that the monarch, while he slackens the reins of his power, still continues to hold and to guide them: for should he once abandon his power, and begin to reign merely by the voluntary submission of his subjects, he would from that moment cease to be a tyrant, and rise into a lawful prince. His power, therefore, must be preserved, as the only foundation of his authority; but while he keeps hold of tyrannic power, he may seasonably decline to exercise it, and with great advantage to his own security, begin to play the part of a king. In assuming this borrowed character, he will first of all pretend to be mightily concerned for the interest and glory of his country. He will not incense the people by lavishing the hard earnings of their sweat and toil, on harlots, flatterers, and fiddlers. Some tyrants have been such admirable actors of royalty, as even to give their subjects a faithful account of their receipt and expenditure. The deluded multitude considered them as stewards, not as masters. Those, however, who have power, can never be in want of property; and an ambitious monarch, frequently engaged in foreign enterprises, acts wisely in not leaving at home a rich treasury

The mode of preserving tyranny by remission, with maxims by which a tyrant may obtain popularity, and appear not a plunderer but a protector.

BOOK VII.

treasury behind him, since those whom he appointed to guard it, would prove his most formidable adversaries. Generous in his own person, he views with complacence inexhaustible treasures, always at his command, in the purses of his subjects; yet, he never demands their money or their services but under pretence of the public exigency. It is the honour and safety of the country, not the ambition of the prince, that summons them to war. They follow his standard readily, regarding him, not as a tyrant, but as a protector. If he proceeds in other instances to act his part well, he will endeavour to inspire, not fear, but respect: this, indeed, is not easy, if his character at bottom be really contemptible; yet, much may be done by pretending a sincere love for his country, and exhibiting himself to the multitude as the guardian and champion of the state. An absolute monarch, who would preserve his power, must, in public at least, keep a watch over his voluptuousness, and take care that none of his ministers or favourites insult the youth and beauty of either sex. His wives and mistresses must also be taught to correct that supercilious and offensive haughtiness, and to repress those insolent airs, which has already caused the subversion of so many tyrannies. As to sensual pleasures, his conduct ought to be directly the reverse of that usual with some princes, who are not completely gratified by the most criminal indulgence in lust and luxury, unless they openly expose their wickedness and emblazon their profligacy; challenging the admiration of mankind, for that drunken debauchery and prodigal whoredom which ought to cover them with eternal infamy. A crafty tyrant will avoid giving

such

such causes of offence; knowing, that he who is drunk or asleep is more obnoxious to a conspiracy than the man who is vigilant and sober. Instead of dissipating his treasures in perishing luxury, he will employ them in embellishing his capital, and improving his country. This will exhibit him under the amiable character of a public guardian; and above all, he must appear to be much addicted to religion, and anxiously attentive to whatever regards the honour of the gods. Persons of this character are less likely to commit injustice, and therefore less the objects of fear: they are, also, less liable to suffer wrong, because men will be afraid of injuring those who reckon the gods themselves in the number of their friends. A tyrant, therefore, must endeavour to appear religious; but this specious shew of religion must not be deformed by abject superstition. It will contribute much to his security, to be diligent in discovering and rewarding merit, wherever it may be found; and to be careful to treat men of eminent talents with such distinguished honour, as will leave them little room to regret that it is not their lot to live under a free republic. Of rewards and honours, he himself must be the dispenser; but punishments must be inflicted by the authority of his courts of justice, or the command of his substitutes[1].

It is a maxim of state in every kind of monarchy, never too highly to exalt any individual subject. When great powers must

[1] See Libro del Principe; particularly chapters 18, 19, 21. Machiavel has neither the merit nor the infamy of the maxims usually ascribed to him, but which he has copied verbatim from Aristotle. Yet, in describing the contrivances for preserving tyranny, whether by the way of intention or remission, the Grecian philosopher is more careful than the Florentine secretary to avoid saying any thing that is liable to misrepresentation or reproach.

must be delegated, it is better that they should be lodged with a commission, consisting of several persons, whose rivalry and jealousy will afford the best pledges of their fidelity; but when the nature of any important function of sovereignty requires that it should be intrusted to one only, the tyrant should take care, that this minister be not of too enterprising a spirit; or if he has imprudently aggrandized such a person beyond the due measure, he must beware not to curtail him of his ample dignities at once, but slowly and imperceptibly. The sudden fall of an ambitious minister has shaken the stability of many a government. All kinds of offensive insolence are to be most carefully avoided, especially such insolence as vents itself in acts of violence or lust. The crafty tyrant must persuade the victims of his outrageous and infamous passions, that they are the objects of his love, and repay their secret submissions by conspicuous honours. But when he suspects that his insolence has really offended, he must particularly be on his guard against men jealous of their honour, incapable of restraining their anger, and willing, as Heraclitus says, to purchase vengeance at the price of their lives.

As every state consists of two principal classes, the rich and the poor, the tyrant must endeavour to make it appear, that his authority is useful to both; or if that be impossible, he must diligently court and gain the strongest party. If *their* favour can be obtained, it will be needless for him to have recourse to the ordinary expedients of emancipating his slaves and disarming his subjects, since the strength of his guards, abetted by a powerful party among the people, will be sufficient to uphold his tyranny. It is needless to expatiate on this subject;

ject; for all the other maxims that might be enumerated must still have the same end in view, to gain popularity, and must be calculated to make the tyrant appear, not as a master, but as a steward; not a plunderer, but a protector [k]. By avoiding blameable excess, and confining his life within the bounds of moderation, he will cease to be the object of fear and hatred; his reign will be more illustrious and more honourable, in proportion as his subjects are less miserable and less abject; his throne also will be the more secure. As to morals, therefore, let him, if it is impossible to be virtuous, be at least half virtuous, and not altogether wicked, but only half wicked [l].

Of all governments, the least durable are oligarchies and tyrannies. The most lasting tyranny on record was that of Orthagoras and his sons in Sicyon. It continued a hundred years. The cause of its long duration was the laudable moderation of those princes, and their cheerful submission to the laws. Clisthenes, besides, was a man of a martial spirit; and, therefore, by no means an object of contempt, which so often proves fatal to tyrannies; and he, as well as the other princes of his family, knew the arts of government, and assiduously cultivated popularity. His impartial equity crowned the honest boldness of the judge who, in a dispute respecting a gymnastic victory, adjudged the prize to his competitor. It is said, that the statue sitting in the market-place of Sicyon, adorned with a crown,

Chap. 12.

That oligarchies and tyrannies are the least durable of all governments. Examples.

[k] How well did the late Frederic II. of Prussia, as well as his model, Philip II. of Macedon, practise the more essential part of Aristotle's maxims! See my View of the Reign of Frederic, c. vi. p. 376, & seq.

[l] Machiavel says more explicitly, "non partirse dal bene, potendo; ma sapere entrare nel male, necessitato." The maxim, if it has any sense, only shews that tyranny being a bad thing in itself, can only by preserved by bad means.

BOOK VII.

crown, perpetuates the remembrance of the judge's integrity, and of Clifthenes's magnanimity. Peififtratus of Athens gave an ufeful leffon to tyrants. When fúmmoned before the Areopagus, he appeared in perfon to plead his caufe, and refpectfully heard the decifion of that ancient tribunal. The fecond example of a durable tyranny is that of Cypfelus and his family at Corinth. It lafted feventy-feven years and fix months; for Cypfelus himfelf reigned thirty years; Periander, forty-four; and Pfammetichus, the fon of Gondius, three years and fix months. The duration of this government proceeded from the fame caufes. Cypfelus was a man of uncommon addrefs, and knew how to practife every feductive and every popular art. He even difbanded his guards, as ufelefs for his fafety. His fon Periander was indeed a tyrant; but his character was ennobled by martial fpirit, and illuftrated by military fuccefs. The third and laft example of a durable tyranny was that of the Peififtratidæ at Athens. It was not, like thofe above mentioned, uninterrupted; for Peififtratus twice abdicated and fled; fo that in the courfe of thirty-three years, he reigned only feventeen; his fons reigned eighteen years; the whole duration of their government, therefore, exceeded not thirty-five years. That of Gelon and his family in Syracufe was ftill fhorter-lived. Gelon reigned feven years; Hieron reigned ten; but Thrafybulus was banifhed in lefs than twelve months. The greater part of tyrannies have perifhed ftill more fuddenly [m].

Thus

[m] When Ariftotle fpeaks of tyrannies, he here means ufurpations of arbitrary power in countries formerly free; whether under a lawful monarchy, or under a republican government. It is ftrictly confiftent with his principles, that fuch ufurpations fhould be fhort-lived, becaufe they are incompatible with the fentiments, principles, and habits of thinking moft prevalent among the people at large.

ARISTOTLE's POLITICS.

Thus much concerning revolutions in monarchies, how they are caused, and how they may be prevented [n].

BOOK VII.

[n] The conclusion of this chapter is employed in refuting Plato's fanciful notions concerning political revolutions; notions founded on the wonderful powers ascribed by the Pythagoreans to periods and numbers. This wild doctrine is explained in the eighth book of Plato's Republic. Aristotle proves, by the facts above stated, that it is totally inconsistent with experience. The revolutions, however, which history describes, and which theory explains, it is the business of policy to apply, that the experience of the past may thus serve for regulating the conduct of the future. While the same causes produce the same effects, nations similarly circumstanced must, it is thought, necessarily run the same political career; obtain by similar exertions the same degree of prosperity; commit, through ambition or insolence, nearly the same errors; and, in consequence of those errors, be liable to nearly equal reverses of fortune. The truth of these general observations cannot be disputed; but in making particular applications of them, either for the purpose of confirming their own confidence, or of inspiring terror into their enemies, men are almost continually deceived by appearances; sometimes mistaking even contrasts for parallels. It is not unusual with the great military republic of recent date, to compare itself with Rome, and its naval and commercial rival with Carthage. Yet it is only under one aspect, and in particulars the slightest and most superficial, that Carthage and England exhibit a false air of resemblance; while in their characterising properties, the two maritime commonwealths form the subject of a contrast rather than of a comparison. The one continental, the other insular; the former depending entirely for defence on foreign troops, the latter exulting in domestic strength; Carthage noted for penuriousness and perfidy; England equally distinguished for probity and profusion; the African republic, addicted solely to lucrative pursuits, considering literature and philosophy as things beyond its sphere; Great Britain, the seat of arts and elegance, of growing fame in literature, and of unrivalled pre-eminence in science.

The parallel between Rome and France is attended with this singularity, that the latter has run through the same stages in a few years, which the former did in as many centuries. It has expelled or destroyed its royal line; abolished privileged orders; laid all honours open to the people at large; displayed the enthusiasm of liberty; proved the connection between this principle and military energy; defeated its neighbours on the Continent; obliged them to supply its armies with pay, corn, and clothing; plundered their altars and temples; carried off their pictures and statues. I need not say more of what France has done; but among the transactions indicating what she in future is likely to do, the reader of ancient history will recollect that Buonaparte is entrusted with nearly the same commission that the Romans bestowed on Cæsar before he became dictator, and in precisely the same countries on both sides the Alps.

(385)

ARISTOTLE's POLITICS.

BOOK VIII.*

INTRODUCTION.

THIS Book is placed laſt in order, becauſe it ſeems to have been written to ſupply the defects of ſeveral preceding parts of the work. Ariſtotle had ſufficiently explained the principles and arrangements of the ſimple forms of government; but he thought it might be uſeful further to examine wherein governments bearing the ſame name, might yet eſſentially differ in their nature. This leads him to enumerate and deſcribe the different kinds of democracies and oligarchies, and to ſhew how the worſt kinds might be improved and corrected; and, when thus happily altered, how they might beſt be upheld and perpetuated. In this Book he alſo examines the different kinds of military or naval force in their relation to the different forms of government; ſhewing which kinds of the former are reſpectively beſt adapted to the different modes of the latter. He concludes the Book with an accurate analyſis of the executive power; enumerating and deſcribing the different functions of magiſtracy eſſentially requiſite in every well-regulated commonwealth. On this important ſubject, the following remarks will not appear unreaſonable.

When

* Commonly publiſhed as Book VI.

BOOK VIII.

When our author first analyfed government into deliberative, judicial, and executive [a] powers, he meant fomething more than merely to explain the fubject as a matter of fpeculation. For it is neceflary, he obferves, not only to know what, and how many are political functions, but according to what fubordination they ought to be arranged and diftributed. That they ought to be as minutely fubdivided as ftate neceflity will permit, he thinks moft evident from this fimple confideration, that each individual will be likely to act his part moft properly, when each has his affigned tafk. The military power ought to depend on the civil [b]; that the army may be formidable only to the enemies of the ftate: and the executive power ought to be clearly diftinct from the legiflature; left tyrannical laws fhould be enacted, and thofe executed tyrannically. All magiftrates ought to be refponfible for the exercife of their authority; and their accounts fubject to the infpection of thofe who never themfelves handle the public money. The office of collecting and applying the revenue ought never, therefore, to belong to the fame perfons who adminifter juftice, and punifh crimes; left the financial adminiftrator fhould abufe his authority to the bafe purpofes of extortion or vengeance. "The law is above the judge; and the judge, as organ of the law, above all other magiftrates. But the office of judge is incompatible with every function, that might pervert his judgment or twift his decifions; for a judge is a ruler, and how can a ruler give ftraightnefs to other things if itfelf be crooked [c]?"

Thefe

[a] The executive is called by him the appointing or electing power, for a reafon above affigned, p. 275.

[b] But to reduce it to this dependence is not an eafy matter, as will be experienced by a great modern republic. Yet unlefs this be done, the commonwealth is a camp, and its liberty an empty boaft.

[c] Rhetor. l. i. p. 512.

These great political principles afford the neareſt approximation which the wiſdom of antiquity ever made to the improvements and perfection which the events of time and chance, co-operating with the virtues of our anceſtors, gradually introduced into the Britiſh conſtitution. But the grand ſecret in policy, of a government, carried on by kings who can do no wrong, and whoſe perſons are ſacred, through the inſtrumentality of accountable adviſers and reſponſible miniſters, was totally unknown to the free ſtates of antiquity; on which account chiefly, none of them could lay claim to that ſtability and perpetuity at which, Cicero maintains [d], all wiſe government ought ever to aim. As this is a point which deſerves the greateſt attention, I ſhall not be blamed for making an unneceſſary circuit, when I take the beſt, or the only, road to eſtabliſh ſo important a truth on authority which demands reſpect, and by arguments which admit not of anſwer.

The learned and judicious Polybius, who was not merely a *ſpeculative* politician, but one converſant from his youth with courts and camps, and the management of great affairs, of unbounded curioſity, and with extraordinary opportunities, explains as the main reſult of his reading and experience, what he calls the theory of political revolutions: revolutions ſo neceſſary in their event, and ſo immutable in their order, that they may be eaſily foreſeen, and boldly predicted. The diſcourſe is contained in the ſixth book of his Hiſtory, and applied to the commonwealth of Rome in the beginning of the ſeventh century from the foundation of the city, the firmeſt and moſt flouriſhing period of the republic; when external victory conſpired with internal arrangement to render the public ſecurity

[d] Fragm. de Repub. l. iii.

BOOK VIII. security as stable, as the policy of the state was profound, and its renown was illustrious.

In that invaluable fragment the historian finds fault with the usual division of governments into monarchies, aristocracies, and democracies; observing that these are neither the best, nor the only, kinds of civil polity. Monarchies are the first governments in their origin, and the work of Nature herself; but they have never yet been so skilfully moulded by art, that they had not a strong and palpable tendency to degenerate into tyrannies. It is the nature of power to corrupt those invested with the exercise of it; and the exercise of hereditary power is, in this respect, still more dangerous than that of any other. When princes, therefore, begin to abuse their prerogatives and authority for the unbridled indulgence of their rapacity, lust, and luxury, their proceedings cannot fail to provoke indignation and anger among the more dignified classes of their subjects, whose temper is the least likely tamely to brook disgrace. The people at large will sympathize with their resentment, and assist in destroying the monarchy, which had degenerated into a tyranny. An aristocracy will naturally rise on its ruins; since the gratitude of the public will cheerfully accept for rulers those by whom the country was delivered from oppression. The new magistrates will continue for a while to conduct themselves with propriety and patriotism; administering justly and wisely the affairs both of the citizens individually, and of the public collectively. But when the exercise of their power devolves on their descendants, who have not the merit of their fathers, nor enjoy like them the advantage of having been trained in the school of adversity, these unworthy successors will begin grossly to abuse their pre-eminent functions; giving loose reins to the most odious

odious and moſt diſgraceful paſſions. The ariſtocracy is thus transformed into an oligarchy; which, ſinking under the weight of its own inherent vices, will be ſpeedily overturned by the firſt leader of the multitude who has courage to aſſail it; ſince the whole body of the people, exaſperated by an accumulation of indignities, will be prepared to abet his meaſures and to ſecond his efforts. The people at large, now taking the commonwealth into their own hands, will eſtabliſh a democracy; and while the greater part of thoſe continue to live, who have experienced the evils reſulting from governments of arbitrary will, the community will flouriſh under the bleſſings of law and liberty. But when the adminiſtration of the democracy is delivered down from father to ſon through ſucceſſive generations, the reſtleſſneſs of man will begin to ſpurn advantages with which he is ſatiated; ambition will nauſeate equality, and ſigh for pre-eminence; thoſe who have accumulated great wealth, will covet a proportional ſhare of political power; and to attain this much envied object, will not heſitate to deſtroy their own fortunes by profuſion, and to corrupt the public morals by bribery, until the whole maſs of the community be ſo deeply tainted with the impatience of rapacity, that the populace will no longer wait for the precarious or tardy dole, but putting themſelves under the command of the firſt daring and unprincipled chief, whoſe boldneſs equals his wickedneſs, will invade the conſtitution; ſubvert the government; confiſcate, baniſh, murder, and plunder, until having filled up the meaſure of their ſavage ferocity, the folly of their own paſſions delivers them enſlaved and bound, into the hands of a ſingle deſpot [d].

Such

[d] The ſame doctrine is maintained by Ariſtotle, b. vii. c. v.; and by Plato in the following paſſage:

ARISTOTLE's POLITICS.

BOOK VIII.

Such is the perpetual round, which, according to Polybius, all unmixed governments are found by experience to run; from monarchy to tyranny; from ariſtocracy to oligarchy; from democracy to the tyranny of the multitude; for every multitude, he affirms, merely as ſuch, is filled with levity and inconſtancy, lawleſs in its purſuits, headſtrong in is paffions, unjuſt in its proceedings[c]. In none of the ſimple forms of government, therefore, is there any conſtitutional firmneſs; their ſtability depends on manners which are tranſient, and on circumſtances which are accidental. They may be kept afloat by a tide of external profperity; while the atchievement and partition of foreign conqueſts, conceal the inherent evils of the conſtitutions under which they are made. But the flame of difcord, the longer it is ſuppreſſed by the mere accumulation of fuel, will finally break out with the greater violence; which has always been experienced by ſtates whoſe inſtitutions were well adapted to the contentious activity of war, but which had never been taught to enjoy the ineſtimable gifts of peaceful leiſure and unambitious ſecurity.

Having rejected and reprobated all ſimple forms of polity, Polybius proceeds to examine thoſe that are complex; governments of reciprocal controul; of which, he maintains, the moſt perfect model was to be found in the conſtitution of Rome, as it ſtood in the beginning of the ſeventh century of the republic. In that conſtitution, monarchic, ariſtocratic, and popular elements

εικοτως τοινυν εκ ιξ αλλης πολιτειας τιμωμις καθιςαται η εκ δημοκρατιας. Εξ της ακροτατης ελευθεριας, δουλεια πλιςη και αγριωτατη. "Exceſſive liberty is not likely to change into any thing elſe but exceſſive ſlavery. Tyranny, therefore, more naturally reſults from democracy than from any other form of government; the higheſt liberty being converted into the completeſt and cruelleſt ſervitude." Plato de Republ. l. ix.

[c] Polybius, l. vi. c. 56. p. 594. edit. Schweigh.

ments were so skilfully combined and so equally balanced, that the Romans themselves could not positively ascertain with which of the three species of governments their own ought to be classed ⁱ. When they contemplated the splendid functions of the consuls, *their* authority seemed equal to that of kings. In the senate they beheld and felt the full strength of an aristocracy. The people at large, headed by their tribunes, appeared imperiously to exercise the plenitude of democratic power. The consuls, our author observes, even before leading their respective armies into the field, carry on within Rome itself the chief administration of affairs. To them all magistrates, except the tribunes, are subject. They assemble the senate, propose matters of urgency for its deliberation, and carry its decrees into execution. They likewise convoke the popular assembly, report to the people the resolutions of the senate, collect and declare the votes, and give efficacy to the will of the majority. When the consuls are at Rome, the ambassadors of foreign states can, through them only, be admitted to an audience in the senate. In military matters their authority is supreme. They appoint the military tribunes, enrol the legions, select the

---

ⁱ The whole of Polybius's observations on this subject seems to have escaped the notice of our great law commentator Blackstone. "Thus these three species of government have all of them their several perfections and imperfections. Democracies are usually the best calculated to direct the ends of a law; aristocracies, to invent the means by which that end shall be attained; and monarchies, to carry those means into execution. And the ancients, as was observed, had in general no idea of any other permanent form of government, but these three; for though Cicero * declares himself of opinion " esse optimam constitutam rempublicam, quæ ex tribus generibus illis, regali optimo & populari, sit modice confusa;" yet Tacitus † treats this notion of a mixed government, formed out of them all, and partaking of the advantages of each, as a visionary whim, and one that, if effected, could never be lasting or secure ‡.

* Fragm. de Repub. l. ii.   † Annal. l. iv. c. 33.   ‡ Blackstone's Commen. Intro. sect ii.

BOOK VIII.

the men fittest for each kind of service [g], and impose their undisputed commands on the allies. All who serve under their standards, are alike liable to their coercion and chastisement; and the questors attend them in the field, merely to disburse whatever sums they may think fit to demand. Such, Polybius observes, are the royal and monarchic powers [h] of the consuls.

The senate is not, however, destitute of its due weight in the state. First of all, this respected council governs the exchequer, into which no sums are received, and from which none are issued, but by the express orders of the senate. By the senate's command only, the questors disburse all monies for the public service, except those sums with which they supply the consuls in the field. Even that heavy expenditure which is incurred by the state at the end of every period of five years, for the repairs or extension of public works, is made by the censors under the authority of the senate; which body also takes cognizance of all public delinquencies committed in any part of Italy; such as treasons, conspiracies, poisonings, and assassinations. To the senate it belongs to settle all disputes which arise in Italy, whether between individuals or communities; as well as to dispatch all embassies to foreign parts, either to treat of peace, or to denounce war; either to offer its advice and protection, or to interpose with its authority and commands. When foreign ambassadors arrive at Rome, the senate receives them

[g] Compar. Polyb. l. vi. c. 12. p. 481. & l. vi. c. 20. p. 496. The military institutions of the Romans called forth the whole energy of the state. With them, the public was every thing; the citizens, nothing. According to their age, strength, and stature, they were draughted into the several legions, and divisions of legions; *cohorts* and *maniples*; without the smallest regard to their partialities and prejudices. Vid. Polyb. ubi supra.

[h] L. vi. c. 12. p. 481.

ARISTOTLE's POLITICS.

them in the manner it may judge moſt fit; and anſwers their demands as it may deem moſt expedient. Thence, to ſtrangers who come to Rome in the abſence of the conſuls, the commonwealth appears in no other light than that of a ſimple ariſtocracy[i].

BOOK VIII.

It may very naturally be inquired, what political functions, then, remain for the exerciſe of the people at large? the greateſt and moſt important of all; for the people are the diſpenſers of rewards and puniſhments. They elect the magiſtrates, they

[i] Polybius, l. vi. c. xiii. p. 482. I abridge the author's narrative as much as attention to perſpicuity will admit; yet I am fearful leſt his analyſis of the Roman government prove tireſome to thoſe, who beſide conſidering the importance of the ſubject itſelf, do not continually keep in view the important conſequence that I would deduce from his elaborate diſcuſſion. Of all mixed governments, Polybius thinks the Roman, as it ſtood in his time, the beſt model of a well-balanced commonwealth. He obſerves, however, that emergencies muſt occur, that would infallibly deſtroy its equipoiſe. His prediction was fulfilled; as all ſimilar predictions had been fulfilled concerning governments ſimilarly conſtituted. I preſume not to maintain, that he choſe for his example, the beſt model of mixed government that could poſſibly have been ſelected. Perhaps the ancient government of the Cretans, whoſe inſtitutions, as well as manners, had ſadly degenerated in his time, might have anſwered his purpoſe better; and the equipoiſe in the conſtitutions both of Carthage and of Sparta was maintained during a period of longer duration, though of leſs ſplendour. But the reſult of his reaſoning, confirmed by that of all the great writers of antiquity, is, that every one of thoſe mixed governments, in many of which there was a nice balance of political powers, and in ſome of which the people (as above proved) acted by their repreſentatives, yet I ſay that every one of them contained in itſelf the ſeeds of its diſſolution. Their radical infirmity originated not in thoſe cauſes to which it is univerſally aſcribed, the want of repreſentation and a balance; but it conſiſted principally in this, that their firſt magiſtrates, by whatever title they might be diſtinguiſhed, conſuls, archons, or kings, were incapable of performing what Ariſtotle conſiders as the main function of royalty, the defending the poor from inſult and the rich from injury, and thus keeping the component parts of a ſtate in their proper places, and thereby giving to the conſtitution inalterable ſtability,

BOOK VIII. they impose fines on those guilty of malversation in office; they alone can inflict the punishment of death. The laws proposed by the senate are either confirmed or rejected by the people; and the people may either ratify or annul all transactions between the senate and foreign states [k].

In this complex form of the Roman constitution, the moving powers are, according to Polybius, admirably adapted to the purposes of harmonious co-operation, and of seasonable counter-action; since the parts reciprocally control each other, linked in a nice chain of mutual dependence. The consuls, at the head of their armies, depend both on the senate and on the people; on the senate, without whose authority their soldiers cannot be provided with corn, or clothing, or pay; which can either prorogue their command, or appoint new generals; which can aggrandize and emblazon their transactions, or depreciate, vilify, and obscure them; and without whose willingness to furnish the requisite expence, they cannot be gratified with the honour of a triumph. The consuls are dependent, also, on the people, to whom, at the year's end, they are responsible for their behaviour in command; and to whom it belongs, either to ratify or to annul their transactions with foreign powers [l].

The senate and the people are held in a connection not less intimate, which compels them mutually to respect each other. The people alone can inflict the most tremendous of all punishments. They can diminish the collective honours of the senate; they can abridge the fortunes of its members; and the *veto* of a single tribune, who is naturally the creature and the organ of the people, can stop all proceedings in the senate, and even prevent the assembling of that council. But the people, in return, must

[k] Polybius, l. vi. c. xiv. p. 484, & seq.   [l] Ibid. c. xv. p. 486, & seq.

muſt reſpect the will of the ſenators, both collectively and individually; for the ſenators are their employers, paymaſters, and judges. In every part of Italy there are innumerable works, conſiſting in buildings and repairs; the culture of lands and gardens; the management of mines, rivers, and harbours, all which objects are let to farm by the cenſors, and undertaken by the people. There is ſcarcely a ſingle Roman who is not involved in theſe contracts; ſome farming under the cenſors at a certain price; others being partners with the farmers; a third claſs being ſureties for them; and a fourth, in ſupport of theſe ſureties, pledging their own fortunes to the ſtate. But in enforcing or modifying all ſuch bargains, the power of the ſenate is ſupreme. This council can extend the time limited for performance; can lighten the conditions of the contract; and when any inſeparable obſtacle occurs, altogether releaſe the contractors. Beſides this, in moſt other civil cauſes of magnitude, judges are ſelected from the ſenate. The people at large, therefore, will be careful how they provoke a body, from whoſe members they have ſo much to hope, as well as ſo much to fear [m]. Nor is there reaſon to apprehend that they ſhould wantonly thwart the inclinations of the conſuls, to whoſe authority all the citizens both collectively and individually are amenable in the field. From this ſkilful adaptation and intimate dependence of the parts, that harmony of action reſults by which the political machine is impelled regularly and rapidly towards its propoſed goal [n]; reſiſting all attacks, ſurmounting every

---

[m] Polybius, l. vi. c. xvi. & xvii. p. 488, & ſeq.

[n] There is a difference between mechanical and moral powers, afterwards hinted at by Polybius. The former, acting neceſſarily and invariably, will, when equal and contrary, deſtroy each other. But in politics two contrary powers may exiſt ſimultaneouſly;

BOOK VIII.

every enemy, and continually extending the dominion of the republic. When the terrors of danger are exchanged for the joys of victory, and the minds of men might be elated and intoxicated through excefs of profperity, the benefit of a government of reciprocal control is eminently confpicuous; fince thofe branches of the ftate that would tower too high, and expand too widely, are checked in their movements, and even anticipated in their tendencies, by the continual preffure of the powers to which they are obnoxious [o].

This is a glorious panegyric of the republic, as then conftituted, and then circumftanced. But Polybius reluctantly acknowledges that the complement would foon ceafe to be applicable;

taneoufly; and the movement of government, inftead of being weakened or ftopped, may be fometimes thereby ftrengthened and accelerated. In the Roman conftitution, befides the *Comitia Curiata*, which was chiefly ufeful in arming military commanders with the fanctions and authority of religion, there exifted in Rome, from the time of the Publilian law enacted in the 414th year of the city, two legiflative powers, the *Comitia Tributa* and the *Comitia Centuriata*; the former founded on the balance of numbers; and the latter, on the balance of property. A dictator might be legally named by the confuls, neither controlable in his exercife of power, nor accountable for his adminiftration in office; which, though limited to the fpace of fix months, afforded time fufficient for the fubverfion of a government. The power of the dictator was occafional and extraordinary; but at all times the veto of a tribune was alike formidable. He might ftop all meafures and all deliberations; and, as the tribunes were the creatures of the multitude from which they derived their authority, they would often be inclined through intereft and vanity, to flatter popular paffions, and to blow up every guft of difcontent into a ftorm of fedition. Yet notwithftanding thefe feeming incongruities, the body politic was held together by the charms of victory and glory, and the neceffity of acting continually againft innumerable enemies [*], in defence of a country in which the great enjoyed pre-eminences and honours, and the people at large more freedom and more advantages than any other nation in the ancient world. Such was the ftate of Rome until that combination of circumftances was produced, which, as Polybius hints, the commonwealth would be unable to furmount.

[o] Polybius, l. vi. c. xviii. p. 492.

[*] Externus metus, maximum concordiæ vinculum. Tit. Liv.

cable; for the component parts of the state would be kept in their proper places through reciprocal counteraction and control, only while the minds of men were neither inflamed by the lust of power, nor loosened from the restraint of principle; and while the commonwealth, continuing in a progressive state of prosperity, could discharge in its colonizations and conquests, those noxious humours which, unless drained by such outlets, must prove destructive to its vitals. But as the measure of national prosperity was filled up [p], the objects of individual ambition would be expanded and magnified; and, while the assailing temptations augmented beyond bounds, the virtues to resist them would continually diminish. The extortion of rapacity would keep pace with the profusion of vanity; and the unworthy proceedings of the Great would finally terminate in their own ruin, and that of the republic; for the people, provoked by the ambition and avarice of one party, and intoxicated by the perfidious adulation of another, would begin to despise law, to spurn authority; and, subjecting the concerns of their country to their own furious passions, would establish under the specious names of liberty and equality, the worst and cruellest of all tyrannies. This political prophecy begun to be verified a few years after it was made, in the seditions of the Gracchi; and was completely accomplished in the future misfortunes of the republic. But it is worthy of remark, that Polybius concludes his discourse, after he has shipwrecked the Romans on democracy; leaving them to infer from his general theory

[p] τις ὑπεροχη και δυναμιν αδριτος, αφικηται, p. 576. I have paraphrased this passage of Polybius by comparing it with what Aristotle predicts concerning the destiny of Carthage. We learn from the Roman historians in general, that the complete colonization of Italy had the effect ascribed to it in the text.

BOOK VIII.

theory of political revolutions, that this tyrannical democracy muſt neceſſarily terminate in the exaltation of a ſingle deſpot [q]. The want of conſtitutional firmneſs in the beſt regulated ſtates of antiquity, produced a very general opinion, that nations, as well as individuals, had their youth and old age; their maturity, decline, and conſequent diſſolution. This opinion is warmly patronized by Plato [r]; it is maintained likewiſe by Polybius; it was firſt refuted by Ariſtotle; and it is alſo rejected by Cicero [s]. But it remained for modern times to ſhew, how the vigour of monarchy, acting by reſponſible inſtruments only, could retain the component parts of a ſtate unalterably in their proper ſpheres; and how the merely executive part of government, though clearly diſtinct from the ſovereignty, might be armed with ſufficient power to uphold law, but without either the power or the will to ſubvert liberty. Had this political arrangement been eſtabliſhed in the free ſtates of antiquity,

[q] According to Ariſtotle's principles, the republic of Rome enjoyed one advantage in common with the great republic of modern growth; viz. its greatneſs: for the parties which neceſſarily prevail in all popular governments rendering them peculiarly liable to the pernicious interference of foreign powers, the ſtability of a great republic conſidered in relation to external cauſes of deſtruction, whether by force or fraud, muſt be much firmer than that of a ſmall one. But the modern commonwealth is deſtitute of two advantages which had a tendency to preſerve the ancient. Firſt, a permanent ſenate, which gave the ſtate continuity of exiſtence, and tranſmitted from one generation to another the ſame plans and purpoſes; and ſecondly, the dictatorial and tribunicial powers, which, however liable to abuſe, ſeem indiſpenſably neceſſary in every populous community governed on the republican plan, for ſeaſonably ſuſpending the adverſe exertion of exaſperated factions; and thereby preventing contrarieties of intereſt from continually degenerating into ſources of ſedition.

[r] Plato de Republic. l. viii p. 712, & ſeq. edit. Ficin.

[s] Debit enim conſtituta ſic eſſe civitas, ut æterna ſit. Itaque nullus interitus eſt reipublicæ naturalis, ut hominis, in quo mors non modo neceſſaria eſt, verum etiam optanda perſæpe. Fragment de Repub. l. iii.

tiquity, they would not have been liable to thofe perpetual abufes of power, which, as Polybius fays, are by *a natural neceſſity*[t], fubverfive of ariſtocracies and democracies; nor would there have been room for that unbounded ambition, which, in all great and profperous ſtates, tends, by a *neceſſity equally* inevitable, to the deſtruction of mixed governments, how nicely foever in other reſpects their texture may be combined, and their elements may be balanced. Enterpriſing demagogues and fortunate generals would not merely have been refiſted in their exertions by the counteraction of equals and rivals, until the bloody conflict ended in the ruin of public liberty; but they would have been repreſſed in their tendencies, and overawed in their hopes, by a power far mightier to fave than they were to deſtroy; but a power, whofe ſtrength would be changed into weakneſs, whenever it attempted to violate liberty, and infringe the laws [u].

BOOK VIII.

[t] The natural neceſſity of political revolutions is maintained by Machiavel. Hiſtory of Florence, l. i. fub initio; whofe opinions on the fubject, and even turn of expreſſion, are copied by Hume. Hiſtory of England, vol. ii. p. 441. Edit. 1767.

[u] Is it neceſſary to obferve as a corollary to this difcourfe, that a neighbouring nation, if ſhe confulted her fuppofed intereſt and the fafety of her republican government, would inſtantly relinquiſh the career of ambition, and diſband her armies more eagerly and more cheerfully than ever ſhe collected them? The ſtability of her democratical conſtitution can refult only from giving to her national guards or militia a decided fuperiority over foldiers by profeſſion. But how many ſtubborn difficulties will prefent themfelves in attempting to realife this project! Should many of the requiſition men be defirous to return to their families, and ſhould the numerous bodies of foreigners in the fervice be difcharged without danger, and without tumult, yet who will be able to perfuade the French veterans to forfake their arms, their generals, and their military habits of life; and prevail on the greater part of them to mix with the peaceful maſs of citizens, while the remainder is diſperfed over an extenfive frontier? Yet unleſs this is done, it is morally impoſſible that France ſhould long enjoy even the name or appearance of a republic. I leave this note as it ſtood before the recent revolution of the fourth of September.

BOOK VIII.

ARGUMENT.

Of republics of husbandmen—Of manufacturers and merchants.— Imperfections of democracy.—Oligarchy.—Military and naval force.—Branches of executive magistracy.—Magistrates for protecting commerce and contracts—Of police—Of revenue.— Courts of record.—Controllers of public accounts.—Different orders of priests.—Superintendants of education and morals.

IN former books, we analysed and examined the complex structure of government, and explained the nature and the differences of the deliberative, the judicial, and the executive, powers. The deliberative power properly constitutes the sovereignty, since the proper office of magistrates and judges consists in obeying its will, and in executing its orders [x]. We shewed, also, what are the political arrangements, which in the appointment of magistrates, and in the constitution of councils and tribunals, are best adapted to each form of government; and described what are the active powers by which every political fabric may be shaken and subverted, as well as what are the resisting forces by which it may be upheld and perpetuated. But as governments, included under the same specific name, differ from each other, in consequence of the different materials of which they are composed, and of the various modes in which those

BOOK VIII.

Chap. I.

Of the elements of government, and their different combinations.

[x] βουλητικὸν καὶ κύριον. Compare above, p. 275 & seq.

BOOK VIII.

thofe materials are arranged, it is neceffary further [y] to examine thofe materials and that arrangement; to confider whether, for inftance, a democracy or an oligarchy contains all the conftituent elements, which are commonly deemed effential to democracies or oligarchies; or whether they contain only a certain proportion of thofe elements mixed with others of a different kind [z]; what is the effect of this compofition on good government in general, and what combinations are beft adapted to each country or nation in particular. We begin by treating of democracy [a].

Chap. 2.

Of the nature and end of democracy.

Liberty is the foundation and fcope of democracy; and it is not unufual to hear that in this government alone, the charms of liberty are difplayed. Liberty itfelf is allowed to be founded on juftice; but the juftice of democracies, being meafured by arithmetical [b] equality, requires that each individual citizen fhould enjoy the fame political advantages with every other citizen, and that the will as well as the intereft of the greater number fhould always be preferred to the will and the intereft of the leffer. It is the nature, therefore, of democracy, that offices of executive magiftracy fhould be held by rotation; and that in the deliberative affembly, the poor fhould always prevail over the rich, becaufe the clafs of the poor is every where the more

[y] Ariftotle having ftated the contents of the preceding Books, goes on to confider the different kinds of governments diftinguifhed by the fame fpecific name, ἅμα τι περι ιχνιων ιι τι λοιπον, " and at the fame time to examine any remaining particulars which bear a reference to the fubject of his prefent work;" which is fufficient to fhew that this Book, as I have obferved in the Introduction, is chiefly fupplemental.

[z] Ariftotle fays that the refult of the συνδυασμοι, " the conjunctions of elements," was not fufficiently attended to in his own times.

[a] I omit fome parts of this chapter, becaufe the obfervations contained in them are afterwards more clearly expreffed.

[b] See vol. i. b. v. c. 4. p. 266.

more numerous. This laft circumftance is confidered as the beft proof, or moft evident fign of liberty; and the fecond is, that each individual may live as he lifts; for to live agreeably to the will of another is, according to the maxim of democrats, to be a flave. On the bafis, therefore, of thefe principles, the following democratical laws may be erected. That every citizen fhould be capable of holding offices; and where election prevails, that every citizen fhould be an elector. That the general will fhould govern each individual; but that each individual, in his turn, fhould be appointed to declare and execute this will. That offices fhould be diftributed by lot, if not all offices, at leaft all fuch as do not require the peculiar advantages of fkill and experience. That a qualification in point of fortune be not requifite for holding any employment; at leaft, that this qualification be exceedingly fmall. That the fame office (military offices excepted) be not held twice fucceffively by the fame perfon; and that all offices fhould be of as fhort duration as circumftances will admit. That all the citizens be capable of being appointed judges of the law as well as of the fact in all forts of caufes, and refpecting all forts of perfons; or, if this be thought too general, in all important caufes, and refpecting all diftinguifhed perfons; for example, in all political queftions, in impeachments, and even in private contracts, where the object is confiderable. That the fovereignty refide in the national affembly, and be as fparingly imparted as poffible to particular magiftrates. Of all magiftracies, that leaft repugnant to the genius of democracy is the fenate; but when falaries and fees are granted for the difcharge of public duties, the authority even of the fenate muft foon vanifh; for the rapacity of the people will fpeedily bring all public bufinefs before

Laws therefrom refulting.

The evils refulting from the form of a fimple democracy, prove that form to be imperfect.

BOOK VIII.

before the national affembly, and draw all law-fuits and trials before their own tribunals ᶜ. Salaries and fees, therefore, are effential to the completion of democracy; magiftrates, whofe uninterrupted functions require that they fhould mefs together ᵈ, muft live at the public expence; and fhould occafional meetings pafs unrewarded, yet the people at large muft be paid for attending thofe ftated and periodical affemblies, the returns of which are regulated by law for the neceffary difcharge of public bufinefs. Birth, wealth, education, morals are the elements of ariftocracies; the elements of democracies, therefore, muft be of a contrary kind; bafenefs of extraction, grofs ignorance, poverty, and profligacy ᵉ. No hereditary, no perpetual magiftracy can exift under fuch a government; and if any thing of that nature had formerly found place in the country, the power of fuch a magiftrate muft be abolifhed; or if his title be allowed to remain, the honour of bearing it muft not be conferred by election, but committed to the blind decifion of chance. Such are the common properties refulting from the form

ᶜ Ariftotle fubjoins, that this had been obferved in the preceding Book; an obfervation which might have led his editors to a better arrangement of his treatife of politics, than that hitherto given.

ᵈ Ariftotle here enumerates τας αρχας και τα δικαστηρια και βουλην; that is, magiftrates refpectively entrufted with executive, judiciary, and deliberative powers; who, as well as the citizens at large convened in the εκκλησιαι κυριαι, or ftated affemblies, ought according to the principles of fimple democracy to be paid for political labours. But if the public revenues cannot fuffice for this profufion of expence, then thofe magiftrates at leaft muft be renumerated, whofe uninterrupted functions require that they fhould mefs together; and with them it appears from B. vi. c. xiii. that he means to clafs, as to this particular, the citizens convened in the ftated and periodical affemblies.

ᵉ The word βαναυσια denotes mean fordid labour; but Ariftotle, by faying that the elements of democracy are directly the reverfe of thofe which conftitute ariftocracy, fhews that he here intends the manners and morals refulting from that degrading fpecies of labour; and what thefe manners and morals are, he explains below in chapter iv. of this Book.

form of a simple democracy, and deducible from the definitions given by the partifans of that government of juftice, equality, and liberty.

BOOK VIII.

The imperfection of thefe definitions appears in the mifchief of their confequences [f]. Yet the number of inhabitants, or populoufnefs, is, doubtlefs, the firft element in the compofition of ftates; and to the intereft of the people at large, due regard, therefore, ought to be had in the diftribution of advantages and honours. But populoufnefs, though the firft and principal, is not the only element effential to the end and purpofe of every political affociation; the well-being, comfort, or happinefs of the affociated members. Towards the producing and fecuring of this comfortable fubfiftence of the community, other powers muft co-operate; property, education, morals; without which it is impoffible that any civil partnerfhip or commonwealth can anfwer the purpofe of the partners [g]. How then are we to combine the other elements or caufes of political advantage with mere numbers? How, for inftance, is the regard due to property, a thing effential to the exiftence of ftates, to be reconciled with the intereft of the people at large, and the rights of the majority. Shall we divide the ftate into the two claffes of

Chap. 3.

How the right of the majority is to be reconciled with the due influence of property.

[f] I have here inferted this obfervation, which occurs below, for the fake of perfpicuity. The fame inducement has made me tranfpofe fome other fentences, and alfo expand the author's brevity by ufing the fame words which he himfelf employs on other occafions when treating fimilar fubjects.

[g] Cicero frequently borrows and adorns this fentiment. Refpublica eft res populi. Populus autem non omnes cœtus multitudinis, fed cœtus juris confenfu, et utilitatis communione fociatus. " A commonwealth is the wealth of the people; but the people are not a mere collection or multitude of human beings; but a multitude affociated according to the principles of juftice, and for the fake of utility." Fragment. de Repub. l. iii.

BOOK VIII. of the rich and poor, and reckon the votes of five hundred of the former, equal to the votes of a thousand of the latter? Or retaining this division, shall an equal number of deputies be chosen from the class of the poor and from the class of the rich; and shall these deputies, united in one assembly, appoint by the majority of voices, the magistrates and judges? According to the partisans of democracy, the political scales ought to be balanced by the mere weight of numbers; according to the partisans of oligarchy, the greatest weight of property ought always to prevail. How can those contrarieties be harmonised into system, but by considering wealth and numbers as elements of equal importance, or mere units, of which the greater number of fractional parts[h] must always prevail over the lesser? Suppose, for instance, twenty poor and ten rich, and that fifteen of the poor and four of the rich are of the same opinion: it is plain, that in this case there is a greater accession of wealth to the side of numbers, than of numbers to the side of wealth. Numbers, therefore, must prevail; but the contrary would happen if the six rich, exceeding half the representation of wealth, had been joined by ten of the poor, which is half the representative of numbers. When the opposite sides are equally balanced, it will be necessary to cast lots, or to have recourse to the expedients employed in doubtful cases by tribunals and assemblies. Difficult as it certainly is, nicely to adjust contrarieties, and to discover the true theory of political arrangements, it is far more difficult to keep the component parts in their proper places, and to restrain the injustice of domineering factions. The inferior party are great

[h] The Greeks, it is known, employed proportion for answering the purpose of fractions; but in explaining Aristotle's sense, I have preferred a language familiar to the modern reader.

ARISTOTLE's POLITICS.

great ſticklers for juſtice; but thoſe that are uppermoſt ſet its maxims at defiance[1].

We have ſhewn that there are different kinds of democracies, neceſſarily reſulting from the variety of materials of which they are compoſed, and the various diſtribution of thoſe materials in the political ſtructure. Every democracy is a government of the majority; but this government may be more or leſs tempered in proportion as wealth, birth, morals, and other circumſtances, beſides the mere ſtrength of numbers, are reſpected by the fundamental laws of the conſtitution, and preferred in the diſtribution of offices and honours. The principal differences of democracies reſult, however, from the different qualities of the people that enter into their compoſition; and communities are thus marked with characteriſtic diſtinctions by their various modes of procuring the neceſſaries of life; or, according to the various occupations of agriculture, paſturage, manufactures, and commerce. Agreeably to this diviſion, the beſt kind of democracy, and likewiſe the moſt ancient on record, is that in which the people ſubſiſt by agriculture; becauſe the beſt claſs of working people are thoſe employed in the rural labours of agriculture and paſturage, eſpecially the former; and the manners and habits of huſbandmen are alſo the beſt adapted to counteract the evil tendency of democratic inſtitutions. From their poverty mixed with ſimplicity, thoſe claſſes

BOOK VIII.

Chap. 4.

Of the different kinds of democracies, and of that which is the beſt.

Of the character of men ſubſiſting chiefly by agriculture.

---

[1] This lamentation is often made by the hiſtorians of Rome, even during the ages moſt diſtinguiſhed for political moderation. " Sed alter ſemper ordo gravis alterius modeſtiæ erat." The reaſon is ſubjoined. " Acco moderatio tuenda libertatis, dum æquari velle ſimulando ita ſe quiſque extollit, ut deprimat alium, in difficili eſt: cavendoque ne metuant homines, metuendos ultro ſe efficiunt: et injuriam a nobis repulſam, tanquam aut facere aut pati neceſſe ſit, injungimus aliis." Tit. Liv. l. iii. c. lxv. In the introduction to this book, I have endeavoured to point out the means by which the evil may be cured.

BOOK VIII.

classes of men are less inclined than any others, to assemble frequently or tumultuously; and summoned to daily labour by the voice of Nature herself, they learn to prefer the certain profits of industry to the precarious acquisitions of rapine. When allowed to retain their own, they covet not the property of others. To them it is a more agreeable task, to cultivate their fields, than to compose laws; and they do not much care to attend the national assembly, unless they be well rewarded for their political labours. The greater part of mankind are, in fact, more desirous of gain, than ambitious of honour. As a proof of this observation, we may allege the husbandmen or peasants of old, who patiently brooked absolute monarchy; and also the peasants of our own times, who quietly endure oligarchy, provided they are not stripped of their property, nor disturbed in their labours; by which some of them acquire opulence, and all of them avoid indigence. The alteration of the government will not alter their propensities and habits, which they will carry with them into democracy itself; where those of them who have any seeds of ambition, will find themselves sufficiently gratified by the right of electing their magistrates, and of exacting an account of their administration. In some democracies, the people at large are seldom convened in the deliberative or elective assemblies. At Mantinæa, the usual magistrates were named by deputies previously appointed, and the nation continued well satisfied with this arrangement; because each individual might become a deputy in his turn, and thus enjoy the advantage of deciding the public resolutions, and of appointing, approving, and judging those invested with executive power. This form of democracy prevailed among the shepherds and husbandmen of Arcadia. But it is usual,

and

and highly useful, in the best sort of democracies, though they entrust to the people at large the election and judgment of magistrates, to enact, however, that the principal offices of government should be held by men of a certain census, or, without specifying any fixed census, to enjoin that such great offices should be conferred on those rich enough to discharge them disinterestedly and honourably. Such a constitution is well regulated, for power will be administered by the fittest persons, whose talents are the objects of public approbation; and whose honours, not bringing with them any profit, will not be the objects of popular envy. The superior ranks of men will be contented with an arrangement which liberates them from the hard condition of being occasionally governed by their inferiors; and they will themselves govern uprightly, because they are responsible to the people at large for their behaviour in office: magistrates not responsible are incompatible with any kind of good government, since power uncontrolled suits not the frailty of human nature.

BOOK VIII.

This then is the best kind of democracy, because resulting from the best quality of the people, the best daily occupations, and the best consequent habits. An important question, therefore, arises, how are we to mould the people into this most useful form? The answer will be found in the legislation of ancient and most flourishing states, whose institutions encouraged agriculture in preference to all other employments. In some countries it was a law, that no individual should possess above a certain measure of ground; in others, this regulation was confined to lands within a limited distance from the capital. Some commonwealths have enacted that no family should be allowed to part with its original lot of land, or ancient inherit-

How agriculture is to be encouraged, and the best kind of democracy to be established.

ance; and a law of Oxylus [k] forbids any man to mortgage beyond a certain proportion of his eſtate. The Aphytæi [l] are a populous community with a diminitive territory, yet are all of them cultivators of the ground; becauſe, though a qualification in land is neceſſary for holding offices and honours, yet is this qualification ſo ſmall in value or extent, that even the pooreſt inhabitants may eaſily acquire it. It is impoſſible to miſtake the ſpirit of ſuch regulations, which, while they prevent one claſs of men from occupying more lands than they can themſelves cultivate, call forth the induſtry of the other claſs by aſſigning to them lands of their own, and thereby giving them a ſubject on which that induſtry is always moſt cheerfully exerciſed.

Of democracies of ſhepherds, manufacturers, ſailors, and merchants.

Next to a community of huſbandmen, a nation ſubſiſting by paſturage is the fitteſt for being formed into a democracy. There is much ſimilarity in thoſe two modes of life; and as a preparative for war, the daily occupations and conſequent habits of the ſhepherd are admirably calculated. He is accuſtomed to ſleep in the open air, to march regularly, to encamp cautiouſly; while his body is hardened by exerciſe, his mind is ſharpened by vigilance.

Why the latter democracies are greatly inferior to the former.

All other democracies are of a far inferior ſtamp; for their materials are not capable of receiving any elegant or laſting impreſſion. They are compoſed of wretched labourers and mean mechanics, of manufacturers condemned to unwholeſome air and diſtorting poſtures, of rapacious ſailors and greedy merchants, who navigate and trade for no other

---

[k] King of the Eliens. See Hiſtory of Ancient Greece, vol. i. c. iii. & v.

[l] In ſome editions they are called Aphetali. Plutarch in Lyſand. p. 444, calls them Aphygæi. They inhabited the peninſula Pallene in the region of Chalcis on the coaſt of Thrace or Macedon. See Hiſtory of Ancient Greece, v. ii. c. xv. p. 196, & ſeq. and Strabo Excerpt. l. viii p. 330.

ARISTOTLE's POLITICS.

other purpose than that of gain; a purpose mean in itself, and meanly or wickedly attained, sometimes by fraud, and sometimes by rapine. Men subsisting by continual deceit and mutual depredation, must live together in crowds, tumbling over each other in populous cities, and ready at the beck of every seditious demagogue to assemble tumultuously, and to act outrageously. But in a commonwealth of husbandmen, families are scattered at due distances by the necessity of their daily labours. The citizens justle not with each other; and their circumstances neither require nor admit the frequency of popular conventions. It is for this reason that a country of great extent, and which easily afforded room for the continual diffusion of colonies at wide distances from the capital, might be improved, fortified, and embellished by agriculture alone and its subservient arts, and might enjoy, under nearly a simple democratic form, the benefits resulting from mixed policy [m].

The properties and habits of husbandmen, as distinguished from mercenary labourers on the one hand, and from manufacturers, merchants, and tradesmen on the other, are so eminently conspicuous and so incomparably better adapted to the peaceful enjoyment of every species of freedom [n], that even in countries where a great proportion of the inhabitants subsists by arts and commerce, the city tribes ought never to assemble separately; every convention, to be lawful, ought to be attended

That the city tribes ought not to assemble separately from those of the country.

[m] Aristotle says, that such people may establish an useful democracy, and a πολιτεία; which he has before explained to be a mixed government, and the best form of republicanism. But the spirit of his observation would evaporate in a literal version.

[n] How much does a great modern democracy mistake its true interest, when it is inflamed by the jealousy of trade, and is ready to begin or carry on war in order to attain commercial superiority, or even commercial equality!

BOOK VIII.

How the inferior kinds of democracy are to be established.

tended by deputies from the country; so that the noxious humours engendered in market-places and courts of justice, may be sweetened and purified by a due mixture of more wholesome materials [e].

Such then is the constitution of the best kind of democracy. The other kinds are more or less praiseworthy, in proportion as every species of venality is more or less completely extirpated; for public functions, gratuitously discharged, are neither the objects of jealousy nor the sources of faction; they are not scrambled for by unprincipled indigence as instruments of profit or pleasure. They are not received as a gift, but undertaken as a task by men of property and integrity, who are covetous of nothing but public gratitude. The last and worst species of democracy, by its political arrangements, admits, and, by the allurement of fees and salaries, attracts and entices all conditions of men to the exercise of every department of executive as well as deliberative authority. It is not every city or commonwealth that is at all susceptible of such a constitution; and to render it permanent in any country, salutary laws and habitual discipline must counteract and control the vicious principle of the government. In order to introduce this form of policy, demagogues think they can never too much strengthen the popular party. Bastards, children descended from the intermarriages of citizens and strangers, all sorts of materials, howsoever impure and corrupt, are considered as proper aliment for such a constitution. Yet it is certain that this progression in degeneracy has its limit. For when the promiscuous rabble too much overpower the rich and noble,

[e] How wonderfully are our author's remarks illustrated by a history, which he could not know, I mean the Roman! See Livy, b. ix. c. xlvi.

noble, these latter classes of men resume courage from despair, and, as happened at Cyrene[p], destroy their oppressors. The regulations once adopted by that African republic, and afterwards employed by Clisthenes at Athens, are useful in establishing democracies. Ancient distinctions are to be done away; ancient associations, civil and sacred, are to be abolished; new tribes are to be created; n w and common solemnities to be instituted; and every expedient to be employed that may have a tendency to stamp the people with one uniform character, and reduce them all to the same level. Democracy may also borrow useful hints from tyranny. The unbridled licence of women, boys, and slaves is conformable to the nature and principle of democracies and tyrannies. Above all, demagogues must never cease to convince the people that under their favourite democracy, they will be at liberty to live as they list; this will procure for them the assistance of the majority; for the greater part of mankind will always be better pleased to live licentiously, than to submit to the restraints of salutary discipline.

It is, therefore, an easy matter to establish a democracy; but the difficulty lies in rendering it permanent. Laws, therefore, of every kind, written and unwritten, must continually be shaped and fitted to those ends and purposes, which, when attained, give stability to the popular constitution; and of laws, those are to be reckoned the best and the most democratical, which tend to uphold the power, not those which flatter the passions of the majority. It is usual with the demagogues of the

Chap. 5.

How they are to be preserved.

---

[p] History of Ancient Greece, v. i. c. viii. p. 347. This country, whose history I shall have occasion fully to relate, flourished as a kingdom or aristocracy, and decayed as a democracy. Vid. Plutarch in Lucull.

BOOK VIII. the present age to gratify the rapacity of the multitude by unjust impeachments and corrupt judgments. But men sincerely attached to popular government, ought to counteract those dangerous and disgraceful measures by getting it established as a law, that confiscated property shall not be divided among the people, but consecrated to the gods; a law by which private peculation might be punished without provoking public rapacity, since the multitude would no longer accuse wantonly, or wickedly condemn, those of whose forfeitures they would not expect to reap the spoils. All groundless impeachments ought also to be repressed by severe penalties; and every method employed to convince the rich and noble, that those invested with power are not their enemies.

How they are to be rendered more moderate and less expensive.

Democracies of the last and worst kind are sometimes so populous, that the public revenues are insufficient to defray the ordinary expences of government, without the dangerous aid of fines and confiscations. When this happens to be the case, no unnecessary assemblies ought ever to be held; and business must be dispatched in the courts of justice with all possible expedition. In consequence of these arrangements, the expences of government will be less oppressive to men of property; and although the attendance only of the poorer classes be rewarded by fees, yet the higher ranks also will for the most part attend both the assembly and the tribunals, because short and unfrequent absences from their private affairs will not prove ruinous to their fortunes; and under the control of the best citizens, deliberations will be more moderate, and decisions more equitable. When revenues, on the other hand, superabound, it is now usual with demagogues to divide the surplus among the poor; but this is pouring water into a sieve. A good statesman, instead

ſtead of being contented with occaſionally relieving the wants of the poor, will continually ſtrive to better their condition; and when he gives them property, will uſe the beſt means for rendering that property permanent and productive. The public ſavings ought not be ſquandered away in temporary and fruitleſs donatives, but accumulated to ſuch an amount, that when diſtributed to the induſtrious and deſerving poor, they will enable them to purchaſe and cultivate a few acres of land of their own, (which is incomparably the beſt uſe of public bounty,) or to acquire the materials and inſtruments neceſſary for carrying on manufactures and commerce. When the national ſavings are too ſcanty to admit of uſeful diſtribution to individuals, they muſt then be divided among the moſt deſerving diſtricts; and the rich, who defray the neceſſary expences of government, muſt be liberated from the burden of uſeleſs entertainments and frivolous but expenſive exhibitions. By ſuch political arrangements, the Carthaginian nobles acquired the affection of the people, whoſe induſtry they encouraged in cultivating the circumjacent territory. It belongs, ſurely, to the good ſenſe as well as to the liberality of the higher ranks of men, to excite, by every means in their power, the productive labour of their inferiors. The example of the wealthy Tarentines is worthy of imitation; who, by communicating many uſes of their eſtates to the people at large, obtained univerſal good-will, and greatly improved their poſſeſſions. At Tarentum, indeed, the populace were farther ſoothed by the law which enacted that ſome public offices ſhould be diſtributed by lot, while others were conferred by ſuffrage. When the ſame magiſtracy conſiſts of ſeveral members, this inſtitution may be uſefully varied by appointing ſome members by lot, and

others

others by suffrage. Such are the arrangements which ought to prevail in democracies.

As to oligarchies, it is plain that they must be constituted on principles totally different; since the highest intension of oligarchy is diametrically opposite to the highest intension of democracy. In proportion as oligarchies and democracies recede from their highest intension, that is, from the worst constitution of each, a tumultuary populace on one hand, and a tyrannical cabal on the other, the distance between them is gradually diminished; each preserving, however, its distinctive character, till, by continual approximations, they finally run into each other, and blend harmoniously in a well-constituted republic. In that species of oligarchy which we call the first and best, because it most resembles a mixed government, retaining nothing of oligarchy but its undue preference of wealth to other political elements, there ought to be a double census, or two sorts of qualifications, of which the lowest ought to entitle those possessed of it to hold all the inferior magistracies. By this means, the best portion of the citizens would have a direct and personal interest in supporting the authority of government, and in defending the honours of that privileged order, which, by enjoying the highest census would be exclusively entitled to form the supreme council, and to administer the great offices of state. Between this species of oligarchy and that which is the last and worst, there are several intermediate kinds; each requiring additional props to preserve it, in proportion to the narrowness of its base. The last and worst kind of all is the most difficultly upheld, requiring the utmost delicacy of management. Bodies well constituted, and hardily disciplined, resist and surmount the vicissitudes and shocks of life; a ship well constituted,

constituted, and well manned, defies the assailing tempest; but a puny habit and a leaky vessel are exposed to the danger of sinking under the least adverse accident. A narrow oligarchy, therefore, can only be supported by the political wisdom of its magistrates, counteracting by moderation and good discipline that tumult of passion and interest which is always ready to assail its security.

Forms of government, we have said, are relative to local circumstances, by which they are often modified, upheld, or subverted. For local circumstances powerfully influence the composition of armies, and the composition of armies often decides the nature of the constitution. As communities are composed chiefly of four classes of men, husbandmen, manufacturers, merchants, and mechanics [p], so there are chiefly four elements that compose national strength; cavalry, heavy-armed infantry, light infantry, and seamen. A champaign country, by its fitness for rearing and maintaining cavalry, is the best adapted for the establishing and supporting an oligarchy, because men of wealth only are capable of rearing and maintaining any considerable number of horses. The next kind of oligarchy may be defended by heavy-armed troops, since to purchase and keep in repair complete and well-tempered armour, only falls within the reach of persons possessed of no mean share of opulence. But light infantry and seamen are, on the contrary, instruments entirely adapted to the establishment or support of democracy; and where the national strength is chiefly composed of such elements, it will be difficult for an oligarchy to subsist.

The

[p] το θητικον, including journeymen or day-labourers, and slaves.

BOOK VIII.

How oligarchies are to be upheld under unfavourable local circumstances.

The best expedient which can, in that case, be employed for propping an edifice always ready to fall in pieces, is to imitate the conduct of good generals, who, by mixing a due proportion of light troops with the heavy-armed men and the cavalry, often supply by arrangement the defect of numbers. This proportion of light troops must be raised from the youth of most honourable descent, and especially the sons of the magistrates, carefully selected and diligently exercised, whose zeal and merit will render them the fittest champions of the oligarchy. But the disease of such a constitution is too dangerous to admit of hope from the application of one single remedy. It will be prudent, therefore, gradually to impart a share of the government to persons chosen from the people at large, either, as before-mentioned, to those who have acquired a certain census; or, as was established at Thebes, to those who have ceased cultivating for a certain number of years all mean and mercenary employments; or thirdly, in imitation of Marseilles, we may associate to government abilities and virtues, in whatever class of citizens they may be found. For the safety of oligarchies, it is necessary that the great offices of state should be burdensome. The people at large will be inclined to tolerate exclusive honours that are dearly purchased, and to pardon generous ambition, that is rewarded by nothing but an expensive pre-eminence. At entering upon office, oligarchic magistrates ought to be sumptuous in their entertainments, and magnificent in their presents. Architectural embellishments of the city, costly dedications in the temples, ought to display and perpetuate their patriotic munificence. But instead of following these salutary maxims, which can alone give permanence to

their

their order, the nobles of the prefent day are equally covetous of wealth and ambitious of honour; and uniting infolent pride with greedy rapacity, the oligarchies, in which they bear fway, are nothing better than little democracies.

Having thus examined the general diftribution of the powers of government, relatively to the principal elements of which communities are effentially compofed, it remains to confider the neceffary divifions of the executive authority, and to explain how many and what kinds of magiftrates ought to be eftablifhed in every well-regulated commonwealth. In fmall ftates, it is plain, there cannot be fo many perfons fpared from employments of productive induftry, for exercifing ufeful but unproductive offices, as in ftates that are larger and more populous. Yet every commonwealth, that completely anfwers the end of its inftitution, muft contain nearly the fame varieties of executive magiftracy; fince, without fome offices, a community could not fubfift at all; and without others it could not fubfift happily. It is neceffary, therefore, to know what are thofe offices that admit of accumulation, and what are thofe that require partition; what are thofe offices that may be eafily and fafely exercifed by the fame perfon, and what are thofe that cannot prudently be intrufted to the fame hands. The folution of this queftion muft be derived from confidering the number and nature of thofe offices that refult from the great purpofes of political fociety; the fubfiftence, accommodation, fecurity, and comfort of its conftituent members.

The general end of the political partnerfhip is the well-being of the partners. Men affociate together and unite their efforts, that the operations of the whole community may terminate as nearly as poffible in the happinefs of each individual citizen.

BOOK VIII.

Chap. 8.

Of the divifions of the executive power, and the different kinds of magiftrates.

Magiftrates for protecting commerce and contracts;

But

BOOK VIII.

But in order to attain, by continual approximations, to this most defirable end, it is neceffary that the citizens fhould enjoy eafy and regular means of communicating mutual affiftance, and fupplying mutual wants [q]. That fpecies of exchange, therefore, which is directed to the purpofes of accommodation and comfort, not to the fenfelefs, becaufe infatiable purfuit of accumulation or gain, is the moft direct and immediate refult of political fociety; and the firft and moft ufeful magiftrates are thofe appointed to protect internal commerce, and to fee that it be carried on freely, regularly, and honeftly.

for maintaining police both in the city and country;

Another concern analogous to the former, and which requires the immediate attention of every ftate, is to take care that boundaries be accurately adjufted; and that ftreets and buildings, whether private or public, be regularly difpofed and folidly conftructed; fo as neither to incommode nor endanger the inhabitants; and that roads be well ftraightened, and kept in conftant repair. Thefe and fuch objects are comprehended under the name of police, which in large ftates is divided into a variety of branches, entrufted to particular magiftrates, who are, fome of them, infpectors of the harbours, others of the fountains, and others of the fortifications; and when their offices bear a reference to the country, they are called keepers of the forefts, and fuperintendents of diftricts.

for collecting and managing the revenues.

Men in their corporate capacity have occafion to effectuate public purpofes, and therefore muft poffefs a common fund. Revenues and contributions thus become neceffary; and there muft of courfe be treafurers to receive and take charge of thefe contributions and revenues, and to diftribute them through the various channels of the public expenditure.

How

[q] See Ethics, b. v. c. vi. p. 271, & feq.

How regularly foever matters may originally be adjufted, diforders muft foon take place, unlefs there be in every country courts of record. Contracts and judicial decifions, as well as actions, fuits, and accufations, muft all of them, when liable to be mifreprefented or difputed, be committed to the faithful regiftry of writing; and this duty of perpetuating the memory of civil acts is plainly the function of one and the fame magiftracy, though the bufinefs is often divided among notaries, recorders, remembrancers, and other functionaries; whofe names have, all of them, a relation to the fame important concern.

Next to this is a function of government of all the moft neceffary, and alfo the moft troublefome. The fentences of courts are nugatory, unlefs they be regularly carried into execution. A magiftrate, therefore, muft be appointed for exacting fines, for inflicting punifhments, and for taking charge of thofe anfwerable to the laws in their bodies or eftates. It is not eafy to find men well qualified, and at the fame time willing, to difcharge this moft important function; for the odium attending it makes prudence and humanity decline it, and it cannot be fafely intrufted to infenfibility or knavery. Knaves or fools require to be continually watched themfelves, inftead of being appointed to watch and take charge of others. Much attention is neceffary in regulating this department of office, which will be beft conftituted when divided among a variety of perfons called to exercife it by rotation, or to the different companies of young men employed to guard the city[r]. The odium attending their employment will thus be diminifhed; and the lefs is the odium that attends thofe appointed to execute the laws, the more eafily and the more completely will the laws be executed. If the fame fet of men were perpetually employed

in

[r] See Hiftory of Ancient Greece, v. iii. c. xxvii. p. 253, & feq.

BOOK VIII.

in conducting all matters of this kind, these men, how proper soever might be their behaviour, would soon come to be regarded as public enemies. The Athenians, therefore, wisely separated the functions of superintending the custody, and superintending the execution, of persons condemned by public justice; and the magistrates of one court may very properly be intrusted with carrying into effect the sentences pronounced by another.

Command of the national force.

Most of the offices hitherto enumerated and explained, may be fitly discharged without any other requisites than those of common sense and common honesty. But there are other employments requiring more than ordinary skill and more than ordinary integrity. To be the general or admiral of the commonwealth; to have the charge of equipping the fleet and marshalling the army; and to be intrusted, either in peace or war, with troops, garrisons, ships, and harbours; all these are branches of one and the same function, the command of the national force; an office that cannot be safely committed except to men of pre-eminent skill and distinguished fidelity.

Comptrollers of public accounts.

Almost all magistrates and officers, civil as well as military, must be perpetually or occasionally intrusted with the receipt and expenditure of public money. In every well-regulated state there ought, therefore, to be a particular board for the specific purpose of examining and controlling the public accounts; and this board consisting of men who never handle money themselves, but who have a right to be satisfied in the name of the public, as to the precise amount of the revenues that are raised, and the exact manner in which they are employed.

The most dignified of all magistracies is that with which important national concerns begin and terminate; which assembles

bles the people; proposes matters for their deliberation; and, by its respected authority, either confirms or annuls their decrees. This magistracy, in which the wisdom and majesty of the state are concentrated, is called in aristocracies the college of censors '; in oligarchies, the council of pre-advisers '; in democracies, the senate.

Religious concerns require also their proper magistrates to take charge of the temples, sacred treasures, and sacrifices; of which some are performed by priests of particular districts, the ministers of particular divinities; and others by those called kings or archons on behalf of the public at large, and in honour of the guardian gods of the commonwealth.

In well-regulated and flourishing states, there are also many offices (all departments of the same function) which have for their objects the education of youth, as well as the morals of every age and of either sex, together with the decency and splendour of dramatic entertainments, and other shows and solemnities. In democracies, there is not any room for several of those magistrates. Inspectors of education and of morals would be altogether useless under such governments; where the wives and children of those dignified with the name of citizens are often, through poverty, employed by them as slaves ". Such is the general sketch of the necessary branches of executive government.[x]

BOOK VIII.

Different orders of priests.

Superintendants of education, morals, and public shows.

' νομοφύλακες, guardians of the laws.
' Resembling the lords of articles in the old Scottish constitution.
" See above, b. iv. c. xv. p. 510.
[x] In some parts of this Chapter, the order of the sentences is changed for the sake of perspicuity; and some imperfect sentences are omitted, the observations contained in them being repetitions of what is said in Book VI.

INDEX.

A

Abydus, how enflaved, page 349.
Achæan league, 64.
Addison, Mr. his obfervations concerning St. Marino criticifed, 138, & feqq. 154, & feqq.
Admiral, high, his undue authority at Sparta, 110.
Advantages, political, according to what rule they ought to be diftributed, 188, & feqq.
Agriculture, how to be encouraged, 409.
Alberoni, Cardinal, his mifadventure in St. Marino, 153.
Alcæus, his reproaches againft the Mitylenians, 194.
Alcidamus, his faying concerning flaves, 26.
Ambratia, how its government was overturned, 339. Why its oligarchy changed into a democracy, 343.
America, United States, their conftitution, 63.
Amphipolis, caufe of diffenfions there, 340.
Amphictyons, council of, 64.
Andreia, what, 112, 113.
Antiffæans, their cruelty to the Chians, 340.
Aphytæi, their peculiarities, 410.
Apollonia, peculiarity in its government, 284. Caufe of diffenfions there, 340. How its oligarchy overturned, 349.
Appius his confpiracy, 336.
Apries, the ftory of his laver, 47.
Archelaus of Macedon, caufe of his affaffination, 359.
Arengo, what, 142.
Argos, origin of the revolution in its government, 343.
Ariftocracies, their revolutions, 350.
VOL. II.

Ariftocracy, its different kinds, 292, 293.
Ariftocrats, their oaths againft the people, 364.
Ariftogeiton overturned the tyranny of the Peififtratidæ, and why, 369.
Ariftotle, his account of the origin of government, or political fociety, 2, & feqq. His doctrine concerning flavery, 6, & feqq. Strange mifreprefentations of his opinions, by his pretended followers, 23. His Œconomics, the nature and defign of that work, 45. Improv.s politics as a fcience, 274, & feqq.
Artibanus, why he flew Xerxes, 370.
Art, political, its end, 177.
Arts, thofe of productive induftry, 44. Their different kinds, 45. 230, & feqq.
Æfymnetes, nature of their office, 191. Difference between them and Afiatic princes, *ibid*.
Affemblies, popular, why tyrannical, 57.
Athenæus cited, 124.
Athenians endeavoured to mould the government of their neighbours after their own model, 354.
Athens, analyfis of its government, 87, & feqq. Tyranny of her democracy, wherein different from Oriental defpotifm, 58. Caufes of her degeneracy, 120. Effect of her naval victories, 121. What changed her form of government, 342.

B

Babylon, its magnitude, 170.
Bacon, his obfervations on political innovation, 101. His unfair treatment of Ariftotle, 102. Not without excufe, *ibid*.

3 I

Barrow,

INDEX.

Barrow, his geometrical analysis agrees with Aristotle's, 19.
Beccaria, his book on style, 156.
Bentley cited, and corrected, 122.
Bern, its government, 330.
Birth, noble, analysis thereof, 293.
Blackstone, his observations concerning slavery not inconsistent with Aristotle's, 30. His overlooked Polybius's discourse on government, 391.
Body, how to be formed and disciplined, 257, & seqq.
Bonelli, Father, 132, & seqq.
Buserich, Father, 137.
Buchannan, his vindication of Christianity against the pretended slavishness of its principles, 328.
Byzantium, dissentions there, 340.

C

Capitals, how they ought to be situated, 235.
Cappadocians, their servile character admired by the Romans, 161.
Carthage, excellence of its government, 115. Proof thereof, *ibid*. Its magistrates, *ibid*. Corruptions introduced into its constitution, 116, & seqq. Undue preponderancy of wealth, 117. Reflections thereon, *ibid*. Dangerous accumulation of office, 118. Reflections thereon, 119. Evils in the Carthaginian government, how palliated, *ibid*. Its military rewards, 218. Carthage and England compared and contrasted, 383, *note*.
Casaubon corrected, 269.
Celts, addicted to unnatural love, 106. Wherein they placed national prosperity, 218.
Census, rule in establishing it, 302.
Chalcis, origin of its democracy, 343.
Charicles, the demagogue of the thirty tyrants, 348.
Charles V. his affection for the commonwealth of St. Marino, 151.
Charondas, 20. 104. Who, 121. His law concerning false witnesses, 122. Bentley's mistake on that subject, *ibid*.
Child, his erroneous opinion as to money, 41.

Children, their virtues different from those of adults, 50. Community thereof, 79. Exposition of, 217. Nourishment, exercises, and treatment, 248, & seqq. Not to be restrained in their exertions, 249. How they ought to be treated till puberty, 249, 250.
China, its principles of government, 326.
Chinese, dissent from Aristotle as to the necessity of a state religion, 29.
Chios, its shipping destined to one employment, 285.
Christianity, the pretended slavishness of its principles denied, 3 8.
Cicero explains Aristotle's account of the origin of government, 5. His definition of a commonwealth, 18. Cited, 102.
Ciradon, cause of his conspiracy, 351.
City, tribes of, their inferiority, 411.
Cities, how to be built for comfort and security, 236. What ought to be their ornaments, 237.
Citizen, how constituted, 166. Different under different governments, 167, & seqq. What ought to be the character of those fitted for the best commonwealth, 238, & seq.
Clazomené, cause of its dissensions, 340.
Climate, how it influences character, 227.
Clisthenes, 293. Crowns the judge who had decided against him, 382.
Clubs, their importance to government, 206.
Cnidus, how its government was subverted, 347.
Codrus raised to the throne by merit, 367.
Colophon, peculiarity in its government, 185. Cause of its dissensions, 341.
Comitia Curiata, &c. 396.
Commerce, its nature and different kinds, 37.
Commonwealth, defined, 17. Its nature and end, 17, 18. Its analysis, 19. Congenial to human nature, 22. Cause of human virtues and perfections, 23, & seq. What constitutes its continuity, 170. Its nature in contradistinction to other associations, 181. Its real happiness, how to be estimated, 220, & seqq. The best, its limits in point of populousness, 222. The extent and

INDEX.

and nature of its territory, 224, & seq. Proper situation for its capital, 225. Its essentials, 229, & seqq. How to be regulated, 231, & seq. Whether naturally subject to destruction, 398.
Community of wives and children, arguments against it, 75, & seq.
Constitution, political, one thing by law and another in fact, 289.
Contempt a source of sedition, 338.
Conversazioni, Italian, their nature, 134, & seq.
Corinth, how enslaved by Timophanes, 349.
Cos, cause of its revolution, 344.
Cosmi, ill regulated, 13. Evils resulting therefrom, *ibid*. Circumstance which has made the Cretans endure that magistracy, *ibid*. The remedy applied to the evil. 14.
Cox, Hippisley, Sir *John*, 125.
Crete, its government examined, 111. Analysis thereof, 112, & seqq.
Cypselus, how he acquired tyranny, 367. Tyranny of his family at Corinth, 382.
Cyrus raised to the throne by merit, 367.

D

Dechamnichus, his resentment of stripes, 169.
Deliberative power, how constituted in oligarchies, 305. In mixed governments, 306.
Delphi, origin of its seditions, 311. A perpetual fair, 20.
Demagogues, their nature and character, 287, & seq. The bane of democracies, 345. How they deceive the people, 346. How their artifices may be defeated, *ibid*.
Democracies compared with tyrannies, 375. Picture of both, 376. How preserved, 413; and improved, 414. Examples, 415.
Democracy, its military energy, 55. Causes thereof, 55, & seqq. Its unjust pretensions, 180. Its four kinds, 285. Those qualified for enjoying its best and cheapest form, 298, & seq. Those fit only for living under its worst form, 299, & seq. How it may be improved, 306. Simple, the evils resulting

therefrom, 403. Its best and worst kinds, 411.
Demosthenes cited to prove the gentle treatment of slaves, 33. His reasoning against political innovation, 103.
Denina, his remarks concerning the republics of Italy, 59.
Denmark, its government, how established, 331, *note*.
Descartes, 273.
Dio, his high-mindedness, 371. Why slain, 372.
Diodorus Siculus cited, 122.
Dionysius, how he treated a monopolizer, 47. How he acquired tyranny, 367. How he became king of Syracuse, 346.
—— the younger, why dethroned, 370.
Dissensions, civil, their causes, 92. Remedies, 93.
Drawing, its uses, 255. Art of, 257.
Drinking, who most addicted to it, 131.

E

Education, analysis thereof, 240. Why it ought to be public, 240, & seq. The ends at which it ought to aim, 241. These ends mistaken by legislators, 241. The education fitted for the best commonwealth, 244. Experience in favour of a public one, 252. Its importance, 253. The forming and sustaining power of government, 253. Political education, wherein it consists, 254. Its different branches, 254, & seqq. Before and after puberty, 259. Democratical and oligarchical, 364, & seqq.
Egypt, its pyramids, why erected, 375.
Elis, its oligarchy, 3.9.
England, the fruits of genuine republicanism best engrafted on its constitution, 164. Aristotle's tests of good government found in England beyond all other countries, 276.
—— its constitution the best model of political arrangement, 62. The admirable principles on which its aristocracy is regulated, 330, & seqq.
Ephialtes, Pericles' instrument in weakening the Areopagus, 120.

Ephori.

INDEX.

Ephori, advantages and inconveniences attending this inftitution, 107.
Epidamnus, revolution in its government, 334. What changed its government, 342.
Epimenides, his hiftory, 21.
Equality, political, its limits, 321.
Eretria, how its oligarchy fubverted, 349.
Erythræ, how its government was fubverted, 317.
Euripides quoted, 365. His ftinking breath occafioned the affaffination of Archelaus, 369.
Executive power, wherein it confifts, 309. How conftituted agreeably to the different forms of government, 309.
Exercife, that adapted to different ages, 259.

F

Fabiano, his unfuccefsful attempt againft San Marino, 150.
Fabius, why called Maximus, 337.
Fear, its operation as a caufe of fedition, 337.
Fees and falaries, their effect on the condition of fociety, 177.
Felori, Counts of, their connection with San Marino, 146.
Flavius, his confpiracy, 337.
Florence, its alliance with San Marino, 145.
Food, different contrivances for procuring it, conftitute the wide variety of manners, 35. Thefe different modes enumerated and explained, *ibid.*
Force, military, rule in eftablifhing it, 303.
France, caufes of its revolution, 326. Its ftates, 330. True intereft of its republic, 399.
Frederic II. of Pruffia exemplified Ariftotle's maxims, 381.

G

Gelon, how his family was dethroned, 372. Tyranny of his family at Syracufe, 382.
General, his principal requifites, 361.
George III., happinefs of the kingdom under his government, 157.
Germany, its diet, 331.

Goods, community thereof confidered, 80.
Gothic nations, their manners, 9. Their governments, 14.
Government, its origin, 2, & feqq. By delegation not fufficient for public happinefs, 66. Illuftrated by the antient hiftory of France, *ibid.* Its different forms, 178. Diftinctive characters, 179. Powers of, 274, & feqq. Practically the beft, how to be regulated, 298, & feqq. What is practically the beft, 296. What hinders its eftablifhment, 299.
Governments, the moft approved of antiquity, 54. Their radical defect, 55. How they ought to be divided and claffed, 281. & feqq. General caufes of their revolutions, 343, & feqq. How preferved, 354, & feq., by avoiding fmall alterations, *ibid.*; by counteracting political fleights, 355; by the virtues of their magiftrates, *ibid.*; by the proximity of danger, 356; by obviating errors in the firft principles, 356; by preventing the difproportionate exaltation of individuals or families, 357; by the cenforial power, *ibid.*; by ftrengthening the middle ranks, *ibid.*; by preventing peculation, 358; by paying with honour, *ibid.*; by reprefling demagogues and fycophants, 359; by gratifying thofe claffes which are excluded from offices of ftate, *ibid.*
Gracchi, their feditions, 397.
Grammar, its ufe, 255.
Great Britain. See ENGLAND.
Great, influence of their manners on fociety, 117, 118. Sleights by which they deceive the people. 301.
Greece, progrefs of government in that country, 30.
Gymnaftic, its ufes, 255. When to be cultivated, 259.

H

Hanno, caufe of his ufurpation, 351.
Happinefs, public, its foundation, 215.
Harmodius and Ariftogeiton, 369.
Harrington, his explanation of the myftery of government, 60. Maintains nobility effential in a commonwealth, 322.

Health,

INDEX.

Health, circumstances most conducive thereto, 235.
Heræa, how its aristocracy changed into a democracy, 339.
Heraclæa, causes of its seditions, 344. How its aristocracy overturned, 347. Causes of its sedition, 350.
Hippodamus, his history and character, 95. His imaginary republic, 96. Examination of, 97, 98. His judicial regulations, ibid. His law in favour of political improvements, 99. Examination of that law, 100, & seqq.
Histiæa, origin of its civil war, 341.
Hobbes, 2.
Honours, political, according to what rule they ought to be distributed, 188, & seqq.
Hooker, his admiration of Aristotle, 169. Quoted, ibid.
Hume, David, his supposed improvement of representative government, 66.
Husbandmen, materials for the best kind of democracy, and why, 407, & seq.
Husbandry, its different branches, 42.
Hutcheson, 2.

I

Impressions, first, their influence, 249.
Innovation, political, arguments for and against it, 99, & seq. Aristotle's arguments against it, 325.
Ister, how its aristocracy overturned, 347.
Italy, antient, revolutions therein, 197. Consonant to Aristotle's theory, ibid. Its history, 232, & seq.
Jason of Pheræ, his loftiness of character, 173.
Judiciary power, the classes of objects to which it relates, 313. Various ways in which it may be constituted, 317. Agreeably to the different forms of government, 315.

K

King, definition of his office, 367. Contrasted with a tyrant, ibid.

L

Lacedæmon, its government examined, 105, & seqq.
Lacedæmonians endeavoured to mould the government of their neighbours after their own model, 354.
Landed property, how to be distributed under the best commonwealth, 34.
Larissa, how enslaved, 349.
Laws, Plato's books concerning them examined, 85, & seqq. Those relative to different governments, 362, & seqq.
Legislation, plans of, how to be examined, 104.
Legislature, argument against a simple one, 323.
Leibnitz, 273.
Letters, their uses, 257.
Limyrnii, their singular institutions, 79.
Livy cited, 277. 336, 337.
Locke, his doctrine concerning government examined and refuted, 3, & seqq. An assertion of the exploded doctrine concerning money, 10. His erroneous opinion as to money, 41. His plan of government for Carolina, 213. His letter to King, 273.
Locri Epizephyrii, their panegyric, 103. Their singular law, ibid.
Lycians, their history and government, 65. Consider taxation and representation as correlatives, 66.
Lycophron, his definition of law, 181.
Lycurgus, his institutions, 105, & seqq.
Lysander, 334.

M

Macedon, its military rewards, 219.
Machiavel, his estimate of the republics of the middle age, 61. His observation concerning the bloodless wars of Italy, 179. Copies Aristotle, 377.
Macpherson, Sir John, 125.
Magistrates, the various ways in which they may be appointed, 310; agreeably to different forms of government, 317. Their requisites, 366. Their different kinds, 310. Those

INDEX.

Those relating to commerce, 420. To police, ibid. To revenue, 421. To farms, 422. Controllers of public accounts, ibid. To religion, 423. Education and manners, ibid.
Majority, rights of, 405. How reconcileable with the influence of other political elements, 406.
M. tella, Sigifmond, 144.
Man...., 2.
Merino, ... republic, account thereof, 126. Infested by smugglers, and why, 129. Its picturefque situation, 131. Its extent, 136. The faint, his history, 143. The commonwealth, its history, 145, & feqq. Character of its inhabitants, 155, & feqq.
Marriage. See WEDLOCK
Mars and *Venu*, foundation of the fable concerning them, 105.
Marfeilles, how its aristocracy overturned, 347.
Mechanics, wherein different from flaves, 51.
Medici, *Cofmo di*, his letter to the magistrates of St. Marino, 151.
Mediocrity, its praises, 276, 277. 296.
Megara, how its democracy overturned, 338. How enflaved by Theagenes, 346.
Metals, the circumstances which render them the fittest measure of value, 37. They are not merely a measure, but a pledge, 39.
Meton the astronomer, 67.
Milton, his plan of government for England, 213.
Mithridates, his confpiracy, 371.
Mytilene, origin of all its misfortunes, 342.
Molyneux, 3.
Monarchies, causes of their revolutions, 366. & feqq. Examples, 369. Limited, how to be preferved, 373. Absolute, how preferved, 374. Examples, 375.
Monarchy, first kind of government, proof thereof, 21. Hereditary and limited, defended, 162, & feqq. Its highest improvements in antiquity, 163. Far furpaffed by those of modern times, 164. Its five kinds, 193, & feqq. Its advantages and difadvantages estimated, 196, & feqq. Hereditary, its inconveniences, 198, & feqq. Defended, 200.
Money, the circumstances that introduced it, 37.
Monopolies, 45.
Mun, his erroneous opinion as to money, 41.
Mufic, why introduced into education by the antients, 255, & feq. Doubts concerning it, 260. Its efficacy in moral discipline, 262. Caufe of this efficacy, 263. Whether children should be taught to perform mufic, 264, & feq. How far they ought to cultivate it, 265. Mufic divided into moral, practical, and rapturous, 267. The last purges the paffions, 268. How this effected, 269, & feq. Adapted to different periods of life, 270, & feq.

N

Naxos, how enflaved by Lygdamis, 346.
Netherlands, causes of their profperity, 63.
Newton, 273.
Nicholaus Damafcenus cited, 79.
Nobles, their turbulence in Crete, 114; or aristocrats, their oaths againft the people, 364.
Nolium, cause of its diffenfions, 341.

O

Oeconomics, what, 34. Its three branches bear an analogy to the three forms of government, 47. Those of Ariftotle, 51.
Oeconomy, political, revolutions in the doctrine concerning it, 9, & feqq. Ariftotle's doctrine concerning it defended againft Hume, &c. 14, 15. Domeftic, its nature and branches, 25. Political often confounded with commerce, 42. Their differences, ibid. Its theory applied to practice, ibid. Political and domeftic, 51. The rules of the latter dependent on the plan of the former, ibid.
Offices, public, requifites for difcharging them properly, 361, 362.
Oligarchies, different kinds thereof, how established and preferved, 416. How to be

I3   upheld

upheld under unfavourable circumstances, 418. Revolutions therein, 346.
Oligarchy, its unjust pretensions, 180. Its four kinds, 288, & seqq. Those fit for living under the different kinds of it, 291, & seq. How it may be improved, 307.
Ombre the favourite game in Italy, and why, 134.
Onomacritus, who, 121.
Orcum, how its aristocracy changed into democracy, 339.
Ostracism, necessity thereof proved, 191, & seq. Its abuse, 193, & seq.
Otho the Emperor, his grant to St. Marino, 146.
Oxylus, 400.

P

Paine, his wild notions of government, 3.
Paper money, its nature explained, 38. Montesquieu and Hume mistake its effect on the exchangeable value of gold and silver, *ibid*. Smith mistaken in thinking that it has no effect in diminishing the exchangeable value of the metals, 39, 40.
Parthenia, why they conspired, 351.
Passions, their purgation, what, 268, & seq.
Patria Potestas, its advantages and inconveniences, 109.
Pausanias, 334. Cause of his usurpation, 351.
Peasants, the character of those fitted for the best commonwealth, 333, & seq.
Peisistratidæ, duration of their tyranny, 382.
Peisistratus, how he enslaved Athens, 346. How he acquired tyranny, 367.
Penestæ, who, 8, *note*.
Penthalidæ, why destroyed, 369.
People at large, of what political functions they are capable, 183, & seqq. Objections thereto answered, 186. Sleights by which they encounter the artifices of the great, 302.
Periander, his advice to Thrasybulus, 368. Why slain, 369.
Periæci, who, 113.
Pericles, his innovations at Athens, 120.
Persia, its despotic institutions, 374.

Phalaris of Agrigentum, what originally, 367.
Phaleas, his plan for equalizing property, 91. Other schemes of that nature, 92. Their futility, *ibid*. Imperfections in his republic, 93. 123.
Pharsalus, why its oligarchy lasting, 439.
Pheidon, his tyranny, 366.
Phiditia, 110.
Philip of Macedon, why slain, 369.
Philolaus, who, 171. His friendship with Diocles, 122. Their monument, *ibid*.
Phocis, origin of its sacred war, 342.
Phocylides quoted, 296. Account of that poet, *ibid*.
Phrynichus, the demagogue of the 400, 348.
Pindar cited, 103.
Piræus, its inhabitants peculiarly attached to democracy, 340.
Pittacus, his law respecting drunkards, 123. His office at Mitylene, 194.
Plato, his analysis of ethics revived by Hume, 17. His republic examined, 74, & seq. His second commonwealth, 89. His paradox concerning the best government explained, 89, *note*. His juridical novelties, 123. His explanation of purging the passions, 268.
Pliny, natural history, cited, 123.
Politics science of, how it ought to be treated, 270, & seqq.
Polybius, his political opinions agree with Aristotle's, 21. His character, 388, & seqq. Account of the Roman government, 390, & seqq. His prophecy verified, 397.
Popes, tendency of their government, 140.
Power, naval, its nature and effects, 226. Executive, its different branches, 419, & seqq.
Price, his doctrine concerning government examined and refuted, 3, & seqq. His mistake concerning representative government, 67. His definition of civil liberty, 327.
Priestley, his doctrine concerning government examined and refuted, 3, & seqq.
Procrustes the tyrant, wherein imitated by the French republic, 325.

Property

INDEX.

Property essential to society, 75. Infers inequality, 82. Injudiciously regulated at Sparta, 106.
Prytanes,
Prytaneum, } explained, 68.
Prytany,
Purgation of the passions, what, 268, & seq.
Pythagoras, his saying concerning education, 52.

R

Ranks the higher, how employed in Greece, 34.
Representation, nature thereof, 9. Not unknown to the free states of antiquity, *ibid.*
Republic, strictly so called, its definition, 293. How established, 294. Examples thereof, *ibid.* Rules by which its excellence may be appreciated, 295.
Republicanism, its connection with martial spirit, 178.
Republics, Italian, 59. Factions therein, *ibid.* Remedies against republican factions, 60. Require virtue more than monarchies, and why, 130. The condition of their subjects less eligible than that of the subjects of princes, 141. Republics, or mixed governments, causes of their revolutions, 351, & seq. Examples thereof, 352.
Revenue of Syracuse, brought the whole property into the exchequer in five years, 375.
Revolutions, three things to be considered in them, 335, & seq. Their general causes, 336. Gradual, their causes, 350. Neglect in little matters, 353. Examples thereof, *ibid.* External causes, 354. Examples thereof, *ibid.* Revolutions in monarchies, their causes, 365, & seq. In limited monarchies, their causes, 373.
Rhodes, revolutions in its government, 344.
Riches, national, Aristotle's doctrine concerning them defended, 12, & seq.
——— real and artificial, 36.
Rights, unalienable, what, 9.
Romans acknowledged they could not subsist without a prince, 162.
Rome, her nice discrimination of military honours, 219. Compared with France, 383.

Its government analysed, 390, & seq. Evil inherent in it lamented by Livy, 407.
Rousseau, his wild notions of government, 3. Cause of his hostility to Christianity, 328.

S

Salaries and fees, their effect on the condition of society, 177.
Smos, its magnificence, 375;
Sardanapalus, why dethroned, 370.
Scythians, wherein they placed national happiness, 218, & seq.
Seditions, their primary causes, 333, & seq. Best means of preventing them, 335.
Senate, constitution and powers of that of Athens, 68, & seq.
——— of Sparta, its constitution examined, 109. Of Rome, 392.
Servitude, a teacher of its offices at Syracuse, 34.
Scuthes the Thracian, his conspiracy, 371.
Shaftesbury, 2.
Shepherds, their character, 410.
Sicyon, its tyranny, why lasting, 381.
Slavery, its origin and nature, 6, & seq.
——— domestic, nature thereof, 26. Defended by the analogy of nature, 28. Requisites for being slaves, 29. Different kinds of slavery, 31.
Slaves, how treated by the Athenians, 33. In what sense endowed with virtue, 49.
——— public, difficult to hit the right policy concerning them, 105.
Smellie, his philosophy of natural history criticised, 23.
Society, political, its origin, 2, & seq.; and progress, 20.
Soldiers, numbers thereof, how limited, 86, *note.* Different kinds, 417, & seq.
Solon, his government, 69. Contrivances for upholding it, 70. Causes of its destruction, 71. His law for preventing the accumulation of inheritances, 92, *note.* His institutions, 120. The abuses of the Athenian government not imputable to him, 121.
Sovereignty, in whom it ought to reside, 181. Aristotle's analysis thereof, 274. More accurate than that substituted in its stead, 275, & seq.

INDEX. 433

& feq. Powers thereof, 303, & feqq. How diſtributed under different governments, 304.
Spain, its Cortes, 331.
Sparta, ſee *Lacedemon*.
Sectariſts always promoters of innovation, i. b. examples thereof, *ibid*.
Statesmen, requiſites for that character, 360.
Statutes cited, 102, & feq.
Stock, the art of accumulation different from œconomics, 34.
Strabo, his digreſſion on mythology, 268, & feq.
Strozzi, Peter, the miſcarriage of his enterpriſe againſt St. Marino, 150.
Subjects, thoſe of republics in a worſe condition than the ſubjects of princes, 141.
Subordination, its different kinds founded in nature, 33.
Suffetes of Carthage, who, 115.
Sweden, its government, how eſtabliſhed, 331.
Switzerland declines working its mines, 41. Its conſtitution, 63.
Sybaris, changes in its inhabitants and government, 339, & feq.
Syracuſe, how ſubjected to tyranny, 338. Origin of its factions, 341.
Syſſities or clubs, their advantages, 206.

T

Tamariſk emblem of ſolitary wretchedneſs, 123.
Tarentum, how its government changed, 338.
Tenedos, its ſhipping deſtined to one employment, 285.
Thales, his expedient for getting wealth, 45.
Thebes, how its popular government changed, 336. Cauſe of its ſedition, 350.
Theodectes, account of him, 32.
Theodorus the comedian, his maxim concerning firſt impreſſions, 249.
Theopompus, his ſmart anſwer to his queen, 374.
Thera, peculiarity in its government, 184.
Thetes, who, 121.
Thracians, wherein they placed national happineſs, 218.
VOL. II.

Thraſybulus, his conſpiracy, 371.
Thurii, cauſe of its revolution, 352.
Traffic, the artificial not for accommodation, but for gain, 40. Its abuſe, 41.
Treaſurer, principal requiſite in that officer, 361.
Tribes, city and ruſtic, 411.
Troops, the different kinds of, ſeverally adapted to different forms of government, 417, & feqq.
Tyrannies, of ſhort duration, and why, 381. Examples, 381, & feq.
Tyranny, its different kinds, 295, & feq. Analyſis thereof, 368. Its maxims, 376, & feqq.
Tyrant, meaning of the word in Greek, 93, *note*.
Tyrteus, his poem called Eunomia, 351.

U

Urbino, Dukes of, protectors of St. Marino, 150.
Uſury, its nature, 42.
Venice, its government, 330.
Vieta, an improver of modern geometry, 273.
Virtue, moral, in what ſenſe aſcribed to ſlaves, 49.
Virtues political, relative to rank, age, and ſex, 172, & feqq.
Voltaire, a citizen of St. Marino's opinion of him, 156.

W

War, laws of war and peace, their foundation, 210, & feqq. Changes effected in thoſe laws by Chriſtianity, 211. Grotius's doctrine concerning them compared with Ariſtotle's, 212.
Warburton, his obſervation on the intention of the Grecian legiſlators, 102. Combated, *ibid*. & feq.
Wards and diſtricts, their number in Attica, 68.
Waring, an improver of modern geometry, 273.

3 K   *Wedlock*,

Wedlock, the principles by which the fitteft ages for it ought to be determined in either fex, 244, & feqq. Fitteft feafon for it, 246. Its rights to be invariably refpected, 247.
Wives, their community, 75, & feqq.
Women, their virtues different from thofe of men, 50. Their undue influence in Sparta, 105. Pregnant, attentions requifite for their condition, 246.

Y

Year, Athenian, how divided, 67.

Z

Zaleucus, 103. Who, 121. His law againft drunkennefs, 122.
Zancle, its inhabitants ejected by the Samians, 340.

THE END.

The following WORKS, *written by* JOHN GILLIES, *LL.D. F. R. S. and S. A. London, F. R. S. Edinburgh, and Historiographer to his Majesty for Scotland, are printed for* A. STRAHAN *and* T. CADELL *jun. and* W. DAVIES *in the* Strand.

I. The HISTORY of ANCIENT GREECE, its Colonies and Conquests, from the earliest Accounts till the Division of the Macedonian Empire in the East; including the History of Literature, Philosophy, and the Fine Arts. In 4 vols. 8vo. Third Edition. 1l. 8s. bound.

II. A VIEW of the REIGN of FREDERIC II. of PRUSSIA, with a Parallel between that Prince and Philip II. of Macedon. 8vo. 7s. bound.

www.ingramcontent.com/pod-product-compliance
Lightning Source LLC
Chambersburg PA
CBHW022147300426
44115CB00006B/381